Open Spaces

OPEN

THE LIFE OF

SPACES

AMERICAN CITIES

A TWENTIETH CENTURY FUND ESSAY

by August Heckscher

with Phyllis Robinson

Maps by Dyck Fledderus

HARPER & ROW, PUBLISHERS
New York, Hagerstown, San Francisco, London

Photo Credits

Louisville Chamber of Commerce, p. 128; Los Angeles City Planning Department, p. 222; Squire Haskins, p. 223; Paul L. Wertheimer, p. 263; Amon Carter Foundation, p. 263; Atlanta Department of Parks and Recreation, p. 272; John Portman Associates, p. 335; Alexandre Georges, p. 335; Victor Steinbrueck, p. 342.

All other photographs were taken by the author.

FIRST EDITION

Designed by Gloria Adelson

Library of Congress Cataloging in Publication Data

Heckscher, August, 1913–
   Open spaces.

   "A Twentieth Century Fund essay."
   Includes bibliographical references and index.
   1. Open spaces—United States.   2. Cities and towns—Planning—United States.   3. Urban renewal—United States.
I. Robinson, Phyllis, joint author.   II. Title.
HT167.H38   1977   309.2′62′0973   76–12064
ISBN: 0–06–011801–6

77 78 79 80 10 9 8 7 6 5 4 3 2 1

The Twentieth Century Fund is an independent research foundation which undertakes policy studies of economic, political and social institutions and issues. The Fund was founded in 1919 and endowed by Edward A. Filene.

Contents

Preface

Since August Heckscher was my predecessor as director of the Twentieth Century Fund and remained a trustee of the Fund while serving as New York City's commissioner of parks and administrator of recreation and cultural affairs, I know that he has had a lifelong concern about urban life and urban living. At the Fund, he worked with Jean Gottman, who wrote *Megalopolis*, and was even more closely involved with Sebastionn de Grazia, who wrote *Of Time, Work and Leisure*. In their different ways both studies reflected Mr. Heckscher's interests in the quality of life and the role of cities in our society.

When he joined the municipal administration, Mr. Heckscher had the opportunity—and the inevitable difficulties—of taking an active rather than an intellectual role in urban affairs, dealing, in particular, with the place of the parks in the life of the city. From the window of his office at the Arsenal in Central Park, he could glimpse one of the great open spaces on Manhattan Island. Of course, parks are just one form of urban space as it is defined and described in this book. And Mr. Heckscher's ideas on this subject had been germinating for a long time. Nevertheless, I harbor the notion that the book really began while he was embroiled in the struggle to make all the city's parks more enjoyable to more people.

Today, urban centers, especially the older cities in the nation, are experiencing serious economic and social difficulties. These problems have been the subject of several recent Fund studies and require still further research. But Mr. Heckscher has brought to this area of concern the perspective of an urbane man who has an abiding interest in the shape and scope of our cities—what they have been and what they could be. At a time when many cities are grappling with harsh options and must search for ways to increase their revenues while reducing their services and facilities, Mr. Heckscher has his eye on the enduring problem and potential of urban design, seeking to make each city more livable for all its residents. Whatever the short-run prospects of our sorely troubled cities, they will survive, and the value of August Heckscher's work is in its affirmation of the survival of the urban environment.

M. J. Rossant, Director
The Twentieth Century Fund

April 1976

Acknowledgments

The first debt is to the trustees of the Twentieth Century Fund, who made possible this study. Adolf A. Berle, Jr., as chairman of the board, first suggested that I undertake such a work; but this dear friend and immensely stimulating counselor died before the book was actually begun. His successor, James Rowe, launched the enterprise; and the Fund's director, Murray J. Rossant, has overseen its progress. John E. Booth, the Fund's associate director, has been constantly supportive in regard to all details.

The book owes much to city officials across the country, to mayors, park directors, planners who gave time for interviews, provided tours and supplied essential materials. Many private individuals, business leaders with deep commitment to the development of their respective downtowns, as well as architects, librarians and plain city buffs, contributed to our understanding and provided a sense of welcome. To list all these would be difficult and would inevitably result in some being left out. We hope that this blanket acknowledgment will be taken as an admittedly inadequate form of thanks. It may recall to individuals scattered in cities across the country two researchers who passed their way, often hurried but nearly always enthusiastic, in quest of the mysterious substance that they described as urban open space.

Much is owed to Christine Shipman, who aided in the research, kept materials accessible and in order, and typed successive versions of the manuscript.

A.H.
(and P.R.)

Open Spaces

Introduction

EVERYONE KNOWS AMERICAN CITIES are in trouble. Many have been losing population; they have been failing to create an adequate number of new jobs; they are subject to crime and beset by racial tension. At a time when the cities face these difficulties, some of their more agreeable aspects bear examining. Without disregarding the cities' troubles, can we not consider their amenities? Urban open space, the subject of this book, is associated with pleasure, with recreation, with human encounters and communal celebrations. It may, as well, play a significant role in renewing and stabilizing the cities' social and economic base.

Open Space as a Positive Force

Imaginative civic leaders have long been aware of a link between a city's amenities and the soundness of other aspects of its life. Efforts to restore and dramatize urban centers have almost without exception been accompanied by a feeling for the importance of well-used parks and other outdoor space. McCoffin of San Francisco, Johnson of Cleveland, Lawrence of Pittsburgh, Clark and Dilworth of Philadelphia, La Guardia and more recently Lindsay in New York, have perceived that the vitality of the city was related to park-building and park use, and to innovative planning of open space. In the administrations of such men new areas have been added to the public domain. In the use of open space the population has found a sense of unity, as well as of pleasure, in revealing to itself the varieties of age, class, nationality and race of which the great city is composed.

1

In today's cities serious efforts to deal with education, housing, jobs and crime are nearly always paralleled by attention to the city's open spaces. It may be an oversimplification to say that the best cities have the best parks. Yet the most progressive cities in terms of social improvements and economic growth are able to show notable physical improvements of their outdoor domain. Minneapolis, Dallas, Seattle, Atlanta, San Francisco can be named as a few of those that, while dealing with social problems, have created new open spaces. Conversely, when parks are neglected, lack of civic leadership and a diminished quality of urban life can be assumed.

The future of cities will, it is clear, be largely determined by the degree to which people develop a positive desire to live in them. Compactness is no longer a necessity (except as energy shortages may ultimately make it so); most essential functions can perfectly well be supplied to a population that is loosely dispersed and relies upon modern technology for transportation and communication. If people continue to gather in tightly knit agglomerations it will be because they enjoy the stimulation and benefits which city life provides. Among these benefits, agreeable open space should not be underestimated.

A Decade of Innovation

The 1960s and early 1970s witnessed striking achievements by both the private and public sector in shaping a more hospitable urban environment. At the start of this period federal aid became available for many forms of open space development. Urban renewal funds were plentiful and procedures were modified so as to permit the retention and restoration of important buildings within the cleared site. Federal support of local planning efforts produced, often for the first time, a clear understanding of a community's open space assets. Meanwhile private investment in office towers, hotels, convention centers and cultural facilities had done much to alter the face of the typical downtown with the proliferation of plazas and small squares. The movement toward historic preservation gathered strong momentum.

In this period, also, urban dwellers took a fresh look at their parks. In most cities physical facilities had been denied adequate maintenance. Encroachments had been permitted and the changing composition of abutting neighborhoods had altered their use. At the same time many parks were being rediscovered by a generation engaged in protests against war and in demonstrations for or against a wide variety of social causes. In 1972 occurred the 150th anniversary of the birth of Frederick Law Olmsted, and amid the significant re-evaluations of his work some park enthusiasts called for a return to the elegantly maintained romantic landscapes he had envisioned as an escape from urban ills. Others saw in the new uses of the parks a fulfillment of Olmsted's faith in their democratizing influence.

When this book was researched and written, in 1974 and 1975, economic recession was bringing many ambitious downtown schemes to a halt. Most federal programs benefiting the cities had been abandoned. In short, it seemed a good time to look at what had been done and to evaluate where the cities were going in terms of their open space developments. The task of making American cities more livable would surely continue in spite of difficulties and setbacks; but it might in the future take a somewhat different course from that which the decade of the 1960s had launched.

The Approach of This Book

This study takes a wide view of open space. It deals with traditionally conceived parks and squares, but does not confine itself to them. In its survey are included areas as essentially different as large-scale natural features within cities and the open space pattern of crowded downtowns. Whatever its form or scale, open space as it is considered here must have some role, actual or potential, for adding to the quality of life in the cities. The disturbing emptiness one finds in so many downtown areas, where land has been cleared but not redeveloped, where open parking lots take the place of buildings, is not treated as open space. On the other hand, a flood basin may be capable of being put to multiple uses, adding limited recreational resources to its basic function. As such, it is entitled to be listed among the open space assets of a community.

Similarly, in these pages we take a broad view of the purposes served by open space. Much writing in the field confines itself to recreation, and usually to active recreation. On the basis of such an approach, it is possible to arrive at fairly exact statistics as to the desirable number of acres per thousand population;[1] it is possible to describe factually the types of facilities needed to serve the neighborhood, the community, the city-wide population. It is not our purpose to add to this already ample literature. Recreation as we see it is only one of the benefits provided by open space.

Additional open space benefits are those that involve the very form and nature of the city. Each city is a place of its own, its uniqueness determined in large measure by patterns created by the alternation of structure and void, of buildings and spaces between. The larger green spaces, parks and parkways, riverbanks and waterfronts, give to a city the coherence that allows the urban dweller to have a feeling for the whole.

Such green spaces may be viewed as the city's skeleton. They are the underlying structure from which depend neighborhoods, institutional complexes and business centers. A man who knows his parks can tell where he lives and should not easily get lost. And because parks are so often the product of basic topography, he should not be ignorant of how his city is related to land, to river, to sea.

The role of open space in clarifying the city's form underlies many of the evaluations of this book; so does its role in enhancing the city's livability. By livability, more is meant than opportunities—crucially important as they are—to play baseball on an accessible field, to find a bicycle path or to go boating. More, too, is meant than the kind of beauty that well-kept lawns and flowerbeds supply.

What is expressed in open spaces is the essential quality of urban life— its casualness and variety, its ability to crystallize community feeling. People find in outdoor meeting places the chance to sense what is going on, to test the mood of the community, to mingle and communicate. Life deprived of these outdoor extensions would lack much of the vitality and savor we associate with city dwelling.

Part One of this book deals with the way open space comes into being and the way it takes the pattern we find in particular cities. It suggests that varying forms of spatial organization—the open-endedness of the boulevard or the construction of the town square—correspond to general tendencies and values within the social order; and then shows how such values are expressed in the structure of today's major U.S. cities.

Part Two surveys the strengths and shortcomings of the more traditional forms of open space, from the town square to the major park and park system. Part Three turns to the central business district of today's American city and to the kinds of space that are developing to suit its new functions.

A Choice of Cities

This book is intended to deal with cities as they exist, not with future plans or abstract concepts. It is based upon firsthand observation of American cities as they stood in the mid-1970s. What has been accomplished in the development of open space is often striking in itself and more interesting than paper proposals. Besides, American cities are too rarely looked at and compared, no matter from what point of view.

In choosing the cities to visit, an effort was made to select those most likely to contain significant open space developments. Factors considered from the start to be favorable to such developments included the following:

TOPOGRAPHY   Cities with a dramatic or strongly molded terrain are apt to have large parks—either because certain of their areas are not suitable for building, or because a natural beauty has led to the land's being set apart and preserved.

WATERFRONT LOCATIONS   Rivers and seashores are favorable to open space and are frequently being reclaimed from earlier industrial and commercial uses.

HISTORIC AREAS   Cities with strong movements for historic preservation are apt to contain significant squares and pedestrian streets. The historic area is generally residential, but may be one of commercial uses or a collection of warehouses.

NEW GOVERNMENTAL, BUSINESS AND COMMERCIAL DEVELOPMENTS   Where a city becomes important to the life of a region, rebuilding to meet a new scale of demands takes place. This rebuilding almost invariably includes new open spaces in the form of plazas, small downtown parks and malls.

A STRONG PARK TRADITION   Certain cities developed in the nineteenth century a pride in parks and parkways, often associated with a local park builder of note. These earlier parks can give a particular character to the modern city; they can also present special problems.

The criteria proved suggestive in seeking out urban spaces. They led us to visit all but two U.S. cities with a population of 500,000 or more and to study a number of others.[2] Most of these cities obviously contain more than one of the factors enumerated above: they will have a waterfront development, new cultural and financial institutions, a historic district now being developed or restored, etc. A few smaller cities were observed because they contained open space developments of particular interest—for example, Savannah because of its historic squares or Binghamton, New York, because of its in-town river.

A word may be said about how one approaches a city and gains relevant knowledge within the necessarily short time available. Camillo Sitte, an outstanding student of cities in the nineteenth century, has left an account of his own method.[3] Arriving at the railway terminal, he would bid the cabman to drive him to the town's central square. First he would ask for the leading bookstore, and next inquire for three things: (1) the best tower from which to view the city, (2) the best map of the city and (3) the hotel where one could most advantageously dine. After thirty years of such observations, Sitte wrote a book on the subject.

Our own course was not exactly of this nature, though an early visit to the central square was imperative, and we did not neglect the bookstore and the tower. A questionnaire addressed to the heads of the parks and planning departments[4] had been a first step in the research and opened the way on arrival to interviews with public officials and concerned private citizens. Thereafter the principal task was to get about the city by every means of transportation available. This included helicopter and riverboat, and made ample use of the indispensable journey on foot. Unlike our predecessor, we were given two years for the study, not thirty.

A Few Questions and Generalizations

A study of the open space of American cities must lead to conclusions concerning its form, its use, its possible future development. Among the questions raised in this book, the answers to which form the substance of the ensuing pages, are the following:

- What is the effect on open space of contemporary urban values? What is the effect of physical geography and of the expressway system? In which U.S. cities can one see most clearly a pattern defined by meaningful open space?
- What makes a lively square? A well-used plaza? What new forms of open space are being developed and how can the needs of the future city be met?
- What is the role of open space in the new downtowns of American cities? What is the value of the open spaces being developed in new complexes for the arts, for government, for housing and for commerce? What contribution does open space make to the city's special role as forum and meeting place?

Answers to these questions run through the text. A few generalizations, applicable to open space as a whole, may, however, be ventured at this point. They reflect issues about which a degree of controversy has been found to exist in almost all cities.

MORE OPEN SPACE?   In the enthusiasm for open space, people overlook the fact that many American downtowns are loosely knit, with as much as half their total area awaiting development or used for parking. In such circumstances it is enclosure that is principally required, not openness.

The fallacy of supposing that open space is by itself and in all circumstances an advantage is shown by efforts to develop plazas, often unusable, at the base of skyscrapers. In return for such patches of open space, zoning laws may allow building bulk to increase unreasonably, bartering away valuable rights to air and sky. An open area, misleadingly called a "pocket park," can be the lure with which a builder gains valuable concessions from city planners.

In each such case it needs to be asked whether the open area is so situated in regard to traffic, to wind, noise and sunlight, as to be a potentially desirable public space. It must be asked, too, whether it is related to other open spaces in a way that makes it part of a pedestrian system. The key must always be careful planning, sensitive to what makes open space a genuine contribution to the recreational and other needs of the urban dweller.

ACTIVITIES   The general rule in regard to urban open space is that it must be used. Emptiness is the curse of open space as boredom is the curse of leisure. What constitutes a proper degree of use will depend on circumstances and it is possible that certain areas may in the future become overcharged with people. But today the danger comes from the opposite direction. The burden of proof is on those who wish to discourage use of the parks, to ban them for festivals and special events, to prohibit food vendors and to demagnetize them as popular attractions.

Squares and parks in the central city are the better for having regularly presented in them such events as concerts, street plays, dance programs, craft shows, sculpture displays, etc. This is particularly true of a new plaza or mall, where well-publicized programs should be considered as important an element in their management as sanitation services and police protection.

CITIZEN PARTICIPATION   A city's open spaces are capable of evoking in the public a strong sense of possessiveness and a desire for involvement. This is obviously to the good in the modern city, frequently haunted by a sense of anonymity and helplessness. A neighborhood should be encouraged to feel a responsibility for the community's open spaces and should be intimately involved in changes in form or use. City-wide park groups formed to preserve the open spaces against encroachment or ill-considered "improvements" can be highly beneficial. Some of these, however, will tend to look upon parks as holy ground where the grass is not to be trod upon and from which strangers ought somehow to be excluded.

NEW KINDS OF OPEN SPACE   The traditional park is often in trouble, being in the wrong part of the city or of a size difficult to maintain and patrol. While such problems are worked on, newer forms of open space must be imaginatively developed. These may include pedestrian and bicycle routes, waterfront areas, walkways through historic areas, or in the central core, the kinds of spaces that open in connection with cultural, commercial and governmental complexes. Streets must be re-examined to develop for them other uses than as arteries for wheeled traffic. In the outer city attempts must be made to combine open spaces of a utilitarian nature—such as flood basins or drainage areas—with recreational possibilities.

Role of Government

Throughout the examples and case studies of this book run statements about the role played by government, federal and local, in connection with new and existing open spaces. Many legal and administrative measures affecting open space exist in the form of tax concessions, easements, zoning and other devices. The federal government, however, has abandoned its direct involvement in the acquisition and beautification of urban open space. By the time work on this book began, the open space programs of the Department of Housing and Urban Development[5] were in abeyance. In Washington a few remaining officials were coordinating reports on the last, often unfinished projects.

Urban renewal funds had also been cut off. Whatever the shortcomings of the urban renewal program, especially in its early days when complete demolition of an area was required by law, it had become a tool capable of being used to impart to downtown a new and often inviting spatial organization. Urban renewal was by then less a program for clearing slums than a means to the reconstruction of major civic institutions. Just when broadened possibilities of urban renewal were being discovered, and when the law had been altered to allow preservation of significant urban features, funds were denied it.

Federal policies for open space are part of a more general problem of the federal relationship to the cities. The administration of President Nixon silently stifled aid to the cities; that of President Ford continued the process. In the bicentennial period it was the official White House view that the cities were not in trouble, and that if they were it was not a concern of the federal government. One looked in vain for programs that might sensitively enhance urban life when the very existence of urban centers appeared to be outside the circle of Washington's responsibility.

A different attitude is bound to prevail in time. Then the open space programs that began experimentally in the mid-1960s should be reinstated amid more enveloping policies designed to help the cities. Revenue sharing, however, must not then be considered a substitute for policies pinpointed at open space planning, acquisition and development. Experience shows that with very few exceptions, the cause of open space and of urban beautification is placed by the localities so low amid seemingly overwhelming priorities as to receive none of the shared funds. In particular, federal programs should be instituted to ensure aid to the cities for ongoing park maintenance, an important form of assistance which has not previously been provided.

The Department of the Interior, through its Bureau of Outdoor Recreation, has been, and can be in the future, an effective instrument in the acquisition and development of urban open space. The establishment of National Seashore Recreation Areas within the urbanized expanses of New York and San Francisco has set important precedents. Grants by the Department to save the Texas bayous is suggestive of a further urban role, particularly on the outskirts of cities where open space for a future population needs urgently to be acquired. Other departments of the federal government can play a significant though indirect role in urban spaces. Thus the Army Corps of Engineers, to the extent it is sensitive to values of conservation and recreation, may modify flood control projects so as to adapt them to multiple use.

Urban open space remains, nevertheless, primarily the charge of local governments. Unfortunately, the more local a government becomes, the less adequate is the level of maintenance. Where the state is responsible for in-city park development and upkeep (as, for example, in Point State Park in Pittsburgh or the historic park in San Diego's Old Town) high standards prevail. County responsibility, as in certain parks of Syracuse and Cleveland, shows disconcertingly better results than in comparable situations where the city is in control. Yet the level of maintenance is not the only factor to be considered in judging what makes a good park. The advantage of drawing for financing upon a broader economic base tends to be outweighed by having a park system unresponsive to community and neighborhood interests.

What is required at the city level is that the voters—as well as mayors and other city officials—give parks a higher priority than has generally been the case. One can understand the temptation to cut park budgets when the needs of police and fire departments, of education and hospitals, are so urgent. Yet nowhere does a relatively small expenditure bring such visible and far-reaching benefits to a city as money spent on parks. The return, dollar for dollar, can be striking as a spur to city morale and even to general economic development.

The weight accorded the park cause is influenced by the degree of active citizen support. Park boards exist in most large cities, composed of representative citizens appointed on staggered terms so as to minimize partisan politics. They can play an invaluable role, especially when a strong chairman works harmoniously with a strong professional director or commissioner, and when local tradition places high value on open space amenities.

Toward a New City

This book, as its title indicates, is not merely a study of forms of open space. It is a study of cities. Its tune is reasonably optimistic at a time when most such discussions are sunk in gloom. U.S. cities are more interesting and each is more individual than is generally taken for granted. The often-stated view that earlier generations of Americans did not like urban living and therefore allowed their towns to grow in ugliness and neglect is disproved by the care with which city after city developed parks and laid out ambitious plans for beautification. The record of the past decades is one of renewed and often strikingly successful efforts along these lines.

American cities have been undergoing changes in their form and function, reflected in a dramatic spatial reorganization. Downtown has become sharply defined as highway routes, designed to expedite traffic, have had the unanticipated effect of sorting out land uses and encouraging a compact central structure. Within this area, new complexes regional in the scope of their services have developed forms of open space suited to the gregariousness and informality of modern life. Parks which were formerly conceived as an escape from the city are now seen as means of enjoying more fully the basic qualities of urban living. Variety, contradiction, unexpectedness—experienced against an undisguisedly urban background—replace the illusion of a pastoral retreat.

The search for new spatial forms has produced some bizarre results, as in skyscrapers isolated upon windy plazas or waterfronts surrendered to recreational uses bearing no relationship to the unique qualities of the site. Pedestrian malls have been left bare of essential programming and adornment, or have been so filled with sculptural forms as to make passage difficult. In many cities the desire to attract tourists and conventioneers has been pursued at the sacrifice of more enduring urban values. Such aberrations are inevitable in a period of innovation. The better examples (which this book tends to emphasize) show that a new understanding of urban amenities is in the making.

While the ultimate fate of American cities may depend upon other factors, political and economic, the importance of attempts to restore quality to city living should not be underestimated as a force setting other forces in motion.

PART ONE

The Nature and Derivation of Open Space

1 Changing Concepts of Open Space

IN THE SHAPING OF CITIES, the communal feeling for a particular kind of space has played a significant role. As much as military, economic or technological factors, the psychic awareness of what makes people comfortable or uncomfortable[1] has influenced the relative disposition and size of closed and open spaces. The cities of one country or of one age will be different from another according to whether bounded or open-ended vistas meet the prevailing mood. Such basic functions as government, marketing and worship can be carried on within various forms of spatial organization; indeed, the history of cities is in no small measure the history of changes wrought upon the outward fabric as successive generations attempt to make them harmonize with an inner perception of space.

This chapter traces historic changes in prevailing ideas about open space. It suggests that we are now returning to something very old—a conviction that at the heart of our cities there must be spaces bounded and contained, in which the pedestrian can feel at home.

From a Closed to an Open System

The medieval space system was essentially closed. Walls surrounded the city and cut it off from the country. The cathedral was rarely disengaged from its surroundings; buildings of the most utilitarian sort ambled up to it and leaned against its walls. Bridges frequently carried shops and stalls, preventing even fleeting glimpses of the river below. The narrow streets wound about and ended in blocked views.

From this tightly packed mass of structures the square or piazza was shaped, providing a central place to which the town's inhabitants came to draw water from the well, to buy from the open-air market and to exchange the verbal currency of day-to-day urban life. The square itself was at best artfully bounded, with a minimum of openings for streets and these usually at the corners, and often with a continuing arcade to give a sense of defined limits. To live in such a city must have been somewhat stifling, but it could also save men from the feeling of estrangement and of amorphous relationships.[2]

Subsequent development was almost entirely in the direction of openness. The Renaissance created in men the sense of movement toward outward ends; the discovery of perspective encouraged the vista leading to a distant horizon. Increasing wealth called for settings where houses and public buildings could be observed and for avenues down which the new classes could disport themselves. Superimposed upon the older cities were the boulevards with their subtle repetitions and harmonies, which gave the city an essentially modern form. With the new constructions of the Baroque period the city moved conclusively from the closed to the expanding space; from implosion to explosion; from "the crystallizing epiphany to the open-ended question."[3]

In the Paris of Napoleon III, a city of modern spaces was dramatically carved out of the still cluttered and compact urban form. By the mid-nineteenth century, Paris had outgrown the structures vital to its administration, its government and its culture, as its traffic had outrun the corridors of transportation. To build on a new scale, and to create spaces suggestive of new values, was a task rarely accomplished with such striking effect and within the span of so brief a time.

The emperor himself laid out upon a famous map, in various colors to indicate the priority he assigned to them, the avenues and boulevards he deemed essential to ventilate and give form to the city. He took a particular interest in the creation of new parks. Baron Haussmann, his lieutenant, a planner of large ambitions and of an innate sense of power, cut through old neighborhoods and bifurcated at least one ancient green space, as he imposed his straight line upon the curving ancient streets. His was the transformation, in the phrase of a historian, "of small-scale complexity into monumental simplicity."[4]

The openness and monumentality of Haussmann's Paris was translated during the 1920s into newer forms by European planners. Taking their cue from technology,[5] they envisioned cities keyed to the massive scale of new commercial and industrial organization, their structures widely spaced and separated by avenues designed for rapid movement. Like the skyscrapers of Le Corbusier's ideal city, their buildings were placed in regular rows within a grid of superblocks. The spaces between, though conceived as gardens, too often resembled the uninviting and sterile lawns of the conventional housing projects of the 1950s.

Progressive opening up of the urban fabric under twentieth-century influences led to a concept of the city completely at variance with its historic role. With space so expansive and pervasive, the city ceased to be the decisive element in defining and containing the major activities of men's lives. As it was no longer necessary for defense (indeed, it was a source of vulnerability to a nation rather than of strength), so it was not deemed essential for carrying on most kinds of business. New technologies of transportation and communication made it possible for men to act while widely dispersed, within a social organization no longer coinciding with the structural realities as they had been known since the Greco-Roman age.

The elite of the social order based upon these new spatial conceptions are individuals with highly developed gifts for interacting with those who do not live in the same neighborhood or the same city, and for dealing with problems having nothing to do with territorial bounds. They are the products of the jet plane, the low-cost long-distance telephone call, the expense account and the endless round of specialized conferences. These rulers comprise a new class of professional nomads, and the city of man becomes coextensive with their rootless wanderings and their inexhaustibly far-flung interests. Left behind, like villagers in the early industrial age, are those who have not gained entrance to this modern elite—children and slum dwellers, the poorly educated and those who still keep an obstinate attachment to the ideal of community.[6]

To such an end, by the latter half of the twentieth century, had come the long process of opening up the city and of creating new kinds of space.

The American Desire for Openness

The town in America, as soon as it could dispense with the stockade and exist with reasonable security, showed a liking for open vistas and an uncomplicated structural form. Streets laid out on a square grid were adopted almost universally in the East, and in the nineteenth-century towns beyond the Alleghenies this pattern was imitated. This was in part because the grid seemed the very image of urbanity (curved roads belonged to the country) and in part because it offered so convenient a means for real estate speculation. But the grid was adopted also because it conformed to the Americans' preferences for spatial openness. A man standing at almost any point within the town could look outward to fields and woods.

The grid was invariably mapped on a scale beyond the capacities of the existing generation to fill up with buildings. Consequently most cities throughout the nineteenth century bore a half-completed look. The inhabitants do not seem to have been depressed by the empty lots and the wide areas of undeveloped land. On the contrary, they viewed them as a challenge and undoubtedly found in them a reassurance against being crowded and contained. When the modern city reverted to this kind of openness as a result of demolition and clearance under urban renewal procedures, people responded as if they had seen it all before.

Ugly as were the spaces left empty while awaiting redevelopment, they did not provide for contemporary city dwellers quite the shock that might have been expected. Where Europeans would have seen anguishing suggestions of a landscape devastated by war, the American was reminded of the unfinished urban landscape in which his grandfather's generation found satisfaction and even pride.

U.S. cities of today are in general loosely organized. They do not lack open space; indeed, if open space is defined to include all areas not built upon, they have too much of it. Rapid annexation of outlying land has left a city like Houston with 45 percent of its total area undeveloped. Parking and streets can take up as much as 50 percent of a central business area, and additional land, cleared and temporarily used for open parking lots, usually awaits construction. The space may be of the wrong kind and in the wrong place, but it imparts to the contemporary American city as strong an impression of openness as the narrow streets and crowded buildings of fourteenth-century Paris imparted their sense of enclosure and restriction.

Today the pendulum is swinging away from the desire for a loose social texture and for unbroken vistas, back toward the reassurance of containment. Before the swing occurred, however, various practical and aesthetic doctrines would affirm the values of motion, of unbounded perspectives and of seemingly endless distances.

The Dream of the City Beautiful

Late in the nineteenth century, a doctrine derived from classical sources sought to give coherence to the American feeling for urban spaciousness. It succeeded because it managed to combine the loftiest ideals of art with a convenient blessing of the business establishment. By then the streets provided by the grid of the average American city were no longer ample enough to ensure rapid movement or to supply unobstructed views. Nor were the structures in which commerce and government had been housed adequate to the needs of a growing population. It became necessary to justify an enlargement of the streets and to discover the forms in which the country's new importance and sense of dignity could be embodied.

The means to these objectives was the movement that came to be known as the City Beautiful. Through it the Beaux Arts style of European artists and architects was brought to this country and given native garb and accent.

The prophet of the new movement was Daniel H. Burnham. Born in 1846 in upstate New York, he fortuitously became involved in rebuilding Chicago after the fire. In the rapidly growing metropolis of the Midwest he found wealth, fame and an opportunity to exercise gifts for planning hardly less imposing than those of Baron Haussmann of Paris.

Burnham and his partner, John Root, put their mark upon a growing number of private residences, buildings that in their solid massing and restrained exterior details were characteristic of the best of the Chicago school. But Burnham was not one to be satisfied with designing houses. "My idea," he wrote, "is to work up a big business, to handle big things, deal with big businessmen and to build up a big organization."[7] It was an ambition perfectly suited to Chicago's expanding economy and to the need for such a shift in scale as led to development of the skyscraper and then to comprehensive urban planning.

The 1893 World Columbian Exposition in Chicago gave Burnham (working with Frederick Law Olmsted and Henry Codman) his first real chance to achieve bigness. For this he adopted a classic style. Low structures, dazzling white in their materials, took the place of the dark-toned brick and high-rise form of his earlier practice. Yet in abandoning what seemed native to Chicago and to the best taste of his day, Burnham captured something deep in the American grain, a feeling that had hitherto lacked authoritative and popular expression.

What Burnham captured was the sense of wide-open space and of liberating vistas which in one way or another—from the laying out of the first grid to the construction of the latest boulevard leading to nowhere—had been congenial to the American consciousness. Burnham's spaces were rather incongruously clothed and delimited, but whether in the Court of Honor at the Chicago world's fair or in the later environments he was called upon to shape, they seemed a happy realization of what Americans desired their cities to be. Burnham was doubly fortunate in that a school of design seeming to be purely aesthetic was so perfectly in keeping with the dominant mood of the business community. The chance for freedom of movement and for the display of conspicuous wealth had been granted an aesthetic sanction consoling to the new imperialists. Burnham was on his way to the goal to "work up a big business . . . deal with big businessmen"; he had also achieved a place as one of America's foremost artistic creators.

Some Practical Applications

The Chicago fair was a make-believe city, but one that was to inspire millions of Americans with a vision of the monuments and the surrounding spaces which seemed appropriate to a land of long vistas and vast potential wealth. The use of formal squares and of avenues laid out in diagonals was not new to the United States. Pierre L'Enfant's original plan for Washington had been based upon such a theme; in Indianapolis, Alexander Ralston, who had worked with L'Enfant, introduced the same classic elements. But the Chicago fair gave to the Baroque a fresh sanction and authority.

Appropriately, after the Chicago triumph, Burnham was called to join with a distinguished team in reappraising L'Enfant's work. (Their approach will be discussed in a later chapter.) Cleveland and San Francisco were also to receive Burnham's attention.

Cleveland in 1903 was under the influence of Mayor Tom L. Johnson, a controversial figure whom Lincoln Steffens called "the best mayor of the best governed city in the United States." Johnson had set forth the vision of an ideal city, "a city built on a hill," and he saw an opportunity to use public architecture and the creation of public spaces as a means to encourage civic pride and even civic responsibility. He turned naturally to Burnham, whose proposals for Cleveland drew heavily on the Chicago fair, taking much of their inspiration from abroad and from the past. Yet once again these borrowings were adapted to the native American feeling for the unconfined and the open-ended. His governmental and cultural center was grouped around a square 260 feet in width which was conceived not only as a setting for the monumental buildings but as a recreational center for visitors, citizens and civic employees.[8]

For San Francisco Burnham projected a grand outer boulevard encircling the city, to which all other arteries would lead. Diagonal streets would unite the older and newer sections of the city. From the civic center the most important avenues would radiate, periodically widening into traffic circles from which further avenues would branch out. The hills for which the city is famous would be circled by roads following their contours. All this might well have given a borrowed splendor to what was at the beginning of the century a fun-loving, somewhat bawdy, high-living town.

For better or worse, the plan was never to be effectuated. In the earthquake of 1906 the drawings and models were destroyed by fire. By the time the plan could be considered, San Francisco was impatient to begin rebuilding and it seemed more expedient to follow the old grid than to attempt a new street pattern. Perhaps, too, there was a psychological need to recreate the city as it had been, preserving what remained of the familiar Victorian atmosphere.

There was left for Burnham the great Chicago plan, completed in 1909. Again there were wide avenues and a magnificent circle to be bordered by the city's public structures. The lakefront proposals, fulfilled in later decades, freed Chicago once and for all of its inward-looking tendencies and added to the spaciousness of parks the gray unlimited spaciousness of water.

A Late Flowering of the Beaux Arts Movement

These spatial concepts in their pure and most extreme form can best be seen in a less familiar plan derived directly from Burnham's ideas but carried out by disciples. Minneapolis is of all American cities perhaps the most interesting today by virtue of its accommodation to the pedestrian and its successful exemplification of late-twentieth-century ideas. The more striking, therefore, is the fact that a plan for Minneapolis developed in the first decades of the century sets forth the most advanced version of the city of vistas and of monumental spaces.

In 1909, still in the afterglow of the Chicago world's fair, a group of city leaders formed Minneapolis' Civic Commission, and a year later they passed a resolution calling for the shaping of a plan which would provide all things necessary for "a well-ordered civic life." Daniel Burnham acted as adviser,

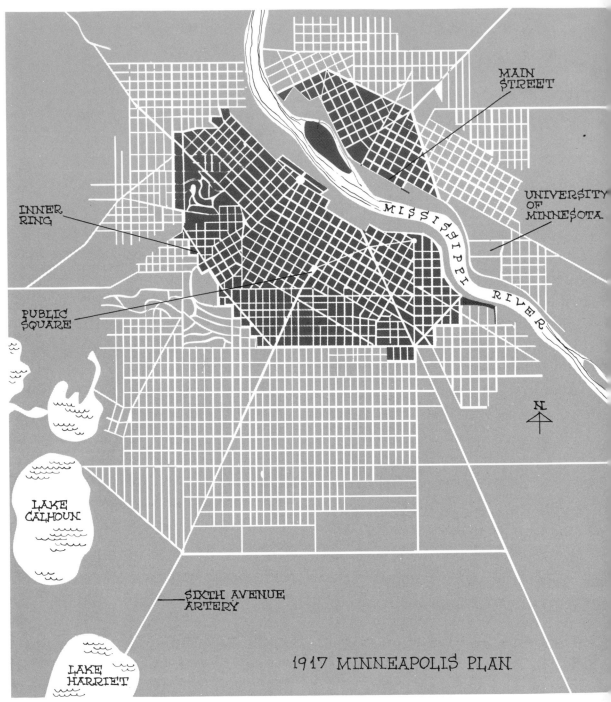

MAIN STREET

UNIVERSITY OF MINNESOTA

INNER RING

MISSISSIPPI RIVER

PUBLIC SQUARE

N

LAKE CALHOUN

SIXTH AVENUE ARTERY

1917 MINNEAPOLIS PLAN

LAKE HARRIET

The diagonals of the City Beautiful imposed upon a traditional American grid. Note the proposed Sixth Avenue artery reaching out to the park at Lake Harriet. An inner ring of boulevards prefigures the later expressway.

but after his death in 1912 the work was carried forward by E. H. Bennett of Chicago. Not until 1917 was the plan published.[9]

The Civic Commission put it forth with great determination and with the air of self-confidence that to this day makes Minneapolis leaders capable of extraordinary accomplishments. Set out in a handsome volume limited to one thousand copies, its illustrations printed in full color, the plan stands today as a touching example of an idea whose time had passed.

The essence of this plan was the creation of two great axes with important civic structures at their junctures. The major artery at Sixth Avenue was in itself a startling concept. Through much of its length as wide as 250 feet, it was laid out on a diagonal across the existing grid, running across the entire city. At the southwest terminus, entering through a huge classic gate into the environs of Lake Harriet, it connected with the principal suburban highways of that day. To the planners it appeared that by such means they could bring rapid economic development as well as monumental order to the city.

Of key significance are the open spaces created at the junctures of the diagonal boulevards. The principal such square is at the site of what was to be a new civic center, a gathering of structures ornately styled and placed around a confluence of streets and avenues. In the official version of the plan is included a view of Versailles from a balloon—"a completed scheme [the caption informs us] somewhat similar to the civic plaza." Elsewhere at the junctures are nodes comprising a cultural center, a city administrative center, a travel center; and there are numerous circles seeming to have no other purpose than to create a circular flow of traffic. The most grandiose of the latter is compared to the Étoile in Paris. For the lesser ones, as at the points where a proposed inner ring meets the diagonals, various ornamentations and embellishments are indicated.

It would be unfair to leave the impression that this 1917 plan is without merit. As in plans for Washington and Cleveland, much that is prophetic is said about parks, especially about parks lying beyond the bounds of the existing city. It lays significant stress on the improvement of the waterfront. In its emphasis upon open space around such major civic functions as government, the arts, the railroad station, it prefigures some of the best of modern developments. The trouble is, the spaces of this plan are monumental. They are designed so that men may confront buildings rather than each other. The splendid vistas would be for the enjoyment of men in vehicles rather than on foot.

The greatest weakness of this plan, however—as of the whole City Beautiful movement—was its creating a situation ripe for the automobile to take over and to deform. By 1917, when the Minneapolis plan was presented, the automobile had already developed to a point where its more dangerous implications might have been discerned. Yet the planners could not alter the presuppositions on which their work was based.

Recognizing that much of the area through which the principal new avenue was to be cut lay within blocks either blighted or only partially built up, the planners supposed that an infusion of traffic would set everything right. What was needed, they said, was "a new artery to send life-blood coursing through the decayed tissues of the city." But we know what would in fact have happened. With the noise and pollution of automobile traffic along the loosely built-up boulevard, the "decayed tissue" would have been replaced by the kind of services and facilities that make up the modern "strip." As for Lake Harriet, where all this traffic was to debouch, it is not difficult to conceive the damage that would have been wrought upon the fragile park landscape.

The 1917 plan for Minneapolis was, of course, never implemented. The First World War intervened, and when another generation took up the task in the early 1950s the ideals and concepts of city planners were very different. The dream of boulevards, monuments, axes and formal circles had vanished. The scale of the central core had been reduced as freeways encircled the downtown area.

Now, instead of traffic "coursing through the tissues" of the city, cars were conceived of as a nuisance to be abated. Instead of boulevards, we find in today's Minneapolis a pedestrian walkway; instead of classic arches, skywalks; instead of endlessly pilastered exteriors, a tower of glass such as the IDS building. In short, within the span of fifty years the whole concept of urban space had altered.

Space and Motion

The City Beautiful movement was responsible for a striking enlargement of the civic scale—for one of those leaps into a new dimension that have characterized planning and architecture at crucial moments. In his best Chicago buildings, the Rookery and the Monadnock, Burnham had already increased the volume and height considered normal at that time; in his later city plans he increased the size of the avenues and plazas upon which buildings fronted—thereby downgrading the traditional street. The avenues which usurped the place of the street might conceivably have become scenes of popular assembly and agreeable pedestrian ways. In Paris many of Haussmann's boulevards did take on this character. But in the United States there was a different context. It was as if Americans had been waiting for a new form of speedway, an in-city corridor capable of carrying them in an unbroken flow of traffic. Indeed, it was as if they had been waiting for the internal combustion engine.

The road to the modern traffic jam was quite literally paved by the good intentions of the City Beautiful movement. The wide avenues, usually lacking strongly defined borders or architectural terminals, seemed to have been devised for one purpose only, and in fact were soon to be given over to the speeding cars at the expense of landscaping and walkways and to the detriment of buildings that bordered them. The exclusive claim of the automobile was formally recognized as boulevards were eventually transformed into express routes.

A new form of space thus came into being—space that was no longer static and bounded; space capable of being sensed only in motion. The social costs of the automobile and of the expressway cutting a wide swath through the city should not blind us to the fact that together these two inventions conformed to spatial predispositions of the contemporary period.

In the plastic arts, transformations have occurred in this century similar to those that have been affecting civic space. Objects that were once designed to exist in themselves, and were possessed of a reality independent of the spectator's position in time or space, became subject to particular circumstances and special viewpoints. A building was no longer a construction to be judged by its exterior façade and represented according to traditional laws of perspective. It became an environment which revealed itself through movement. Indeed, it was not something to be viewed at all, but to be felt in its entirety as one passed around and through it.

Similarly, kinetic sculpture moved into new configurations before the eye; or moved as the spectator moved to surround and penetrate its form. Modern painting created by various devices the impression of seeing different aspects of a thing simultaneously; or, more subtly, of keeping in the mind receding layers of vision, the residues of overlapping impressions.

The traditional city space, like the traditional sculpture, had been made to be enjoyed by people remaining more or less stable. The street, which is often thought of as a channel for motion, was almost as often a fixed place—a site where things happened. People gathered in the street to talk or to stop, they ate at tables set outside its cafés; children played in it, old people sat on benches. Even more clearly, the square was a location where one was supposed to be at rest. Approached through the city's byways, the square formed a natural destination or stopping place. Let the street be widened to a boulevard, however; let the boulevard erode the square's seclusion—now a whole new kind of space comes into being. This space is no longer passive. It exists only when we keep going; it is sensed only in motion.

The Highway as Space

The parkways and boulevards of the nineteenth century introduced the idea that in urban planning, motion and space are complementary. The parkways became means of progressing through linear extensions of the romantically conceived countryside, under shady trees and often along cooling waterways. The boulevard provided a new means of experiencing the urban scene. In both cases the carriages were in themselves elements of a moving sculpture—while for those being thus transported, the landscape unfolded with the subtle variations one discovers in passing through any finely modulated structure.

At a different scale and with a vast increase of speed, the modern highway provided a new spatial adventure. At best, the automobile gained the sensation not only of uninterrupted motion but of motion through an environment of contrasting images. Though the highway engineers too seldom took advantage of their opportunities, there were moments when the car's rapid movement presented an exciting alternation of man-made and natural features, and when glimpses of the whole emerged from the crowded details. Cities revealed themselves at a glance, as Cincinnati and Seattle do on approaching them from the airport. If the view is lost behind a hill almost at the instant of its being exposed, the experience is even more in the nature of a revelation and its brevity is compatible with the speed at which modern time is passing.

The descent from the highway into the streets of the city provides a different experience. The change in speed, and then the change in scale, make an instantaneous transition from one kind of space to another. In several cities, design efforts are being made to identify this moment of change. "Portal parks" at the exits from the inner loops of expressways become a means of marking and celebrating the passage from space experienced only as motion to the contained and bounded space of the more traditional civic order. Elsewhere, as at Houston, a number of elements combine unexpectedly to create the sense of having arrived.

To one's right, upon coming from the Houston airport, is a major park. To the left is City Hall, with its own deeply shaded small park. The red tile roof of the old library is a welcoming accent; and beyond it lie the tightly gathered skyscrapers. Though a closer inspection will reveal much that bears an inhuman aspect, nothing can quite dispel the sense of momentary excitement as one descends from the expressway into the narrowness and crowdedness of Houston's city streets.

This change of pace and this sense of arrival are not to be confused with mere cessation. To pause on a street or in a square is to be rewarded by being in the midst of comprehensible space; to be stopped on a highway is to be lost. Experiencing a traffic jam on an expressway is to have spatial pleasures converted on the instant into a feeling of enclosure and even of imprisonment. The exhilaration of continuous flow, of a varied and changing visual composition, gives way to seeing and feeling nothing. The kinetic nature of the experience has been destroyed, and in its place is the deadening sensation of being nowhere.

The Strip Cities

A related but different form of space as motion has been discerned in the contemporary, or postmodern, development of the strip. Having begun modestly enough and for purely practical reasons, the strip has become, like a Campbell's tomato soup can, something of an art object, as its appreciators have grown into a cult. It started at the edges and on the outskirts of towns, but has threatened to take over the city itself and to become its dominating form of spatial organization.

Originating along the main roads leading from the center, these strips were a direct linear extension of the existing city frame. Here land was cheap, so that demands for the large floor areas needed by furniture stores and automobile showrooms could be met. Here, too, parking was available. The absence of zoning restriction in such areas made it easy for the sprawling and nondescript buildings to attract the eye of the motorist by flamboyant signage. One was compelled for lack of alternate routes to pass through these weird assemblages, where like highway robbers of old the proprietors stood athwart one's passage.

The freeway system might have been expected to eliminate the strip form of development. This was not to be the case. By the 1950s strips had become so firmly established, and apparently answered so effectively the shoppers' practical and emotional needs, that they continued as a particular form of shopping area, some being granted a semireligious aura through designation as a "Miracle Mile."

If the strip had once prospered because it was impossible to escape, it now became a place people took pains to go to. Even more ominously, it began to be replicated under changed conditions. The roads leading from the freeway exits, like the roads once leading from the center city, became lined with glaring lights and seedy signs. It is significant that in Atlanta the planners find little in the way of industrial development integrated with the freeway exits, but find instead at those points "a linear form, ubiquitous parking areas, and visual chaos."[10]

This very chaos may be interpreted as a form of urban space. Prolonged and generalized, the strip is taken as representing a new kind of city, of which Las Vegas is the most stunning example.[11] Gone from such a city are the spaces that we have traditionally supposed gave form and limits to the urban agglomeration and that provided for the citizens special pleasures and recreations. Gone are the streets, squares, parks; the avenues and boulevards. Gone are the monumental buildings with their open spaces around them. In their place is the broad right of way lined by flashing signs, symbolic representations of familiar objects, and a blinding array of overlapping graphic configurations.

All this, we are assured, is not chaos. It is a "new spatial order," abandoning form in favor of the mixed media. The dominance of signs over objects, of billboards over structures, has no antecedents and no equivalent in our concepts of urban form and space; it has nothing to do with historical styles, yet is a style, the architect and critic Robert Venturi asserts, that stands for values of its own.

Las Vegas space is neither enclosed nor contained, nor classically balanced nor symmetrically ordered. It does not flow around free-standing urban space-makers, as modern space is often supposed to. It is, rather, space defined by the impact of crude sensations, measured by the intervals of time between visual stimuli. Within such a medium we surrender the use of the ordinary senses, the awareness of objects and the feeling for distances, much as one does when entering a complex cloverleaf.

In the older organization of space a crossroad was plainly visible as such. It imposed upon the individual a choice—to go straight ahead or to the right or left. It actually was a cross; and it called for the agony of decision. But the modern cloverleaf finds the individual impelled forward in directions to which his senses bear no relationship. In order to go north he may very well have to follow a sign leading him south. His reliance on "communications" must become total.

Postmodern space calls for this same surrender, for a similar substitution of the symbolic for the real. Along the perfected strip we do not see the hot dog in the window; we see the giant representation of a hot dog standing out in front. We do not see the structure, but only an advertisement of the structure—a sort of spiritual emanation, while the object itself recedes and vanishes. This is the world as it is experienced by men and women for whom time is a succession of dazzling lights seen through a windshield, and space is defined by the last light flickering at the desert's edge.

Conceivably the strip may represent something valid in American experience, as pornography and graffiti may represent something valid in art. Like the pop artist, Venturi has performed a service in opening the eyes of his generation to neglected aspects of modern life. Taste is rarely the arbiter of relevance. What is taken for blight may conceal meaningful impulses struggling to be embodied in new forms. Indeed, where the iconography and graphics of the strip are sufficiently bold and concentrated, they can be quite overwhelming in their effect. A fault of most such areas is not that they have too much in the way of signs and lights, but that what they do have is not sharply enough contained. The visual litter runs out in attenuated form to become a parody of itself and a source of infection for other neighborhoods.

The strip is not to be condemned because it is loud and gaudy, any more than the expressway is to be condemned because it affords so rapid a form of motion. The serious objection is that the kind of spatial experiences they afford, while undoubtedly novel, satisfies only a small part of what the present generation of urbanists is seeking. The vision of a Burnham and a Venturi both fail, and they fail for the same underlying reason, even though one may appear on the surface very out of style and the other very "in." They propose the kind of space that can be known only in motion, while today's city dweller seems determined to combine this with measurable and bounded spaces, built to the human scale.

Toward New Pedestrian Spaces

The spatial organization of today's cities is being largely determined by the fact that people like to be on foot as observers and participants in the urban scene. They are increasingly prepared to park their cars and take part as individual human beings in the movements of the city, its comings and goings, its meetings and its dispersals. The force of pedestrianism has caused urban planners to re-examine most of their basic assumptions and to shape an urban environment basically different from that which a few generations ago was considered the ideal.[12] Where the basic issue is posed— wheeled traffic versus foot traffic—the latter is in a surprising number of instances winning out. The shift in values may be seen in a process so simple as the widening of a sidewalk, or in developments as ambitious as those that are setting the pedestrian upon skyways, giving him landscaped malls for his domain, and creating new city squares and parks.

The force of the pedestrian movement may be judged by the way it has taken advantage of technological developments. Two dominant features of contemporary urbanism, the skyscraper and the arterial highway, appear to be unrelated—and indeed adverse—to the interest of the man on foot. The scale of the skyscraper is at odds with the buildings that framed the earlier town square, as the highway negates the spatial values of older forms of open space. Both have been deplored by urbanists who have tended to look at the objects themselves, rather than at the quite unexpected effects they have had upon the city's character. In fact, these two essentially modern developments have been used to restore small-scale spaces and to tip the balance in favor of the pedestrian. Humanly designed spaces do not, as we shall see, belong to the past; space as motion is not necessarily imposed by modernity.

The skyscraper may be attacked on many grounds, aesthetic, ecological, humanistic. But for one simple reason it has helped preserve a compact city. Basically this is because vertical transportation is swifter and better organized than horizontal transportation. So far as the individual is concerned, the ride is also free. Where skyscrapers are clustered it is possible to go easily on foot from one urban destination to another. A city like Houston, despite the immense spread of its suburban areas, is tightly knit at the core, with a system of underground pedestrian tunnels uniting most of its commercial buildings. The Wall Street area of New York, overpowering in the scale and mass of its buildings, nevertheless provides some of the most dense pedestrian passages to be found anywhere.

The City Beautiful movement was basically hostile to the development of the skyscraper. Burnham, a pioneer designer of the high-rise tower, in his later Beaux Arts phase needed buildings horizontal in form to line his spacious courts and boulevards. The shapers of the 1917 Minneapolis plan, that climactic expression of the City Beautiful, viewed the skyscraper as a "disease." They denounced the new towers of New York's Broadway as a menace to public health—a source of "unventilated, sunless business offices." A more profound objection went to the root of what the Beaux Arts planners conceived to be the ideal city. "The immediate effect of the skyscraper," they declared, "is to limit the number of buildings needed." It was also to create nodes of intense activity, as opposed to the "justice" of having buildings evenly disposed and property values equalized throughout the city.

Where high buildings were erected, it was maintained with some logic, the space around them should be proportionately large. This, however, was thought undesirable because it would break the line of the boulevards of the City Beautiful. It would erode the classic boundary of its plazas. In due course Le Corbusier's solution made of this supposed defect the central feature of a new image of space. His skyscrapers were placed upon open areas sufficient to assure sun and air for each; and as a result they erased completely the concept of court and boulevard, leaving the pedestrian with spaces too wide to cross comfortably on foot.

The contemporary solution is to accept the economic pressures making for clusters of high-rise buildings, and then to maximize at ground level the advantages produced by the concentration of people. Architects have been experimenting with ways in which the skyscraper can most effectively meet the ground, some of this work makes important contributions to the street-level landscape. The skyscraper plaza at best can provide pedestrian areas quite different in form, but no less picturesque and animated, than those of the old marketplace or cathedral square. Even where older buildings descend without plan and in apparent disorder, we tend nowadays not to see oppressive canyons, but street scenes of reassuring liveliness.[13]

The transportation system is a second major factor inducing a healthy form of urban density and compactness. In combination with the skyscraper, the expressway encircling the downtown core has been creating environments scaled to the short journey made on foot. Despite its overpowering dimensions and often crude engineering details, it has had the effect of making the city dweller conscious once again of the psychological and practical pleasures of enclosed areas, narrow streets and bounded distances.

The city walls of medieval towns were likewise the product of technological needs. They were massive works of engineering seemingly unsuited to making life more pleasant for the urban individual on his daily rounds.

Yet in the case of both military fortification and automobile highway the original concept was touched by humane values. The walled towns became the picturesque centers within which existence attained a unique liveliness and intensity, contained as it was by a tight spatial organization. The modern city core, confined by its inner traffic loop, at least begins to mitigate the looseness and dispersal which have long been characteristic of American cities. Contrary to conventional expectations, the modern downtown is apt to be quite a small place, easily grasped and readily traversed. Within it, open spaces of modest proportions are significant focal points of communal life, and many streets play a role more diverse than that of corridors of traffic.

This is accomplished despite the unprecedented numbers of people necessary to sustain the organizational forms of contemporary society, and despite the numbers of cars considered essential to bring them from the suburbs. The crowds of people are accommodated by high-rise towers. The cars (at least potentially) are accommodated in ramps at the periphery. The space of the central city then becomes inward-looking and centripetal.

Discoveries and Rediscoveries

Such visible developments as the clustered skyscrapers and the arterial loop have been accompanied by new theoretical formulations in regard to civic space. Some of the most significant of these have been in the form of perceptive second looks. The cities of ancient Greece and Rome have been re-examined, their agoras and forums seen as precursors of the modern town square. (It is interesting to be reminded, for instance, that no wheeled vehicles were allowed in the vicinity of the forum at Pompeii, the most subtly developed of the open spaces of the ancient world.) Vitruvius has been reread. The hill towns of modern Greece and Italy have been viewed with a fresh eye, and the medieval city has been revisited in the imagination.

The virtue of crowded street life within the compact neighborhood was affirmed notably by Jane Jacobs in her now classic book on American cities. Not since Rousseau had found in his native Swiss canton an image of universal democracy had any writer so effectively generalized the qualities of a particular environment. Jane Jacobs' Greenwich Village was seen as the ideal form of spatial organization, one where urban inhabitants could know one another and watch one another, where sidewalks were broad and traffic lanes narrow. Another urban enthusiast, William H. Whyte, used close observation and time-lag photography to discover within the contemporary plaza a milieu rich in human encounters. Landlords might try to thwart the populace by prohibiting vendors and providing a minimum of seating space; but the people still gathered to watch one another, to argue, to eat and to conduct mysterious small deals.[14]

One of the most significant rediscoveries of urban space was contained in a book first published in 1889. Camillo Sitte's *The Art of Building Cities*[15] appeared in Vienna at a time when Americans were still in love with their visions of wide-open spaces, and when they were prepared to be seduced by the City Beautiful. The book was not translated or published in this country until 1945. Then it found a ready audience and a sympathetic atmosphere. Its message is the importance of open spaces conceived from the beginning as elements of the city at least as important as its buildings, and designed according to basic architectural principles.

The modern city, Sitte argued, completely reverses the proper relationship between built-up areas and open space. In former times the open spaces—the streets, squares and plazas—were designed to have an enclosed character and to create a predictable effect. "Today we normally begin by parcelling out building sites, and whatever is left over is turned into streets and plazas." The sole reason for the existence of most modern open space, he maintained, is to provide more air and light, or to break the monotony of oceans of houses. Sometimes, too, it serves to enhance a monumental edifice by freeing its walls.

But the point of open space, as Sitte saw it, was not to serve or enhance a building, but to *be* a building—or at least to be something so like a building as to be chiefly distinguished from it by lack of an actual roof. In the eye of the medieval or Renaissance city-builder, "the difference between the public square and other structures was so slight," he wrote, "that it is amazing to our modern minds, accustomed to a very different state of things." In the time of those earlier builders, public squares were inseparable from the buildings that enclosed them (as the wall is inseparable from the room); and they formed the principal settings for public life. It was not the open spaces that served the buildings, but almost the opposite. The buildings served the open space as enclosures, providing backup facilities by their indoor warmth and shelter.

With the dissipation of the earlier conception of open space, modern cities (in Sitte's view) had become too loose and open. The intersecting streets made for too many breaks in the continuity of their fabric; they created the effect of isolated blocks and sacrificed the enclosed and enclosing

1. Bern.

Three European squares from
The Art of Building Cities by Camillo Sitte.

2. Venice.

3. Florence.

nature of the street. Modern squares were too big. Although the square should be adapted to the size of the structures surrounding it, there were squares too vast for even the large-scale buildings that modern commerce and government required. Indeed, as a result "the fear of squares had become a modern nervous disorder. Many people suffer from it. They become ill in crossing a large square."

Sitte's book is full of practical formulations for the creation of effective open space. A few acres of ground not being yet a square, it is necessary to deal with the unformed environment as artfully as if designing a room. Among the important rules was the need to avoid too many wide openings. At Ravenna the streets enter at the corners so as to leave unbroken the central line of buildings. An arcade providing visual continuity at the street openings is recommended. The "rage for isolating everything" is, above all, to be overcome. Sitte even has interesting comments on the way sculpture or a fountain is to be placed within a square—not in the traffic routes, but at those points where pedestrians tend naturally to pause and gather. One might discern such points by noting the pattern of footprints after a light snow. Squares should follow the ancient precedents in not being too regular, and could well open into other squares, as at St. Mark's in Venice.

This analysis, we must recall, dates from the last decade of the nineteenth century. It fails to suggest the spatial complexity and the dynamic quality of the best of today's open spaces. Yet it is recognizably modern in most of its insights. Venturi and his followers apart, today's architects are turning away from the open-endedness of the conventional American city. Corporate and architectural arrogance still combine to build the isolated high-rise structure and to place it amid undefined space. But the search is for spaces in which the human being feels at home, and where his interrelatedness with other human beings is affirmed.

Modern Space—An Example

American cities in their current phase of development present us with many examples of this kind of space. We shall see this concept at work, sometimes well and sometimes poorly expressed, at many points in this book. But we begin with an example in the field of campus rather than city planning, so as better to see the concept in a precise form.

The campus that Edward L. Barnes designed for the State University of New York for its college at Purchase asserts strikingly that a public place

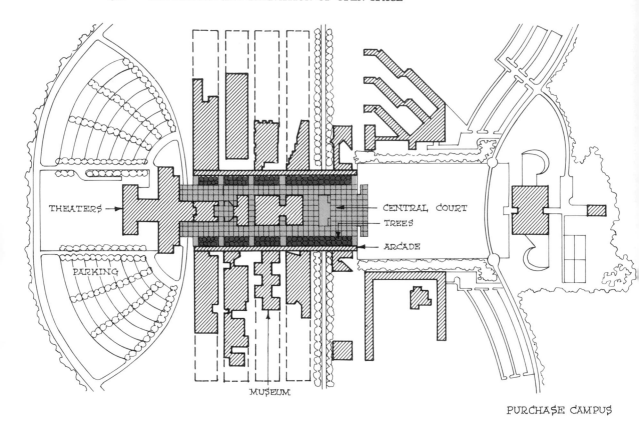

THEATERS

PARKING

CENTRAL COURT

TREES

ARCADE

MUSEUM

PURCHASE CAMPUS

A tightly bounded plaza at the heart of the Purchase college is combined with a dynamic capacity for growth. The buildings, placed with their narrow ends on the court, can extend backward to almost any length, with narrow "streets" running between them. The boundaries of the court are assured by a strong arcade and triple rows of trees.

must be created from the start, not merely left over after the structures have been shaped. It represents the subordination of architecture to urbanistic qualities; the subduing of the parts to the whole; and the assignment of private and public realms, of closed and open forms, to balanced and harmonious relationships.

The planner began with the college square. He wanted it to be large enough to receive the entrances of all major academic buildings, yet not so large as to provoke the kind of illness which Sitte had noted. He wanted it to allow for expansion and growth: as the population of the college increased, the use of the square was to become more intense, rather than its size extended. Finally, he wanted it to have enclosure and continuity while allowing for a variety of structures around its edge.

To achieve these objectives, Barnes placed the surrounding buildings so that their narrow ends face the square. This allows the perimeter to accommodate the maximum number of buildings. It has the secondary effect of de-emphasizing the architecture of the structures. The buildings can be of virtually any design, and they can be of any size, as the site allows them to extend backward to the required length, or farther in the same direction if later expansion is required. Between the buildings, "streets" open to the countryside, thus adding to the tightly ordered center that feeling for distance which characterized older American towns. All this is held together by the use of one material—a dark brick—and by a strongly delineated arcade (reminiscent of Jefferson's at the University of Virginia), which ties in the separate buildings and bridges the openings between them.

The planner had created the square so that it could be framed by anonymous structures; he then asked some of the architects least known for their practice of anonymity to be the buildings' designers. Among these were Philip Johnson, Paul Rudolph, Gunnar Bickerts and Robert Venturi. They submitted in varying degrees to the discipline of the overall plan. Philip Johnson, who might have been thought the last man to be amenable to the imposed restrictions, conformed most strictly; and his museum, unforced and unmannered in its interior spaces as in its exterior massing, is a happy example of how building and square can interact. There has by and large been achieved a fulfillment of seeming contradictory aims—uniformity and diversity; anonymity and the liveliness contributed by outstanding talents.

The square itself is a paved area three hundred by nine hundred feet, its long sides flanked by rows of trees running parallel to the arcades and open at its eastern end to an expanse of green field. A performing arts center—

four theaters included in one cruciform building—closes the square to the west. Giving the area form and breaking its otherwise excessive expanse is a group of partially underground structures running down the center, designed to contain library, bookstore, post office, and an open-air stage for meetings and performances.

A basic idea of the planner was to spread the nonacademic facilities of the college around the square rather than to conceal or centralize them in a single student union. The square will express its nature only as these activities spill over into the open space—as sculpture, banners, kiosks and bookstalls supplement the comings and goings of the students themselves.

The Purchase campus is small and isolated, compared with the vast enterprises which, as will be seen later, are transforming American cities. But it is significant in affirming what Arthur Drexler, commenting on it for the Museum of Modern Art,[16] called "the pre-eminence of the public sphere." It is significant, too, because in terms that are thoroughly contemporary, it corresponds to concepts of space that Vitruvius would have understood and that Camillo Sitte reinterpreted at the end of the last century. If the modern city has much of Las Vegas, it also has in it much of which Purchase is an illuminating abstraction.

2 Spatial Organization
of U. S. Cities

THE PROCESSIONAL CITY

SPATIAL CONCEPTS, as described in the first chapter, have been influencing
the forms of American cities, sometimes directly and sometimes as a
largely unconscious force. They have made the oldest cities what they are—
essentially monotonous in their original plan, but transformed by later shaft-
like spaces and parks on a large scale. They have shaped newer cities to
the desire for movement and openness. Finally, these changing concepts are
at work in the latest development of pedestrian-oriented environments.

The present chapter deals with selected American cities in terms of their
spatial organization: cities characterized by sequences of open space; by
a linear composition; and by a nuclear core from which corridors thrust
outward to reach satellite space. The reader will be invited to imagine
himself on a journey by foot, by bicycle or by automobile. With the aid of
illustrative maps he will explore the experience of moving through different
types of U.S. cities.

Philadelphia—A Classic Case

One begins, perforce, with Philadelphia.[1] No other American city has so
deliberately shaped its environment to provide the sense of passing through
varied spaces, all of them related and yet different in scale and function.

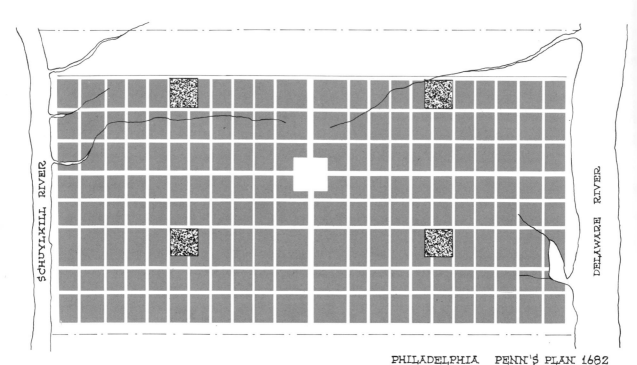

PHILADELPHIA PENN'S PLAN 1682

Historical contingencies have contributed to the outcome; yet at crucial points men with a strong feeling for urban design have imposed order upon the processes of change and growth.

The first planner was, of course, William Penn himself. He laid out his city at the narrowest point between the Schuylkill and Delaware rivers, bounding it on the north by the greenbelt of "Liberty Lands." Within this area a strict grid pattern was laid down, but with two wide avenues, Broad and Market streets, crossing at the center. The grid was further broken by a central square and by four squares placed symmetrically around it. Open space was thus made from the beginning the essence of the plan, providing Philadelphia with an identity readily fixed in the mind.

The city's development was somewhat different from what Penn imagined. He had supposed settlement would occur equally along the two riverbanks, progressing toward the center. Accordingly the houses were to be numbered from both the east and the west sides of the town, with the numbers mounting as the streets progressed inland. In actuality, settlement took place almost exclusively along the Delaware to the east, with the present-day Society Hill being the principal residential section of the eighteenth century. The center of gravity then moved westward, leaving the older city to decline in neglect while banks, offices and department stores clustered around the point where Broad Street and Market intersect at the central square.

By the early 1900s two developments pinned down the center: the construction of City Hall in the central square and the placing of the new subway system beneath Broad Street and Market Street. A third development decisively broke the grid and altered the whole spatial development of the central city. This was the construction, at the high tide of the Beaux Arts movement, of the Benjamin Franklin Parkway.[2] Incorporating one of Penn's five squares as a circle reminiscent of the Étoile in Paris, the parkway brought the tip of Fairmount Park's four thousand acres into the ambience of the central city. At a stroke, a new dynamism was introduced into the city's spatial organization.

Such were the conditions when in the 1950s and 1960s, under two remarkable mayors—Joseph S. Clark, Jr., and Richardson Dilworth—and under Edmund D. Bacon as executive director of the Planning Department, the concept of a modern center city was vigorously set forth. The 1963 master plan for Philadelphia's core stands as a classic document,[3] embodying the idea of a dense, multilevel central city, scaled to the pedestrian and responsive to essentially urban pleasures. Spatially the plan is based upon concepts that Bacon shortly afterward refined in his own pioneering study, *The Design of Cities.*

The plan is rooted in historic forces. The strength of the center is acknowledged and reinforced, with the eclectic City Hall made to stand dominant amid the taller buildings which were to surround it. Removal of the elevated tracks leading to the center gave opportunity for the commercial complex of Penn Center to be built, and new squares, promenades and underground concourses were provided. Restoration of the old residential area was given high priority.

The sequence of spaces may be followed on the map on page 46. Starting below the Museum of Art, classic and apart upon its hill, one descends the kind of avenue of which the Beaux Arts designers dreamed, past the kind of circle (superimposed on Penn's original square) that seemed to them essential as a means of altering the pace and providing a change in the vista. Benjamin Franklin Parkway still functions as a grand break in the

urban landscape, bordered by trees and flowers and in recent years strengthened by the edge accorded by new buildings. The edifices that close its two
ends—the Museum of Art and City Hall—are rare pieces of architecture in
themselves, and are placed at the right distance from each other to give
a sense of enclosure to the great space.

Density and liveliness are assured at the center by the transportation
systems that converge upon it; these qualities are expressed in tall buildings
and in a profusion of courts and plazas. Terraces below the street level lead
to the underground complex of transportation and pedestrian routes. To the
east past the central complex, the busy commercial area of Market Street
creates its own atmosphere and pace of movement.

In the Market Street East development, a wholly new environment—a
glassed-over and multileveled space four blocks in length—is moving beyond
the planning stage into visible forms. This will be the place of arrival, the
explosive point at which a population emerges from the confinement of cars
and subways, buses and commuter trains, to greet the city of quick pedestrian movement and bright confusion. A block to the south and parallel with
Market Street is the malled pedestrian space of Chestnut Street.

Cutting across the built-up grid, Independence Mall provides a greenbelt
tying together two of Penn's original squares. From Independence Hall the
National Historic Park leads east, and parallel to this runs the spine of
Society Hill. The passage is now through streets and walkways among the
restored eighteenth-century residential buildings and the modern town-
houses designed to fill the breaks. The open space texture is one of intimacy
and charm, while three residential towers designed by I. M. Pei break the
scale with carefully planned juxtapositions. All this leads to the new parklands along the river and the still incomplete Penn's Landing development.

The passage has been over a distance of about four miles. Penn had
cared from the beginning that his city be one that people could traverse
comfortably on foot; the area as he conceived it was to be 1,130 acres. The
central city remains compact to this day, yet the spatial experiences it
provides have become more varied, more complex and more sharply con-
trasted than anything the eighteenth century could have conceived.

Boston—An Emerging Sequence

Boston has a very different history; it grew without a plan, and much
of it stands upon land that did not even exist until the mid-nineteenth
century. Yet the present-day form of the central city is in its spatial

sequences no essentially different from Philadelphia's.[4] A journey across environments of different scales and different historic epochs will be of approximately the same length, and, as in Philadelphia, will pass from a wedge of parkland to a riverbank.

By the 1850s Boston possessed no open space except the original Common, to which the contiguous Public Garden had been added; the latter bordered on the waters of Back Bay. Dammed to provide water power for mills, but without means for the town's sewage to escape into the sea, this Back Bay became a source of noxious odors. A second, more successful effort filled in the whole Back Bay area. New sites for housing and residences were thus created by one bold engineering stroke, an operation that easily paid for itself through profits derived from the new land. Boston was now in possession for the first time of a level expanse lying along the Charles which could be laid out in broad avenues and bordered by town houses with lawns and gardens.

On this land was created Commonwealth Avenue, a tree-filled space extending nine long blocks (about a mile and three-quarters). The first addition to Boston's open space was thus brought about by an engineer, Loammi Baldwin (who also developed the Baldwin apple); the second—likewise resulting from a gentle modification of the terrain—was the work of the great park-builder Frederick Law Olmsted.

Discouraged with political interferences to which he was subjected in New York, Olmsted had settled in Boston in 1876 and was given the task of creating a new park system. A wide green arc was to have its base in the fens of the Muddy River, at the point where it debouched into the Charles. In a later chapter we shall examine this system in some detail. What is important for the present is that the new Fenway connected with the outward end of Commonwealth Avenue. A map on page 196, showing Boston parks, illustrates the downtown connections.

Today the essentials of this system survive, though suffering degradations imposed by changed social conditions and by thoughtlessly designed expressways. At the same time the spatial system has benefited from having superimposed upon it developments that belong peculiarly to the twentieth century and to a new pedestrian scale. Upon the old spine has been grafted a series of dense, complex developments; and the scope of the open space system has been extended eastward through the historic town to meet the waterfront.

The new sequence of open spaces is less formal than the old. It seems to be saying that space is not a continuum to be crossed at a uniform speed (as in the horse-drawn carriage), but is shaped to the multiple and random speeds at which urban man moves today—by car, by bus and on foot. It suggests moments of pause, as when we are caught in a web of small streets and bounded squares, and then the release of the long vista or the broad avenue.

To speak first of the less fortunate developments: The point at which Commonwealth Avenue intersects the Fens has been obscured and rendered impenetrable to pedestrians by the construction of a freeway and its approaches. The Fens' juncture with the Charles has been similarly mishandled. Indeed, today there is no way that a bicyclist moving along the shore of the Charles can turn inland to enter the Olmsted park system.

Both these interruptions could have been avoided by a more sympathetic design of the freeway. The fact that not even an underpass allows the river walk to connect with the park walk can only be attributed to a total insensitivity on the part of the highway designers. They gave absolute priority to the automobile, not recognizing that one characteristic of modern urban space is the accommodation of different speeds and modes of transport. As it is, pedestrian and bicyclist are ignored.

Referring now to the map of the central city on page 46, we look at some of the better modern developments. Coming out of the Back Bay Fens, one passes Symphony Hall to go a block down Massachusetts Avenue to Norway Street. Here the Christian Science Church has created a pedestrian environment on an impressive scale, a reflecting pool 670 feet in length bounded by church-related buildings designed by I. M. Pei and focusing on the historic structure of the Christian Science Mother Church. These spaces connect with the plazas and passages of the Prudential Center, a thirty-one-acre complex of hotel, department stores and office buildings. The Prudential environment is contemporary in its mixed uses; it is mediocre in design, but shaped for the pedestrian and effective in its spatial sequences.

Emerging into Boylston Street, the pedestrian next enters Copley Square, a famous and traditional city space walled on two sides by the Public Library of Stanford White and Trinity Church, designed by H. H. Richardson. The silver-blue shaft of Pei's John Hancock Building impinges on the square but does not dominate it. From here one turns to walk down Clarendon Street and into Commonwealth Avenue.

The transition is dramatic. Coming from the spine of skyscrapers at the edge of the Back Bay area, one is now in an environment of an entirely different scale—the nineteenth-century city of low brownstone buildings, of trees and lawns. Three blocks, and Commonwealth Avenue opens to the large green space of the Public Garden and the Common.

In this progression we are still only at the hinge, at the midpoint in the sequence of Boston's downtown spaces. From Tremont Street (or perhaps from the relatively narrow, shop-lined Washington Street—a proposed mall) one enters the space of the civic center. A pedestrian bridge takes one past Faneuil Hall and the Quincy Market. From there under the expressway, a "walkway to the sea" leads to the new waterfront park and to the wharfs being renewed for housing and shopping.

The course of a little more than three miles from the Fens to the waterfront has been replete with various sensations, with contrasts and discoveries. There has been a sense of progression through changing environments and indeed through different periods of time. Along the way notable buildings have added to the rewards of the passage.

The City's Internal Form

To a striking degree Boston has revealed a spatial organization similar to that of Philadelphia. In each case the root of the system is in a major park; this gives way to a landscaped artery (Benjamin Franklin Parkway, Commonwealth Avenue). Each artery is broken by a new spatial form embodying governmental authority (Philadelphia's central square with its City Hall, the Common with its State House). From here in both cases the passage is through the intimately scaled streets of a historic district and down to a waterfront park.

It is illuminating to note how in Paris the same sequences occur within a frame of similar dimensions. The map on page 47 shows central Paris drawn to the same scale as the two American cities. Here, too, we have a system anchored in a large park (the Bois de Boulogne); the procession down a grand boulevard (the Champs Élysées). The gardens of the Tuileries again provide a major open space within the processional route and serve as the historic seat of power. Beyond the Tuileries and the palace of the Louvre lies the ancient city with its small winding streets; and the whole culminates in the green space of the Luxembourg gardens.

In each of the three cases there has been a similar course of development; an outward thrust into relatively undeveloped lands, carrying the city forward to culminate in a major park. We have seen how the Benjamin Franklin Parkway was cut across Philadelphia's original grid; how Commonwealth Avenue was laid upon newly formed land. As if driven by similar forces, the Paris planners pushed outward from the Tuileries, which in the eight-

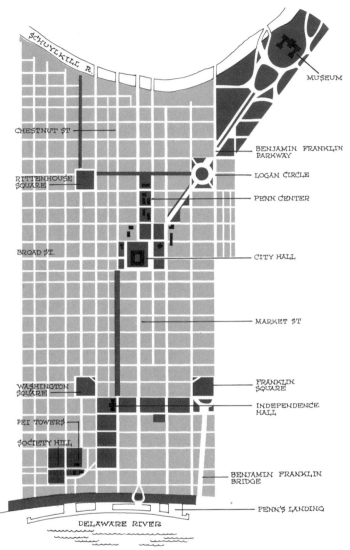

Map labels (Philadelphia):

SCHUYLKILL R.
MUSEUM
CHESTNUT ST
BENJAMIN FRANKLIN PARKWAY
LOGAN CIRCLE
RITTENHOUSE SQUARE
PENN CENTER
BROAD ST.
CITY HALL
MARKET ST
WASHINGTON SQUARE
FRANKLIN SQUARE
INDEPENDENCE HALL
PEI TOWERS
SOCIETY HILL
BENJAMIN FRANKLIN BRIDGE
PENN'S LANDING
DELAWARE RIVER
PHILADELPHIA

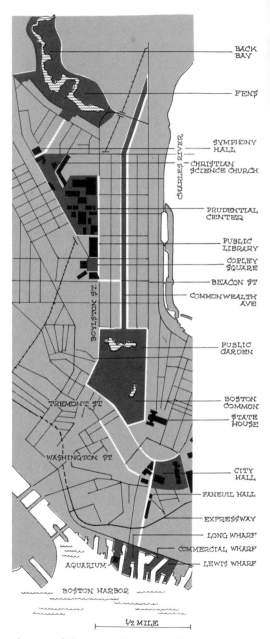

Map labels (Boston):

BACK BAY
FENS
SYMPHONY HALL
CHRISTIAN SCIENCE CHURCH
CHARLES RIVER
PRUDENTIAL CENTER
PUBLIC LIBRARY
COPLEY SQUARE
BEACON ST
COMMONWEALTH AVE
BOYLSTON ST.
PUBLIC GARDEN
BOSTON COMMON
STATE HOUSE
TREMONT ST
CITY HALL
FANEUIL HALL
WASHINGTON ST.
EXPRESSWAY
LONG WHARF
COMMERCIAL WHARF
LEWIS WHARF
AQUARIUM
BOSTON HARBOR
½ MILE

Philadelphia's Fairmount Park (left) leads into the Benjamin Franklin Parkway, cut diagonally across the old city grid to William Penn's central square at City Hall. From here the spaces become complex and intricate, as one moves past Independence Hall through the old residential section to the river.

In central Boston (right) the path runs from the Fens to the river, passing through Copley Square, down Commonwealth Avenue to the Common. Beyond lies the historic heart of the city, with the spaces around the new city hall and recent developments at the riverfront.

BOIS DE BOULOGNE

PALAIS DE CHAILLOT

EIFFEL TOWER

ETOILE

AV. DES CHAMPS ELYSEES

INVALIDES

TUILERIES

LOUVRE

LUXEMBOURG

NOTRE DAME

PARIS

1 MILE

This rendering of the classic space sequences of Paris, from the Bois de Boulogne to the Luxembourg Gardens, is drawn to the same scale as the two adjacent maps of Boston and Philadelphia. All three cities are shaped to the pedestrian, beginning and terminating in notable open spaces, with a variety of spatial experiences and directional changes occurring along the way.

eenth century stood at the edge of the old city. In the mid-nineteenth century Haussmann completed the construction of the Bois de Boulogne, as the good citizens of Philadelphia started Fairmount Park and as Olmsted a generation later completed the Fens. Thus in the three cities parks were formed to terminate the new forward thrust and to provide a dramatic change of scale. Here was openness where there had been constraint, and nature where there had been the works of man.

In most cities with an interesting spatial organization, contrasts will be found between the small scale of the older settlement and the greater openness and formality of later additions. In many of them, too, a bold city-builder will at some point have created a dramatic extension to an outlying green space. We shall observe in Brooklyn another such extension; and in St. Louis we shall note the failure to achieve a bold visual breakthrough to its major park. But in these resemblances we are not suggesting the existence of an ideal urban pattern. The succession of spaces revealing so marked a similarity in Philadelphia, Boston and Paris may be taken as no more than a satisfying coincidence, though undoubtedly brought about by comparable historic forces and by prevailing fashions in design.

More significant than the similarities is the fact that within many American cities a spatial pattern of one kind or another may be discovered. Such cities are distinguished by a quality that may be called processional; they reveal an interior organization formed by a variety of connecting and inter-related open spaces. These spaces invite movement at changing speeds through environments varied in their form and function, in their degree of openness and constraint. Because the central city is much smaller than is often realized—and because it returns in its contemporary form to the dimensions of its historic counterpart—the sequences can often be covered on foot. To do so is to sense most sharply the relationships of the different spaces and to have a feeling for the way the separate elements form part of one whole.

The weakness of American cities, in contrast to the cities of Europe, is the lack of care devoted to making the transition from one spatial experience to another. The "gate," which should indicate a change, either does not exist or has been allowed to be obscured by incongruous developments; the "hinge" between separate parts of the system remains unclarified. As a result two types of contrasting space may lie near enough to provide the potentiality of exciting contrast and the stage for a continuous and varied passage; yet in practice the juncture is so overlaid as completely to disrupt the movement.

Classic city design called for monuments, circles, arches and other devices to mark and celebrate such transitions. It is not suggested that these be imitated (although many of them merit preservation); rather that by contemporary urban planning the same effect be secured. The means available to today's planner include such devices as "portal" parks, malls, walkways and plazas, lighting and landscaping, and, not least, an adroit use of modern sculpture and wall paintings.

Available maps and guidebooks for American cities are of little use in uncovering an inherent spatial sequence. The maps are keyed to automobile traffic; they play down parks and squares. Guidebooks emphasize isolated buildings or at best the isolated square. Even when they trace out interesting walks, they show little awareness of the open space design that can run through a central city. One must find the pattern for oneself, as one would find a path through a maze. One must uncover what all too often neither the urban planner nor the urban guide has taken care to make plain.

The fact that American cities are so generally formed upon a regular grid makes it the easier, in some ways, to discern a processional aspect within them. The street pattern with its even blocks and repeated right angles is an open space plan in itself, requiring only slight variations to create noticeable contrasts. A busy intersection can show some of the qualities of a square; deliberately shaped openings are impressive precisely because they are approached through the relatively narrow and confining street. Elsewhere the grid gives way to the superblock, is widened to form an avenue or boulevard, or is overlaid by a diagonal. Larger parks, waterfront developments, commercial complexes, will totally shatter the grid, yet leave the street as a means of approach and as the vital connecting link.

Even Manhattan with its tyrannical grid can reveal any number of half-concealed spatial sequences. From the plaza at the southern end of Central Park one can move down Fifth Avenue to the pedestrian-scaled spaces of Rockefeller Center; thence across to Madison, where the projected mall may be imagined to exist; and down toward the intricate complex of the Grand Central area. Again, one can take the imperfectly formed axis of Forty-second Street, running from the United Nations at its eastern end, past Bryant Park and Broadway, to the Hudson River where the new convention center should logically stand. Moving north from Columbus Circle (to take a further example), one follows the diagonal of Broadway past Dante Square and Lincoln Center, up to Verdi Square at Seventy-second Street.

The exercise can be pursued as well in almost any city, within any grid where variations and interruptions have been permitted to occur. The search

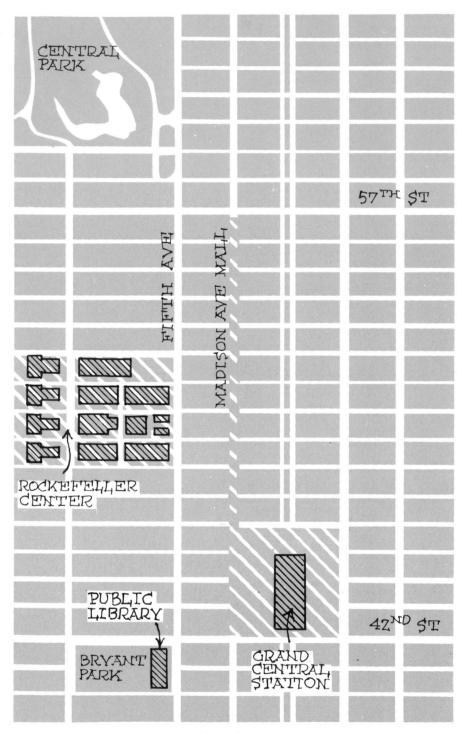

Midtown Manhattan

for sequences and processions sensitizes the citizen to the possibilities of the environment; it helps one see what lies half-formed beneath the seemingly undifferentiated urban scene. But the reader, before being released for such a search, is asked to consider two further cases in which grand spatial sequences, though incomplete, give a special character to their respective cities.

Scaled for the Carriage

The passage through Brooklyn, New York,[5] begins at Brooklyn Bridge, a sort of aerial park across the open space of the East River, and continues down the green spaces of the ambitiously designed Civic Plaza. Following the map of Brooklyn on page 52, we note to the east the narrow streets and picturesque views of Brooklyn Heights; ahead is Fulton Street, soon to be made into a pedestrian mall, a scene of crowded commercial activity; Flatbush Avenue is beyond. The avenue is nobly conceived, being anchored at one end in the soaring towers of the Manhattan Bridge and coming to a visual climax in Grand Army Plaza at the entrance to Prospect Park. In recent years blight has taken possession of this whole area, but today the first evidences of renewal are visible. Cultural and commercial institutions are being freed from dilapidated surroundings, while such small amenities as landscaped triangles at the intersection of side streets speak of citizen concern.

Prospect Park is itself one of the great open spaces of any city, and driving through it today one still can realize the designers' dream of seeming to be completely in the country. No buildings rise above the surrounding trees; the vistas down the Great Meadow appear endless. Where one emerges from the park at the southwestern end, another circle forms the transition to Ocean Parkway.

The parkway, one of the achievements Olmsted shared with Calvert Vaux, was a thrust into lands still undeveloped, which lay between the park and the expanses of the Atlantic. Having designed Central and Prospect parks, Olmsted had envisioned a system of green spaces extending throughout the city—linear parks which would enable the seeker for tranquillity to reach his rural enclaves along paths more agreeable than city streets. But New York was then losing its first enthusiasm for parks; it was turning to other social and political concerns, and Olmsted himself was soon to be engaged in the design of Boston's park system. He did, however, succeed

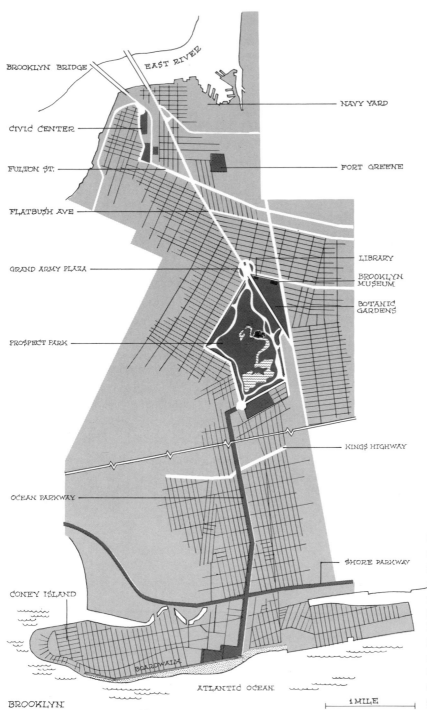

BROOKLYN BRIDGE — EAST RIVER

NAVY YARD

CIVIC CENTER

FULTON ST.

FORT GREENE

FLATBUSH AVE

GRAND ARMY PLAZA

LIBRARY

BROOKLYN MUSEUM

BOTANIC GARDENS

PROSPECT PARK

KINGS HIGHWAY

OCEAN PARKWAY

SHORE PARKWAY

CONEY ISLAND

BOARDWALK

ATLANTIC OCEAN

BROOKLYN

1 MILE

Scaled to the nineteenth-century carriage rather than to the man on foot, Brooklyn nevertheless shows a striking processional aspect. The terminal spaces are the Hudson River and the ocean. Midway, Prospect Park provides a dramatic change of pace and scene, while boulevards and avenues on both sides of it give form to the urban landscape.

in building Ocean Parkway, a broad link between Prospect Park and the Coney Island beaches. It survives as a wide tree-lined boulevard, with two grassy malls flanking the roadway, and with lanes for cars, pedestrians, bench-sitters, bicyclists and, until recently, horseback riders.

If the parkway is not what it used to be, it is still an effective part of the city's spatial system.[6] Driving down its four miles of length, with the recollection of Prospect Park in mind and with anticipations of the ocean ahead, is even today an experience to be savored. The beaches to which the parkway leads are a poor image of the gay resort area the nineteenth-century citizen ventured toward. But still the sand and the sea are there; and Ocean Parkway now makes lateral connections with the later parkways which encircle the bay shore.

This journey from the Brooklyn Bridge to the ocean, with its alternations of classic and romantic spaces, its passage from the densely built up shopping areas to the wide parkway, is a fine example of how space by itself can give form to a city scene. If this sequence of spaces is too long to be readily traversed on foot, it nevertheless lends itself easily to a bicycle ride, as it was once scaled to the carriage.

A Flawed Spatial System

In St. Louis, the organization of public spaces has been given much thought over the years.[7] Glancing at a map of the city, a semicircular area confined to a mere sixty-two square miles, one is immediately aware of two elements—the broad river and the large expanse of Forest Park. Add to these the famous Mall, which runs from the river due west in the direction of Forest Park, and one begins to conceive of a fine succession of spaces waiting to be traversed. In fact, the city's pattern is rather different from what this preliminary examination would suggest.

The first illusion to be dissipated is that Forest Park is meaningfully co-ordinated with the other spatial elements. When created in the 1870s, Forest Park lay outside the central city. It seemed so far in the country, indeed, that doubts were expressed as to whether it would ever be useful. The five miles lying between the river and the park have since been densely built up; yet the park remains aloof from the central business district and is tied in, rather, with residential neighborhoods surrounding it to the west, north and south.

The eastern side of the park, facing downtown, has been the least attractively developed. Here no monumental approach, comparable to the Grand Army Plaza in Brooklyn, creates a forecourt to the park. Instead a highway, following in the route of an old railway track, cuts off one corner, and across the eastern edge another highway was recently widened, taking park land without arousing serious opposition. In short, a wall, rather than a gate, confronts anyone who approaches from downtown.

Nevertheless, St. Louis does have an impressive series of spaces, and it has at its heart one of the most ambitious concepts of any American city. A photograph shows the central Mall, which was conceived as organizing the downtown area and giving access to the Mississippi River. This Mall was not originally thought of as a pedestrian place, but as a dramatic break in the urban landscape along the edges of which the principal public buildings of the city would be lined up. It stands today as a partially fulfilled idea. It does indeed give space to the civic and cultural center of the city. The old railroad station (preserved and soon to become the entrance to an office and residential complex) fronts upon it. It contains the much-loved sculptural fountain designed by Carl Milles, which symbolizes the meeting of the waters of the Missouri and the Mississippi.

The vertical thrust of the Mall had been intended to meet the horizontal green space at the riverbank and in recent years this has actually been achieved. Where the Mall is basically defective is in its termination at the other end. Having begun so grandly at the river, it leads nowhere. Market Street, which forms the backbone of the Mall, dips south beyond the railway station; expressways cross the area, neither bounding it nor being bridged boldly enough to lead forward into a new space. Forest Park, to which the Mall might have led, seems remote and isolated. The land rises beyond the expressway into the Mill Creek renewal area. Here there has been tentatively sketched a large square, which could make a fitting end to the thrusting space.[8] The likelihood of its attainment is remote.

The Mall escapes a Beaux Arts sterility by diverse and interesting lateral connections, still in need of being fully developed. To the south is the historic district centered upon Lafayette Park; also the nearby Soulard Market (in course of revival), as well as a planned new town in-town. South, too, will stretch the new development connected with the railroad station. To the north opens the business district, dark in tone and compact in texture, forming an effective contrast to the sunny openness of the Mall. Careful attention to this area, with the development of skywalks and pedestrian streets, could make a striking series of spaces leading past major department stores to the new convention center. Finally, as one progresses

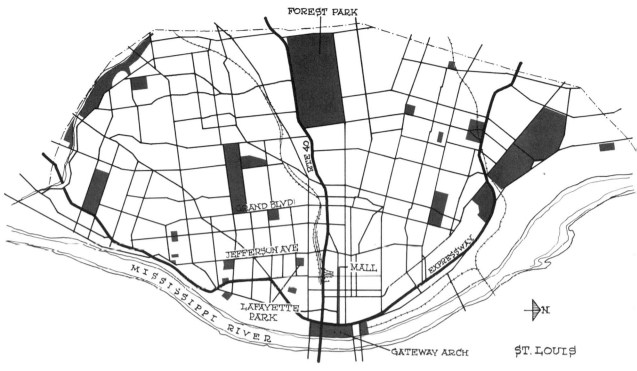

FOREST PARK

RTE 40

GRAND BLVD

JEFFERSON AVE

MALL

EXPRESSWAY

LAFAYETTE PARK

MISSISSIPPI RIVER

GATEWAY ARCH

N

ST. LOUIS

4. St. Louis Mall beginning under the shadow of Jefferson Memorial Arch.

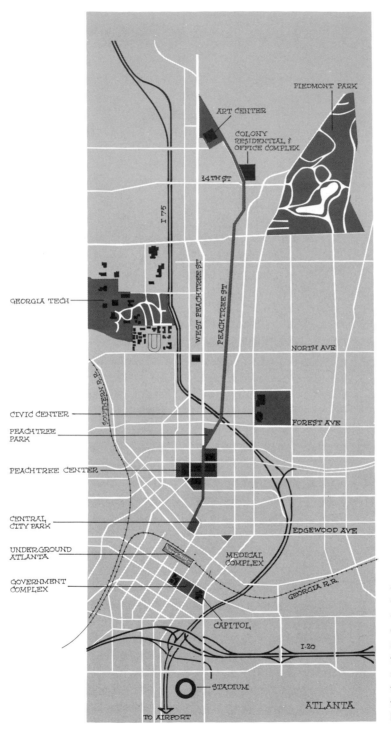

PIEDMONT PARK

ART CENTER

COLONY
RESIDENTIAL &
OFFICE COMPLEX

14TH ST

I 75

GEORGIA TECH

WEST PEACHTREE ST

PEACHTREE ST

NORTH AVE

CIVIC CENTER

PEACHTREE
PARK

SOUTHERN R.R.

FOREST AVE

PEACHTREE CENTER

CENTRAL
CITY PARK

UNDERGROUND
ATLANTA

EDGEWOOD AVE

GOVERNMENT
COMPLEX

MEDICAL
COMPLEX

GEORGIA R.R.

CAPITOL

I-20

STADIUM

ATLANTA

TO AIRPORT

Atlanta is a city stretched along a ridge, once the path of a railroad and now of an expressway. The separate spatial features of the city, from Piedmont Park to the stadium, are situated along this spine. Peachtree Street forms a connecting link parallel to Interstate 75.

west toward the major cross-artery of Jefferson Avenue, lively residential spaces open laterally.

If these developments are recognized as having a relation to the Mall, if the connections and entrances are effectively delineated, we may yet see in St. Louis a combination of spatial forms lively enough to make the central city outstanding. The linked Mall and riverfront will stand as the grand organizing theme, while juxtaposed to these classic spaces will be the dense, the small-scaled, the bounded areas which characterize contemporary urban planning at its best. Such are the possibilities that St. Louis balances against the economic problems it faces.

LINEAR AND NUCLEAR CITIES

In the cities just considered, space itself forms the organizing theme. Large parks, formal openings and small enclosed squares are part of a total system linked by linear parks and pedestrian ways. However flawed may be the development of such a system—overlaid by expressways or obscured by incompatible land uses—the observer senses within the urban context the possibilities of spatial variety and coherence. Certain other cities, however, take their form less from internal spaces than from natural or man-made features which impose a strong pattern of their own.

In such cities space is not continuous but occurs at intervals along a structural chain. Three examples from different parts of the country show effects upon a city's spatial organization of a geographic ridge, an extended coastline, and a river.

ATLANTA   The city has an interesting urban history, having begun as a railroad depot and developed along the railway lines, which followed the natural ridges. An 1870 map shows a city defined as a perfect circle, with three railroad lines coming together at the center. Such a plan was easily imposed upon the ruins left by the Civil War. Slow recovery and delayed development were, however, to bring about a city quite different from this early form. Today the central city may best be conceived as a string of urban features placed irregularly along the north-south ridge defined by Interstate 75.

Coming from the airport (closely integrated with the city and just south of it), one leaves the stadium behind, to pass in succession the state and city governmental complex, the hospital complex and the downtown node. Peachtree Street now becomes a principal north-south lane, reinforcing the alignment of Route 75. It links the downtown center with the high-rise development of John Portman and leads to a second group of skyscrapers half a mile beyond. Along this route lie such features as the Exhibition Hall, the cultural complex, the Colony residential and office complex, and Piedmont Park with its surrounding residential areas. Each of these has spatial dimensions of its own; each generates its own kind of openness. But together they are like beads strung loosely upon a thread rather than an integrated and continuous system.

Within downtown Atlanta there are spaces of interest in themselves; their terminals and linkages are now receiving thoughtful attention from the city planners. A small park being constructed at the juncture of Peachtree and West Peachtree creates a beginning for the internal open space system. Peachtree is being malled; a green square named in honor of Atlanta's Margaret Mitchell will mark an important juncture five blocks to the south. Most important of all, the small but vital Central City Park has been created at Five Points, the heart of the business district. Thus there exists an inner system of spaces, although the overarching form of the city is linear and its major features are distinctly separated.

SAN DIEGO A pacific coastline of twenty miles is the unifying element in the chain of alternating open spaces and settlements that forms the city of San Diego. Reaching down from the southernmost extensions of Los Angeles's vast sprawl, the regional city extends from a complex of institutions and universities as far as the Mexican border. Centers as diverse as La Jolla, Ocean Beach and Coronado are strung along this benign coast.

The first settlers in the area were drawn by the mild climate and dazzling views to live near the sea. Today, when San Diegans are asked what feature of their urban landscape they consider dominant, it is to the sea that their thoughts return.[9]

Actually, settlement has pressed well inland, covering the level mesas while leaving the canyons between them in a more or less unspoiled state. One invasion of valley lands resulted in the dismal landscape—shopping centers, strip developments and parking lots—of the present-day Mission Valley. Now controls are in effect, and the canyons are viewed in the San Diego open space plan as part of a system of natural parks.

Further inland, east of the mesas, a mountain range forms a barrier to settlement—a curtain against which the drama of the city is played out. The coast runs in a long arc, bounded by bluffs or penetrated by salt lagoons. At two points outgrowths of the mountains break the arc, extending out toward the sea at Mount Soledad and Point Loma. Related to these are two bays,

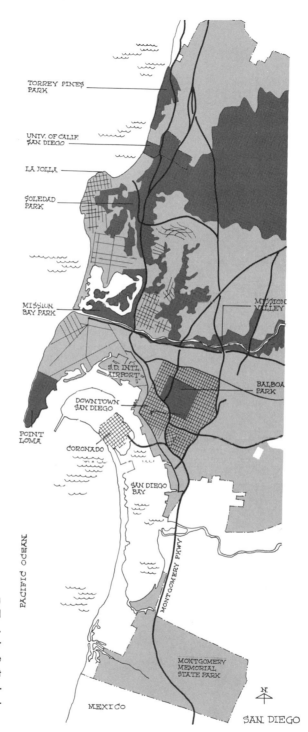

San Diego is a city strung out between mountains and sixty miles of the Pacific shore. Consciousness of the water gives unity to what otherwise would be a diverse assortment of communities and institutions. Two major bays punctuate the extended seacoast.

TORREY PINES PARK

UNIV. OF CALIF. SAN DIEGO

LA JOLLA

SOLEDAD PARK

MISSION BAY PARK

MISSION VALLEY

S.D. INTL. AIRPORT

BALBOA PARK

DOWNTOWN SAN DIEGO

POINT LOMA

CORONADO

SAN DIEGO BAY

PACIFIC OCEAN

MONTGOMERY PKWY

MONTGOMERY MEMORIAL STATE PARK

MEXICO

N

SAN DIEGO

important both as open space in themselves and as a means of breaking what might have been a continuous line of undifferentiated communities. South of Mount Soledad is Mission Bay, in recent years developed into a large aquatic park. On the inner shore of San Diego Bay, the central city is located.

The bay, with its islands, its beaches and its facilities for boating, is an urban open space which is supplemented inland by the thousand acres of Balboa Park, easily accessible to downtown San Diego. Southward from the bay stretch residential communities which are part of the regional complex; and the long chain ends in a state park at the Mexican border.

Nature has created this succession of spaces—a city pleasantly fragmented by bays on the seacoast and inland by valleys and canyons. Yet nature is subject to being overruled by the bulldozer and the dredge. A remorseless population spread could make it profitable to create a pattern of homogenized settlement. San Diego, fortunately, seems at least as concerned to avoid Los Angelization as San Francisco is to avoid Manhattanization.

Besides controls on use of the canyons, the city has taken a stand against unconstrained growth. Backed by the voters in the 1975 municipal elections, Mayor Pete Wilson was that rare phenomenon—an effective opponent of urban sprawl. Under his leadership San Diego passed legislation compelling new development to be co-ordinated with existing city services. Prospective developers would bear the burden of developing any new services, including schools, required by their projects. The city also blocked a massive flood control project, which would have made possible conversion of agricultural acreage to housing. Vigorously pursued, such policies could enable San Diego to show the best features of a linear city—a succession of bounded settlements, given coherence by the long stretch of a truly golden coast.

SAN ANTONIO A river forms the unifying chain of Texas's most charming city, while a waterway threading the downtown area creates small-scale amenities. Through most of its length this is in fact a man-made canal (it will be discussed in detail when we examine the open space features of downtown). The San Antonio River, from which the downtown waterway springs, is on a different scale and is the organizing feature of the larger city. For about six miles this river in its wandering course forms the connecting link for a number of urban features which otherwise would seem to be quite disparate.

Starting at the north, we confront the first major open space, unique to San Antonio. This is the Aquifer, a body of land endowed with subterranean water easily tapped, a sort of earth-covered reservoir. To prevent this land from being built upon and developed is considered by most ecologists the

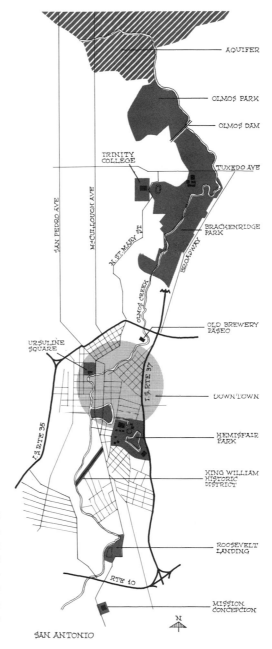

AQUIFER

OLMOS PARK

OLMOS DAM

TRINITY
COLLEGE

TUXEDO AVE

SAN PEDRO AVE

McCULLOUGH AVE

N. ST. MARY ST

BROADWAY

BRACKENRIDGE
PARK

OLMOS CREEK

OLD BREWERY
PASEO

URSULINE
SQUARE

I.S. RTE 37

DOWNTOWN

HEMISFAIR
PARK

I.S. RTE 35

KING WILLIAM
HISTORIC
DISTRICT

ROOSEVELT
LANDING

RTE 10

MISSION
CONCEPCION

N

SAN ANTONIO

San Antonio's spatial system is organized by the river. Down its main length from the Aquifer to the Missions stretch parks, institutions, historic complexes. A loop of the river penetrates downtown and gives this area a distinctive character.

plain course of prudence and good sense. The whole city, as Olmsted's shrewd eye observed when he visited the area on his Texas tour,[10] is tipped upward toward the north, so that the waters of the Aquifer drain toward the settled areas. Farther south, the San Antonio River becomes the axis of the city, passing through Los Olmos and Brackenridge parks, past points of picturesque and historic interest, through the downtown and out into the sites of the Spanish missions.

The river corridor contains many areas of potential development. The Old Brewery, the landmark Ursuline Academy, the presently underused Hemisfair park, the King William historic district—these await, along with others, the fulfillment of their cultural and recreational potentialities. The river system lends its livening touch, but what has been missing is access in a continuous flow to the various activities spaced along its bank. Indeed, an imaginative development of the river could convert this from a purely linear area to one having many of the aspects of a processional sequence.

With such a fulfillment in view, a river corridor study was made in 1973.[11] This proposes making the river throughout its six miles a channel of communication by footpath, bicycle and boat; it urges strengthening the nodes that this channel will connect, and also the development of better access to facilities that extend laterally from the river. At its base, the linear path is to be marked by an enlarged Roosevelt Park and a more secure preservation of the mission properties.

The 1973 plan does not deal with the problem of the north expressway, long stopped by citizen action at the southern entrance to Brackenridge Park. If it is to be true to its nature, San Antonio should remain a city whose significant places are spread at intervals along a river, not overpowered by an expressway.

A Molecular Agitation

Cities blessed neither by planning nor by natural features tend to organize themselves in their own haphazard way. Usually such cities find their central business districts surrounded by a powerfully expressed inner freeway loop. The loop acts as a constraining force, tending to drive buildings upward to skyscraper heights, and diminishing the distances between them. The separate features of the central city, each quite often with its own open space—its plaza, courtyard or small square—stand about at random within the constraining ring. Movement between them is not systematic and is not suggested by any directional current. A residential tower will be adjacent to offices, hotels adjacent to shops. Indeed, the newer complexes mix everything up; and one advances through such a city not so much by orderly procession as by bouncing from one feature to another.

Characteristic of such cities are outward thrusts, penetrating the sprawl and establishing further centers of activity or interest.

The diagram of Houston's downtown illustrates the connections, by underground tunnel or by pedestrian skywalks, that have been created (or are in a few cases projected) between Houston's principal public buildings. Pictured abstractly in this way, the core's spatial organization becomes more evident than through any other graphic means. What we see gives a sense of a random placement and molecular agitation which are characteristic of this type of city.[12] In actuality there are several well-conceived green spaces. But the essential pattern is revealed in the bridged circles of the diagram: an urban landscape with structures dotted indiscriminately upon the grid, and with hurried crowds passing back and forth between them. The diagram suggests the inherent force that leads to breaches in the constraining ring and the establishment of open spaces beyond it.

The area map indicates two principal outgoing routes. The first of these is to the northwest along the Buffalo Bayou. The bayou enters the city from the east. At the end of Main Street, the point where ships coming up the river formerly discharged their cargoes, is a small park, poorly designed but correctly conceived to mark and celebrate a historic place. From here the bayou flows unnoticed along the city's eastern edge until it widens into the green space of Sam Houston Park. The park forces itself out under the expressway, for a distance of three and a quarter miles providing linear space for walks and playgrounds, until it joins with the city's largest single open space, Memorial Park.

The second major breakthrough occurs where Main Street passes south under the expressway to reach after two miles the congeries of cultural and educational institutions that border Hermann Park.

Dallas reveals a somewhat similar pattern. Here the major breakthrough occurs westward toward Fair Park—once the site of an international exposition, now a place where cultural and athletic facilities are somewhat incongruously jumbled.

Dallas planners have a scheme to clarify through better land use and landscape design the way out of the ring and toward the park. At present it is extremely difficult to find the connection between downtown and Fair Park; the way is lost in a maze of disorganized street patterns, parking lots

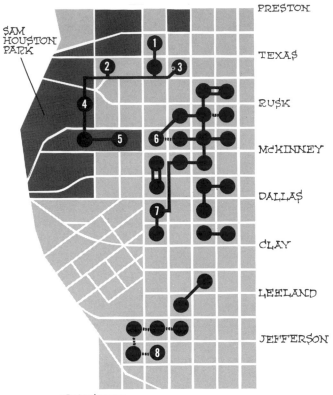

HOUSTON
DOWNTOWN

LEGEND:
1 ALLEY THEATER
2 EXHIBITION HALL
3 JONES HALL
4 COLISEUM & MUSIC HALL
5 CITY HALL
6 ONE SHELL PLAZA
7 REGENCY-HYATT HOTEL
8 CULLEN CENTER BANK BLDG

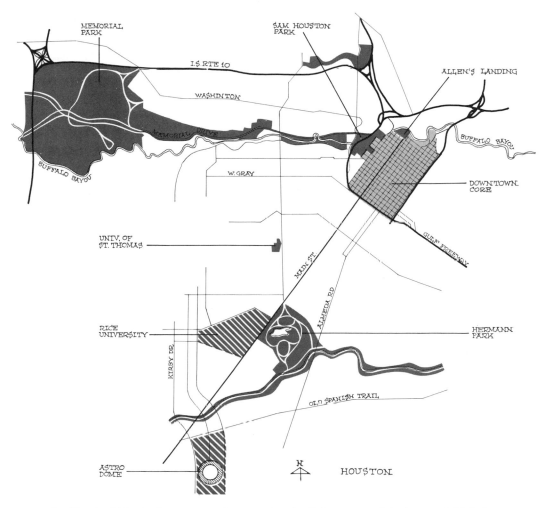

Combined within its freeways and expressing itself in a powerful cluster of high-rise buildings, Houston breaks out in lateral axes down the old Main Street and the Buffalo Bayou. These spatial thrusts terminate, respectively, in Memorial and Hermann parks.

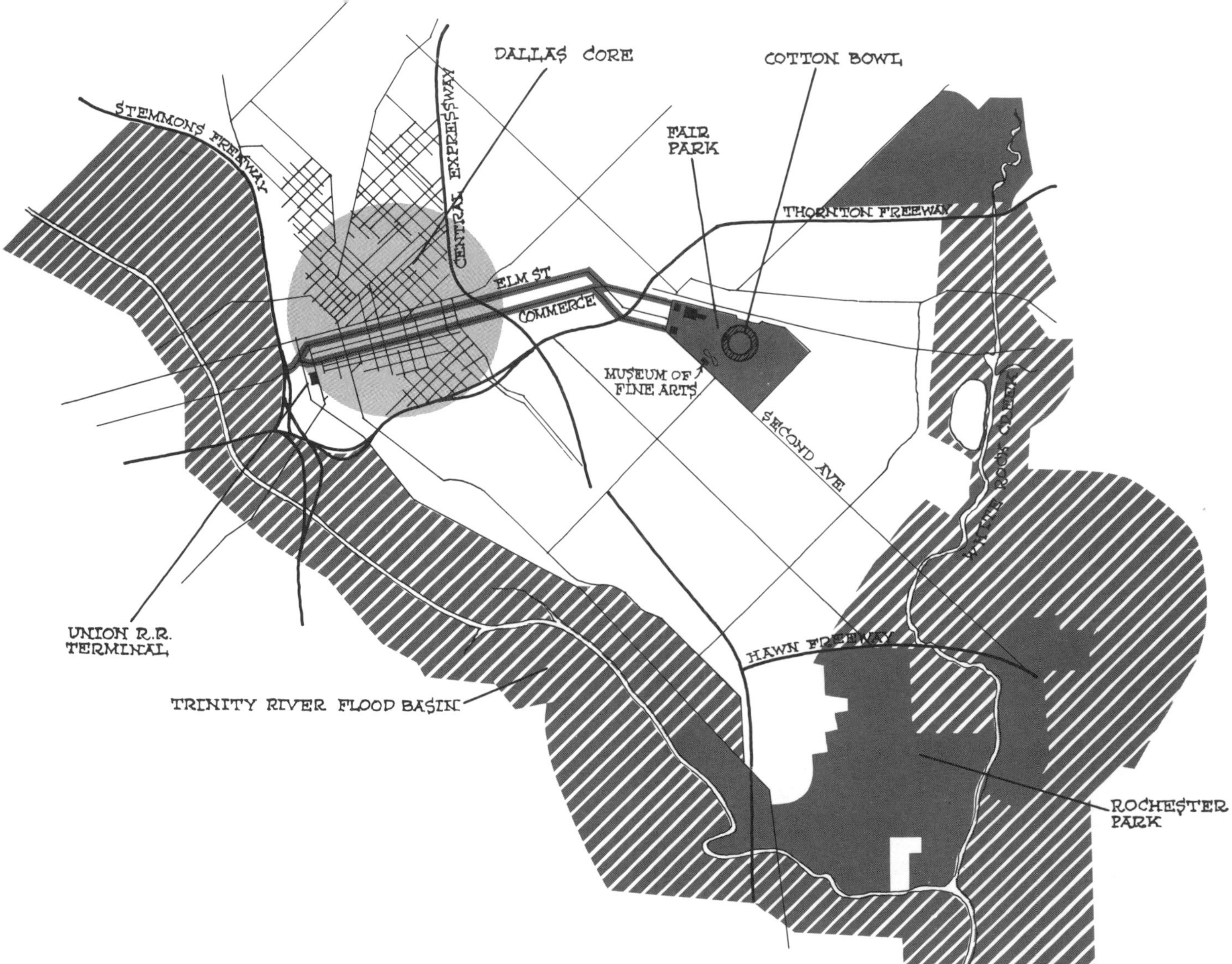

COTTON BOWL

ROCHESTER PARK

THORNTON FREEWAY

FAIR PARK

SECOND AVE.

WHITE ROCK CREEK

MUSEUM OF FINE ARTS

HAWN FREEWAY

DALLAS CORE

ELM ST.

COMMERCE

CENTRAL EXPRESSWAY

STEMMONS FREEWAY

UNION R.R. TERMINAL

TRINITY RIVER FLOOD BASIN

DALLAS

Dallas is a city walled by freeways and surrounded by the greenbelt of the Trinity River basin. On the East of downtown lies Fair Park, containing the city's principal cultural institutions. The spatial linkage of this downtown area and the related park waits to be developed.

and automobile repair facilities. Indeed, in both of the Texas cities the exits from the ring are concealed or partially blocked, lacking the design elements to mark a conjunction which on the map appears logically assured.

Why, for example, should there not be a clear indication, as one passes out of the inner core along Main Street in Houston, of the approaching change in land use and urban character? Why, in Dallas, as one passes in a northeasterly direction along Main Street, should there not be vivid indications of the spatial thrust lying beyond? A strongly conceived span under the freeway in one case, boldly landscaped green spaces surrounding the cloverleaf in the other, could orient the motorist and express the sense of escape that should be felt at this point.

Sensitivity to the city's changing spatial pattern is a first requisite to bringing about the kind of design features that make a city legible and coherent. In too many American cities the opportunity is neglected and the underlying spatial form remains an enigma.

3 The Role of Topography

THE NATURAL SITES of American cities are more diverse, and often far more beautiful, than is generally recognized. The casual visitor going from the airport to his motel may find little to distinguish one city from another. He assumes that all of them are drawn to the same plan and exist upon the same sort of convenient tableland. Even those who live in the cities fail too often to sense the underlying topography or to appreciate the relation of man's work to nature's.

Some Notable Settings

Yet each city exists upon its own piece of earth and in some measure or other derives its character from land and water. A few of the major cities we see as inseparable from their settings—San Francisco with its bay and its in-town hills; New York with its two rivers embracing Manhattan Island. Chicago's lakeshore is fixed indelibly on the mind; the river that played so important a role in the city's early history is still visible at its core, the focus of new efforts to create a downtown of significant amenities.

Other settings are less well known, but their uniqueness strikes the eye of the sensitive observer, as in the past they have evoked the astonishment and praise of travelers. Some examples:

LOUISVILLE, KENTUCKY For a thousand miles, from Pittsburgh to New Orleans, the inland river system of the Ohio and Mississippi flows unobstructed by any sizable obstacle—except for the Great Falls at the site of

Louisville. Here a city was destined to grow, accommodating the transshipment of goods and men. Inland the land opens in a circle of plains, and rises to the east and north to form the rolling country that has long been the city's most desirable residential section. (By comparison, Cincinnati lacks the dramatic interruption of the river's flow, but reveals a plain of four square miles pierced by rivers and rising to a commanding crescent of hills.)

MADISON, WISCONSIN   Nothing excels the classically appropriate setting of this midland city of 172,000 population. Between Monona Lake and Lake Mendota an isthmus rises in a gentle elevation; on its crown stands the capitol of Wisconsin, surrounded by the financial and commercial sections of the town, with the university opening along the lakeshores to the west.

PITTSBURGH, PENNSYLVANIA   Two rivers, the Allegheny and the Monongahela, flow together at a level triangular plain to form the start of the Ohio. Holding the key to access to the West and drawing produce from the settled East, the site was contended for by three great powers. To the east of the triangle rises a spine of hills, and the banks of the two rivers are bordered by sharp bluffs. Coming suddenly upon the city of clustered towers as one emerges from a tunnel is today a breath-taking sight; and so it was from the beginning. "It must appear an enchantment to a stranger [so wrote a traveler of 1786] to see, all at once, and almost on the verge of the inhabited globe, a town with smoking chimneys, halls lighted up with splendor. . . ."[1]

BINGHAMTON, NEW YORK   This small upstate city stands where two rivers, the Susquehanna and the Chenango, meet at right angles—in "a valley, hill encircled." The land runs back from the Allegheny for a mile and a half, before the hills rise to a height of five hundred to eight hundred feet: "they engirdle the city with a natural loveliness of the softest, gentlest, most unwearying kind."[2] Upon the plain itself, in the residential area west of the Chenango, varieties in the conformation of the terrain helped keep the railroads away from the river shore and laid the foundation for a lively urban landscape.

NEW ORLEANS, LOUISIANA   If the sites of other cities are made by their hills, that of New Orleans is made by its declivities. Much of the city lies fourteen feet below the level of the Mississippi, which passes in a sharp curve at the city's front door, and Lake Pontchartrain, which forms a northern border. This land between these two waters is penetrated by bayous and canals. The low-lying site requires a constant pumping operation and has resulted in a compact pattern of settlement. Until recent advances in building technology, New Orleans was spared the skyscraper, and its low skyline suggested the city's watery roots.

Unfortunately, the settings of these and other American cities have been obscured by sprawl and overrun by insensitive economic developments. The falls at Louisville are cut off by the elevated expressway; the origins of Louisiana are betrayed by particularly barren high-rise buildings; the hillsides of Cincinnati are threatened with being misused for construction sites.[3] Along the shores of most American cities railroads and industrial structures block the views and prohibit access. Elsewhere skyscrapers dwarf the hills, and the implacable grid masks the nuances of topography.

Yet land and water, if not fatally abused, wait in silence to make their presence felt. The present chapter deals with the way these elements can affect the open space of cities. It examines four representative American cities to see in what measure their free lands reflect and enhance the underlying structure.

The Claims of Nature

A basic issue before recent generations of city-builders has been their approach to given topographic conditions. They could largely disregard topography, or they could make use of it in sensitive and imaginative ways. The possibility of ignoring topography has grown with the power of machines, until today there is little practical limit to what may be altered or abolished if the economic incentives are sufficiently strong. Land can be rendered formless by regrades or by cut-and-fill techniques. Streams can be put in sewers underground, shores built out to the pier line and edged in concrete.

Here and there citizens have taken a stand against the advance of the dredge or the bulldozer. If San Francisco Bay survives in its familiar shape, this is not because developers lack either the will or the means to fill it in. It is because a few resolute men and women have determined that some limits be set to the power of technology. Elsewhere the story is less happy, as by slow degrees or by some audacious gesture the original shape of things has been made over.

Conservation and a respect for natural beauty are strong forces, yet they are not absolute, and within the complex fabric of the modern city should perhaps *not* be. Other interests—commercial, industrial, residential and touristic—also have their legitimate claims. The diversity of a city's population expresses itself in mixed land uses, often in incongruous uses, and nearly always in uses less than ideal from the conservationist's point of view.

Even where the cause of recreation is nature's only competitor, the question of land use is not necessarily simple. Groups advocating active recreation may be strongly at odds with the advocates of leisure in its passive forms. Consider, for example, an unspoiled wetland. It may be so lightly developed for walking or bird watching as to have the necessary facilities scarcely impinge upon the natural setting. In the name of recreation, others will urge that it be filled in for ballfields, tennis courts or a golf course.

However much the balance may appear tipped in favor of minimal development, it must be acknowledged realistically that many of the country's important recreational facilities exist—and could only have existed—through resort to landfill operations. The loss of a marshy shoreline may well seem in such circumstances to be compensated by the opportunities for exercise and fresh air provided for the pent-up masses of the inner city. Besides, the landfill is usually in answer to a secondary but not to be despised urban need—that of space for disposal of the city's wastes.

This having been said, the cause of ecology and of the inviolability of a fragile natural terrain needs to be stressed. When hillsides are reshaped by the bulldozer to accommodate housing, when flood basins are encroached upon or the delicate interdependence of shore life harmed by fill, the city-builders risk nature's retribution. They risk, too, the loss of their city's character. In ways the citizen may not always be able to put into words, this character—the unique and basic quality of the environment—is important to him. When it is eroded he can no longer say with quite the old assurance: "This is the place where I live—*this* place with its own river, its particular hills."

Man-made features, which so often obliterate the form of the terrain, may also in some cases preserve or actually reinforce it. Towers upon the horizon; low buildings upon an upland; a consistent roof material, like the red tile of Palos Verdes Estates of Los Angeles—these can give emphasis to a contour or repeat the submerged patterns of the land. In the imagination of at least one planner, buildings can create an artificial topography of their own. Thus, in a significant planning document, Charles Blessing sees Detroit's river plain as a canvas on which hills and valleys are formed by structures, by their varied heights and by the relationships between them. The city as a whole becomes on the landscape a vast "outcropping"; the central business district is described as "mountainous" and the space along expressways as "valleys."[4]

Structures may thus in some measure become a delineator of natural form, or may provide form where it is naturally lacking. Yet they have their limits. For the citizen there will continue to exist nothing so reassuring as the sight at the end of his street of a plain hill, or so comforting to the urbanized senses as a sudden glimpse of blue water.

Parks as Form-Givers

The most direct and obvious way of preserving the natural site, of keeping a sense of the terrain, is through the establishment of parks. Certain other methods may be additionally employed. Views can be protected through zoning corridors; open space can remain outside the park domain, being combined with functions that leave the land relatively open. Mapped parkland, however, remains fundamental in its capacity to preserve the city's frame.

Park-builders of the nineteenth century were aware of this role for parks, though they often used arguments more closely related to the interests of their time, such as improvement of morals and of health. Today it is possible to trace the relationship of their work to the underlying terrain. This relationship is sometimes direct and sometimes subtle and tenuous, but rarely is it separated entirely from a concern with natural features of the landscape.

The site for a park may be chosen because the land is cheap and inhospitable to other kinds of development. Golden Gate Park in San Francisco and Central Park in New York are examples of the triumph of the engineer and landscape architect over deficiencies of soil and environment. If the original proponents of Central Park had been primarily concerned with preserving nature, they would have persisted in their first choice of a site—the agreeable area along the East River known as Jones Wood, then an irregular shoreline watered by streams. Yet in its actual location Central Park made a statement about the character of Manhattan Island. It indicated among other things that this rocky stretch of terrain, pockmarked and marshy, was somewhat less than desirable for the kind of real estate development envisioned for the growing city.

More often the location of Manhattan's parks has been a direct response to underlying topographic conditions. A close observer of these parks gets an impression of what the island was once like, being reminded even amid the changes which steam shovels and bulldozers have wrought, and even amid the obscuring mass of tall buildings, that this had been a beautiful and varied terrain. To the north of the island Inwood Park, though now sundered by the West Side Highway, keeps the steep slopes and caves famous since Indian days. Just south of Inwood are the natural ledges of Fort Tryon Park, in this case with more formal landscaping skillfully superimposed. Farther down Manhattan are the spaces carved out of a continuous rocky spine, uninviting as building sites in an earlier day, which now are preserved by the four linear parks of Morningside, Colonial, High Bridge and St. Nicholas.

Such naturalistic areas are protected by their park status from being developed commercially even when construction techniques would make it feasible. The urgent present-day problem becomes preventing their natural features from obliteration by structures for active recreation.

Open Space of a New Town

The preservation of form through parkland may be seen in a modern counterpart where new cities are being developed. Here the planners begin by setting aside those aspects of the terrain which will give the future town its shape and will provide those who live there with a strong feeling for the integrity of the site. Woodlands, streams, slopes, drainage areas and marshlands are among the areas designated as immune to development. The structures that form the new town take their place within a context systematically determined by natural features. For the new planners, nature can indeed be said to be foremost, with man slipped in unobtrusively so as to cause as little damage as possible. Open space—the land not built upon—becomes the essence of their community, the first element to be defined and the most consistently to be guarded.

The new town of Jonathan in Minnesota, begun in 1970, may be taken as an example of the way topography and open space interlock. Jonathan unfortunately fell upon evil days financially; its once-bright hopes have not been realized. But that has nothing to do with the premises of its plan and the elegance with which these premises were articulated. The natural environment of Jonathan—a 6,850-acre site of small hills, streams and lakes about twenty-five miles southwest of Minneapolis—is viewed not only as an integral terrain but as an ecological system. The preservation of this system is, the planners assert, a paramount goal.

The plan is essentially a process for maintaining the natural balance *"while accepting man into the equation."*[5] The shores of the three lakes are kept clear for public access. The ravines are taken for pedestrian walkways; the marshes, tree stands and steeper slopes for various forms of recreation. The resulting space creates a greenway system which not only links centers within the community but separates areas of conflicting and different land uses. In short, the open spaces of the town of Jonathan, when compared with the land's natural features, show an almost perfect congruity.

No city that has grown amid the processes of change and the pressures of divergent needs will show such a pure relationship. Parks have to stake out their claims amid conflicting interests; they are defended, even at best, amid battles that have an uncertain outcome. The relation between green space and topography will be relative and will vary from city to city. It is useful to take a few examples.

Seattle—Parks in a Dramatic Landscape

Seattle has a natural site as strongly molded as that of any city in the United States; it lies in a part of the country where men and women are unusually aware of the beauties of earth and sea. We should expect to find here a clear expression of the interdependence of open space and natural forms. And indeed we do find it, notwithstanding all that man does, even in an enlightened community, to obscure and deface his heritage.

The city of Seattle lies between two principal bodies of water, Puget Sound and Lake Washington, which provide a shoreline of fifty-three miles. Within the city lie Lake Union and Green Lake. In the southern area the Duwamish River establishes a north-south axis. These waters are one of the dramatic natural features of the city; the other is formed by the ridges or elongated hills that were shaped by ice moving southward in the glacial period. The combination of the two makes for the city's extraordinary sense of openness and identity.

Bodies of water within a city or along its edges are themselves open spaces of great value. They purify its airs, reflect its towers, provide for the city dweller strong directional points as he glimpses their expanse down a street or avenue. In Seattle the lakes and the bay powerfully organize its linear form. On a flat terrain such waters have a limited visual effect, enjoyed chiefly by those close to their shores. When combined with hills, however—and hills that in general run parallel to the shorelines—they can be a daily source of visual refreshment and a constant point of reference to people in their homes and places of work.

In Seattle the views of water and of mountain peaks do much to make the city what it is. While less favored cities find occasional corridors of visibility, and (if they are wise) protect these as important aspects of their openness, Seattle has been given by nature such wide perspectives on blue water as to make its citizens keenly aware of spatial values.[6]

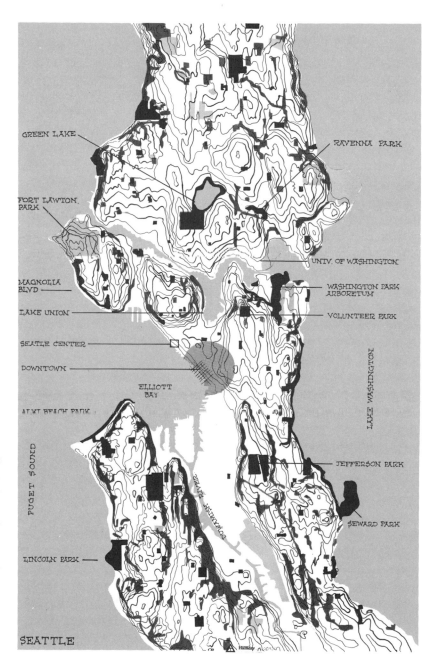

The strong topography of Seattle with its combination of hills and water calls plainly for some areas to remain free of construction. Hilltops, promontories overlooking the sea, lake-shores, stands of forest, suggest the outlines of a coherent open space system. This map shows how parks, greenbelts and restricted areas have in fact been used to preserve a sense of nature.

Parks Superimposed

Such is the terrain of the city of Seattle and the possibilities of open space its people enjoy. What have they done with these possibilities? In 1903 the park commissioners of the city requested a plan for a park system from the landscape firm of Olmsted Brothers of Boston.[7] The planners found a large number of parks in existence, but scattered widely in a city undergoing rapid growth. They proposed to add to these and link them by parkways into one organized whole reflecting the existing contours and open spaces of the city's site. "The primary aim," said the 1903 report, "should be to secure and preserve for the use of the people as much as possible of these advantages of water and mountain views and of woodlands. . . . An ideal system would involve taking all the borders of the different bodies of water . . . and to enlarge these fringes at suitable and convenient points."

In practice, something less than the ideal was recommended, but the proposals were nevertheless far-reaching as well as consistent in aim. In 1909 the park commissioners could report that the Olmsted plan had been adopted, that a bond issue of one million dollars had been passed "almost unanimously," and that "wonderful progress" had been made toward development.

The 1903 plan called for a major new park and extended the system by means of lakeshore drives and connected parkways until it touched nearly all the city's natural features. The start was to be at Bailey's Peninsula, jutting out prominently into Lake Washington. "This topographical feature should be taken as a whole," the original report recommended. The peninsula today forms Seward Park. From here the green chain can be followed northward along the lake to the University of Washington, the Arboretum and Washington Park. At this point the system branches westward down the wild and beautiful Interlaken Drive and takes command of the hilltop on which Volunteer Park is situated. From this, the star of Seattle's park system, a striking view opens westward across Elliott Bay into Puget Sound. In the near foreground—a dividend the early planners could not have anticipated—is the Space Needle of the Seattle Center.

A second branch of the system, reaching northward from Washington Park, follows a proposed parkway to Ravenna Park. Further parkways would extend to parks overlooking the sea. By this means a chain of green would be placed around the major hillsides of the area and the public would be given permanent access to a major in-city lake.

This well-planned system is incompletely realized, being flawed by gaps and by incompatible land uses. Even so, it is a fine illustration of how parks and an unusual terrain can complement each other. The existing park system may form a weak chain in comparison with the dominating forms of nature; yet it can still impart to the city the reassurance of geography. Along the interconnected system the park builders have successfully established reminders and preserved residues of the city's essential frame.

The shores of Elliott Bay and Puget Sound are less effectively preserved. Here, as in so many American cities, the land close to the sea was left for commercial development, and an elevated expressway was allowed to usurp immediate access. But parks exist along the two outer arms of Elliott Bay, and plans call for strengthening the parkways. For the rest, strong efforts are required to save the steeper hillsides from exploitation and to preserve the seaward and lakeward views. These views, as has been indicated, are in themselves a form of space and a powerful reinforcement of the city's natural features. Downtown skyscrapers of the scale and mass of the Seattle First Building are a threat to these views and endanger qualities that make Seattle unique.

Mention should be made of the two principal waterways that pierce the city. The Duwamish River in the southern portion has been obscured by industrial uses and its original course has been altered by landfill. It is past being recovered, though an important greenbelt follows the upland ridge and serves as a buffer between it and the nearby residential section.

More interesting is the man-made waterway that connects Washington Lake and Puget Sound and gives access to both from Lake Union. The lake is a busy scene of commercial activity, enlivened by the numerous houseboats that are permanent living quarters for a segment of the Seattle population. A small park upon its northern shore is planned to enshrine a picturesque and abandoned gasworks. In this instance open space will at the same time celebrate the work of nature and man's industrial achievements.

Washington—Beyond Malls and Monuments

Older cities of the eastern United States lack Seattle's bold contours and its dazzling profusion of waterways; but in these cities, too, we can often discern the role of geography in shaping open spaces. Boston, for example, is comparatively flat and would seem to be topographically uninteresting. Yet when Frederick Law Olmsted was asked in 1872 to create a system of parks for the city, he found in the Muddy River and its related fens at least one natural feature that gave strong direction to his plan. Working on a comparatively small scale, he used not seas and mountains, but tides and indigenous grasses to give identity to his open space.

Another eastern city of modest topographical assertions is Washington, D.C. Here, also, a succession of planners sensitive to the natural environment were able to respond to nature, shaping open space to accentuate the city's basic form.

Washington may be said to be two cities. There is the monumental city with its man-made spaces—its squares and avenues and its great mall. And there is the naturalistic city of plateaus, ridges, small valleys, hills and riverbanks. These two overlap and are related in interesting ways.

The familar plan of Pierre L'Enfant is an odd-shaped sort of rectangle. Within this irregular form L'Enfant laid out his city, grandly conceived to give an appropriate setting to structures embodying the institutions of free government. A series of diagonally placed avenues derived from the Baroque overlies the grid characteristic of American towns, opening into formal circles and squares.

Even within this area of monumental spaces, L'Enfant was feeling for another principle, that of space related to natural features of the landscape. His diagonal axes of Massachusetts, Pennsylvania and Virginia avenues parallel the escarpment that edged the city to the northeast; his other strong axes, particularly the Mall and the long meadow south of the White House, were oriented toward views of the Potomac. Principal squares and open spaces took advantage of elevations within the flat terrain.

L'Enfant's Washington, as has been noted, was irregular in outline. It was not circular, like the First Atlanta, nor a square or rectangle like the conventional American city. The reason for the irregularity is immediately discernible when the one-dimensional plan is laid upon a topographic map. Besides the rivers which bound the original city on two sides, a series of ridges and escarpments continues in a broad arc to form the northern and western limits of the plan. Within the area thus defined, the original drawing fits with startling exactitude.[8]

The city developed slowly, its avenues long unpaved and bare of trees, its grand squares through most of the nineteenth century lacking buildings to border them. Yet the main features of the L'Enfant plan formed the scheme by which the city grew. When a second look became necessary, the planners went back to principles laid down in the eighteenth century. One notable defect, however, was faced up to. L'Enfant neglected the riverfronts, evidently expecting them to be occupied by the normal development of wharves and piers. The McMillan Commission of 1900 shaped and firmed up the riverbanks, creating new parks of formal design.

Subsequent planning efforts returned with increasing emphasis to concern for topography and for the enhancement of a natural site. Charles W. Eliot II (nephew of the Charles Eliot whom we shall meet in connection with Olmsted's Boston work) worked in the 1920s with Olmsted's son; and the two carried on the naturalistic approach that had been characteristic of the older generation.

The perspective of these planners reached well beyond the city of institutions and monuments, to embrace a region of connected open spaces. First the gorge and the Great Falls of the Potomac above Washington, and then the shores of the estuary below it, became a major preoccupation. The beautiful scenic highway connecting Washington and Mount Vernon was designed. As director of the Washington Planning Commission, Eliot prepared the 1929 plan which aimed at protection of stream beds along the Potomac and their conversion into recreation areas; he was instrumental in securing passage of the Capper-Cramton Act, which provides funds for the acquisition of important parkland.

Washington's major parks outside the downtown area are Rock Creek, Anacostia, and the Fort parks system, all closely tied in with the natural terrain. Funds for Rock Creek Park, running due north from the Potomac in one of the valleys that break the escarpment's rim, were first secured in 1890. The park has been extended several times and forms an invaluable green space piercing the built-up city.

Anacostia Park, running along the banks of the river northeast of the original city, lacks many advantages associated with a park. Railroad tracks and yards, freeways and large building complexes, reduce the available parkland and cut it off from the Capitol district. Yet plans for dealing with this relate it to the axis running east from the Capitol, and combine urban uses with pedestrian paths and facilities for active and for passive recreation. The arboretum, bird sanctuary and ecological reserve in the upper sections of the river would be preserved and restored.[9]

Interesting in its combination of natural and man-made features is the ring of old forts built upon the high land encircling the city for protection during the Civil War. These forts and their surroundings make a potential system of open spaces following the natural contours and providing constantly changing views of the city. The necessary land has been acquired, but the whole awaits an agreed-on concept and a determined development.

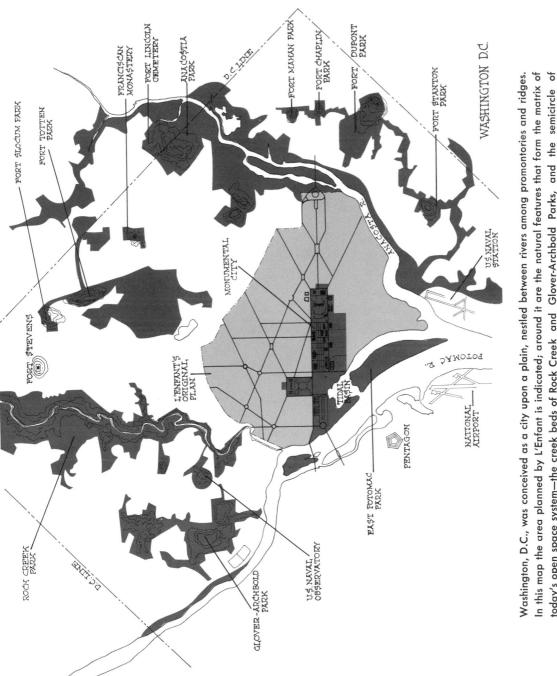

Washington, D.C., was conceived as a city upon a plain, nestled between rivers among promontories and ridges. In this map the area planned by L'Enfant is indicated; around it are the natural features that form the matrix of today's open space system—the creek beds of Rock Creek and Glover-Archbold Parks, and the semicircle of ridges running from Fort Stanton across the Anacostia to Fort Stevens. These latter points, along with the river-banks, are touched by the green of parks and by the presence of institutions. Within this outer ring lies a second open space system, that of the monumental city.

ROCK CREEK PARK

D.C. LINE

GLOVER-ARCHBOLD PARK

U.S. NAVAL OBSERVATORY

EAST POTOMAC PARK

L'ENFANT'S ORIGINAL PLAN

MONUMENTAL CITY

FORT STEVENS

FORT SLOCUM PARK

FORT TOTTEN PARK

FRANCISCAN MONASTERY

FORT LINCOLN CEMETERY

ANACOSTIA PARK

D.C. LINE

FORT MAHAN PARK

FORT CHAPLIN PARK

FORT DUPONT PARK

FORT STANTON PARK

ANACOSTIA R.

U.S. NAVAL STATION

PENTAGON

POTOMAC R.

TIDAL BASIN

NATIONAL AIRPORT

WASHINGTON D.C.

The 1967 master plan wisely rejects the idea of a motor parkway, reserving the rights of way connecting the forts for pedestrian and bicycle paths. The old earthworks would be cleared to provide the alignment for a portion of these. Starting at Fort Greble on the Anacostia River in the southeast of the city, the system of connected open spaces would follow the line in a wide semicircle, passing through partially restored historic sites and through existing parklands such as those of Rock Creek, to end in Palisades Park on the northwest.

The system would not only provide a grand tour but would be linked to neighborhood recreational facilities. Not least, it would disengage the topography that has played so large a role in the varying phases of the city's life. The rim that L'Enfant saw as a boundary giving Washington an identifiable form, and that the generation of the Civil War saw as a natural defense line, would become in the city's maturity an unparalleled leisure resource.

San Francisco's Urban Landscape

Two major cities on the West Coast have faced up in quite different ways to the problems and opportunities posed by their topography. San Francisco and Los Angeles are interesting not only in terms of the scale, disposition and character of their open spaces, but as cities that reveal a dependence upon underlying topographic conditions. This dependence is indicated in the use or misuse of open space.

San Francisco is small in area—only forty-four square miles; and it is so strikingly situated upon its sea and its bay that little of added natural advantage or man-made beautification might have been deemed necessary. But San Francisco also has its hills. And through thoughtful accretions over the years it has gained the benefit of features that add up to an urban landscape singular in charm and legibility.

A topographical map of San Francisco shows Telegraph Hill dominating the downtown area and the port. Its summit is crowned by a small park. Moving westward on the city's grid, the streets rise steeply to Pacific Heights and then lead to the sea. The three major open space areas of the Presidio, Lake Merced and Golden Gate Park are linked by boulevards to form a strongly defined open space system along the Pacific.[10]

The lay of the San Francisco land, combined with the grid that overlies it, has the effect of creating views independent of formally designated open

Ocean and bay contain San Francisco on three sides; and three hills—Nob, Russian and Telegraph—crowd its downtown section. Behind these the land rises to Pacific Heights, and southwest progresses to the complex topography of Mount Sutro and Twin Peaks. Open spaces of the city are related to these elevations, but more significant is the way the streets climb uninterruptedly in straight lines over the hills. The major San Francisco park is on relatively flat land, defying topography and natural conditions rather than taking advantage of them.

spaces. Down a hundred streets occur glimpses of land and sea, combining to build up a feeling of how the city is composed. It will be recalled that the Burnham plan for San Francisco, made immediately before the earthquake, proposed modification of the grid with broad avenues, and with routes on the hillsides following contours in the conventionally approved manner. For various reasons both practical and sentimental, San Franciscans decided to keep the grid. They also have managed through the years to keep large expanses of traditional small-scale buildings. As a result—in ways that could not have been wholly anticipated or planned—one is constantly confronted by views of the city and its surroundings. The steepness of the inclines has not proved a serious deterrent either to wheeled traffic or to people on foot.

In addition to its many natural advantages, including a shoreline which even today is saved from being completely cut off by highways, the early San Franciscans felt they needed a big park. The site chosen in 1870 under the leadership of the city's progressive mayor, Frank McCoffin, was a long, narrow stretch of dunes reaching from Divisadero Street westward to the sea. It was not only barren of growth; its sands were subject to constant shifting under the force of Pacific gales. William Hammond Hall designed the park with its serpentine roads (in themselves a device to thwart the winds) and tamed the sands with plants and grasses carried down from the hills and imported from abroad. Thousands of seedlings of cypress and pine in turn provided anchorage for further plantings.[11]

In 1890 Golden Gate Park came under the control of one of those extraordinary figures, gifted with longevity and natural authority, that great park empires seem to require for their development. John McClaren was the presiding genius of this green domain for more than fifty years, until his death in 1943. A Scotsman who had learned horticulture at the Botanical Garden in Edinburgh, he found no detail of park management too small to escape his attention; and no dream too visionary to be pursued. He hated the "stookies"—statues of would-be famous figures donated to the park—and ordered his gardeners to screen them from view with natural growth. He withstood encroachments, setting gardeners to work through a famous night so that the engineers of a proposed trolley line found in the morning that their path lay across newly planted shrubs and beds of flowers. The engineers withdrew. McClaren's public support ensured his survival through various political administrations and provided him with funds for needed park improvements.

The care lavished on this principal park did not divert McClaren from the other green areas of his domain. San Francisco's smaller parks show the hand of the careful gardener rather than of the comprehensive city planner; but McClaren knew the wisdom of taking a hilltop or seizing a bit of coast. The hills of Buena Vista or of Diamond Heights to the south are marked and encircled by his green touch. The city as a whole (except where it has been "Manhattanized" by tall buildings in the downtown) remains surprisingly unspoiled, its parks serving to underline a topography still telling its own story in neighborhood and street.

A Regional Terrain Obscured

Los Angeles is a city whose natural features are on a far vaster scale than San Francisco's, as they are altogether different from Boston's or Washington's. The city comprehends mountain ranges and indeed whole wildernesses, and in area is built upon regional dimensions. Yet Los Angeles has never had the care of men like Olmsted, father and son, or like Charles Eliot or McClaren. When the men of their generations were shaping or reshaping the older cities, Los Angeles was absorbing its multitudes of settlers from the American heartland.

These settlers flooded the valleys with their bungalows and then climbed the foothills; they constructed the system of rails and roads that was to spin a fabulous web of intercommunication. The natural environment in its mute imperatives thwarted some part of the human invasion and gave, in spite of all, a form and limit to the city's growth. But in the end even the most rugged natural features stood in danger of being overrun. And still no planners of the highest stature possessed vision or resource sufficient to disengage what belongs to nature from the things that belong to man.

Los Angeles in its modern form is a metropolis encompassing 463 square miles. It cannot be said so much to spread in four directions from a center as to constitute a network of settlements more or less equidistant from each other and all (with the possible exception of the socially immured and isolated Watts) in a state of animated suspension within the urbanized environment. In Los Angeles, it has been well said, people think of space in terms of time; and the freeway system to a large extent equalizes the time it takes to range over near or far distances. A Los Angeles city center exists; yet Reyner Banham makes a valid point when he says that everyday commuting tends less and less "to move by the classic systole and diastole in and out of downtown, more and more to move by an almost random or Brownian motion over the whole area."[12]

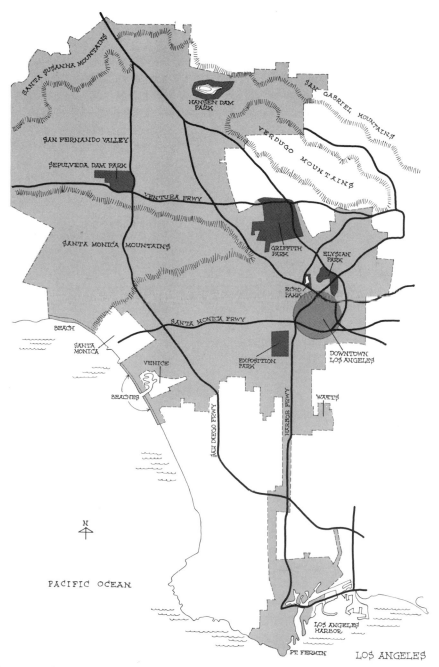

This map of Los Angeles, reduced almost to a diagram because of the city's immense spread, shows the major open spaces related to large topographic features—the Santa Monica Mountains cutting athwart the city and tying in to the 4,063-acre Griffith Park; and to the north the strong rim of the Santa Susana and San Gabriel chains. The center city is independent of the sea, but reaches down through a narrow corridor to Los Angeles harbor at the south. Expressways tie the fabric together.

This "whole area" must be grasped conceptually.[13] It lies in the level lands reaching southward to Los Angeles port, southwest to the Pacific beaches, northwest into the San Fernando Valley, and east toward Pasadena. Along these level lands between hills and mountains the early railroad ran, and the freeways later fortified the pattern. The little houses proceeded up the foothills; the grid of the conventional city gave way to gently curving streets and then to a tangle of mountainous roads as home-builders sought the privacy and the fine views of the higher slopes. The natural features, except for the high Verdugo Mountains to the north, are less effective in defining the city than in placing obstacles more or less temporary in the way of its dynamic sprawl. Rivers and stream beds are increasingly placed within concrete troughs, and the beaches are cut off from use by pollution and erosion.

The Los Angeles parks lie within canyons and upon hilltops; but instead of clarifying the topographic structure, the park planners tended to take the easiest way. Where the pressures for immediate development were least demanding they built the minimal parks that the city required. One cannot blame the city fathers too harshly. In that ideal climate, where every house would have its own verdant space, parks did not have the priority they received amid the crowded tenements of New York or Boston. Besides, when the country-wide park movement was at its height, Los Angeles was still a settlement of uninhabited open spaces.

Today's planners are faced, as a result, with large deficiencies of parkland, not only for the existing population but for that anticipated in the future; not only for present life styles but for the life styles of a postindustrial tomorrow. The city is threatened, moreover, with having its natural features increasingly overrun.

When the freeways came to Los Angeles there was no strong tradition to turn them from the existing parklands. Freeways have encroached upon or have divided Griffith Park, Elysian Park, Hollenbeck Park and Victory Park. Only after the invasion of Echo Park did the citizens awake to the irreversible dangers and begin to demand at least equivalent recreation lands for the condemned rights of way. Such lands, however useful for community needs, were not likely to reinforce the city's natural form. Development of park space in conjunction with freeway building, facilitated under programs of the federal government, may be more effective in this regard, particularly where the freeways themselves follow natural contours.

The hills and mountains of Los Angeles, covering 150 square miles, offer open spaces of the most dramatic kind; but they are often inaccessible even to motor roads; and where they are accessible, encroachment by subdivisions seems inexorable. The Santa Monica Mountains alone cover an area larger than the city of San Francisco. A study by Harland Bartholomew in 1930 emphasized the city's shortage of recreation space and recommended that 74,000 acres in these mountains be acquired. The only action taken to implement this and subsequent recommendations of the same kind has been the acquisition of scattered tax-delinquent properties. Meanwhile new techniques of earthmoving have resulted in "mountain cropping" —the reshaping of the terrain into large building pads—while both the need for open space and the natural appearance of the land are ignored. Considerations of drainage and stability of the earth have also been disregarded.

The highest mountain lands seem safe against this kind of ecological mayhem. Through the spine of the Santa Monica Mountains, now crossed by Mulholland Drive, a chain of parks and recreation sites is in need of being formed. Zoning laws to assure private development in conformity with the open space system, especially in the form of guest ranches and camps, and the use of lightly clustered residential units, could further assure the visual openness and the naturalistic development so essential if Los Angeles is not to lose the grandeur of its setting. In the Verdugo Mountains, along with horse and pedestrian trails, the use of aerial tramways could well be tried.

The land thus speaks to the city-builders; sometimes it is listened to, sometimes blithely ignored. The next chapter considers the waters. In the vast American continent the principal cities were located first along the seashores, and afterward upon lakes and rivers, which provided them with means of transportation and communication. These sites shaped the physical forms of the cities, as they molded their economic life. They also provided opportunities for open space, which are at last being recognized and are sometimes being fulfilled.

4 Waterfront Sites

UNTIL THE COMING OF THE RAILROAD, American cities were almost of necessity situated upon waterways. The extreme difficulty of overland transportation left no choice to the first settlers other than to use coastal and inland waters as routes for trade and, as much as possible, for travel.

Of all forms of intercity transportation, the overland stagecoach in America must have been the least comfortable, the least expeditious; it is surely the one that lovers of the past should least want to resurrect. Romance may color the coastal steamers plying between New York and Boston; nostalgic feelings may attach to early railways, canal boats or Mississippi side-wheelers; but the stagecoach remains unblessed in memory. At least until the coming of the railroad, the way to travel was by boat, and the place for a town to be was upon a rivershore or seacoast.

Waterfronts and the Shape of the City

The strong incentives for locating cities upon waterfronts had important effects upon the disposition of open space and the form of the typical American city. Often the waterfront was thought to provide by itself adequate open space for the health and recreational needs of the citizens. In the New York plan of 1811, for example, a neglect of parks was justified on the grounds that "the large arms of the sea" embracing Manhattan made other recreation facilities unnecessary. Waterfronts, however, were gradually monopolized by facilities for transportation and commerce and were rendered useless for any other purposes.

88

Louisville, which had the good sense to set aside some of its waterfront lands for parks, early in its history sold these off to pay municipal debts. They were never recovered. New York allowed most of its unparalleled waterfronts to be taken over by shipping and manufacturing. It did, however, keep the point of the island for a park, and the Battery from the earliest days became a favorite spot for promenades and entertainments.[1] Even now, encroached upon as it is by memorials and hemmed in by skyscrapers, it remains the one open space that has consistently marked the relation of the city to the waters from which it draws its life.

The development of the typical waterfront in ways incompatible with public access or public pleasure caused the city dwellers to move in other directions. Stirred by new standards of civic beauty or new social ideas, the park-builders of the nineteenth century turned inland and endeavored to make over the hearts of their cities. The major parks laid out in Louisville were spaced in a wide circle roughly equidistant from the center of river activity.[2] St. Louis built Forest Park on a broad piece of land three miles west of the levee, and George Kessler's 1907 plan for Cincinnati wrote off the waterfront as unreclaimable.

A reverse action was nevertheless destined to set in. This was caused in part by man's ineradicable enjoyment of the waterside; in part by changing economic conditions, which rendered obsolete many of the structures and land uses that had once monopolized the waterfront sites. The most recent trend has been toward recapturing the banks of rivers or the shores of the sea, developing them for mixed uses or setting them apart as open spaces for the enjoyment of the public. The circle is completed as plans begin to call for the shaping of new open space systems which tie in the waterfronts with the older landbound parks.

The Lure of Water

So categorical a sketch, while generally true, omits one aspect of waterfront development. Shipping and its many related activities became in themselves a source of excitement, even of inspiration, beyond that which any park-builder could devise. In the early days of a city a busy waterfront was the best place for a youth looking for adventure, or for couples out to take the air. Exceptionally noble watersides were made use of by commercial interests. Louisville and Minneapolis were situated at waterfalls; Cincinnati and Memphis stood upon handsome bluffs; yet it was not their natural features, so much as the excitement attendant upon ships and their comings and goings, that provided the ultimate lure.

In comparison to this, how tame could be an inland park, how lacking in picturesque variety! To watch the paddle-wheelers exchange their cargoes along the Mississippi or Missouri; to see the sailing vessels go out across the bay in Boston or New York, was better than to be surrounded by green meadows. And the waters themselves, endlessly changing—sluggish and peaceable along the river in summer or carrying threats of destruction as they rose in the spring—were more stirring than a forest grove.

In characteristic style, Melville in *Moby Dick* invokes the spell of the Manhattan waterfront.[3] "Right and left," he says, the streets of the island "take you waterward." At the extreme downtown "that noble mole [of Manhattan] is washed by waves, and cooled by breezes, which a few hours previous were out of sight of land." Everywhere are the water-gazers. "Circumambulate the city of a dreamy Sabbath afternoon. . . . What do you see? Posted like silent sentinels all around the town, stand thousands upon thousands of mortal men fixed in ocean reveries. Some leaning against the piles; some seated upon the pier-heads; some looking over the bulwarks of ships from China; some high aloft in the rigging, as if striving to get a still better seaward peep." Yet "these are all landsmen," Melville continues, "of weekdays pent up in lath and plaster—tied to counters, nailed to benches . . . How then is this? Are the green fields gone?"

Still the crowds come on, "pacing straight for the water, and seemingly bound for a dive. Strange! Nothing will content them but the extremist limit of the land . . . They must get just as nigh the water as they possibly can without falling in." Melville tells us, after another page or so of wonderful invocations to the rivers and oceans, that all these Manhattoes (like artists, and like the old Greeks and Persians) discover in the sea "the image of the ungraspable phantom of life."

Perhaps in the sea they merely were discovering pleasant relaxation and a source of cool breezes. In any case the Manhattoes and all those intent on walking to "the extremist limit of the land" were soon to find themselves cut off. The brief period when commerce and recreation, when transportation and public enjoyment, coincided had passed, as first the railroads and then the highways took over the waterfronts. It was left for later generations in a few picturesque reconstructions to try to recover the long-vanished magic; or for developers of oddly assorted interests to give back to the citizens in new forms some inkling of what a waterfront had once been.

The Growth and Decline of Industry

A typical waterfront town had its Water Street or Front Street. The names, and indeed the streets themselves, have often disappeared from the modern map, the area having been pre-empted by transportation and industrial facilities or having decayed into a slum and been cleared for modern developments. The railroads were the earliest force to shatter the city's configuration and to efface the lingering uses of the waterfront for recreation. They came in along the level land to connect in the most direct possible way with the waterborne traffic. The business community welcomed the railroad, with its assurance or prosperity. Even those who regretted the loss of a natural heritage recognized the demands of transportation as irresistible.

Not the rail line alone, but the varied facilities it required for servicing and the secondary employment it generated, blighted the waterfronts. Switching yards and freight terminals—combined with repair sheds and foundries, with mills and factories—compelled residents to flee the shores and made it difficult for anyone to approach them on foot. Minneapolis provides a representative example of these changing land uses.[4] Its whole early history was closely related to the Mississippi; it drew prosperity from this source at the sacrifice of amenities it then had to seek elsewhere. It is also a town which in the course of time saw its river-based economy decay.

Within the confines of the modern city, the river at Minneapolis drops a hundred feet. The early settlers thus found power in abundance. They also found conditions providing them with raw materials, with markets and with transportation. A forest covering more land than the state of Maine, with trees reaching more than two hundred feet in height, stretched to the north. Southward, the land opened into wide prairies waiting for the plow. In 1847 a skilled millwright from Maine built a wooden dam seven hundred feet long between what are now Hennepin and Nicollet islands. The logs collected in the millpond above, and a sawmill was soon the basis of the settlement's growth.

By the 1880s, however, the milling of flour had become Minneapolis's major industry. Its "new process" flour was known worldwide. The bridging of the river and the development of more efficient river transport added to the city's growth. Then the railroads came in, moving along the river shore, taking over large areas of additional land for multiple trackage and secondary services. The beginning of the twentieth century saw a metropolis having successfully attained a stable economic base. In terms of environment it had suffered, however, by turning its back upon the river.

Now we can observe the second crucial phase of so many waterfront cities. The mills and factories faltered; use of the railroad trackage declined. In Minneapolis the last lumbermill closed in 1920. In the 1930s the city's flour mills came into competition with those of Buffalo and Kansas City. Obsolete mills and warehouses blocked off the river completely, while sewage on the waters acted as a final deterrent to its enjoyment. The famous Bridge Square deteriorated, and business moved southward along Nicollet and Hennepin avenues. Thus, like so many others, the city had abandoned the waterfront, but it had not, as we shall see, entirely forgotten it.

The Road and the Waterside

The second major element cutting the cities off from their waterfronts was a transportation system keyed to the private automobile and the heavy truck. The highways came in upon the path of least resistance, where the railways had already laid out their routes. They took over parkways, obliterating earlier attempts to thread picturesque roads through the landscape. In a state of hopelessness or under misapprehension, the citizens of many cities stood silently by while the later freeway system cut them off from their waterside heritage, making future rehabilitation of the area virtually impossible.

In Seattle a citizenry ready today to do battle against even the most plausible encroachments could not avert an elevated roadway between the downtown area and the animated border of Puget Sound. "We just didn't know it would be so bad," is the kind of explanation offered for their submission. In Portland, Oregon, an elevated expressway similarly blights the right bank of the Willamette River. The citizens had been expecting what one of them later described as "a sort of parkway." When they woke up it was too late. Following earlier transportation routes, the freeways marched in, bringing their promise of easy access and only faintly hinting at their environmental damage.

The "sort of parkway" expected by the Portlanders was not altogether a figment of their imaginations. In many cities there had been hope of combining a waterside route with attractive vistas and compatible recreational land uses. H. W. S. Cleveland, the famous park planner of Minneapolis, had looked upon such a route as a real possibility. "The river," he said in a famous address to a meeting of the park commissioners in 1883,[5] "is the grand natural feature which gives character to your city." He suggested capturing the high bluffs, which then had little economic value but which, he warned, could with time become "the most unsightly and irreclaimably squalid quarter of the whole city." His proposal: "Let a broad avenue be laid out upon each side of the river near enough to its banks to admit views into the depths below, and reserve for public use every foot of the land between the avenue and the water."

Cleveland envisioned "costly mansions and public buildings" in a row along the inland side of the boulevard, while along the river would extend "a continuous park of such picturesque character as no art could create and no other city can possess." This idea came to nothing at the time, though other boulevards proposed in the same address were built and remain a principal feature of Minneapolis. In New York City, however, an almost exact replica of Cleveland's vision came to reality. Along Riverside Drive appear his hoped for mansions (now, alas, in their faded glory); they face, along the river, the sort of picturesque park he had described (though now traversed by the West Side Highway and threatened by an interstate truck route). In Chicago and Milwaukee the lakefront provided landscaped drives co-ordinated with parks.

The combination of park and waterfront highways reached its fullest development in New York, where Robert Moses was convinced he had the key to coexistent recreation and transportation. He ringed Manhattan with drives, and then linked them by bridges to parkways around the shorelines of the other boroughs. Wherever possible and often in imaginative and effective ways—he combined these roads with parks.

Moses saw that by itself the demand for parks could not be sufficiently strong to ensure land acquisition and development. Created simultaneously with the roads, however, the parks could often be built on land reclaimed from the sea and shaped with "sanitary landfill." Typically, along the shores of Brooklyn the highway passes along baseball fields and playgrounds on the landward side, and carries a footpath along the sea wall. Constructed in more dense urban conditions, East River Park, though neglected and somewhat inaccessible, adds significantly to Manhattan's green space. Carl Schurz Park with its esplanade is extended over the Franklin D. Roosevelt Drive, so that driver and park user go their separate ways in peace.

The debit side of these developments is the virtual encircling of the city's shoreline with a wall of concrete. Looking down Manhattan's streets, one sees most often the elevated highway rather than the waters apostrophized by Melville. It is not only the view that is interrupted, but physical access. On Manhattan, for example, not a single waterside restaurant exists. A considerable portion of the island's perimeter is blocked to the pedestrian.

Moses constructed his parkways not in the infancy of the automobile age but when the high speed of modern traffic, with its accompanying noise and pollution, was fully evident. He never actually grasped the fact that his roads would be used very differently from those dreamed of in 1883 by H. W. S. Cleveland, and that they would create a wholly new kind of disturbance within the surrounding parkland. His parkways came to be more and more like expressways (except that trucks were still kept off them); they tended seriously to harm the character of the related parks, and they paved the way for the intercity freeways that in the 1950s would run with devastating effect along the waterfronts of so many cities.

The Waterfront and the Freeway

Louisville is today a city largely cut off by highways from the river to which it owes its origin. The elevated expressway inhibits the pedestrian's most determined efforts to see the water and the falls. Those who make their way to the Belvedere, a new riverside plaza, and climb up terraces of pools and flowers to its highest point, will find a small outlook higher than the freeway's elevated structure. There, and there only, the river becomes visible.

Hartford is not even this fortunate. Upon Constitution Plaza the pedestrian moves as by a natural instinct to the east, where the Connecticut River runs. At the parapet the view is stopped by the serpentine framework of Interstate 91.

Many other examples exist, for the principle is almost universally applied: a waterfront and an expressway must coincide.[6] Nevertheless, in a few places the route has been at least temporarily interrupted.

In Milwaukee, I-94 and U.S. 141 lack a connection along the shore of Lake Michigan; a parkway, however, runs along the lakeshore area and through the much-used Lake Park. If the conventional system is completed, the parkways will be destroyed and the park bifurcated. But this is not the end of the damage. A grand avenue, conceived to make the connection of the city and the lake dramatically visible, will suffer irreparable damage if the expressway cuts across it.

In Memphis, the Mississippi is at its grandest, and, passing the city, is bordered by parks and a parkway. Downtown's main axis runs parallel to the river. Plans call for a strong cross-axis at Court Square on Main Street, opening this area to a river view and making possible a new residential development along the bluff. Yet a freeway is projected along the river at this very point, to connect two major bridges. If constructed, this freeway will not only damage the parks but fatally detract from the plans for a more effective use of Memphis's river site.

Finally, in San Francisco, a link of the freeway connecting the Bay Bridge and the Golden Gate Bridge has stood uncompleted for years. A connection between these two bridges is logical. Equally logical, to all who care for the city's amenities and for its invaluable waterfront, has been the freeway's abrupt termination—its structure cut off and left hanging in the air. Here, for almost the first time, citizens took their stand against a freeway under construction. And here they won. In 1974 it was announced that the freeway along the waterfront would not be built, and that the existing structure running in the front of the old ferry slip would be torn down.

In each of these instances a case can be made for the completion of the highway system. Although in theory traffic can detour around existing expressways—a distance at most of a few miles and a matter of a few minutes' time—in practice, the incomplete system does tend to become overcharged. The San Francisco master plan, sensitive as it is to aesthetics and to the keeping of the urban scale, recognizes the needs for improved traffic flow circumventing the downtown area.[7]

San Francisco planners advocate restudy of the problem, with tunneling suggested as one alternative. In cities like Memphis and Milwaukee the topography might permit a variant of the scheme developed effectively at Brooklyn Heights, where two levels of traffic hug the steep bank and carry a promenade above them. Whatever the solution—except where the best solution may be to do nothing—careful design of the freeway is essential.

The design standards adopted for crossing open countryside are simply not adequate to a stretch of highway along a waterfront and closely related to a downtown area. More thought and more money are both required for a solution to the design problem. Tunneling, or at least the depression of the roadway, is often feasible. The alternative is other Louisvilles and Hartfords—cities cut off from their major visual and recreation asset.

Early Efforts to Recapture the Waterfront

The first serious efforts to recapture a waterfront go back to the beginning of the century. The 1901 plan for Washington tidied up the banks of the Potomac. It set the pattern for waterside parks and green spaces, which has gradually been completed as land has been filled and sites for monuments established.

The example of Chicago is the most striking. The opportunity to open up the lakefront fell to Burnham at the peak of his career. His vision was of a lakefront park extending along the entire length of the city, combined with drives, recreational facilities and cultural institutions. Fortunately, a tradition running well back into the nineteenth century had decreed a public use for at least part of this area; fortunately, too, Chicago was a city looking for a splendor of form to match the intensity of its business life.

As early as 1835 a group of citizens campaigned to have Fort Dearborn, the military reservation on the lake, converted to a public square.[8] Four years later the U.S. government officially divided the Fort Dearborn lands, with the secretary of war certifying that the ground between Randolph and Madison streets and fronting on Lake Michigan "is not to be occupied by buildings of any description." This area, together with land set apart in 1836, became Lake Park, later known as Grant Park. Though only a small part of the lakefront was involved, this designation of parkland was ambitious for its day.

The integrity of the park was challenged when the state legislature endeavored to sell part of this land to the Illinois Central. The Lakefront Act of 1869 granted to the railway owners all submerged lands for a distance of one mile into Lake Michigan, and authorized the city council of Chicago to provide necessary local ordinances to accept payments for the parkland. To the great credit of the city, the comptroller refused the first payment. The case went to the U.S. Supreme Court, which denied the legislature's right to make such grants of parklands. Four years after its passage, the Lakefront Act was repealed.

Later court tests to resist encroachments on Grant Park were launched by the prominent Chicago businessman A. Montgomery Ward. With the exception of the Art Institute, he succeeded in removing existing structures and blocking new ones, the courts going back for their precedents to the ban against buildings on early land maps. Ward himself was perhaps less moved by dedication to parks than by a determination to keep unobstructed views of the lake for the property owners he represented. But from such mixtures of motive good causes frequently benefit.

By the time Burnham presented his plan for the city in 1909, considerable support existed for his proposal to develop the lakefront as park. His own commitment to the concept was so deep he placed improvement of the lakefront first among the six principal elements of his planning document. He depicted a new shoreline of beaches, lagoons, islands, harbors and cultural facilities, a vision that shaped much of the subsequent development. Today nearly twenty-four of the city's thirty miles of shoreline consist of public parks and beaches. In addition, a 1923 zoning ordinance, periodically revised, has succeeded in keeping the residential character of all the public and most of the private portions of the lakefront.

Cincinnati and St. Louis—Large-Scale Planning

In the 1950s, improvement of waterfronts became part of accepted planning doctrine in most cities. By then several policy tools had been devised and federal funding was available. Urban renewal in particular was applicable to most of the deteriorated waterfront sites. The federal highway program disclosed its own possibilities for altering land uses; federal housing programs offered an obvious lever. The Cincinnati and St. Louis waterfront projects depended heavily on combining these and other sources of U.S. funds as well as on the powers of excess condemnation provided by federal policy. Typically, land would be cleared and basic improvements assured under urban renewal procedures; access would be provided by the Federal Highway Act, and housing would be made possible as part of a total complex. Private investment could then be counted on to provide such facilities as hotels and luxury apartments or town houses.

In Cincinnati these tools have been employed skillfully to give substance to urban planning which started in the early 1940s with the participation of local groups. A disastrous flood in 1937 had raised the basic question about the use of the waterfront and its advantage to the downtown area. Yet flooding, it was recognized, did not alone account for the area's decline—waterfronts in Detroit and Buffalo, unaffected by floods, were similarly decadent. "The real root of the trouble," the 1948 Cincinnati master plan stated, "is that the whole layout of streets and structures has become obsolete, resulting in a conglomeration of marginal uses."[9] To avoid the pollution emanating from this area, to avert the spread of blight into the adjacent business section, and at the same time to provide needed facilities for the city, the plan called for a broad-scale scheme of clearing and renovation, which has governed all subsequent developments.

The first decision was to place a stadium on the land between the expressway and the river. This was to be combined with a park, with a hotel and a residential complex. The 1948 plan also proposed a grouping of public buildings in a new civic center. Today the Cincinnati waterfront effectively combines most of these large-scale elements.

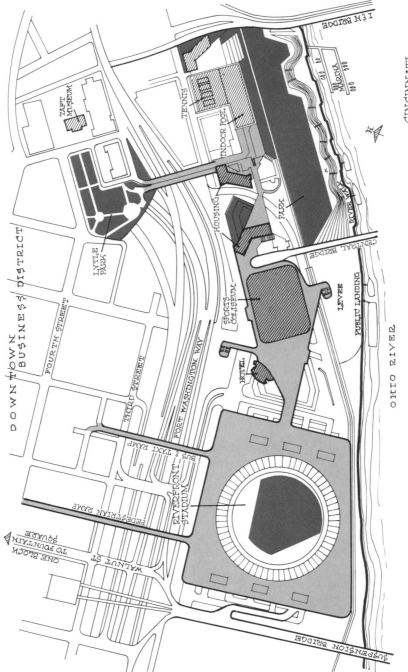

This rendering stresses the connections by footbridges to Cincinnati's downtown area. (Fountain Square is one block to the north of the map's edge.) The plaza of the stadium connects with a Coliseum plaza and a proposed hotel, and leads into the new riverfront park. From here a footbridge crosses back over the swath of highways to lead into the green space of Lytle Park.

5. Cincinnati Riverfront.

Whether the development might have taken a different direction, reclaiming and rehabilitating the traditional Water and Front streets once adjoining the levee, it is now useless to debate. The area cleared under urban renewal was certainly a slum—perhaps, indeed, as Cleveland had said of the Minneapolis waterfront, "the most irreclaimable squalid quarter of the whole city." Instead of efforts at rehabilitation, an expressway, depressed through most of its length, introduced a new dimension, serving both to contain the business section of the city and to provide easy access to the proposed new amenities.

Among these amenities a waterfront park was a priority. When its design became a question agitating civic groups, the New York landscape architect Robert Zion was consulted; he rightly perceived that everything connected with the waterfront development was big, and warned against trying to introduce small-scale elements. The newly erected stadium was big, he pointed out. The freeway and the bridges were big; the river was big. So was the scale of the nearby city buildings. He conceived a riverside park (now going forward) of which the principal feature would be a long serpentine wall—an element in keeping with its surroundings, giving access to the river and unity to the features within the new open space.

In addition to the stadium, an indoor sports complex is planned, along with a hotel and new housing. (Only the civic center of the 1948 plan has failed to materialize.) Downstream to the west, areas once given over to industrial uses will be salvaged. The freeway is bridged by an extension to Lytle Park, connecting an in-city green space with the new park on the waterfront. Lytle, recently redesigned upon somewhat conventional lines, is attractively surrounded by residences and is bordered by the handsome Taft Museum.

This waterfront scheme, though incomplete, works well. The stadium, a strongly defined structure, is easily reached by the freeway system. It is also accessible to pedestrians coming from the adjacent downtown area. On the day of a major event it is pleasant to see the crowds pressing on foot through the city streets and out toward the river across the freeway overpasses. Observed from the river or from the Kentucky side, the stadium with its podium appears oversized, interrupting the view of the city's otherwise harmonious skyline. Yet if the texture of the old city has been compromised, at least there has been envisaged a new city bold in scale and answering to acknowledged needs.

Waterfront renewal in St. Louis has been in many particulars similar to that of Cincinnati. Here, too, there had been seemingly irreparable decline

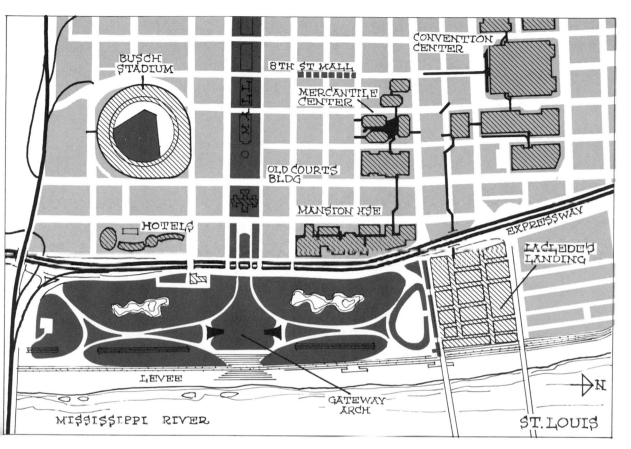

St. Louis's waterfront shows the national park with Memorial Arch and the adjacent Laclède's Landing historic district. These front on the levee and are backed by new hotel and mixed business-residential developments. The mall feeds into this area, with Busch Stadium to the south and the business district to the north. Projected walkways and pedestrian links are under construction.

along the Mississippi; a freeway created a prominent dividing feature, and a long-standing locally inspired plan sanctioned a riverfront development characterized by important open spaces.

The need for a development along the river that in its scope would match the concept of the St. Louis mall was met in 1964, on the one hundredth anniversary of the founding of the city by Pierre Laclède, when President Lyndon B. Johnson dedicated a ninety-one-acre park built entirely by the federal government and destined to be permanently maintained by it. Within the park rose one of the few successful monuments of the modern age, the shimmering arch of stainless steel designed by Eero Saarinen to memorialize the country's westward expansion.

The commemorative arch with its height of 630 feet appears almost too slight to carry its own weight—far less to carry the complex machinery by which millions of tourists are lifted to the summit to peer from small but precisely placed windows on the city below and on the wide river. The arch is visible from almost everywhere within downtown St. Louis. Unexpectedly it frames otherwise commonplace views, reminding walkers in the city's streets of the river's timeless existence.

The park within which the feet of the great arch are placed gives access to the levee, where modernized versions of the old riverboats provide agreeable restaurants. But the park itself is quite destitute of interest, formal in layout and undistinguished in landscaping. It contains the old cathedral, the one building salvaged when the riverfront slum was cleared—a somewhat forlorn historic reminder, bereft of the urban surroundings that once gave it life and meaning. (Still, it is an honest building, better where it is than destroyed, like so many other landmarks in so many cities!) Otherwise the park serves mainly as an approach to the memorial. On one Fourth of July, as a result of concerted civic efforts the space was filled, but mostly it has little relation to the daily life of the city's residents.

Twin skyscrapers form a kind of gate to the waterfront. On one side, parallel to the river, run the curved façades of the Stouffer Inn; on the other is the long axis of Mansion House, an office and residential development. Along the river just south of the park is Laclède's Landing, a congeries of old brick warehouses, fronting upon narrow cobbled streets and lending itself to the kind of small-scale development St. Louis lacks—a place for restaurants, studios, galleries and craft shops. There has been ominous talk of "renewing" this area. The need is for preservation—for the kind of sensitive rehabilitation that can slip new uses into an environment whose primary functions are no longer being served.

Henry Ford Plans for Detroit

These two examples of Cincinnati and St. Louis show riverfront development upon a large scale, heroic rather than intimate, each fulfilling a long-standing sense of what the community conceived to be its mission and its identity. One may mourn a lost feeling for history, or criticize the planners' failure to create for present-day users the multiple options and the complex interrelationships which once made the waterfront the most fascinating section of any city. Yet it is better to have a stadium on the river than to have the area remain inaccessible and blighted. It is good to have a park, even if it is unimaginative in design—especially if it is the site of a breath-taking monument. However you look at them, the riverfronts of Cincinnati and St. Louis are superior to those at Hartford and Louisville. When we come to Detroit, however, we face a very different situation.

Detroit is unlike the cities we have been discussing because, among other things, its capacity to dream—and certainly its capacity to plan—has been killed by the dominance of its powerful business community. Detroit does not boast, as Houston does, that it has no zoning; but the ascendancy of the private sector over governmental processes is so complete as to create a similar situation. While Charles Blessing was head of the planning department (1953–1974), a number of highly imaginative and professional documents were produced. Most of these remain doomed prophecies. Meanwhile the most far-reaching riverfront development was set on foot by private interests without any real concern for its relationship to the rest of the downtown area.

Along the Detroit River are found again the typical elements of large-scale renewal—the expressway running several blocks inland from the waters, with the intervening land cleared of a deteriorating neighborhood. An exhibition hall as architecturally undistinguished as the city's other civic buildings has been built here, along with a privately donated music hall. A large riverfront plaza is under construction—too large, one fears; but at least space will be provided for the ethnic festivals that draw huge crowds in the summer and provide an occasion of genuine civic celebration in that otherwise fractured community. Yet these features were not enough to fill the empty land. Besides, a no less powerful figure than Henry Ford felt that he ought to "do" something for the city.

The automobile manufacturers centered in Detroit have been struck periodically by the realization that they perhaps owed more to the community than they had rendered. In this mood they have contributed generously to its cultural institutions. Yet they failed completely where they might have made a contribution truly innovative and unique, demonstrating how the automobile could be made to harmonize with modern urban needs. Their offices and residences remaining far from the central city, they have not been interested in developing parking patterns or pedestrian systems and spaces that might have made Detroit a showcase. Indeed, they opposed, more openly here than elsewhere, the development of rapid transit. And when they moved to create a huge new complex on the river, they paid so little attention to parking needs that some of the projected office buildings are being considered for conversion to this use. Detroit stands today as an object lesson not of solutions, but of evils wrought by the automobile upon the fabric of a once elegantly designed city.

In keeping with the way things are done in Detroit, Henry Ford, when he decided the time had come to make significant business investments in the city, went not to the city authorities and to the planners, but to his own real estate specialists.[10] He asked them to look about for property in Detroit where he could create something at once profitable and symbolic. After a search they came back with property on the river. It was available; the site was appealing and the space large enough so that something spectacular could be done with it. There was no problem of relocation. Ford asked his board of directors to set aside $500,000 for preliminary work and engaged John Portman, well known for his work in Atlanta and San Francisco, to create a development plan.

This was in the early 1970s. Detroit had been picking up the pieces since the 1967 riots. The disastrous unemployment that was to hit the city in 1975 could not then be imagined. Two leadership groups, Detroit Renaissance and New Detroit, had quietly been urging a major move by Ford; and the time now seemed ripe for other companies to join in. This was to be a privately financed, money-making venture, without aid from the federal government. The call went out for investors. Henry Ford was as a man seized with a vision. He brought fellow automobile executives to see a film of Portman's work; groups traveled to Atlanta and San Francisco; Boston's Prudential Center and Atlanta Underground were examined as examples. On the day before Christmas, 1972, Richard G. Gerstenberg, board chairman of General Motors, announced that General Motors would invest in the project the same amount as Ford. After that the other investors, mostly auto manufacturers and suppliers, followed quickly.

The concept of the new waterfront development was large and went beyond

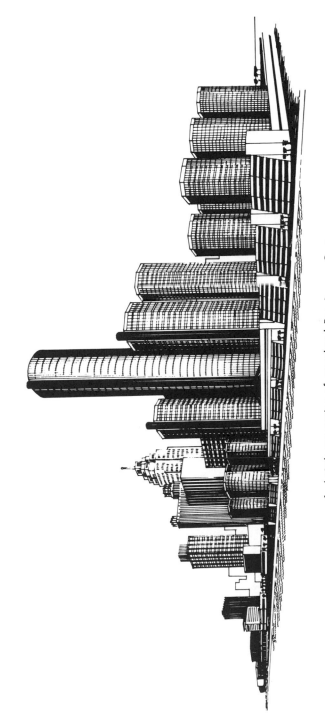

6. Artist's conception of completed Renaissance Center.

immediate self-interest. "It could happen," Henry Ford mused on the day of the ground-breaking for Renaissance Center: the whole riverfront from Cobo Hall to Parke Davis "could be like Chicago's lakefront." The first phase to be put under construction includes the Detroit Plaza Hotel, designed in the Portman style, a glass-walled cylinder seventy stories high. The hotel is flanked by four octagonal office towers of thirty-nine stories each, the whole set on a podium which is described as containing within its five levels "enormous interior vistas, covered walkways, escalators, gardens, fountains, promenades, specialty shops, theaters and restaurants." Amid inflationary costs and the tight money market, this complex found itself in mid-1975 running into severe financial difficulties.

The Center as ultimately completed will create a new waterfront scene for Detroit, one that no doubt will generate a large convention trade. But the question of what this will do to downtown remains unanswered. The area is already suffering from low occupancy, and a greater strain will be imposed before the day comes (if ever it does) when the overflow from Renaissance Center fills up existing office buildings and causes new ones to occupy the numerous open lots.

Will the average Detroiter benefit from covered walkways and the enormous interior vistas of the new riverfront development? Perhaps. But one gets the impression from present-day young Detroiters, those who would like to come in from the suburbs and find pleasures in their city's downtown, that what they would really choose to see are environments more like Greek Town—that one narrow street nestled among downtown Detroit's broad avenues, lined with unpretentious small shops and restaurants, where everyone feels safe even at night, and where somehow once again city life seems human and rewarding.

Historic Waterfronts

It is possible, of course, to give pre-eminence to the values embodied in a Greek Town. We would then see fostered along the cities' waterfronts an entirely different kind of space from that which has been reviewed.

Frequently there remains an environment capable of being restored rather than demolished. Seattle, despite the elevated highway that runs between downtown and the waterfront, keeps along the bay a variety of pleasant uses, a general medley of the urban and industrial. Old wharves still serving the movement of ships and ferries are interrupted by restaurants and a seaside shopping center. The famous market gives unexpected views across the water. In Savannah, the waterfront of the past has been regained for restaurants, antique shops and galleries. These huddle in the basement of old brick buildings whose upper stories, at the level of the street, once contained the cotton market. Across the roughly paved esplanade the ships of the port still come and go.

Boston has approached its waterfront as part of a city whose past is hardly less important than its present. Wharves are reclaimed as open spaces for living and walking; parks are inserted upon a modest scale, linking the waterfront to the inland green spaces, to Faneuil Hall, and to the openness of the new civic center. New York might seem a less likely example of historic waterfront preservation. Lower Manhattan has been so bent upon destruction of older buildings and is given over so largely to skyscrapers, it comes as a surprise to find on South Street an area of several blocks keeping the scale of the nineteenth-century city, with many of the old buildings intact.

From John Street north to the Brooklyn Bridge, salty names like Front Street, Water Street, Peck Slip and Burling Slip evoke the life of the old port during its heyday. A working waterfront community is in being; the low profile of brick buildings survives, and the ships that tie up at the piers are schooners and barges gathered from as far away as Argentina and Finland. The buildings, some of them, like Schermerhorn Row, dating back to 1812, are open for business, with offices and craft shops and museum headquarters.

South Street Seaport was the dream-child of private citizens who felt that New York, a city born of the sea, was ignoring its heritage. In 1966, when the group first met, led by Peter Stanford, an irrepressible if landbound mariner, the primary aim was to save the old buildings in the Fulton Market area. Interest grew into a determination to preserve the entire area. The Seaport found support in a sympathetic city administration, which developed the tools to make the project economically feasible through the device of selling off the unused development rights from the historic tracts ("transferring the air rights") to builders in the surrounding area.

The heart of the project is the South Street waterfront itself.[11] Here the bows of clipper ships once projected deep into the streets. Today an elevated highway unfortunately runs between the waterfront and South Street, which has itself been built on fill, thus putting the old Water Street inland. For a time it was hoped that the highway might be depressed at this point; but being realistic, the Seaport planners have reconciled themselves to its presence, and foresee a striped canopy to brighten its effect. The piers have been treated as still-unfinished parks. "A certain amount of activity and display of interesting objects is envisaged as a kind of 'meaningful clutter,'" the Seaport enthusiasts report: "kiosks under the elevated highway and pushcarts selling things to beguile a stroller or to quench an August noontime thirst." But on the piers the clutter is to become "historic and monumental." Here between the moored ships are carts, machines, piles of materials.

South Street is part of a total environment where the visitor will more and more become part of a lively, ongoing community. The blending of residences and craft shops, commercial stores, restaurants and theaters is not so much a reminder of the past as it is a living example of the way the past and present are connected. Mixed in with the boat whistles are the sound of jazz and rock. Poets read their modern verse and transcendental meditation goes on along with contemporary dance. The young feel at home in this oldest part of the city. For young and old alike the water becomes a lure once again, a feast for the eyes and a stimulus to the senses.

The Open Space Component

In the modest approach of the South Street Seaport, in the mixed uses of Seattle, Savannah and Boston, questions are being asked that the planners of Cincinnati and St. Louis never faced. What is the "river character" of the waterfront area? What role did it play in the origin and history of the city? What peculiar visual and sensory experiences does it foster? What activities are uniquely dependent on a waterfront site and which could as well be located elsewhere? A stadium, however well it may work as a stadium, would not have been the answer to the last question.

Waterfront planning based upon the preservation of historic areas has generally been more successful than efforts starting from a clean slate. In too many cities waterfront renewal has meant no more than turning over a cleared site to developers, whose projects provide scant benefits for the people at large. Whatever attractions waterside housing may possess for those who live in it, they are not to be compared with a many-dimensioned plan that adds significantly to the open space of a city.

The space contributed by an expanse of water is realized as a resource only when it can be enjoyed by the public. It must be open to view and also approachable. Architects and planners, even when aware of the degree to which an urban waterfront is "affected with a public interest," seem uncertain how to combine economic necessities with a larger good.[12] Low buildings extending along a waterway help keep the form of the city, yet may effectively block pedestrian access. In theory, towers maintain a desired effect of openness, but unless controls are rigidly enforced they tend to merge into a massive wall.

Several methods other than those embodied in historic-preservation ordinances have been used to control waterfront development. Urban renewal procedures permit local authorities to determine an overall plan. Zoning, and most recently the establishment of special zoning districts, can establish guidelines. Both these approaches, unfortunately, are more effective on paper than in practice, as local political and economic pressures tend to bring about results quite different from the original plan. In California, a 1971 state law attempts to meet the problem by requiring review by a state planning board of all projects within one thousand feet of the sea. This has obvious implications for a city like San Diego, with its twenty miles of coastline.

In waterfront developments, the following standards should be observed if the open space possibilities are to be realized:

- Maintenance of visual connections between the central city and the water.
- Access by pedestrians to waterside promenades and parks.
- Limited-use drives and landscaped parkways providing views of the water.
- Abatement of water pollution to allow use of the waters for recreational activities.
- Preservation of historic areas with their long-standing orientation toward the water.

If these criteria are observed, waterfronts may be utilized for a variety of other purposes—residential, commercial, industrial. It is important to emphasize, however, that the open space component must be put first. If it is not, the waterfront becomes merely one more area for development—the benefits that should belong to all the people either going to waste or being kept for the pleasure of the few.

The Waterfront as Image of the New City

For a model going beyond historic restoration as it goes beyond the satisfaction of large commercial interests, we turn to Minneapolis. This is a city that in the past owed everything to the river, and in the present has totally neglected it. This book aims to deal with cities as they exist, not as

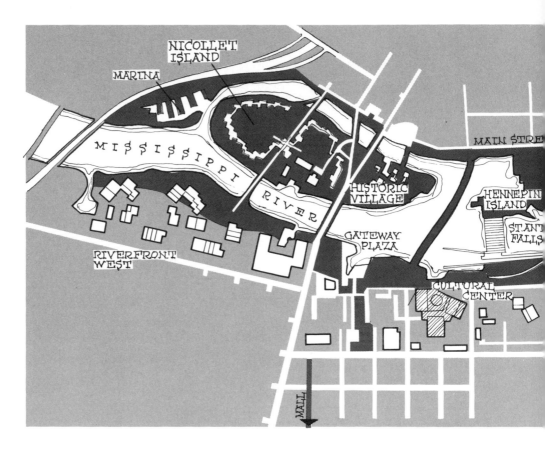

Plan for the Minneapolis waterfront shows key areas which come together in one complex whole. At St. Anthony Falls the city had its beginning; here Nicollet and Hennepin islands provide important opportunities for recreation and for recovering the city's past. On the north bank lies the old Main Street; on the south, the projected Gateway Plaza, tying in with Minneapolis's famous mall. Housing reclaims deserted railroad lines and yards; the university's new campus becomes a means of creating parkland along the shores.

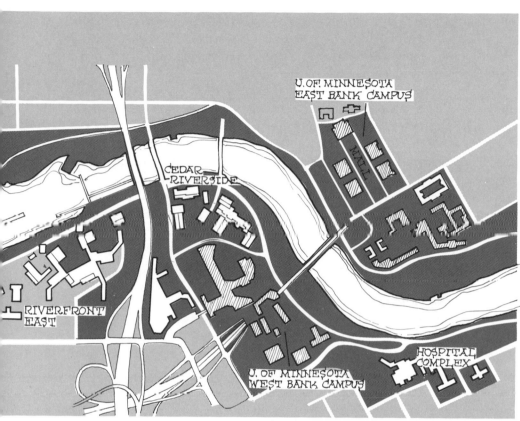

U. OF MINNESOTA
EAST BANK CAMPUS

MALL

CEDAR
RIVERSIDE

RIVERFRONT
EAST

HOSPITAL
COMPLEX

U. OF MINNESOTA
WEST BANK CAMPUS

MINNEAPOLIS - WATERFRONT

visionaries might dream of their being. Nevertheless, Minneapolis presents so striking a case of a riverfront lost, and makes out so good a case for its recovery and renewal, that its riverfront plan is worth serious consideration. Minneapolis is, moreover, a city that has shown a striking capacity to make plans that turn out to be realistic and achievable.

The city in the past decade and a half has been so busy creating a new downtown that it has turned little of its creative energies toward the riverfront. The old Gateway Park along the river is neglected, and much of the cleared land of the Gateway Renewal Project is vacant. The railroad yards and the decaying, underused industrial facilities make it virtually impossible to pass from the Nicollet Mall to the riverfront. At the university, on the east bank of the river, where Cass Gilbert once proposed a grand neoclassic, river-oriented façade, the Mississippi is now cut off, and the university mall is closed by the Coffman Student Union. Along Main Street, running on the east bank, the cobbled streets echo to the roar of trucking and its nineteenth-century brick storefronts are largely unused. In 1974 a young architect established his home and opened a restaurant there—the single flicker of new life in that otherwise dreary and abandoned neighborhood.

Minneapolitans have neglected, but they have not forgotten, their riverfront. A brilliant planning department document of 1972[13] lays the groundwork for a complex series of steps, involving all segments of the private and public sector, which could put their city at the forefront of urban achievements. The plan is based consistently on the idea that the river area should be dedicated to river-connected uses: no monuments, no stadiums, not even recreation facilities that do not call for a high sensitivity to the environment. On the other hand, certain industrial and commercial uses still are dependent on the river, and these are given a top priority. The planners look upon the river and its adjacent areas not as space to be filled up, nor as space to be cleared and vacated, but as a more rare and valuable resource, to which every element must be subtly adapted and among all of which clear relationships must be established. Seeing the opportunity in this way, they move toward a concept of multidimensional renewal, in which history and education, industry and transportation, beauty and power and refreshment of the spirit, all play their part.

The elements available to these planners are unusually rich and various; and some of the handicaps admittedly remain formidable. Of the latter, the railroads and railroad yards seem most obvious. Though their economic importance has declined as the industries they have supported change or move away, certain lines must be placed underground and properties must be disposed of in a way that puts the railroads to a hard test of statesmanship. The essential vision is, however, so persuasive as to make even this obstacle seem not insuperable in the long run.

Consider the resources waiting to be reshaped. Around St. Anthony Falls, the site of the city's origin, are clustered four major points of renewal. Nicollet Island offers the opportunity for open space and outdoor activities; Hennepin Island, with its rough topography and its fine view of the falls, suggests a different open environment; the Gateway area can bring downtown excitement to the river's edge; and finally Main Street on the opposite shore, envisaged as a traffic-free mall with two squares to mark its limits, allows history to be recreated and the needs of today's artists, craftsmen and small shopkeepers to be served.

Upriver, Gateway housing is proposed, keyed to Bassett Creek—one of those unfortunate waterways now buried in a culvert, which the planners mercifully intend to liberate. Downriver, the bluffs of the Mississippi rise steeply and indicate a somewhat different type of housing, with the fine stone Arch Bridge in view and some of the old grain elevators maintained as sculptural reminders of the past. The University of Minnesota faces the prospect of growth to fifty thousand students by 1980, with expansion projected to cross the river to the west bank. Public and private planning is in progress, with a view to relating this new development to the Cedar Riverside renewal area, and to open space along the riverbank. River parkways would be extended on both banks to the downtown Gateway area, opening up fine river and city views, and thus fulfilling one of the old dreams of Minneapolis's first park planner.

Important as are the individual projects, the spirit and general approach of the plan give it unusual distinction. The reconstruction of the riverfront is seen as the grand opportunity to convert the remains of a nineteenth-century city, with its emphasis on the workaday aspects of life, to a twentieth-century environment of leisure. It substitutes the city of delight for the city of necessity—or even better, combines the two. Everywhere the emphasis is on individuals exercising their free choice, given wide options of recreation, of means of transportation, of views and types of outdoor settings. It makes the past visible in the present. The pedestrian is freed from the tyranny of the automobile, and even mass transportation loses in this plan the somewhat ominous stress on "mass." It becomes specifically related to what men and women want to do and where they choose to go.

This river redevelopment, it should be noted finally, is for the benefit of those who live in the city, not primarily for the tourist or the visitor. One looks in vain in the plan for a convention center or for the standard exhibition hall. One does not even find a mention of hotels. The riverfront becomes the heart and symbol of the city; indeed, in its mixture of uses, its variety of pleasures, it becomes a city in itself, and an image of what all cities ought to be.

5 Transportation Shapes Open Space

"THE FORM OF THE CITY IS, or must be, derived from the necessities of locomotion." So wrote Soria y Mata, a Spanish engineer inspired in the last century by the invention of the trolley car.[1] He went on to envisage a future city with a single street some fifteen hundred feet in width, running from Brussels to Peking, bordered by structures whose inhabitants would have the benefit of constant proximity to the countryside. Others have similarly projected an endlessly stretched out city, from the "roadtown" of Edgar Chandless (1910) to Paul Rudolph's plan for a linear development following the Penn Central right of way in Brooklyn.

The particular vision of Mata was not, for better or worse, fulfilled; but his generalization remains in large measure true. The "necessities of locomotion" are a powerful force in organizing the city and determining the nature of its open spaces. The forms of locomotion are various, including pedestrian, cycling, buses, rapid transit, trains and above all the automobile. How these are combined and put to use makes the contemporary city what it is—in most respects a muddle, but with gleams of rationality and with some hope for the future.

Railroads and Their Terminals

The railway was the first major transportation development to disrupt the older city, whose scale and pattern had been fixed by men on foot and in carriages. Its coming was as shattering to the traditional American town

115

as was the coming of the expressways a century later. The more densely formed and tightly organized European city kept the railway terminal at its gate, letting the city as it expanded slowly grow up around the tracks. In the United States, however, the railroad lines tended to slash through the loosely knit fabric of the older town, dividing neighborhoods and obliterating open lands.

So anxious were the citizens to receive within the urban bosom this sign of progress and this promise of prosperity, they would, as we have seen, encourage it to pass along choice waterfront sites. Meanwhile subsidies were being demanded by the railroad companies from new towns beyond the Appalachians, on pain of having the tracks by-pass the settlement, with fatal consequences. The objective of the developers was to have the trains pass directly through the town, as roads and canals had done earlier, and as expressways were to do later.

The railroads, once they had penetrated a city, extended their claims for all kinds of secondary purposes—the more easily because their soot and noise rapidly made the area unsuitable for commercial or residential uses. Having thus weakened the urban fabric, the railways then became a principal means of dispersing the population into suburbs.

Here and there, in a grand terminal with a square before it, the railways contributed to the open space of a city. As the main point of entrance they had the opportunity to give the visitor a favorable first impression and to influence the nearby development of hotels, restaurants and other urban amenities. By the beginning of the twentieth century, however, an observant student of cities, Charles Mulford Robinson,[2] could note that in contrast to Europe, almost all American cities had their terminals in "squalid" surroundings. Most of the best terminals were built later, in the aftermath of the City Beautiful movement, and one of the most striking— the masterpiece of Art Nouveau in Cincinnati—was completed when the days of passenger transportation were already numbered.

A rare instance of railway trackage contributing to the city's open space is to be found in New York's Park Avenue. The tracks running into Grand Central Terminal were covered over by 1913; the New York Central Railroad developed its air rights in the uniform and handsome apartments that lined the lower avenue until replaced by office towers after World War II. At the center of this broad avenue there was originally a system of linear parks, broad enough to afford shelter from the traffic, containing curving paths and pleasant seating places. Unfortunately, these were progressively cut away to meet the demands of automobile traffic. Today a vestige of the park system remains in the form of narrow strips lending themselves poorly to the minimal planting that a harassed Parks Department endeavors to maintain.

In their decline the railways may do more for open space than they accomplished in the days of their glory, and may even compensate for some of the damage they did to choice lands. Pittsburgh has recaptured for park uses the abandoned tracks and sheds that stood until the 1950s at the point where the Allegheny and Monongahela rivers meet; Philadelphia has created a new city center where the "Chinese wall" of the Pennsylvania Railroad once invaded the heart of downtown.

The old railroad stations, lightly used or abandoned, provide other sources for public space, both outdoors and under cover. The terminals are often picturesque in style, like the imitation of Carcassonne upon the St. Louis mall, or classically noble, like Burnham's great portico in Washington, D.C. The former is now to become the entranceway to a new mixed development of residences and offices; the latter is a visitors' orientation center. Elsewhere stations saved as landmarks, house markets, shops, a school, an educational center, and in at least one instance, a transportation facility. The once-crowded concourses, and the neglected open space before them, can in many cases provide an ideal focal point for the mixed uses of the new downtown.[3]

Atlanta, originally a railroad town, has taken unique advantage of the almost ghostly residues of its central terminal. The tracks have long since been covered, first by bridges, which traversed them, and then by complete streets; a second city grew up at this new street level. Below, like a city waiting to be unearthed by archaeologists, lay the foundations of old railroad stations with their nearby hotels.

On one corner of this subterranean world stands a bank, its solid masonry gently rounded to accommodate the passer-by; across the way is a drugstore, a Coca-Cola sign dating from the early years of this century still vivid on the exterior wall. Here in the 1960s came a group of imaginative young developers, well organized and soon adequately financed, who filled the streets and the shops with new activities. Atlanta's night life became focused around this old railroad station—a railroad station that long since had disappeared from sight.

Invasion by Expressway

Similar in effect to the railroads, but more devastating because they entered cities hardened and matured in form, were the expressways of the 1950s. The interstate system was conceived as a means of moving traffic between cities. This vast construction, comprising 41,000 miles of multilane, limited-access highway, was the most costly public works program ever undertaken by this country. At the beginning no one saw it as a development that would alter the shape of cities and crucially affect their spatial organization.

In 1931 the concept of the "townless highway"[4] was elaborated by Benton MacKaye. This system was to avoid the mistakes of the railroads, leaving the cities whole by by-passing every urban center. The highway engineers began with this idea. The pioneering New York State Thruway, planned in the late 1940s, skirted the towns along its way. But portents of the future could already be discerned in the way local politicians used their influence to have the route come as near as possible to their own cities. Rochester, for example, was left several miles from the nearest thruway exit; Syracuse, whose politicians apparently were more adroit, managed to have the right of way penetrate into its downtown area.

By the 1950s, mayors and congressmen were fighting to have the interstate routes become part of their local arterials, and the system was taking the form everywhere evident today. Once again, as with the railroads just a century before, the hearts of cities were ripped open, neighborhoods were divided or wiped out, and normal lines of communication were broken. Designed to cross open country, the expressways were being brought without change into the most heavily built up areas of towns and cities or along the precious waterfront lands.

That all this should have been allowed to happen seems incredible today, when the devastation of the in-town expressway lies plainly exposed. The old fear of being left outside the route of the canal or railroad was a factor; so was the failure of the citizens to imagine exactly how the expressway would affect their communities. The 1948 Cincinnati master plan discusses the new "motorways" as logical successors to the parkway concept: ". . . these routes will have much of the esthetic quality formerly associated with 'parkways,' which traditionally were regarded as ways for pleasure driving."[5] Nor did the planners see incompatibility of trucks and passenger cars. The use of the new routes "by heavy, slow-moving commercial vehicles is neither a hazard nor a hindrance to other traffic," they declared.

So little was the nature of the modern expressway understood that in Chicago it was brought along the very route Burnham had set aside for a grand avenue, with an obliterating cloverleaf taking the place of his nobly conceived plaza. Similarly in Minneapolis, the in-town expressways follow routes once held sacred for boulevards.

The devastation wrought upon the city's form was unnecessarily intensified by the arrogance of the highway engineers. They allowed for no modification of design, no refinement of details, so that the same large-scale, brutal structure that might be at home crossing an uninhabited countryside was introduced amid the city's architectural works and its landscaped parks.[6] Sensing the first tremors of citizen opposition, the engineers and planners plunged the more stubbornly ahead. "Cities need expressways so badly," said the U.S. Commissioner of Public Roads,[7] "that they are worth almost any cost." He urged buying and clearing wide swaths of in-city land—"with plenty of emphasis on the word 'wide.'" The incorrigible Robert Moses, addressing the National Highway Users Conference as late as 1964,[8] asserted that whatever latitude might exist in building a new city such as Brasilia or Canberra, "when you operate in an overbuilt metropolis you have to hack your way with a meat ax."

Such attitudes produced two reactions. The first was outright opposition to the in-town freeways; the second was a series of attempts to come to terms with the invader. In much the same way that the cities had surrounded, lidded over and otherwise adapted themselves to the railway trackage, they began to absorb some of the most disruptive manifestations of the freeway. The cities, after all, are living organisms; their physical form is capable of responding to, and sometimes rejecting, a foreign substance.

Rejections and Accommodations

Resistance to the in-city expressway was most easily expressed where the issue could be dramatized by public groups resolved to save a park, a waterfront or a functioning neighborhood. Such efforts have not always been successful; but in San Francisco the abrupt termination of the freeway separating the Embarcadero from downtown; in Hartford and San Antonio, the freeway lying like a cut ribbon at the edge of major parks; in Queens, New York, the Clearview Expressway running out like a spent stream where it met an integrated and resistant community—these scenes could be repeated in other cities. Two of the more interesting examples of the way expressway plans have been modified exist in Phoenix and Baltimore.

Phoenix shows from the air an open but greening swath directly across its downtown area. This was to have been the route of the Papagos Expressway. It was rejected by the citizens.[9] In that automobile-oriented city the

grid of superblocks, with traffic regulations strictly and rather brutally enforced, is considered a better way of getting around, and one that more
effectively disperses traffic, than the monolithic expressway. Parks and a
parkway will eventually make use of the land that was cleared for the
freeway.

Baltimore, lying in the path of the eastern seaboard's populous cities,
seemed doomed to have the heart of its downtown area torn apart by the
connecting expressway. The firm of Skidmore, Owings and Merrill was
brought in, with Nathaniel Owings at the head of the team of professionals
charged to find a way of reconciling the New York–to–Florida freeway
system with preservation of the city's historic core and of its neglected but
potentially invaluable waterfronts. In less than a month's time a plan was
conceived which took less land, made fewer intrusions on the vital parts
of the city, and incidentally cost less to built. It by-passed the solid residential community of Rosemont, with its 7,500 blacks, eliminated the crossing of the inner harbor and rescued important Federal Hill.

"Freeways," said Owings,[10] who could well take pride in the accomplishment of his team of experts, "must go under or around, never through the
fragile fabric of the city." This was the very opposite of the "meat ax"
approach.[11]

Elsewhere existing highway structures are being looked at by civic
designers as open space resources. In Dallas the right of way of the encircling expressway is being treated as a potential greenbelt, and the descending ramps as the site of "portal parks." In Seattle the expressway that
bisects the downtown area has recently been bridged over by a park
(designed by Lawrence Halprin) which is a delightful amenity in itself
and reunites with the downtown area apartment houses and a church that
had stood isolated across the divide. In Los Angeles the master plan includes
an extension of open space running across the freeway to connect the historic Pueblo with the City Hall complex.

Such compromises between the needs of the inner city and the needs of
transportation would have been easier to accomplish had they been conceived from the beginning. The Federal Department of Transportation has
indeed been aware since the 1960s of the crucial impact of freeways upon
the cityscape; the location of rights of way was made subject to environmental review under Section 4 (f) of the Department of Transportation Act
of 1966, and architects and landscape designers were consulted on details
of the roadways.[12] But by then the period of major expressway building was
over. The often blighting structures lay upon the cities, capable only of
being softened in their effect by the belated efforts of local urban planners.

Unforeseen Results of Traffic Engineering

The aspect of freeway design most significant to the spatial organization of the modern city is not, however, the highways crossing through them; it is the inner circumferential route which draws a tight noose around the downtown area. The cores of cities have, as already noted, been given a new form by the wall thus created. They have been made more dense, more closely knit, more inviting to the construction of high-rise towers, and more amenable to being traversed by people-movers or pedestrians. Yet the extraordinary fact is that these developments took place unawares, as a result of considerations having little to do with the design of cities or the determination of their spatial texture.

The concept of the inner loop arose, quite simply, out of a desire to move traffic more efficiently.[13] The overall system, which had been conceived originally to move traffic between cities, became increasingly adapted to helping relieve congestion within the cities. The arterials were extended as far as possible into the heart of downtown, with as many as five or six converging routes tending toward the center. Now, it is impossible to have spokes without a hub; it is impossible to have roadways from different directions come together at one point. An inner circumferential route was therefore devised, its size and form entirely the result of engineering calculations.

In the preindustrial city, too, it was not possible for routes leading into the city to meet at a mathematical point. They joined at a square or plaza, usually at the center of town. The square at Santa Fe is a perfect example; here was the end of the trail, and in this open space men tied up their horses and set out for a favorite place of refreshment. The monumental circle was also a device for handling converging routes, keyed to the slower pace and less concentrated traffic volume of the pre-automobile society.

The open area brought into being at the hub of such a traffic web has almost invariably been pedestrian space. In the same way the area enclosed by the inner loop of today's expressway system—an area comprising the modern downtown—is (or ought to be) largely pedestrianized.

The method of fixing the circumference of this loop has had little regard to urban form. The exclusive aim was to speed traffic and then properly to distribute it. If the loop was too large, traffic was dumped at too early a point into streets not able to carry it. If the loop was too small, the number of access routes was limited. These required about ten acres of land each, and could occur only at two-thousand-foot intervals.

The resulting circumference of these loops varies from eight miles in Washington, D.C., to slightly over three miles in Kansas City and Fort Worth. The diameter varies from one to two miles, and the area contained from 4.3 square miles to .7 mile. Despite the lack of an urban philosophy in fixing these limits, the results in terms of the city's form have been better than might have been anticipated.

What the highway engineers and most of the city planners had not taken into account was the fact that these inner loops, beside acting as traffic regulators, would play a crucial role in establishing the size and nature of the central city. Sometimes elevated and highly visible, sometimes exerting a relatively unseen effect upon land values and land uses, these circumferential routes tended to produce a tight downtown area, containing within it a core and supporting services, whose distances were easily traversed.

The effect of the freeway wall is seen in any comparatively young city that does not have a waterway for its edge. The central business district is sharply defined, and development tends to move outward to borders set by the freeway. Land use differs at this edge—on one side of the freeway, high-rise office buildings or land temporarily vacant, waiting to be developed; on the other, buildings of a traditional scale, two or three stories tall, with their backyards and scattered greenery. At ground level the motorist crosses the encircling freeway, moving from a highly built up, almost futuristic cityscape into a commercial avenue which still shows traces of its residential past.

The constraints work well in a city like Houston. Here the need for 100 million square feet of office space is foreseen, compared with the 50 million now existing. The large amount can be met comfortably within the defined area. Dallas, too, finds a congruity between the predicted working force of its center and the space provided by the inner loop of the freeway system. Louisville, however, seems to suffer from a poor fit. The inner loop creates too large an area to be built up or sustained by the economy of the city. The result is a looseness of the urban fabric, with expanses of undeveloped land lending themselves neither to business and institutional use nor to the residential patterns that prevail beyond the expressway ring.

Parking at the Perimeter

Victor Gruen, who in his Fort Worth plan of 1956 first detected and publicized the role of the circumferential route as a modern form of the city wall, went on to elaborate its defensive nature. He saw the automobile as the enemy, and decreed that it should be halted and housed in enormous ramps at points where it descends from the freeway. From there to the center, ideally a distance of less than a mile, various forms of people-movers should take over. It was thought not impossible that many would go on foot, through an urban environment made colorful by courts and gardens, and under the shelter of skywalks and arcades.

The concept of highly visible and symbolic parking ramps at several points on the periphery of downtown has never been fully realized. Minneapolis has such a scheme in its master plan; Atlanta officials claim to be watching carefully the number of cars entering downtown, prepared to take action when a saturation point is neared. All too often, as in Rochester, the principle of perimeter parking is well understood, but the planners succumb to pressures and allow a large parking garage in the very center. Houston seems to feel that each major building must have a satellite parking garage attached to it by bridge or tunnel, so that the individual will never feel uncomfortably far from his means of locomotion.

With an approach that tells us much about the character of San Francisco —its pluralism, its worldly sense of realism, its mistrust of simple solutions —officials of that city have concluded that the parking problem never will be solved. There will always be too many cars. The only way to deal with them is to let them proliferate under more or less severe restrictions and with the option of mass transportation available when the problem becomes too burdensome.

Whatever the various approaches dictated by a particular city's physical situation or its basic attitudes, the image of an inner loop furnished with parking ramps has taken deep root. It has influenced a number of other aspects of urban design. The "necessities of locomotion" which determine the form of a city now include pedestrianism along with private automobiles or long-range mass transport.

The ultimate locomotion of man on foot, or man in some individualized and localized conveyance, is a force of absolutely major significance. It is no less capable of affecting and indeed of transforming the inner cities than the highly visible force of the freeway system. It is linked closely with that system. The expressway, the inner loop, the interception of automobiles at the point of entrance and continuance of the journey on foot or by people-mover—these are all part of one vision, and together they are making the modern city what it is.

New Functions for Streets

The concept of the circumferential loop once established, it becomes necessary to take an entirely fresh look at the city's streets. For these now play a part different from the one they played in older cities. They are no longer prolongations of routes into downtown; they are not ways of passing through it. Their functions may be diverse—a street for shopping, or a street for loading and unloading vehicles, a street for playing or just for walking. The important point is that many of them have specific functions, and that these need to be identified and sorted out from the undifferentiated confusion that marks most downtown areas.

An important study for New York City grasps the interrelationship between exterior loop and internal street, coming up with surprising conclusions in regard to open space. In 1970 the planning firm of van Ginkel Associates was asked by the city authorities for help in dealing with downtown traffic flow.[14] Their study began with the movement of automobiles, it ended with proposals for numerous streets confined to pedestrians, including the recommendation that all automobile traffic be kept out of Central Park! Seeing stalled cars, blocked streets, trucks rendered helpless by congestion, the report did not propose that sidewalks again be narrowed, but rather that traffic arteries so seemingly indispensable as Broadway and Madison Avenue be made pedestrian malls. How did the planners reach this conclusion?

Basically they reached it by adopting the radical assumption that "movement" in midtown refers not only to wheeled traffic but also to foot traffic. Of these two "necessities of locomotion," they see the latter as no less important than the former in shaping the central city.

The midtown area of New York City shows major expressways along the riverbanks on east and west. The planners identify these not as portions of an inner loop, but as bridges carrying traffic across midtown. They then develop what is essentially an inner loop by giving a particular function to existing avenues—First and Second avenues on the east, Eleventh and Twelfth avenues on the west, with Fifty-seventh Street and Thirty-fourth Street bounding the north and south. The area thus contained is a little over a mile in each direction, roughly the area of the ideal downtown.

Within this area most streets are used for the conventional combination of pedestrians and automobiles—except that the mix is seen as being significantly altered by the fact that much traffic is drained away from the

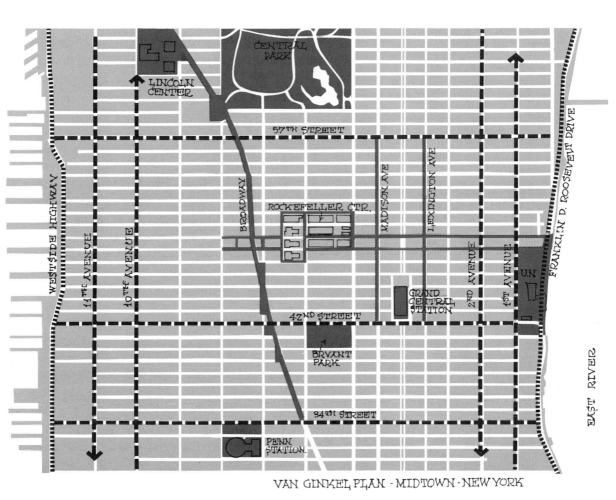

VAN GINKEL PLAN · MIDTOWN · NEW YORK

▪▪▪▪▪▪▪▪   PRINCIPAL NORTH-SOUTH HIGHWAYS
▬ ▬ ▬   INNER-LOOP
▬▬▬▬   PEDESTRIAN ROUTES

This simplified version of the van Ginkel Plan shows the principal north-south highways or "bridges" across mid-Manhattan. The "inner loop" is superimposed on the existing city grid; pedestrian routes are made possible by the redistribution of traffic. Thus without major construction an apparently formless central core can be given sharply defined functions. The effects on pedestrian space are impressive.

interior by organizing particular streets and avenues to serve as a loop. Other streets are unexpectedly set aside as pedestrian ways. These include such present channels of traffic as Broadway, Madison Avenue and Lexington Avenue. They are not entirely closed to cars; many variations of design allow for cross-traffic, the passage of emergency vehicles, provisions for loading, and minibuses. The exclusion of all wheeled traffic is not considered essential to a pedestrian path. What is essential is that the pedestrian should have a balance in his favor—a balance of space, of quiet, of urban amenities.

Significantly, the van Ginkel plan does not require engineering feats in the form of elevated expressways or depressed by-passes. The most complicated "hardware" called for is a small minibus which people can enter and leave with ease. The plan discerns the nature of downtown within the existing configuration of expressways, avenues and streets. Clarifying the functions of each by traffic regulations as well as by modifications of landscaping, pavement and street furniture, the planners reveal a downtown form that is characteristic of the modern American city. From within that form, important new open spaces emerge.

The Mall as Open Space

Most dramatic of such new open spaces are pedestrian malls. Essentially these involve closing streets or a portion of an avenue to vehicular traffic and developing the area as a pedestrian concourse. The result is something like a park and something like a square—an important addition to the hierarchy of spaces available to the urban dweller. These malls are usually viewed as downtown amenities, but their nature is more fully disclosed when they are seen in the context of a balanced transportation system.

The mall concept is so attractive that it may too readily be adopted as a supposed cure-all for downtown ills. What a few cities have accomplished through wise traffic planning and carefully nurtured business co-operation, others have tried to impose more or less arbitrarily on shopping areas not ripe for the change. If there is a lesson to be learned from observation of malls in a number of cities, it is that the street, like many elements within the city, is a delicate organism relying for its commercial viability upon a variety of half-understood factors, some physical and some psychological; and that merely to "dress up" a street is not necessarily the first answer to its needs. So apparently desirable an addition as trees can obscure the merchants' signs; new street lighting can be an invitation to vandals. Elimination of wheeled traffic can in some cases kill the illusion of vitality which sustained at least a reasonable level of economic activity.

The mall is best seen as one tool among many in restoring the attractiveness of downtown and should come as the capstone upon other related improvements. Cincinnati rejected the mall concept in favor of skywalks; St. Louis has given priority to the freeing of its central vista toward the Mississippi. Louisville, on the other hand, has put high hopes in its downtown mall along with its river-oriented Belvedere. If Louisville fails to go forward with additional civic improvements, this mall—too fragile by itself to counter downtown deterioration—will almost certainly decline into an area of second-rate shops and entertainments. A mall in another city has been taken over by senior citizens, and one proved so commercially successful that it was bought up for a developer, who will construct a shopping center on the site.[15]

Two examples, of a mall that failed and of one that succeeded, illustrate the complexities inherent in this form of open space and suggest how important it is that they be closely co-ordinated with overall plans for transportation.

MADISON AVENUE, NEW YORK   In the early 1970s New York began plans for what would have been the most spectacular of big-city malls and could have greatly influenced for the better the character of midtown Manhattan. In 1971 Mayor John V. Lindsay announced a decision to convert Madison Avenue from the mid-Forties to the mid-Fifties into a street carrying only two lanes of traffic, these being restricted to buses and minibuses, with truck deliveries being made in off-hours. The sidewalks would be widened to accommodate extra plantings of trees and street furniture and to allow for awnings and arcades in front of individual stores. This area, running roughly between Grand Central Terminal and Rockefeller Center, is naturally thronged with pedestrians, though existing sidewalks are narrower than a hundred years ago, when the avenue was lined with four-story buildings. Experimental closings of this portion of the avenue had shown in what numbers and with what apparent joy pedestrians accepted this enlargement of their domain.

The Madison Avenue Mall, as the project was known, fell heir to the kind of controversy that has attended the closing of shopping streets both in this country and abroad. Though most have decisively benefited local merchants, fears have regularly been expressed that trade will suffer and that "undesirable elements" will take over. In New York the conventional-

The Mall becomes a popular form of open space.

7. In Louisville, the River City Mall awaits the extensions and connections that can assure vitality and a necessary population mix.

8. In New Orleans, a mall is created by the simplest of means—placing a barrier at certain hours across Royal Street.

9. Lexington Mall in Baltimore benefits from being adjacent to Charles Center.

10. Nicollet Mall in Minneapolis showing skywalks and kiosks—a model for other cities.

minded Fifth Avenue Association expressed its opposition, strongly abetted by the taxi industry. The Association brought the dispute to court, winning a decision that moneys for the purpose of the mall could not be expended without approval of the Board of Estimate. Taxi drivers, a large number of whom live in the Bronx, put political pressure on the Bronx borough president. The mayor was then near the end of his term, with his political strength greatly diminished. The vote of the Bronx representative on the Board of Estimate was decisive in defeating the plan.

Such are the surface facts. More significant was the mayor's failure to convince the public that the mall was not an isolated if spectacular amenity, but was the direct outcome of the van Ginkel study of midtown traffic. Even those most anxious to see its accomplishment asked how the wider area would be able to absorb the additional load. Actually, as has been seen, the traffic problem had been dealt with in the first instance, and the mall was a part of the solution.

The mayor had taken the position with his advisers that the best way to prepare the ground for the van Ginkel traffic reforms was to go ahead just with the mall. He believed that its high visibility and its popularity would help generate the consensus necessary for further moves. In this tactic he erred, losing both the mall and the traffic plan. But he was profoundly right in associating the two and seeing their interrelationship. Only when a pedestrian mall is viewed in the context of downtown as a whole, when problems of movement and parking are recognized as part of it, can there be a lasting gain.

NICOLLET AVENUE, MINNEAPOLIS   The best example of a mall functioning to the satisfaction of both merchants and the general public, and the best case history of how such a result can be reached, is that of Minneapolis. The Nicollet Mall has become a prime factor in the city's downtown renewal. Running from the Gateway Center along the riverfront, the length of the city's retail core, it is a sensitively landscaped street, shaped to a gentle curve through much of its extent.

All traffic save buses are banned from it, but cross-traffic at the intersections allows the close approach of cars and taxis. The pavement is heated to melt snow. Separate blocks are designed to be different in their street furniture and planting, giving almost the appearance of a series of plazas; yet the whole has the harmony of a single design. Among the features incorporated into the street scene are bus terminals heated by infrared lamps with benches and phone booths, fountains, floral displays and trees, an automatic post office and a weather station. This mall is crossed at various points by second-level skywalks, and it ties in with the enclosed spaces of the IDS Center.

The immediately visible aspects of the mall are hardly less important than the long process of planning that went into its making. Of its nearly four-million-dollar cost, roughly two-thirds was spent on the installation and improvement of underground facilities. The figure may be taken as indicative of the essential nature of such a mall. Not only is a large portion of the physical improvement unseen, but the greater proportion of its benefits lies outside the direct grasp of the observer. However pleasant its spaces to the window-shopper and pedestrian, its secondary and deferred results are the more crucial to the city's economic life, to the restoration of a viable downtown, to the reform of traffic, parking, mass transit and other urban systems.

The proponents of the Minneapolis mall understood from the beginning that this work was to be the apex of a pyramid whose wide base lay in a master plan for the central business district. In the mid-1950s a number of forces were coming together to suggest that unless common action was taken, the changes in the downtown area would be out of control and could accelerate the first signs of deterioration in a hitherto strong commercial district. The interstate freeway system was being planned, a major shopping center was being constructed in the suburbs; General Mills, one of the city's chief industrial plants, was moving out of the city. In this atmosphere of concern the Downtown Council of Minneapolis was formed in 1955.

The Council's first experience was with the impact and the detailed planning of the freeway system. The limited nature of the city's input convinced the Council that a greatly strengthened planning department within the city government was essential. Decisions being made by the city engineer, in whose hands rested the general management of the city, were simply not adequate to the scope and complexity of the new urban needs. A well-staffed and well-funded planning commission was established and immediately began on studies. Its first concern was the midtown area.

Two years later, a subcommittee of the Downtown Council proposed the redesign of Nicollet Avenue into a series of enclosed plazas. The concept was too grandiose to be immediately practicable, but the idea had been launched that was to issue in the mall and was to influence such a later development as the IDS Center. For the time being, the Council insisted upon the underpinning of a more comprehensive plan by outside consultants.

This 1960 report examined five proposals for Nicollet Avenue, from minor cosmetics to the ambitious union of a mall and transitway. The Downtown Council now involved all affected interests in a broad consideration of alternatives; and after a year's discussion the idea was generally accepted of a mall broken at the street intersections, designed to serve as the focus for a bus transit system linking downtown with every Minneapolis neighborhood. A general plan was then shaped and adopted by the Downtown Council; Lawrence Halprin and Associates was engaged to do the landscaping; and the scheme was given official standing by approval of the city council and the county board of commissioners. "Some three years had been consumed in conceptual planning and the gaining of both private and public approval," writes Frederick T. Aschman, whose firm had done the basic planning for the mall. "Few suspected in 1963 that another four years would transpire before the mall became an operating reality."[16]

To finance the mall, a complicated system of assessments was worked out. Because it was recognized that the benefits extended beyond the mall's actual frontage, roughly half the total assessment fell to owners of frontage property; the remainder to properties not directly on the mall. Construction and maintenance costs were further refined so as to impose a variable burden. Two sources of federal funds were made use of, an urban beautification grant and a mass transportation demonstration grant. The ultimate cost was $3.8 million, shared by the city and the federal government.

The Minneapolis mall has today taken its place as a central and seemingly indispensable feature of the city. Together with other improvements which it has stimulated, it brings to the downtown area a sense of what is special and exciting in city life. Yet it has its shortcomings. Proceeding for several blocks from its terminus at the Northwestern National Life Insurance Building, the mall is lined by uninviting walls such as those of a bank and a parking garage; and the public library–science museum presents, unfortunately, a lifeless face. Only in the area of the department stores near Third Street does the full impact of the mall make itself felt. And then the seductive entrance of the IDS complex adds its own dazzling burst of life.

At night, apart from passengers warming themselves in the little bus stations while they await transportation, the mall is empty. The traditional entertainment section of the city, on adjacent Hennepin Avenue, now featuring "adult" bookstores and X-rated movies, is by comparison crowded.

The ultimate success of the mall depends upon still further extensions, so that it connects with the plaza in front of the new Music Hall at Twelfth Street, and in altered form makes its way through a residential complex to the green spaces of Loring Park. The Minneapolis city plan projects additional developments in the way of heated arcades and pavements, further skywalks linking it to the entertainment district and the civic center, and a skyway route for pedestrians leading from a massive parking garage at the freeway exit.

It seems to be the fate of modern cities that they cannot rest on such improvements as they have attained at any one point. They are not static, as the classic or medieval city was intended to be, but dynamic in their growth and change. Each environmental gain interacts with other factors; the most sought after results generate in their turn new necessities and often new problems. The Minneapolis mall, despite the enlightened efforts that have gone into it and despite its success to date, is a good example of this compulsion to keep going forward. It stands as a major achievement; but it stands truncated and incomplete. It will resist the encroachments of blight or decline only if a comprehensive downtown plan moves steadily toward fulfillment.

Rapid Transit Reshapes Main Street

Central in the downtown plan of several cities is a rapid transit system, one further form of locomotion to be viewed in its effect on the city's open space.[17] Following most often the routes of existing rail lines and highways, and serving existing concentrations of population, rapid transit schemes are not likely to alter the existing form of the city. In the terminals and stations of the system, however, open space implications may be significant.

The idea that some better way of entering a subway than descending (as at most New York City stations) down a steep stairway through a hole in the street originated—like so much else in urban design—in Philadelphia. At Penn Center it was seen that various levels could be combined, the outdoors and indoors, the upper levels and lower levels integrated, so that the individual would find it a pleasant experience to make the transition from going on foot to moving by mechanical means at an extremely rapid rate. At the same time, since such a station fell naturally at busy intersections, the entrance could become a civic square in its own right, used for sitting and resting.

The meeting of transportation routes has always been a factor in the carving out of open space, from the square where the old roads joined to the nineteenth-century railway terminal. In Philadelphia the process reaches a culmination, using entirely modern procedures and embodying the results in innovative forms. Thus at Market Street East occurs an interface

11. BART subway station creates a square on Market Street in San Francisco.

of subways and commuter railways, of buses, automobiles and streetcars. Within the field of density and movement thus generated, on land provided by urban renewal, a vast downtown shopping mall surrounded by office buildings has come into being.

The pleasant effect of underground routes on the cityscape may be noted in three cities[18] where rapid transit plans and projects are well advanced.

SAN FRANCISCO At Market Street and Powell, within a few blocks of the civic center, a sunken plaza creates a pause in that busy area. Handsomely laid up granite walls planted with trees and vines echo the granite arches of the bank building on its west wall. Across Market Street the scale and texture of long-standing commercial buildings complete the plaza's frame. Benches at two levels accommodate the habitués of the neighborhood, a class much given to sitting and thinking. At the lowest level, reached by moving staircases, is the entrance to one of BART's new subway stations.

As a result of the subway construction, Market Street itself is being refurbished extensively, at a cost of thirty million dollars. New pavement, new lighting and street furniture, a new parking system and a further square at the Embarcadero station are all dividends of the transportation system. Market Street is expected to maintain its popular, middle-class aspects, keeping many of the existing street-front buildings and upgrading its down-to-earth department stores. The city, more than almost any other, contains shopping areas for a specialized clientele seeking arcane merchandise. Market Street can well afford to remain a place where ordinary people (including the habitués mentioned above) can pursue their ordinary pursuits in an agreeably renovated but not overromanticized environment.

ATLANTA A city that plans seriously and imaginatively where its vital interests are at stake, Atlanta has seized upon the stations of its new rapid transit system as a way of making significant improvements in its downtown area. The subway, says Allen Hardin, chairman of the Rapid Transit Authority, "is an opportunity to cause things to happen."[19] Peachtree and other streets will be torn up, and "when things are put back they should be put back differently." The earlier intention to make Peachtree Street a complete mall, with cross-traffic passing below grade, has had to be abandoned. But traffic will still be barred except at the cross-streets. Margaret Mitchell Square, now an adequate juncture at the fork of Peachtree and West Peachtree streets, will become the site of a new plaza giving access to the tracks below. And the park at Five Points will go down in terraces to the station level.

BUFFALO The boldest effort to make use of a rapid transit system as a lever to remake downtown is found in this upstate New York city. A covered mall extending six blocks is projected for the core. The glass structure running to the building line on each side and incorporating fire-fighting and other safety measures is in effect the roof of a vast subway concourse, with the street level becoming the subway's mezzanine. (For this reason the subway excavation has to be only one level belowground.) The combination of enclosed mall and rapid transit terminal is an example of the results that may be achieved when the overlapping interests of transportation and open space are combined. This joint approach offers a solution to financing the project.[20]

We have now seen some of the underlying forces that have played upon American cities, giving them form and shaping their open spaces. Social and aesthetic concepts, topography, transportation—these have all been at work, sometimes asserting themselves boldly, sometimes ignored but still powerful influences. Open space comes alive to the observer when he can feel its source and origin; cities, in turn, achieve a meaningful landscape when they are viewed as a subtle combination of structures and of voids.

Part Two of this study will look at some of the recognizable and traditional forms that open spaces assume: among them the square, the park, the natural reserve. Each of these forms has its own role to play within an urban complex; and each, in the well-designed city, is related to the other forms. Squares and parks may not present to contemporary urban dwellers the novelty and challenge of newer pedestrian spaces in the revitalized downtown areas. Yet they are important as part of the city's tradition and many of them are capable of dynamic new uses. These spaces deserve more thoughtful examination than they often get.

PART TWO

The Enlarging Scale

6 The Town Square

No FORM OF OPEN SPACE is older than the square. The park is a later creation, a clearing deliberately conceived and then artfully landscaped so as to enhance the city or to relieve its ills. But the square was there in the beginning, more humble in origin than the park, more down to earth in its daily uses. It survives today often at the oldest part of the city, and is inseparably connected with contemporary historic districts. It has had the capacity to inspire other forms of open space, not only the urban park but the skyscraper plaza, the shopping-center mall, and the courts and commons of today's housing developments.

For Europeans the design of the city was in large part the design and placement of squares. The proportion of the open space, the way it was bounded or walled and connected with the neighboring streets, its relationship to the entrances or gates of the city—these concerns preoccupied town builders. In America these same concerns lay at the heart of many town plans. The French, the Spanish and then the English sought to create in their New World towns such a central meeting place as in Europe had stood before the church or the town hall or had provided a setting for the local market.

The Square in America

Philadelphia's five squares gave the city of William Penn its special character. George Oglethorpe's Savannah was laid out with a single central

12. Mt. Vernon Square, Baltimore.

13. The Plaza at Santa Fe.

14. The Plaza, Old Town, San Diego.

15. Jackson Square, New Orleans.

square, but with the provision that this form should be replicated as the grid was extended. By 1856 there were twenty-four squares spaced equidistantly within the growing city. The French in New Orleans, the Spanish in Santa Fe, built their towns around a place d'armes or a plaza.

Many American squares were not planned and may be said to have existed before the town.[1] They were the land around which the first buildings were placed—the natural openness that the village enclosed. Here cows were grazing and men and women were passing on their daily rounds when only country existed. These same activities continued as the town took form. Thus New England settlements were built around informally shaped greens—often used for burying grounds as well as for grazing cattle and later as parade grounds. As leading citizens came to build their houses fronting on this open space, sharp white forms contained within white picket fences, these greens became places of great charm and served new uses in the town's social life.

Quite often public buildings were placed within the green. New Haven is famous for its three churches, sculptural elements under the shade of elms. Frequently it was a courthouse or city hall that occupied the central portion. The pattern was followed in different parts of the country. Today in Texas the old courthouse squares remain an unexpected amenity at the heart of many small towns that were never to grow in size or population. In the Ohio towns of the Western Reserve, immigrants from New England reproduced the village squares they had known, surrounding them with well-designed houses.

When the town developed into a city, the squares in New England and elsewhere passed through various transformations. Occasionally they continued to be the center of a residential district. More often the open space remained intact but the surrounding land use changed. Thus many squares survive as downtown parks surrounded by high-rise buildings, removed from their origins but still playing an important civic role.

Most American cities of today contain squares that are worth searching out. The sampling on the following pages briefly sketches some squares not fully described in the text. In these and others, the character of the city can often be sensed and its story quickly read.[2] The best of them are filled not only with historic residences in the form of monuments and plaques, but with varied expressions of contemporary life. They provide a stage where people meet and mingle, where children play, and where the commonplace rituals of city life are carried out.

HISTORIC CITY SQUARES—A SAMPLING

BRYANT PARK—New York This formal landscaped square at Forty-second Street and Sixth Avenue makes a grand courtyard behind the New York Public Library. It was the site of the Crystal Palace built for America's first world's fair in 1852. At noontime on a warm day the park becomes a magnet for shoppers, office workers and students, who bring lunch and settle down on the grass or on the steps to hear a concert or poetry reading, or just to read or snooze in the sun. The stone figure of William Cullen Bryant stands under the library at the park's eastern border.

MOUNT VERNON SQUARE—Baltimore An urbane square formed by the crossing of Mount Vernon Place and Washington Place. A monument to George Washington sits atop the small park, which contains fountains, flowers, formal walks and benches. Greek Revival town houses flank the Peabody Institute and the Walker Art Gallery to frame the elegant square. Only a short walk from Charles Center, Mount Vernon Square serves as a link between the older residential city and the new downtown.

HEMMING PARK—Jacksonville A much-abused space in a decaying retail district, it had long ceased to function as a park. Planners today see Hemming Park as a valuable open space asset with the capacity to anchor development in downtown Jacksonville. Present plans call for a more urban approach to landscaping, repaving, new lighting, new street furniture and the addition of covered arcades and walkways.

CLINTON SQUARE—Syracuse Once the Erie Canal ran through Clinton Square; today the canal has been replaced by a four-lane roadway. Some good buildings survive and downtown development plans include the square as a hub, even suggest restoring a part of the canal. Nevertheless, it stands as a sad reminder of a once-animated pedestrian place.

NIAGARA SQUARE—Buffalo A classic square dating from the earliest design of the city in 1799 by Joseph Ellicott. Influenced by the L'Enfant plan for Washington, the square was combined with radiating diagonal boulevards. Today it is ringed with government buildings, including the high-rise city hall. Vistas to the outer city may be glimpsed down the boulevards.

MARKET SQUARE—Pittsburgh A gift of the William Penn family in 1784, the square was the site of the first public market, the first county courthouse, the Pittsburgh city hall, a concert hall and theater. Until 1960 a part of the square had been used continuously for public marketing. In contrast to the dense high-rise development of the Golden Triangle, Market Square is loose-textured, low-scale and pleasantly tawdry. While the area awaits renewal, Market Square provides a touch of green, a place to sit, a change of pace in downtown Pittsburgh.

LAFAYETTE SQUARE—St. Louis This residential park, the oldest west of the Mississippi, and the surviving row houses that border it have been rediscovered by the young, who are attracted by the convenient center-city location as well as by the square's historic character.

OLD MARKET SQUARE—Houston In the oldest part of town, this historic square is now used for parking, though a border of grass recalls its former character. Meanwhile surrounding warehouses are being converted, old buildings restored and restaurants and boutiques are pushing out the seedy bars and X-rated movie houses. The next thing is to put the cars underground.

THE PLAZA—Santa Fe   The end of the Santa Fe Trail, since 1610 the core around which the history of the city has unfolded. Spaniards, Mexicans, Indians as well as the Confederacy left their mark on the Plaza. To this day Indians come in from the pueblos to sell their crafts under the portico of the Governor's Palace. Historic ordinances protect the Plaza and the adobe buildings, among the oldest in the country, that surround it. Recent renovation has caused local controversy but left the Plaza much as it was.

HORTON PLAZA—San Diego   Originally the forecourt of the lavish Horton House Hotel in "new San Diego," where townspeople gathered for celebrations, band concerts and political debates. Five thousand people filled the plaza in 1891 to hear President Benjamin Harrison. Today buses from all over the city make a stop there; bars, X-rated movie houses and pornographic bookstores face the U.S. Grant, successor to the Horton House. Horton Plaza is included in redevelopment plans for the area.

PERSHING SQUARE—Los Angeles   An attractively landscaped downtown park in a city that isn't supposed to have a downtown. In the heart of the city's retail area, walled by miscellaneous commercial enterprises, Pershing Square is the mixing place where businessmen and bums, shoppers and tourists, take time out on a sunny afternoon.

PORTSMOUTH SQUARE—San Francisco   A small historic park where the American flag was first raised in 1846 and Mexican rule of the city ended. Redesigned to accommodate an underground parking garage, it is on the border of Chinatown and is connected by a wide bridge to the Chinatown Hilton Hotel. Habitués of the square, resistant to change, play their interminable games; the monument to Robert Louis Stevenson, though relocated, still presides over the busy scene.

PIONEER SQUARE—Seattle   The old commercial heart of the city, once a setting for flophouses, saloons, hiring halls and missions, today enjoys a new life as the center of a restored historic district. The square, with its brick-paved sitting park, its fountain and flamboyant iron pergola, provides Seattle with an agreeable open space in an otherwise dense downtown. The historic Pioneer Building, which serves as one wall of the square, has housed the popular Brasserie Pittsbourg.

THE PLAZA—Old Town, San Diego   The original settlement of San Diego is now part of a state historic park which recreates the city of Mexican and early American times. The square has been known by many names, depending upon which flag flew over the town; today it is simply called the Old Plaza. The cannon in the center was imported from Manila by the Spanish in 1800 to serve their fort at the entrance to San Diego Bay. Pleasantly shaded by cork oaks and eucalyptus trees, the Plaza is bordered by low buildings housing shops and professional offices, and by carefully restored adobe *casas*, once the homes of prosperous Spanish families.

RITTENHOUSE SQUARE—Philadelphia   One of William Penn's original squares, named for an old Philadelphia family. Long the very symbol of an aristocratic way of life, this still elegant, formally landscaped green square today proves hospitable to an astonishingly varied population. Despite changes in the neighborhood and a new clientele, Rittenhouse has managed to survive as one of the best-used, busiest places in the city.

LOUISBURG SQUARE—Boston   Carved out from the lands of John Singleton Copley, which were purchased by the Mount Vernon Proprietors in 1795, Louisburg Square was designed in 1826 and developed under careful restrictions in regard to the surrounding building types. It stands today as a small jewel in a prime historic section, discreetly fenced and enhanced by sculpture.

JACKSON SQUARE—New Orleans   See text and map on pp. 148–150.

What Makes a Good Square?

Four characteristics of the successful square may now be noted.

THE SQUARE EXISTS IN AN URBAN CONTEXT   For this reason, attempts to create squares detached from the urban fabric almost invariably fail. They may be attractive in appearance, but they possess neither a life of their own nor a capacity to generate new urban forms. Suburban developments or isolated business complexes frequently strive to reproduce the image of the town square, but the result is a mere stage set so long as the open space is cut off from infusions of popular life and from connections with other city spaces. Only occasionally, as in the picture-book Lake Anne Square of the new town of Reston, does the artificially created central place become truly alive as populated areas grow up around it.

As the town has produced the square, so the suburb must find a form of open space adapted to the loose texture of its settlement. The most appropriate suburban spatial organization seems to be the open cluster—a configuration of dwellings where land extends freely to join with other lands undefined in scope.

THE SQUARE IS LINKED TO THE STREET SYSTEM   This linkage is clearly shown where the simplest form of European square has been formed by merely widening the street at a certain point, permitting pedestrians to flow around a church or fountain. The typical American square—a hole in the checkerboard—was derived from the prevalent grid, being a block (or occasionally a group of blocks) from which buildings were permanently excluded.

In its internal organization the urban square has been plainly related to the grid, being formal and geometrical, with entrances and pathways in line with the streets and with ornamentation placed at the axes of traffic. This relationship to the narrower streets is the source of much of the attractiveness of the urban square; drama arises from the contrast of scales as one passes from confinement to breadth, from comparative darkness to sunny light.

Occasionally the square transcends the street system, by its size or prominence creating a new urban element, an open space that is like a square but has many of the features of a small park. The Boston Common and Public Garden, as well as Bushnell Park in Hartford, are of this kind and will be treated later.

The square, typically at the center of the town, often becomes part of a pattern of similar dispersed openings in the grid, as in the classic town plans of Philadelphia and Savannah. The streets then are included in a total open space system; they may broaden into avenues or boulevards to become linear spaces connecting the broader spaces of the squares. The design history of U.S. cities is marked by a tendency to shape a pattern of open space more complex and varied than the original plan of similar right-angled streets and a central square.

THE SQUARE IS A THREE-DIMENSIONAL CONCEPT   It relies upon a surrounding wall to enclose it and give it form. By contrast, the classic park is content to be left alone, asking nothing of the city except that it be recessive and relatively invisible.

American architects and planners have been surprisingly insensitive to this three-dimensional aspect of the square. Rarely do they see that the buildings that line a square have two roles to play: one (and usually the less important) is as objects in themselves; the other is as a wall to contain the open space. In city after city examples could be given of new buildings designed with no regard for this second role. The charmingly located and well-proportioned Travis Park in San Antonio is defaced by a bank building whose high-rise form and inappropriate use of glass break the scale and fail to provide a sense of continuous enclosure. The New Haven Green suffers from a building of similar defects; and the General Motors Building at the Grand Army Plaza in New York shows a startling incomprehension of the proper role of a structure in defining and giving form to an open space.

The most effectively walled squares are those for which a historic district provides an enduring frame. In Savannah, New Orleans, Santa Fe and some other cities, historic-preservation ordinances prohibit destruction or modification of existing buildings around the traditional open space. Other squares, not situated within such historic districts, should be made the focus of a special zoning district[3] and subjected to the kind of controls that define the form and height of surrounding buildings. Only in this way can a continuous and harmonious enclosure be assured.

The wall of one such square, Lafayette Square in Washington, D.C., was saved by an enlightened sense of urbanism, nothwithstanding official doctrine that would have changed it radically. Long an ideal forecourt to the President's mansion, Lafayette Square had inevitably changed in usage— from being a residential place to a focus of governmental activity. The 1903 Washington plan recommended the destruction of the charming nineteenth-century buildings bordering the square and their replacement by monumental architecture. Fortunately this part of the plan failed of realization, and not until the 1960s did the issue again present itself for action. At that time the President's wife, Mrs. John F. Kennedy, led the forces of preservation, and John Carl Warnecke was commissioned to provide the desired office space and at the same time to save the small-scale Federal façade.

The architect's solution was to preserve the original row of buildings and to fill in gaps with new buildings exactly in the style of the old. Behind these, and having access through a few of their period entrances, were constructed contemporary buildings of dark brick, sparsely windowed except for bays at their higher levels. The result is to retain the character of the square, with the small buildings appearing to nestle under a hillside. The new buildings do not so much loom over the old as rise gently and somewhat mysteriously behind them.

Important as was the actual achievement—this square is, after all, at the very heart of the national capital—hardly less so was the establishment of a clear principle. At Lafayette Square the lesson is taught that a city square is not mere two-dimensional openness, but is openness appropriately and sensitively walled.

THE SQUARE IS A MIRROR OF THE COMMUNITY   It is, and should be, colored by the neighborhood of which it is a part.[4] Efforts to limit the patronage and use of a square, to make it conform to someone's idea of order, can only destroy its essential character. Conversely, the expectation that the tone of a community may be improved by the existence of a small park or square is based on oversimplified though frequently held assumptions. Because such an open space reflects community life going on around it, it is not likely in itself to change the social aspects of its surroundings and may actually intensify underlying problems. It plays a role in renewal only when it is part of wider forces working together to improve housing, education, social services and employment opportunities. The square then may be the symbol, but not truly the fulcrum, of reform.

The urban square at its best, however, does not reflect one neighborhood alone. Like the city writ small, it draws a diversity of people, bent on many errands and pursuits, and mixes them in an atmosphere of mutual toleration.

In specific instances the square may be burdened beyond its capacity to assimilate or digest this variety of social and racial elements. Washington Square in New York has suffered from overuse and from the multiplicity of demands constantly made upon it—mothers demanding play space for their children, students demanding space for outdoor campus activities, welfare recipients demanding their rights to be at ease in their own way. Not far off is Tompkins Square, containing a mixture of races and nationalities, of humans and dogs, of cultures and generations, which during the hot summer season have brought it to the point of social explosiveness.[5] Whatever the problems posed by such conditions, they are more human, and perhaps in the end more soluble, than problems resulting from underuse.

In general, a city square benefits from multifarious and contrasting activities. Merchants and hotelkeepers often object to vendors, but these need not be competitive with their own interests, or harmful to the atmosphere of the open space. Certainly it does not seem wise for the self-appointed defenders of public order to object to the presence of such agreeable intrusions as bookstalls, flower carts or small groups of entertainers.[6] Even cars need not be considered altogether incompatible with the life of the urban square. The automobile has become so dominating and objectionable that it may be forgotten that it, too, is part of the urban scene. In the Grande Place in Brussels, automobiles make their way discreetly around the flower marts and the jostling crowds; in the fine square in the Crown Center development of Kansas City, cars passing through are not an incongruous or distracting element.

Such are the basic elements of the square: its need to be part of a large whole, its relatedness to the city streets, its three-dimensional design and its varied uses. Three squares in three different cities of the United States will now be sketched briefly. In each the criteria outlined above are embodied to a greater or less degree. Of these three squares, one shows unbroken historical continuity; one shows adaptation to the needs of the modern downtown; one in its survival shows its capacity to reinvigorate a residential neighborhood. All these come down to us from the American past.

A Historic Square

Jackson Square in New Orleans stands today unsurpassed among the effective open places in the nation. It has managed with grace the transition

Jackson Square, New Orleans, is shown within its striking urban environment. The old city of the Vieux Carré surrounds it, and is in turn surrounded by the contemporary downtown, bounded by expressways. All the life of the city seems to press on this small and intensely used space.

from one of the oldest of city squares to one that satisfies the contemporary need for a civic gathering place of young and old. The central area, a city block in size, is landscaped well enough, with ample trees and pleasant green mounds. A statue of Andrew Jackson provides a conventional sculptural note. The asphalt paths are too wide and there appears to be an inadequate number of places to sit. But these defects are not serious: the wide paths accommodate the busy public that crowds the small park, while the grass provides ample space for informal sitting and reclining. Around the square on all four sides is a well-maintained iron fence.

This square once looked out upon the Mississippi, its own small space giving upon the large space of the river. It thus provided one of the best examples of an open-ended square. Today, as it has been since the coming of the railroad and the building of the levee, this view is lost. However, the ignominy of an elevated freeway along the riverfront was narrowly averted. The scale of this structure, the noise and the sight of automobiles passing across it at swift speeds, would have seriously disturbed the atmosphere.

The fight to save the riverfront at Jackson Square is one of the classic examples of how a small group of determined private citizens can defeat city hall and take on successfully the federal government itself. In 1964 the city council of New Orleans committed itself to construction of the riverfront expressway, a project that had been in the interstate highway plans since the 1950s. This expressway was tied in with a proposed new cross-river bridge, which would have carried traffic through the historic "garden district." An insurance agent, Claude Kohler, had just bought a house in the area affected; Mark Lowrey was an architect practicing in the French Quarter. Both were early leaders in the fight and both saw their careers hurt as they set themselves against the establishment and the political powers. They were joined by a lawyer, David L. Campbell, and by Marta Lamar, described in the press as "a diminutive, fire-breathing red head."[7]

In the end, according to those who had worked hardest for the cause, it was the changed attitude toward historic preservation that killed both the bridge and the expressway. "The fear of being a preservationist is lost," Lowrey could say at the conclusion. "Now they feel it is an honor to be one." Public meetings, political upheavals, court proceedings—all proved in the end to have been part of a holding operation which allowed the currents of public opinion to change direction.

Historic preservation is precisely what gives Jackson Square its aesthetic value and also its extraordinary vitality. The square succeeds as an open space, first, because it is magnificently surrounded and walled by buildings that have not altered their outward aspect for more than a hundred years; and secondly, because it draws on a public that filters through the narrow streets of specialty shops and restaurants, of antique stores and bars, in the surrounding Vieux Carré. In short, the square does not exist by itself, but by the things of which it is a part.

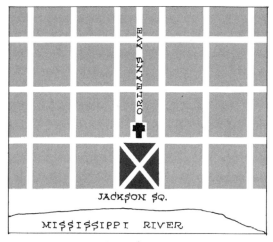

PART OF VIEUX CARRÉ FROM PLAN OF
NEW ORLEANS - 1815.

Plan of New Orleans, 1815

The wall of buildings on three sides, just outside the iron fence, has for its focal point the St. Louis Cathedral, flanked by the identical classic façades of the Cabildo and the Presbytère, both begun in the eighteenth century. The two sides of the square are framed again by identical buildings—here the low colonnaded brick structures of apartment houses built in 1850 by the Baroness Pontalba. These have survived as dwellings, with shops on their lower floors. The fourth side of the square, which should be opened to the sea, at least presents no strongly incongruous element. One feels the gentle rise of the levee and senses the trains passing just out of sight. Northward extend the brick sheds of the old market.

Behind this wall of harmonious structures stretches New Orleans's unbroken historic district. Its streets, without ever quite revealing it, suggest the nearness of the square. From the first the plan of the old town provided for a wide central street as an approach to the square. This was achieved by having Orleans Street break the otherwise uniform grid. Orleans Street actually ends at the rear of the cathedral, from which narrower passages branch out to take one around the church, moving toward the square and the river. This is a marvelously subtle and appropriate way of coming to the old town's central place, as effective now as when it was first laid out in 1765.

If the square sets up a magnetic force drawing one riverward through the streets of the old town, the old town itself is a magnet operating upon the surrounding contemporary city. The New Orleans map shows the double envelopment—the square enveloped by the Vieux Carré and the Vieux Carré by the city. Just outside the major boulevards which bound the historic center—and which were once the site of its ramparts—lie such powerful urban elements as the new World Trade Center, the Civic Center, the Cultural Center, and the Superdome with its related hotel complex. The boulevard at the southern border of the old city is, moreover, Canal Street—according to local lore the widest street in the world, and the focus of burgeoning commercial activity. All these elements generate activity which presses upon the old city and upon Jackson Square at its heart.

The question is not whether Jackson Square will remain populous and busy. It is, rather, whether the whole area of which it is a part will not be so inundated by visitors and tourists as to lose its essential character. Today Bourbon Street is on the verge of suffering such a decline as has overcome Chicago's Old Town or San Francisco's Haight-Ashbury. But the controls over the historic district may be sufficiently strong to save it, and indeed there is some evidence that it is less tawdry than it was in the 1960s.

Meanwhile the square can present an ideal aspect, delightful in its use as it is aesthetically pleasing. On a day of late winter a group of young people will be playing guitars; a girl in bare feet dances absent-mindedly. Others of all ages sit or lie upon the grass; people stroll in the new warmth of the sun, and a gathering of tourists comes by to gaze for a few moments on one of the rare and picturesque moments of urban living.

Old Square in Today's Downtown

The Public Square of Cleveland, Ohio, presents another example of an open space which has played a notable part in the history of a city—in this case not by remaining constant but by changing its use and aspect as the years passed.[8] When the city was laid out under Moses Cleaveland in 1796, the plan was that of a typical New England village, a grid pattern with a square of ten acres at its center. No other provision was made for public land. Numbered lots ran to the lake and to the river, the only concession to topography being two irregular roads leading down the bluff to the river's bank. Designed as a village, the future city lay undeveloped, its role unglimpsed until the coming of the canals and the railroads.

The Public Square in this early period was surrounded by houses in the Federal style, dominated by a church, as well as a courthouse and jail. It was used for pasture and as a parade ground. As the city grew into an industrial and transportation center, the square became increasingly the focus of its social and political life; the New England–inspired architecture gave way to Victorian and the space was filled with trees, flower beds and sculpture.

The square suffered from the beginning from a major defect. It was crossed by two extremely wide avenues, Ontario and Superior, so that the green space was cut into four quadrants. Today's traffic intensifies the problem. The square is bounded by a chain-link fence, and surrounded by commercial buildings of various materials and differing heights. At the southwestern corner rises the Terminal Tower, a dominating Cleveland landmark, but one that casts a long shadow across the green. Higbee's department store and the Sheraton Hotel supplement the transportation nexus.

This is a vital civic place, less because of its use by pedestrians than because of its role in giving structure and form to the downtown area. Whatever its deficiencies, it remains a major amenity; it *is* the center, a hub around which everything else revolves. Visually one is constantly oriented by the Public Square, and as the core takes on new nodes of activity, they relate themselves to this primary open space. This is well illustrated by the Cleveland map.

The first and most impressive example of such a new open space relating itself to the old was the famous civic mall created by Daniel Burnham. Not emphasized in the earlier reference to this mall was the fact that it lies directly at the northeastern corner of the Public Square. Burnham's classic spaces reveal themselves suddenly as one passes around what seems a conventional corner; one looks for a bounded street, and there is an unexpected grand openness, set off by the play of the War Memorial Fountain. Moving on a diagonal line from the Terminal Tower of the Public Square to City Hall at the far end of the mall, one has traversed a distance of four blocks, through two large and subtly related outdoor rooms.

From another corner of the square Euclid Avenue exits on a diagonal line, the major shopping street, which after four blocks comes to a pause where it intersects with the newly malled Huron Street. This is Playhouse Square, undergoing a healthy renewal as Cleveland State University builds to within two blocks of it. On the opposite side of the Public Square—moving westward now—an easy pedestrian stroll brings one downhill past old warehouses and nineteenth-century commercial buildings to the riverbank site

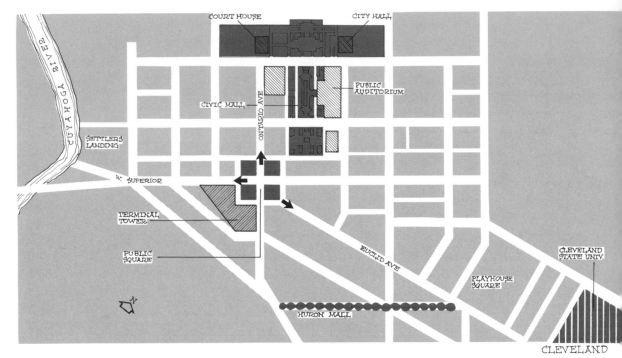

A traditional town center as seen in many settlements of the Western Reserve, Cleveland's Public Square has enhanced its importance by becoming part of a related system of open spaces, including the Burnham civic mall and new pedestrian areas to the east and west.

where a complex of hotel, shops and restaurants is planned, a Ghirardelli Square on the Cuyahoga River.

Thus the square works—not so much because it is in itself a handsome space, but because it has shown over the years a capacity to remain central to the changing developments of the city. Recently Lawrence Halprin has been working with the business leaders of the city upon a downtown plan stressing further pedestrian linkages and open spaces which by their small scale are to contrast with the wide streets and monumental plazas of the existing core. Redesign of the square has been proposed, so as to make it more hospitable to pedestrians and to accentuate its historic role. If Clevelanders want to make a serious effort to save and restore downtown, they could do worse than begin with this symbolic space.

An Old Square Saved and Renewed

Wooster Square in New Haven is a third example of an open space that has survived through profound urban changes, to play a significant part in the city of today. It is different from the two squares just considered because it is surrounded by domestic rather than public buildings and has been the focus of an immensely successful renewal effort.

New Haven, of course, has another famous open space, like Cleveland's entitled the Public Square on early maps. This is the green, site of three churches standing within it. New Haven's original plan of 1784 was unique in dedicating one-ninth of its area to be held forever for public land. This green remained the heart of the growing city. Yale College was established along its western border; churches and public buildings came to surround it, and when after World War II New Haven became a pioneer of urban renewal, the new construction was concentrated here. Less well known and less secure was another open space, Wooster Square, some four blocks to the east.

The origins of this second square are interesting.[9] New Haven was once a seaside city; along Water Street in the early nineteenth century stretched "a lovely promenade of shade trees and flower gardens graced by elegant town houses facing the waterfront." In summer families came by boat from as far away as New Orleans and Charleston to benefit from the cool breezes and the pleasant vistas. Water Street is now a half-mile inland, and all traces of its past are gone. But the resort development spread north and east, to create a settlement called Newtonship, adjacent to the nine squares of the original New Haven.

In the 1820s the citizens of Newtonship, honoring a hero of the American Revolution, created a six-acre open space in the center of their new community. This became the Wooster Square of today's New Haven. Large mansions were built around it—the homes of merchants and retired sea captains—some of them showing the influence of the New Orleans summer visitors. With the industralization of the 1860s and 1870s, a desire for proximity to the water and to rail lines drew the new factories to the very areas thus agreeably settled. Large brick and timber buildings were set among the frame houses, their noise and smoke driving the residents to seek new homes. The immediate surroundings of Wooster Square were spared; but the merchants vacated their houses, which were then subdivided and taken over by factory workers. Later many of them were converted to storefronts.

Italian laborers were brought over in great numbers after the 1880s and by 1900 Newtonship was an entirely Italian neighborhood.

That the open space of Wooster Square remained intact is in itself extraordinary. In the 1940s serious planning began in New Haven, and an urbanist of wide international reputation, Maurice E. H. Rotival, was engaged as consultant to the new City Plan Commission staff. Rotival was a man of large vision, who saw the future of cities in terms of sweeping transportation systems and massive reconstruction. Wooster Square became for him the location of a two-level vehicular rotary, a huge gateway for travelers from Boston, Hartford and New York. A helicopter landing field and a stadium were combined with a reorganization of lateral streets to spread traffic through the city. It seemed inconceivable to Rotival—as it did to almost everyone else at that time—that the old buildings of Wooster Square should be considered worth saving. It did not even seem possible that a community remained of sufficient importance to be worth consulting.

The next years saw a drastic change in the general approach to planning and to the Wooster Square area particularly. Richard C. Lee became New Haven's progressive mayor and soon brought in Edward J. Logue to be in charge of development. The New Haven map shows how the new highway was aligned to bring the Connecticut turnpike close to the river and to make the new north-south route run east of Wooster Square. This had the advantage of eliminating the worst of the slum areas and also of dividing what remained of the residential community from the most intensely industrial district. At approximately the same time the U.S. Housing Act was amended to include rehabilitation as an accepted renewal tool, instead of relying entirely upon demolition and clearance.

It now became clear that around Wooster Square existed the core of a viable community, capable of playing a shaping role in its own preservation and renewal. Father Hugo Cavicchi, pastor of the Italian Mission Church, drew the interest of the Yale University Planning Department; a representative of the city's planning commission was given the assignment of working with the neighborhood. A plan for the area was developed, giving the old square a central role and placing a heavy emphasis upon restoration of the older buildings. At the same time connections between Wooster Square and the area surrounding the old New Haven green were improved. Court Street, which had become one of the most squalid imaginable sections of rooming houses, was narrowed to a mall where it entered Wooster Square, and with the upgrading and rehabilitation of its houses became an attractive gateway to the area.

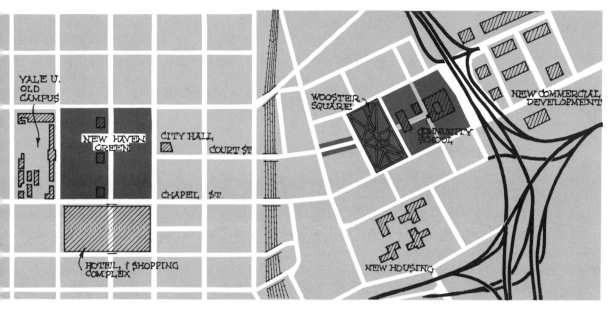

WOOSTER SQUARE
NEW HAVEN

Wooster Square, a focus of residential renewal in New Haven. The expressway has been placed to save the community and to separate it from commercial development. The square and the New Haven green, once centers of two distinct towns, are now vitally related.

At the far side of Wooster Square, opposite the Court Street Mall, a community school was planned. This was to be innovative in the services it provided, but it was unusual, too, in the care that was taken to make certain that it reinforced and complemented the square. Skidmore, Owings and Merrill went through half a dozen schemes, as they sought to create a wall continuous with the older buildings and in scale with them; to place upon the border of the square elements that should be accessible to the public (a coffee shop, a library), and at the same time to provide a secluded walkway and play space for the students. The final design was not successful in all respects (the community abandoned the idea of the coffeehouse, fearing it might become a "hangout"); but the completed scheme shows a rare understanding of the relation between open space and its surrounding structures.

In the blocks neighboring the square a similar concern for the nuances of open space expressed itself in small parks, in housing developments, and even in the treatment of parking areas. The old square, having survived so many changes in fortune and resisted the seemingly irresistible tide of progress, united a whole community and inspired it with a sense of what city living could mean. Today Wooster Square has fulfilled the hopes of its planners. The little houses on Court Street are in much demand; the mansions surrounding the green are almost all fully restored and converted to desirable apartments. New in-fill housing keeps the scale and texture of the neighborhood. The square itself is a green oasis, considered safe and obviously well maintained.

Toward the City Park

The square, as has been noted, takes its pattern from the grid and is necessarily shaped by the formal lines of the streets and of the enclosing buildings. In a few cities, however, something different occurs.

"Here and there" wrote the landscape architect Charles Eliot,[10] "is found a small public ground of such strongly marked shape and character that it by right rules its surroundings." It "calls a halt to city structures."

An instance of the small park that "rules its surroundings" might be the Boston Common and Public Garden. Taken together, this seventy-five-acre expanse retains many of the aspects of a public square; yet by its design it seems to become a place of its own, standing outside the city and apart from the basic urban form. The Common and Public Garden exist amid the small-scale buildings of Beacon Hill and the Back Bay. While the contemporary city encroaches, it has so far avoided the massive and regularized intrusions that can reduce a natural landscape to subservience. The Friends of the Public Garden, a citizens' group working to conserve and protect the park, has fought acrimoniously against an adjacent high-rise development, and has had some success. A law dating from the nineteenth century limits the height of buildings around Boston's parks, but has been too often breached to be effective.

The emergence of the square into the park—a transition between the original urban open space and the newly invented romantic landscape—is also well shown in Hartford, Connecticut. Bushnell Park lies at the very

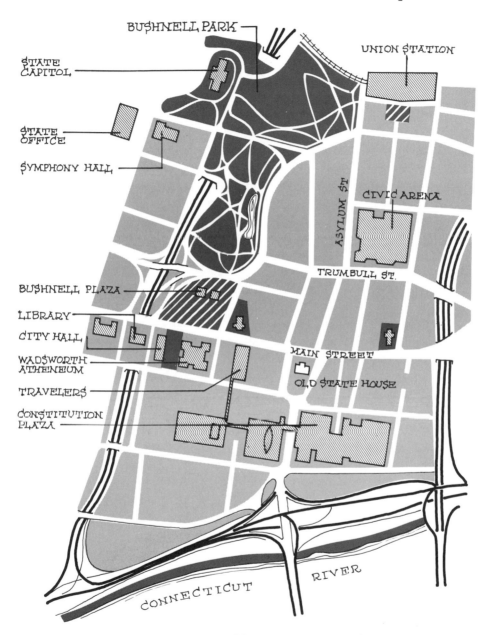

BUSHNELL PARK

UNION STATION

STATE CAPITOL

STATE OFFICE

SYMPHONY HALL

ASYLUM ST

CIVIC ARENA

TRUMBULL ST.

BUSHNELL PLAZA

LIBRARY

CITY HALL

WADSWORTH ATHENEUM

TRAVELERS

CONSTITUTION PLAZA

MAIN STREET

OLD STATE HOUSE

CONNECTICUT   RIVER

HARTFORD – BUSHNELL PARK

The middle-sized Bushnell Park has become in effect a town square as the diverse elements of the city—governmental, commercial, cultural and residential—have grown up around it.

heart of downtown: an enlarged commons, or a miniature Central Park. It is the focus of the kind of gatherings and encounters we associate with a place like Manhattan's Union Square.

The map of downtown Hartford on page 159 shows Bushnell Park in relation to the city core, which sweeps in a wide arc around it. Containing thirty-eight acres, the park is crossed at its western end by a still important passenger railway. At two points may be seen the abruptly broken route of Interstate 84. The expressway has tunneled under the library, but the plan was to cross the park at grade. The plan has been aborted, and ugly scars are left where the cement terminates.

The park formerly contained an open river, giving life and focus to the landscape. Unfortunately, upstream flooding led to the burying of the stream in a culvert. Today the bridge that once arched its waters can be seen incongruously just above the filled-in land. Until now Bushnell Park has remained without the enclosure of a structured wall. The buildings that contain it are low, and their line is broken by towers against the middle sky. Churches still have a part in this composition; such a high-rise office building as the Traveler's is not inharmonious; and the twin towers of Bushnell Plaza, the apartment complex designed by I. M. Pei, enhance rather than exploit the scene.

Unhappily, the solid, turreted façade of the YMCA was torn down in 1974. Many mourned the passing of this fine old landmark—a familiar object gone from downtown. But few perceived how important it had been in enriching the park, and how regrettable a gap it had left. Similarly, few seem to realize how grave a detraction from the park are the badly designed hotels that have arisen on its northern edge.

Various forces have thus done their worst to Bushnell's fragile and charming scene. Yet a fountain was able to attract the young to this place—in those recent years when the young liked to gather in the open to perform their tribal rites; a lake still reflects the surrounding trees and towers, a memorial commemorates the Civil War. In winter the benches of the little park are removed by the Parks Department and the paths and lawns seem deserted. Let the mild days come, however: Bushnell Park plays its part as the center and bull's-eye of the city's compact core.

7 The City Park

NOT EVERY CITY has a surviving central square; but virtually every city in the United States has a park that can be called its central park. For the stranger in a city, this central park is a first feature to be searched out and explored. Much may be learned from it about the mix of the population and the condition of government, about the city's history and about the citizens' current mood and habits. Rarely will it be difficult to identify this park, or will there be much dispute about which of many parks deserves the priority. If not always the most central in location, it is first in use and in its standing with the public.

Every City's Central Park

On the following pages appear the names of central parks in major U.S. cities. Most of them have the following principal characteristics:

- Age—dating back to the second half of the nineteenth century.
- Location—conveniently accessible to the downtown area.
- Size—from 150 acres to as many as 4,000.
- Facilities—major cultural institutions of the city; often a zoo or a botanical garden.

In addition, these parks are almost invariably "sensitive areas." Since they were carefully designed, any change of form or use becomes a matter of public controversy. In the late 1960s and early 1970s these central parks were the gathering place of the hippies—the scene of protests, demonstrations and festivals.

CENTRAL PARKS OF SOME AMERICAN CITIES

ATLANTA—Piedmont Park   185 acres; site of the Cotton Exposition of 1870; original design by Olmsted; golf course, rose garden, greenhouse and conservatory, pavilion and grill; in a residential neighborhood close to downtown.

CHICAGO—Grant Park   304.7 acres; donated to the city by private citizens in 1844; contains major cultural institutions: Art Institute, orchestra shell, Shedd Aquarium and Field Museum of Natural History; on the lake and fully accessible.

CINCINNATI—Eden Park   185 acres; a cultural center containing Krohn Conservatory, art museum and art academy, zoo, theater and bandstand; hilly terrain with curving roads; affords views of Mount Adam and the Ohio River and overlooks downtown.

DALLAS—Fair Park   189.6 acres; site of the first Texas State Fair in 1886; original plan by George Kessler, 1904; most buildings date from Texas Centennial celebration, 1936; museum of fine arts, museum of natural history, horticultural center, music hall, amphitheater, aquarium, Cotton Bowl; close to downtown but needs to be better connected.

DENVER—City Park   314.3 acres; a flat landscape embellished with fountains, flowers, statuary; site of museum of natural history, planetarium, zoological gardens; summer evening concerts by the Denver Symphony Orchestra.

FORT WORTH—Trinity Park   252.75 acres; purchased in five acquisitions from 1892 to 1913; original plan by George Kessler; a bike and hike trail following the bank of the Trinity River; miniature train running through park; contains Japanese garden and botanic garden; site of annual Mayfest.

INDIANAPOLIS—Garfield Park   128.5 acres; the first county fairgrounds, purchased by the city in 1873; the site of regular Sunday concerts, an amphitheater, swimming pool, tennis courts, sunken gardens, a controversial pagoda; contains twelve lighted horse-show courts; in recent years the gathering place of hippies; in a residential area a mile from the central business district.

KANSAS CITY—Swope Park   1,769 acres; gift to the city from Colonel Thomas A. Swope, 1896; zoo, nature center, "starlight" theater, golf course, lake and boathouse; for history see pages 199–203.

LOS ANGELES—Griffith Park   4,063 acres in the Santa Monica Mountains overlooking downtown; five golf courses, observatory, zoo, Hall of Science, Greek Theater, riding trails. Highway department paid three million dollars in compensation for portions of the park on the north and east lopped off for freeway.

LOUISVILLE—Cherokee Park   409.3 acres; designed by Olmsted and dedicated as "a place for artists to paint and for poets to sing about"; strong citizen protest unsuccessful in keeping freeway out, but did succeed in getting a portion of the route tunneled; severely damaged in tornado of April 1974.

MEMPHIS—Overton Park   342 acres; site of Brooks Memorial Art Gallery, city zoo and aquarium, Academy of Arts, open-air theater, golf course; subject of 1971 Supreme Court case (see page 186).

MILWAUKEE—Lake Park   136.8 acres along the shores of Lake Michigan; site of the Saarinen War Memorial, used as museum and community center; unresolved question of planned expressway through park; hippies encouraged to gather in park during 1960s, though the fountain on the bluffs above had been their first choice.

MINNEAPOLIS—Loring Park   32.5 acres; acquired in 1883 as part of park system designed by H. W. S. Cleveland; originally called Central Park; freeway skirts the park but leaves it intact within downtown; Walker Art Museum and Guthrie Theater outside park.

NEW ORLEANS—City Park   1,460 acres; created by Louisiana legislature in 1895 with its own board of commissioners; a flat, grassy peninsula surrounded by water; expressway on railroad right of way alongside park; forty-four tennis courts, five golf courses.

PHILADELPHIA—Fairmount Park   4,079 acres on both sides of the Schuylkill River; from its establishment in 1865 the park has grown through gifts and purchases from 28 acres to be largest in-city park in the country; six restored historic mansions in park; contains art museum, Playhouse in the Park, zoo, aquarium, Robin Hood Dell.

PHOENIX—Encanto Park   219 acres; acquired through purchase and donation in 1934; an oasis in the desert; a romantically landscaped park in a residential neighborhood close to downtown; contains lagoons, tennis courts, swimming pool, recreation building, band shell.

PITTSBURGH—Schenley Park   456 acres; 300 acres donated by Mrs. Mary E. Schenley in 1889, the rest acquired through purchase and donation between 1891 and 1929; contains ball fields, tennis courts, golf course, swimming pool, ice-skating rink; cultural facilities include Phipps Conservatory, nature museum and outdoor theater; major vehicular arteries cut across the natural landscape of hills and ravines.

SAN ANTONIO—Brackenridge Park   248.78 acres; donated to the city by the Water Works Company in 1899 and named for the company's president, George W. Brackenridge; a largely natural landscape; contains zoo, museum, a miniature train, a sky ride, open-air theater; the Sunken Gardens, once a rock quarry, has been developed into a botanical garden; the San Antonio River runs through the park.

SAN DIEGO—Balboa Park;   set aside in 1868; a lush landscape of 1,158 acres created; hosted the Panama California Exposition of 1915–1916 and the California-Pacific International Exposition of 1935–1936; buildings of Spanish, Mexican and Indian architecture remain, housing the Fine Arts Gallery, the Museum of Man, the Natural History Museum, the Balboa Park Club, the Spanish Village; famous for its zoo.

SEATTLE—Volunteer Park   45 acres; oldest park in the city; designed by Olmsted Brothers; once hippie gathering place; a "pitched battle" was waged over attempts to change the wading pool; contains art museum, water tower, reservoir, tennis courts, baseball fields; reached by Interlaken Boulevard, overlooks downtown and Seattle Center.

Other large parks in the city have specialized uses. They may be important as centers for sport, as areas conserving natural resources, as regional recreation facilities. The central parks, however, are essentially mixed in use and multiple in their appeal. At their best they mirror nature, they invite play, they offer a choice of cultural and recreational diversions. They draw a public of various ages, races and economic backgrounds. Being so closely tied in with the character of the city, so revealing of its existing conditions and its prospects, they are a form of open space that deserves from municipal governments better maintenance and more intelligent planning and programming than they usually get.

The Park Movement

The central parks of American cities were the product of deeply held social and economic beliefs. The Old World might look upon parks primarily as amenities; the cities of the New World were looking for means to uplift and moralize their citizens—particularly the immigrants. Crowded into tenements under conditions that denied them light and air and (it was believed) rendered them particularly susceptible to crime and vice, these newcomers were to be saved by access to nature. The romantic landscape developed by park builders was at least as important in its capacity to affect men's character as it was to delight their senses.

"A grand park within the reach of every citizen would do more in preventing disturbances and vice than half the sermons preached"; it would "keep away the poor and the young from the temptations scattered all about them." Thus spoke a San Francisco editor in the mid-nineteenth century.[1] More sophisticated spokesmen for the park cause echoed the theme. Olmsted saw the growth of big-city parks as the expression of a self-preserving instinct within society. President Charles W. Eliot of Harvard asserted that parks produce the best means to restrain the vices of men coarsened by the factory system and urban crowding, and also to feed their "mental and spiritual growth."[2] In Philadelphia, the tenth annual report of the City Parks Association asserted that "whatever furnishes innocent recreation and amusement exerts a potent influence in checking crime, and the public square and playground must be given prominent places among the agencies favorably affecting the moral condition of society."[3]

Besides these idealistic factors, a strong economic argument was made for the construction of parks. Within a decade after the completion of Forest Park in St. Louis, Andrew McKinley (who was, incidentally, the first president of the park's board of commissioners) was advertising the sale of building lots near its eastern edge. He claimed that the value of the lots had already risen from fifteen dollars per foot in 1873 to forty dollars in 1885.[4] The building of Central Park in New York resulted in a quadrupling ot rates from surrounding houses, so that within twenty years the whole cost of the park was recouped.[5] Other cities found their parks yielding similar economic benefits.

Nevertheless, by the 1880 census, parks existed in comparatively few cities. Of 210 cities enumerated, twenty made no report of public spaces (presumably because they had none).[6] The examples of New York, Boston, Philadelphia and Buffalo had not yet been generally followed. Pittsburgh, with a population of 156,000, had less than one and one-third public acres; Kansas City, in those pre-Kessler days, had two acres of parks for its 56,000 souls. A broad movement, however, was soon to begin. Playgrounds and athletic facilities would be built; but the park most desired by the citizens, highly visible and usually the recipient of generous funding, was that which was to continue its pre-eminence and to become the central park of the contemporary city.

Conflicts and Tensions

From the beginning conflicts developed between the romantically conceived central parks and the needs of the rapidly changing cities. The parks had been created not so much to enhance or beautify the city as to provide an escape from it—indeed, so far as possible to deny the city's very existence. The ideal park was designed to render the surrounding city invisible; New York's Central Park had a wall of trees which were to grow higher than any likely residences. Within, long meadows, trees casting a deep shade and shrubbery massed to create a sense of mysterious distances, were combined with expanses of water reflecting the sky. Roads and paths followed a curving course. Specialized uses were decried and buildings were kept to a minimum.

Here was a Walden for the multitudes; but the accomplishment was not readily understood by the politicians of the Tweed ring or by city people clamoring for places to engage in active sports and mass entertainments. A tendency toward depression accentuated Olmsted's own gloom. He saw his New York masterpiece bordering on failure; and in looking back over a life's accomplishment he could assert with a characteristic mixture of pride and pessimism: "There are, scattered through the country, seventeen large public parks . . . upon which, with sympathetic partners or pupils, I have been engaged. After we have left them they have in the majority of cases been more or less barbarously treated."[7]

Olmsted's concern was deeply based. The nineteenth-century park, beautiful and refreshing as it could be, was a fragile oasis in the midst of a city that was demanding specialized forms of recreation and whose citizens were increasingly able to make their group interests felt. Open spaces created to meet precisely defined needs—bird sanctuaries, nature preserves, beaches, golf courses, athletic fields—could be maintained with comparative ease and could preserve their integrity in the face of opposing pressures. But the many-faceted park of romantic configuration contained at its best a large number of smaller attractions harmoniously related to each other and dependent for their charm upon subordination to the overall design. Yet special groups pressed for the satisfaction of their claims—the baseball players, the swimmers, the ice skaters, the spokesmen for the elderly, for cultural institutions, for schools.

The demands became more insistent as these parks—most of them originally outside the built-up areas—found the city encroaching on their very borders. The hoped-for impression of rural quiet was lost. Commercial towers and high-rise apartments destroyed the scale. Even more seriously, the original concept of the central park was frequently strained by change in the social composition of the surrounding neighborhoods. Large mansions converted to apartments, crowded with the poor and with racial minorities, created a park public with other interests than the enjoyment of a romantic landscape. As time went on, many of these parks become a patchwork of special uses. And then the slow process of decay set in. Masonry steps and terraces proved difficult to restore; ancient trees suffered from the city's polluted airs; the earth became compacted and thin.

New generations of park users rebelled against restrictions imposed by older social mores. Litter, graffiti and vandalism signalized that the parks were neither being adequately supervised nor satisfying needs of the current population.

In many cities groups formed to defend and renew the historic green spaces. They were composed of well-intentioned citizens, often thoroughly informed on the objectives of the original park-builders and motivated by an earnest desire for restoration. They saved the parks from many hasty and ill-considered invasions. Yet many of them were not capable of seeing that contemporary city life had its own justifiable claims, or realizing that some compromise with modernity was necessary.

Efforts of public-spirited citizens were not sufficient to stem the tide of deterioration. Neither private philanthropy nor strained city budgets could effectively repair, maintain, supervise and police these vulnerable and menaced parks. The danger was that they would come to stand in the modern city as a somewhat pathetic anomaly, cared for grudgingly and with a sense of guilt. Meanwhile in the newer forms of urban open space— in the restored riversides, the busy plazas and malls—men and women would find the sort of urban experiences most congenial to the twentieth-century mood. They would discover their pleasures in the heart of the city, amid its turbulence and diversity, and not (as the earlier park builders had proposed) in a flight to pastoral illusions.

CENTRAL PARK, NEW YORK

We turn now to an examination of certain of the major parks—brief case studies pointing up the assets of these historic open spaces and their problems.

No choice exists but to begin with Central Park in New York City. This was the first large-scale park created in this country. Its impact upon other cities was immediate. Its principal designer, Frederick Law Olmsted, became a national figure, calling into being a new species of park-builder. Central Park presents today the whole range of problems with which authorities in other cities are contending.

The map on page 168, besides recalling the park's scale and essential features, shows something that is not often taken into account. Central Park does not stand isolated. At its northern end there is a series of topographic features that could, if the links were developed, make it part of an extended chain of green spaces. Within a few hundred yards Morningside Park begins, running along the ridge that also underlies Colonial Park. Directly north of Central Park, Cathedral Parkway runs westward to Riverside Park. (Morningside and Riverside parks were designed by Olmsted, and it was he who envisaged the "parkway"—now a crowded street uninviting to pedestrians or cyclists.)

At its southern end Central Park opens into a different kind of urban space —especially where the Grand Army Plaza leads to Fifth Avenue and down toward Rockefeller Center.

Two other important aspects of the situation of Central Park need to be noted.

First is the encircling ring of major cultural institutions. The Metropolitan Museum of Art has been in the park since its establishment in 1870. The Museum of Natural History is on parkland just outside the park's borders. To the west are Lincoln Center and the New-York Historical Society; on

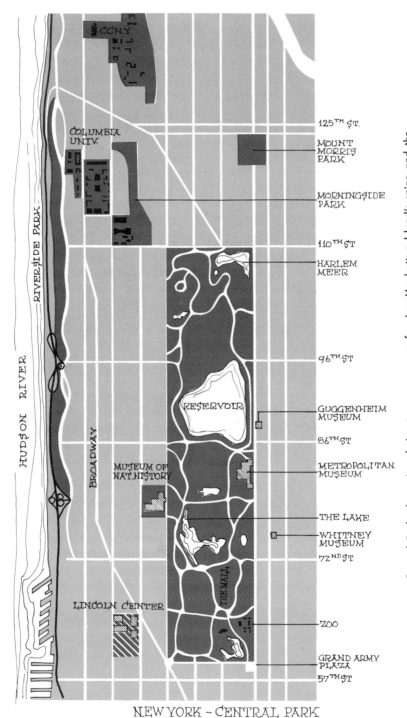

NEW YORK – CENTRAL PARK

Central Park, shown in relation to green spaces forming Manhattan Island's spine and the Hudson riverfront. In addition to Central Park, Olmsted designed Morningside and Riverside parks.

the east, the Guggenheim Museum faces the park, while the Whitney is a block away. The strong affinity between parks and cultural institutions is thus expressed, while a minimum of Central Park land is made use of.

Second is the way in which diverse neighborhoods surround the park. To the south are outstanding hotels and commercial developments. To the north, centering on Mount Morris, is Harlem. Two more different communities, both feeding into the park, could hardly be imagined. The east and west sides have also long been dissimilar in economic and social characteristics. Thus the park is located so as to draw a varied population. Today's widespread use of the bicycle has helped ensure that no group will remain isolated in a particular geographic location.

Origins of the Park

When Central Park was first envisaged, Manhattan Island was poor in open space. A few squares—Bowling Green, Union Square, Madison Square—broke the grid extending northward from the Battery. Broadway's slanting progress up the island left in its wake small triangles not suited for being built upon. The New York plan of 1811, though boldly providing for a city of far greater size than then existed, did little to cure the deficiency of open space. Anxious not to disappoint the hopes of real estate speculators, it counted upon the waterfront to provide a substitute for parks. Not until the middle of the century, when built-up areas were moving steadily northward, did the need for a large public park begin to make itself felt.

The park movement was fortunate in having at that same time a group of strong civic leaders, and having in William Cullen Bryant a powerful editorial voice convinced that a large park or "pleasure ground" was essential to the growing city. Two principal sites were considered, a location known as Jones Wood, along the shore of the East River, and the other at the center of the island. The latter was selected in 1857, and the planning and construction of the new park was begun.

The several hundred acres acquired for park purposes (the ultimate size of Central Park was to be 840 acres) were as uncongenial to development as could have been imagined. At once rocky and marshy, this site of abandoned farms and wretched hovels might well have been difficult to conceive as a place of any utility, far less of beauty. Yet here was to take form a setting of romantic vistas and rural perspectives in a style that was to be followed in city after city throughout the remainder of the century. The practical and artistic accomplishment was due in large part to the genius of a man whose name was to become synonymous with landscaped parks.

Olmsted was cast more or less by chance into the role of park-builder. He was not trained as a horticulturist. Little in his early experience suggested that he would become the country's foremost landscape designer and the founder of a new profession.[8] Something of a wanderer in youth, he tried his hand at many things before settling down to the one big thing that was to form his career. He had had, like Melville, his season before the mast. Like Thoreau he had hoed and planted. He was one with many of his generation in being troubled throughout his life by depression and by unresolved psychological drives. Yet when the chance arose to act as supervisor of construction in the new Central Park, and then to compete in its design, he stepped in as if born to the work.

In partnership with the British-born architect Calvert Vaux, he won the competition. He oversaw the park's development and (despite many threats to quit) was its manager during most of its formative years.

For Olmsted and his contemporaries there was little doubt about what the new park should be. It should provide a contrast to the existing city, a refuge from its noise, its oppressive darkness, from the crowdedness and the inhuman surfaces of streets. The concern for picturesqueness and for country amenities was not an aesthetic judgment alone. In a typically American way it was a moral judgment, rooted in the conviction that men's outlook and character could be changed for the better.[9] It would be the workingman's park (as well as that of the swells and dandies), and all would benefit spiritually as well as through pleasures received.

The design of Central Park showed many important innovations. The park drives; the separation by grades of various forms of circulation; the sunken transverse roads; the careful substructure of irrigation and drainage and the use of natural outcroppings as design features—these were to prove suggestive in the future. For the visitor, however, the park gained its special character from the shaded views, the long expanses of grass, the sense of a wide yet subtly mysterious landscape in which a man might find a sense of peace and a recollection of his earlier roots.[10]

Olmsted's Influence

Completed just after the Civil War, in a period when many American cities were entering upon a period of dramatic growth, New York's Central

Park created a profound effect. It seemed that everyone wanted a park, and wanted it to be as much like New York's as possible. Olmsted's views were accepted as the true gospel, and his disciples multiplied. A young Texan, George Kessler, had worked briefly as a gardener in Central Park, but grew homesick for the spaces of his native West. It was Olmsted who recommended Kessler for the job of laying out a railway excursion park near Kansas City. The latter went on to design Kansas City's famous parks and park system. He also made plans for Cincinnati, Indianapolis and Dallas.

H. W. S. Cleveland, whose Boston firm had competed unsuccessfully in the Central Park competition, met Olmsted in 1868 and the two became friends. When Cleveland was fighting to establish the Minneapolis park system, his board asked the famous landscape designer for advice. Olmsted, in a classic letter to the park board, backed Cleveland.[11] The system became one of the outstanding achievements of nineteenth-century urban planning.

In San Francisco William Hammond Hall worked in what he believed to be the Olmsted tradition. He submitted the plans for Golden Gate Park to the older man and received a reply giving general approbation of the design but expressing doubts whether it could be executed on such a site in such a climate.[12] Olmsted's misgivings later gave way to optimism and generous praise.

Mention should be made, finally, of a young man who came to Olmsted's Boston office to serve as an apprentice just after his graduation from college. Charles Eliot, the son of Charles W. Eliot, president of Harvard, had been determined from youth to become a planner and landscape architect. The apprenticeship served both men well. Eliot learned much, and had opportunity to work on Belle Isle Park in Detroit as well as on the Boston parks with which the firm was at that time chiefly occupied. He accompanied Olmsted on his trips around the country and must have added much to the journeys of the older man. Eliot left the firm to travel in Europe. In 1893, when he joined in a partnership with Olmsted and his son, the creator of Central Park was entering upon the mental decline that darkened his last years. Eliot himself was to be victim of a rare disease only four years later.

Charles Eliot's career, though brief, was one of genuine accomplishments in his field. We shall meet him again when we deal with open spaces at the perimeters of modern cities. Here we emphasize his basic agreement with Olmsted on the nature of the central city park. The square, said Eliot, was a proper place for monuments, for decorations, for gardens. But the true park is to be kept free of "townlike things." Parks are intended for the recreation of people "by means of their rural, sylvan and natural scenery and character."[13] Thus he expressed the ideal underlying Central Park in New York and many of the other central parks that were established afterward across the country.

The Park Today

The public devoted to the cause of Central Park is prone to exaggerate the abuses that have overtaken it in the more than one hundred years of its history. Like Olmsted himself, they see the park as "going to the devil"; they may even echo his "grave doubt whether the undertaking to provide a rural recreation ground upon such a site in midst of a city like this was not a mistake. . . . The park," Olmsted added, "can easily become a nuisance and a curse to the city."[14] Today's park devotees become similarly preoccupied with shortcomings of upkeep or restoration, and are often troubled by the number of people Central Park attracts.

In fact, the park has survived remarkably well, considering the changes in the city around it and the variety of social and political pressures to which it has been subjected. Friends of the park like to circulate a map indicating the various outrageous and bizarre proposals—including a huge hotel, an automobile speedway, a landing field for airplanes and a permanent world's fair—which have been made over the years. But the surprising fact is not that such proposals have been made; it is that they were never implemented. They were effectively resisted in some cases, simply laughed out of court in others. A vigilant public makes the park as safe today from major changes or encroachments as is any piece of land in any city of the world.

This is not to deny that there are severe problems—problems of adequate maintenance, of safety, of architectural and horticultural restoration. There are also difficult and delicate choices to be made in the management of the park. The underlying difficulty stems from the basic nature of Central Park and of the parks that were made in its image. "A rural recreation ground" (to use Olmsted's words) is bound to have problems when placed "upon such a site in midst of a city like this." But the problems need not be insuperable. The underlying concept should not be considered an anachronism. At least it can be said that New York has made better use of its Central Park, and dealt with its problems more sensitively, than many cities in similar circumstances.

Examples taken from the experience of other cities help give us insight into the dimensions of these problems and some of the measures required.

FOUR PARKS REVISITED

Forest Park—Piecemeal Change

The central position of Forest Park within the semicircle of present-day St. Louis has already been noted. The two square miles of green dominate the urban expanse and form with the newly recaptured waterfront two nobly proportioned and complementary open spaces.

Not surprisingly, a park so large and so centrally located has a lively historical background.[15] The acquisition of the tract was subject to controversy and its subsequent development was under the impulse of varied and often contradictory pressures. In 1871 enterprising citizens in the western part of the city secured legislative authority to acquire the park, and three years later the city purchased it for the sum of $849,058.61. Property owners sued against what seemed an act of folly and a derogation of their natural rights to speculate in the land. The basic legislative act was, however, declared valid.

The next problem was to design the park. The names of two relatively unknown men, M. G. Kern and Henry Flad—one a park superintendent, the other an engineer—appear on the original plan, now in the possession of the St. Louis Historical Society. These men were evidently familiar with Olmsted's work, and in the winding roadways, the rustic bridges, the deference to natural forest areas, the master's influence is visible.

Another aesthetic force was also at work—the tendency toward the grand and the classical, which has long inspired the citizens of St. Louis and may be seen today in the city's central mall. A hippodrome with a monumental figure of a horse at the center, a bizarre music stand, a castle (subject to being redesigned as the "ruin of a castle") and a statue of Edward Bates, a local political luminary, were among the incongruous features included. For better or worse, the plan—unlike that of New York's Central Park—was not one to which there was ever any strong commitment. The depression of the early 1890s drastically cut the funds available for development—though leaving enough for the statue of Mr. Bates. Then the St. Louis Exposition of 1904, the centennial of the Louisiana Purchase, changed the park's physical aspect and turned the city's thought to new social concerns.

The exposition authorities promised to return the parklands "as found."

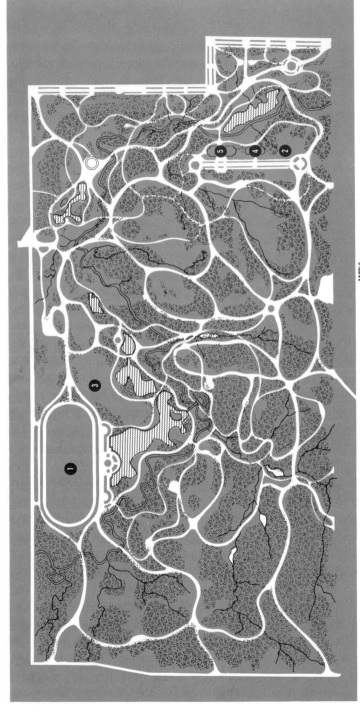

FOREST PARK - ST. LOUIS

KEY:
1 HIPPODROME   4 AQUARIUM
2 FLORAL WALK   5 TROPICAL GARDEN
3 THE MEADOW

Original design of Forest Park, greatly influenced by Olmsted, with formal elements at Hippodrome and Flower Walk.

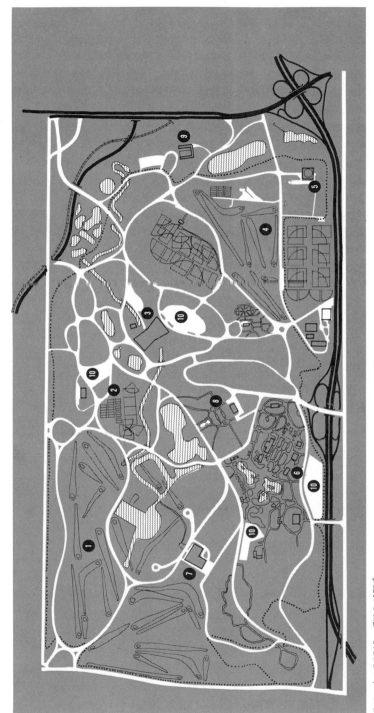

FOREST PARK – ST. LOUIS

The park today, showing multiplicity of special uses, traffic lanes, parking spaces, etc.

But in clearing sites for their buildings they felled seventeen thousand trees; and they left structures that are in use to this day. In addition, to compensate for the destruction of the trees, a new Jefferson memorial was constructed, a formal portal to the park at the De Baliviere entrance. The two wings of the building now house the Historical Society, and a monumental figure of Jefferson looks down upon the park from the pillared loggia.

The loss of the forest and the introduction of new man-made elements opened the way to an avalanche of "improvements." Thereafter, every time a new institution was created or a new entertainment devised, Forest Park seemed the natural place to put it. Today the park contains a zoo—an excellent one—using seventy of its acres, a fine arts museum, a planetarium, an ice-skating rink, a municipal opera and three golf courses (one of them semiprivate), as well as much space given over to parking. The River des Peres, once thought of as a natural feature of great potential beauty, but subject to flooding and unpleasant smells, has been placed underground in a sewer. Here, a local historian asserts, it has "ceased to be a source of annoyance to visitors to the park."[16]

The adjoining maps on pages 174–175 form an instructive contrast. One shows the original plan of the park; the other, the park as it now exists. The features singled out for reference suggest how widely separated are the interests of today's park users from those of a hundred years ago. In one case, the "floral promenade," the "sheep folds," the "terrace," the "rustic shelter"; in the other, "model airplane field," "golf course," "skating rink," "baseball field," etc.

Before dismissing Forest Park for its apparently piecemeal and haphazard accumulation of special features and programs, we must take into account the very real interest in social causes that animated St. Louis and affected its outlook on parks. The 1904 Exposition may have occasioned the cutting down of trees. But it also made articulate a new emphasis on social processes and humanitarian reform. If man the creator was on display, so were the forces shaping man. Instead of only showing the wonder of scientific invention and consumer gadgetry that the new century was ready to pour out, the fair became by the conscious decision of its sponsors an opportunity to present to its visitors the latest theories of social scientists. Forest Park itself became a laboratory in which new ideas of education and recreation were explored.

Installed as part of the fair, a model playground was retained and became a pattern for others throughout the city. Hundreds of small plots were marked out at the edge of the park and assigned to children for growing vegetables. In 1911 something even more revolutionary in the use of the park took place. The "Keep Off the Grass" signs were removed. To the sociologically oriented park officials, grass was no longer something to be looked at from a distance and surveyed from paved pathways. "To the element of natural beauty," states a park report of 1915, "has been added the conception of social utility. . . . The primary purpose of the park system has become the raising of men and women rather than grass or trees." In that same year the name Department of Parks ceased to be used and the agency became known as the Division of Parks and Recreation of the Department of Public Welfare.

The emphasis on "social utility" may seem naïve; yet one should not minimize the degree to which Forest Park has served the communal interests of the city around it. The strong tradition which persists to this day of outdoor pageants, festivals, concerts and ethnic celebrations has worked as a unifying force in St. Louis; and the many facilities for sport and culture give the park a lively, well-used appearance. In short, if Central Park in New York has survived as a powerful civic asset because it resisted change, Forest Park has survived and on the whole has prospered because it accommodated itself to new needs and to new social doctrines.

Belle Isle—Park with a Social Problem

No one of the country's larger parks presents today a more tantalizing challenge than Belle Isle in Detroit. The Belle Isle map shows it as an island in the narrow Detroit River, which separates the United States from Canada, situated a few hundred yards off the U.S. shore and no more than half a mile downstream from the business core. Belle Isle was set aside as a park in 1881 when Olmsted came out from Boston to survey the land and make a plan. The design was in his characteristic style, with a formal area toward the end of the island nearest the city, an elaborate water system with canals fed from the river, and with a natural forest carefully preserved and pruned so that sun could penetrate to the undergrowth.

Olmsted does not seem to have been entirely happy (he rarely was entirely happy) with the way his plan was implemented by the city authorities. From the beginning there was a disposition to place within the park more buildings than he thought desirable and to set land apart for such specialized uses as ball games, swimming, tennis courts and formal gardens.

Today Belle Isle, enlarged by landfill to a thousand acres, is in many of

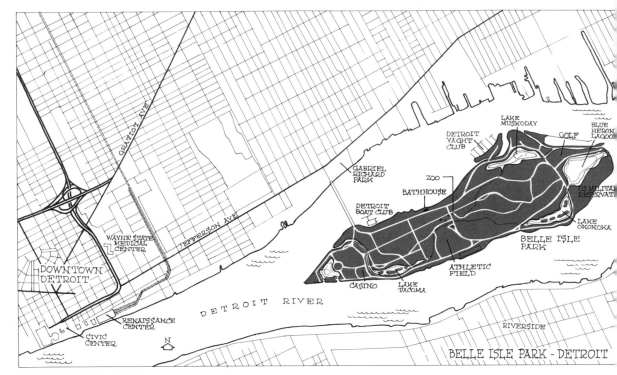

Belle Isle Park, shown in relation to downtown Detroit and to existing and projected waterfront development.

its areas a hodgepodge of inharmonious and tasteless structures, while delicate wrought-iron bridges from the last century decay and rust.[17] The casino, an exotic period piece, shelters the elderly and a third-rate eating place. More recent additions like the Scott Fountain and the Nancy Brown Peace Pavilion serve less to provide an air of elegance than to make everything else look the more shoddy.

Yet the park is well used, and in a strange sort of way is well loved. As many as 23,000 people per day, most of them black, come over the one bridge from the city that the whites left behind when they fled to the suburbs. A small but intense group of such suburbanites constitutes the Friends of Belle Isle Park, determined to restore it to something of its former natural charm and man-made splendor.

The park has become a symbol to both blacks and whites. Coleman Young, the black mayor elected in 1974, echoes the dedicated Ray Rickman, chairman of the Friends, in calling Belle Isle "a top priority"; yet one has the feeling that each has a somewhat different picture in mind. The mayor sends in city forces to pave the roadways and enlarge the parking places; while the Friends struggle to get a city contract with an outstanding landscape architect, whose first recommendation would probably be to narrow or eliminate the roads and to restrict parking. Yet for everyone this grand open space is a test of the city's capacity to survive; and the Friends, fortunately, are not so blindly devoted to a past tradition that they cannot see the need to meet the interests of new racial and economic groups.

Delaware—Park with a Plan

The location of Delaware Park within Buffalo is indicated on the map on page 180. It will be seen to the northeast of the downtown area, at a distance from Niagara Square of some two and a half miles. It is bordered by institutional developments, an attractive residential area and a cemetery. It is cut through by a modern expressway. The accompanying large-scale map of the park shows the expressway route and the principal areas as they exist today.

This was clearly intended to be the central park of Buffalo, a city in the last half of the nineteenth century immensely civic-minded and immensely ambitious. The business leaders heading the park movement would have no one but the designer of New York's Central Park to create their own. Olmsted stopped off in Buffalo on a Sunday in August 1868 and spent the afternoon driving about looking for an appropriate site. He discarded suggestions that involved land too expensive to transform into the desired rural pleasure ground. But coming to an elevation overlooking the city from the northern countryside, "Here is your park almost ready made," he exclaimed.

"The Park" (or Delaware, as it came to be known later) was laid out with diverse facilities and wide areas of lakeside and meadow. By the late 1880s it was a popular gathering place; old photographs show its use by large crowds strolling on a Sunday afternoon or taking drives along the carriage roads. The Pan-American Exposition of 1901 was sensibly placed just outside the park, and left as a residue within it only the agreeable building now used by the Historical Society. In 1905, when the Albright-Knox Art Gallery was built, Delaware was still a pastoral park and sheep grazed in the meadow.

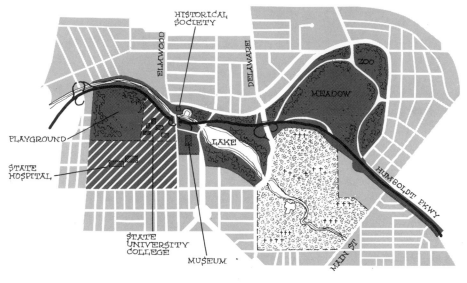

An Olmsted park divided by an expressway, Delaware is the only such park now the subject of a comprehensive master plan.

The original design had carefully separated competing or incompatible activities. Opportunities for active recreation, for passive pursuits and for purely social encounters were provided with minimal intrusion of one upon the other. In the early years the 350-acre park assured ample room to satisfy diverse needs. With time, however, sports made increasing demands on the park's open space. Ball fields pre-empted a portion of the Meadow; an eighteen-hole golf course was added; playgrounds for neighborhood children appeared along the park's edges.

The most traumatic change came in the early 1960s with the construction of the Scajaquada Expressway and its interchanges. This was a shock from which the park has not recovered. The nineteenth-century landscape was drastically altered; the entire area was bisected. Mirror Lake and the Historical Society found themselves cut off behind the expressway barrier. Other pieces of parkland were fragmented and isolated.

With portions of the park rendered inaccessible, intensity of use came to vary widely. Some areas were heavily overused; others fell into forlorn neglect. As the park's natural environment deteriorated, its man-made facilities fell into a state of disrepair. A hundred years after Delaware Park was created for a city alarmed by its dwindling open space, Buffalo woke to the need to re-examine the park's condition and to consider what could be done to minimize the expressway's inexcusable encroachment.

Buffalo became the first city to have a carefully drawn master plan for its central park.[18] New York has not been able to achieve this for its own great park despite the obvious need for an appraisal of each acre, monument and structure. San Francisco's city-wide plan calls for such a re-examination of Golden Gate Park; so far nothing has been done. In Buffalo, however, a citizen's advisory group worked closely with professional planners in a major effort to accommodate to twentieth-century conditions a park designed according to a nineteenth-century philosophy. If this master plan had been done twenty years earlier, the encroachment of the expressway would surely not have been tolerated.

As it is, the planners accept the expressway as a fact of life, though with the faint hope that in the future it may be depressed in at least some sections of the park. In addition, they propose softening its impact by the removal of entrances and exits that bring traffic directly into the park.

The plan emphasizes the underlying dilemma posed by the differences in urban living—in life styles, recreation preferences, modes of transport—between two historic periods. How can the park be assured of "relevance" for today? How can a rural pleasure ground retain its character and at the same time satisfy contemporary tastes? Accommodation with the automobile is the first major concession to modernity. Parking spaces are included for "a greatly increased number of cars." The Meadow is to be ringed by a continuous one-way Meadow Road with parking and support services provided. The planners assume that without convenient automobile access, the park will not reach its full use. Public transport to the park is indeed lacking, but the possibility of providing it in some attractive form might have been examined.

Aspects of pedestrian and bicycle traffic within the park are effectively dealt with. The interior barrier created by the expressway is at least to be broken through at crucial points by pedestrian underpasses.

Circulation problems thus disposed of, the report concentrates on activities. It makes the explicit assumption that there will be more facilities adopted to special uses, more participant and spectator sports, more communal events and more indoor recreation. Yet it seeks to embody these functions within a landscape retaining its original flavor and set in definite contrast to the surrounding urban environment. It seeks to embody them, also, without doing violence to the neighborhoods that edge the park. Sensitive to the park's context, the report shows how recreation for small children and the elderly is to be kept close to residential areas, while active sports and spectator events are confined to the park's more central areas.

The Delaware Park plan can well serve as a model for other cities. It deals with basic issues of park philosophy in a practical and realistic way; it recognizes the validity of contemporary values without discarding the past. A strong infusion of citizen thinking has been skillfully combined with professional judgments. As with all plans, the ultimate question is whether it will be followed up and implemented.

Franklin—The Park That Got Lost

The inclusion of Boston's Franklin Park in this discussion of "central parks" may be thought surprising. It certainly does not meet all our criteria—the Common and Public Garden are located at the heart of the city, while Franklin seems comparatively remote; it is those, not Franklin, that attract public ceremonies and arouse the people's fanatic involvement where any change is contemplated. But Franklin was *intended* to be Boston's great rural pleasure ground. In design it was considered the equal, if not superior to, Olmsted's two other masterpieces, Central and Prospect parks in New York and Brooklyn. Though farther out than the Common and Public Garden, it was still no more inaccessible to Bostonians of the last century than was Forest Park to the people of St. Louis or Delaware to the people of Buffalo.

The question is, what happened to Franklin Park? Basically it got caught within a social context that made it the province of a single community rather than a city-wide resource. And that community has not been sufficiently sure of its identity to make effective use of what it possessed.

Franklin Park's general location is best seen on the map of Boston's park system, page 196. It stands as the climax of the series of green spaces that begins with the Common at the heart of the city. This greenbelt has suffered as its once pleasant drives have become subject to the strains of modern traffic. The transformation of the park's basic access route has played a part in Franklin's isolation. Yet it may be noted that the privately maintained Arboretum, along this same belt system, is visited by hundreds of thousands who have grown accustomed to spurning Franklin Park as a no man's land.

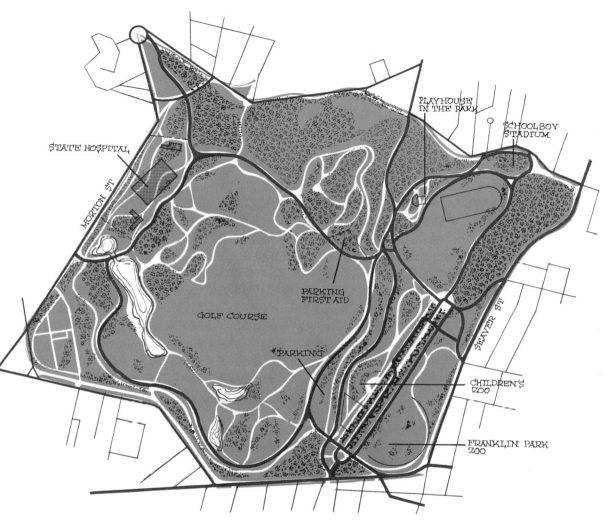

STATE HOSPITAL

MORTON ST

GOLF COURSE

PARKING
FIRST AID

PARKING

PLAYHOUSE
IN THE PARK

SCHOOLBOY
STADIUM

SHAVER ST

CHILDREN'S
ZOO

FRANKLIN PARK
ZOO

OLMSTED'S FRANKLIN PARK - LIGHT
PRESENT PARK - DARK

Olmsted's conception of Franklin Park, with land uses of today superimposed.

The accompanying map of Franklin Park is drawn at a scale to show
the disposition of the park's interior spaces—the original woods and meadows, remarkably unchanged today—with some contemporary uses overlaid.
Olmsted, who had first proposed the site in 1876 as the location for Boston's
major park, admired the way the land lay, finding its ridges, its natural
groves and its expanses of meadow so agreeably combined that he avoided
the use of lakes and running water. (Later park commissioners, feeling they
had been slighted, added their own ponds.)

The park is the same overall size as Prospect Park in Brooklyn, but
chunkier in dimensions. The core is a large central space formed by a relatively level meadow. A curving space called Ellicottdale draws one toward
the north, and between are gentle hills—Schoolmaster, Hagborne and Scar-
boro. A circuit drive winds around the park. On the east is the kind of
formal space—known here as the Greeting—such as Olmsted often included
within his rural landscapes, but which in this case he seems to have assented
to reluctantly.

In declaring this "the best piece of work done by its designer," Olmsted's
son commented: "The topography and ridges and trees lent themselves not
only to many picturesque bits of landscape designing but afforded, with
moderate grading, excellent fields for such sports as are permissible in a
landscape park."[19]

Over the years the number of "permissible" sports has grown; the park has
been subjected to various encroachments and invasions. An edge was lopped
off for Shattuck Hospital. The North Meadow was pre-empted by a stadium
and parking lot. The Metropolitan District Commission claims a significant
portion for the zoo and is hoping to acquire more. Nevertheless, a largely
rural atmosphere prevails, and the absence of surrounding high-rise buildings gives the park an agreeably isolated feeling.

This isolation, however, is a major reason why Franklin Park is in
trouble. Although once surrounded by middle-class homes, the park never
spurred the development that might have been anticipated. When the middle
class moved on to the suburbs, the poor, mostly black, took their place.
Services in the area declined and today the surrounding homes are deteriorating. With this change in the neighborhood the park began to suffer.
Harassment, muggings and acts of vandalism increased, until the number of
visitors began to drop off. Fewer families came out on a Sunday afternoon
to picnic or play; even the zoo failed to attract them.

The Great Meadow had long since become a municipal golf course. Here
levels of maintenance were relatively high and the clubhouse on the slopes
of Refectory Hill was well cared for while other park buildings deteriorated.

Even so, fewer and fewer people came out to play golf, until a few years ago it was decided to use only the nine holes nearest the clubhouse, which seemed to offer golfers some measure of protection.

The basic issue in regard to Franklin Park is whether in fact it is a city-wide park or belongs to the adjacent Model Cities neighborhood. In 1975 a $900,000 appropriation was withdrawn by the city council when the chairman of its appropriations committee, Louise Day Hicks, argued against the expenditure on the grounds that city-wide tax money ought not to be spent on a park so exclusively within the domain of a minority.

The park does have a constituency, however—one that is fighting hard to secure restoration of city funds and to get on with necessary improvements. It has been led by a remarkable woman, Elma Lewis, who devoted herself to providing programs for Franklin Park. She conducted a dancing class for children and trained them rigorously. During the summer, in an outdoor theater that had been named for her, she ran nightly programs of music and dance. Standing directly in opposition to Louise Day Hicks, Mrs. Lewis went beyond encouraging her own community to use the park and take care of it. She did not lose sight of the park's place in the total city and demanded that the city fulfill its obligation.

Mrs. Lewis and her friends were joined by a much larger and less defined constituency—those Bostonians conscious of the city's historic heritage, not willing to stand by and let Franklin Park decline. The park touches a raw nerve because public officials and citizens alike feel some guilt at having seemed to abandon the masterpiece in their midst. "If it weren't for Elma Lewis and her group," said one civic leader, "nobody would care about Franklin Park."

The way back is not easy to find. Certainly the expenditure of public funds cannot by itself guarantee a cessation of vandalism or assure greater use for the park. The lack of development in the surrounding area suggests that long-range planning for the park ought to wait a little longer until the future of that part of Boston is assayed. Meanwhlie Franklin Park must receive proper maintenance and policing. Otherwise there will be little left to plan for when the nature of its constituency, their interests and requirements, are finally determined.

SOME BASIC ISSUES

The parks just sketched raise certain issues about the historic central parks which can now be placed in a wider perspective.

All the parks show the strain of adapting to new conditions; all have suffered to a greater or lesser degree from a gap that has developed between their original conception and their present-day situation. In some cases the result has been overdevelopment, in others a falling off in use. The strain may manifest itself in so obvious a deformation as bifurcation by a major highway, or in ways so subtle as neglect and creeping vandalism. Yet in none of these cases—nor in any we know of—is there an intention to give up the land. In none is there serious argument for surrendering a major park's central status, or abandoning its character as a landscaped oasis.

The danger is not that officials or private groups will advocate these things, but that by a compromise here and there, or by a single major alteration presented under the guise of necessity, a park will lose its unique aspects. An opposing danger is that through a doctrinaire and inflexible attachment to the past on the part of its supporters, a park may prove unable to provide what a new generation is seeking. The young people may then come to look upon it as being without significance and will cease to be concerned for its future. In acts of vandalism certain groups may actually set out to destroy the park.

Other threats to these old parks come from a slow decline in upkeep, to the point where they seem shabby and uninviting; and, perhaps most pervasive, from a sense of fear among their users. Some special problems:

Encroachments

Use of central parks for plainly nonpark purposes is comparatively rare, though schools and hospitals, as well as some dubious commercial enterprises, have been allowed to intrude. Today's public is apt to resist in a historic landscaped park the kind of pressures to which outlying green spaces are often highly vulnerable.[20]

From one major form of encroachment, however, even the central parks have not been immune. In a half-dozen instances roads have lopped off portions of a central park,[21] and in others a road stands poised to pass through the city's most cherished open space. The likelihood of this threat's occurring in the future is diminished by the review provided by Section 4(f) of the Department of Transportation Act of 1966, and by the strong support this has received from the Supreme Court in the case of the proposed highway across Overton Park in Memphis.[22] Such protection, however, cannot be absolute, as has been shown in the case of Brackenridge Park in San Antonio.

Brackenridge stands in the line of a north-south expressway which is presently stopped dramatically at the point where it enters the park. The Department of Transportation ruled against the road, as having adverse environmental effects. However, the local San Antonio legislature voted in its favor. The case is still in the courts, and the future of the park is uncertain.

Balboa Park in San Diego lies close to the downtown, greatly treasured by the citizens and highly attractive to tourists. Unlike the Olmsted-type central parks seen elsewhere, Balboa is developed with elaborate structures, housing cultural institutions and the world-famous San Diego Zoo. It would seem most unlikely that here, of all places, a highway could be let pass through. Yet the Cabrillo Freeway cuts off a broad edge of the park and pre-empts at least forty acres with its cloverleaf. San Diegans tend to be apologetic about this encroachment, claiming that it gives the motorist (as indeed it does) a beautiful entrance to the city. The freeway is elaborately landscaped—a pioneering concession won from the federal highway authorities as a result of citizen protest. Yet nothing really seems to justify this use of parkland. It can only be hoped that a movement to widen the expressway will be permanently staved off.

Special Uses

More difficult than the problem of encroachment on lands of the central park is the question of what facilities and structures can properly be located there. Most of the proposals made for special use—ball fields, golf courses, museums, recreation centers, stadiums, etc.—can be justified as having a park purpose. Nearly all of them can be plausibly presented and will be defended by public-spirited citizens. The question is whether a particular facility belongs in a particular park. That makes each case delicate and each one unique.

A park designed from the beginning as a coherent work of art, preserving its original character into the present, would seem to eliminate all difficulties of choice. The obvious decision when changes are proposed would appear in each case to be a negative one. New York's Central Park presents the best example of this situation: to keep the original form of the park, to restore as may be necessary its horticulture and its architectural monuments, to resist attempts to add new features and "attractions"—this has been accepted by successive park commissioners as their charge. Nevertheless, even here a line is sometimes hard to draw.

In recent years much controversy has occurred over the completion of the Metropolitan Museum within a master plan occupying hitherto open parkland. A scheme to restore and relandscape the dilapidated area around the bandstand was defeated by park groups. More understandably, the gift of a restaurant for the southern end of the park was rejected by one mayor after having been accepted by another. In the near future decisions will have to be made—upon which Olmsted can offer no direct guidance—regarding what to do with a reservoir that becomes obsolete as part of the city's water supply.

In parks less sanctified by tradition, the question of what is a legitimate improvement and what is an unwarranted diversion becomes less clear. Many past decisions achieve acceptance and even favor, though they represent a course we would not want to see continued or repeated. Few, for example, would find that Delaware Park in Buffalo suffers from having the Albright-Knox Art Gallery within its borders. Nevertheless, if one were to build such a museum today, the case against taking parkland would be very strong. A location along the edge of the park or in the downtown area would seem more desirable from many points of view. The use of central parklands for zoos has long been accepted; but today one must question whether the small zoo usual in such a park is justified as an institution, and whether the land could not better be left free for general park purposes.

Cultural institutions are taken for granted as fitting adornments to a city's principal park, but that is no reason for adding to their number. Too often a park location has been the easiest, as it is obviously the least expensive, to acquire. With more justification than a school, but creating hardly less of an intrusion, a museum or theater has taken the place of trees and grass. Afterward the full effect of the required parking is felt, and then begins the almost inevitable pressure for expansion. If the citizens of our cities care about their green spaces they will insist on keeping them green, notwithstanding plausible arguments as to the merits of mixing art and nature.

Active and spectator sports are another major source of difficulty for the central parks. Here, too, the arguments for compromise are persuasive and often insistent. Many of the larger parks do indeed incorporate ball fields, golf courses and tennis courts without any sense of incongruity. Ice-skating rinks and swimming pools, while theoretically compatible with a historic landscape, are usually of such poor design and require so many supporting facilities as to become visual blights. A stadium is obviously out of place, yet not beyond the range of what sports fans may demand.

A separate sports park, centrally located and accessible by public trans-

portation, is the real answer to these claims. It is significant that in designing Prospect Park Olmsted created a special area for active sports just
outside it (as he created another for cultural institutions). In the Buffalo
system he urged a large park for sports on the south side of the city, balanc-
ing his landscaped park at its north.

The nature, size and location of each central park will finally determine
what special land uses are justified. A master plan, formulated by professionals with effective public participation, is essential. Many desirable
services and functions can be incorporated if their design and placement are
thought through in advance, whereas they would do violence to the park
if introduced piecemeal, according to the wish of a donor or the pressures
of an intransigent community. A clear sense of direction, combining traditional values and contemporary needs, should emerge from the process
of park planning. That sense of direction will confirm not only the park's
identity but the city's.

The Public Order

The parks under discussion are the showplaces of their cities and, with
major exceptions, they are better maintained than might be supposed in a
day when municipal budgets find it difficult to supply bare necessities. The
exceptions, unfortunately, include New York's Central Park. An example
to so many others in its design, and the envy of others because of its
popular appeal, it shows what happens when repairs are deferred and the
years are allowed to take their toll. The soil, always thin, has been compacted
by intensive use; erosion jeopardizes many of the old trees. Structures and
monuments await restoration. Belle Isle Park shows a more frowsy face, and
Franklin Park declines more somberly in its neglect. But it is a municipal,
and indeed a national, disgrace that the first and foremost central park
should have to be compared with the worst, and not with the best, of its
kind. In contrast, Golden Gate is a well-maintained oasis; Eden Park in
Cincinnati, Encanto Park in Phoenix, are decent images of city pride.

There are disadvantages in setting apart one park in a city and giving it
special treatment. A showplace spruced up and well-maintained, while
neighborhood parks are overrun by weeds and falling prey to vandalism, is
not conducive to the city's peace. Nevertheless, there is something to be
said for singling out the park that is so often a major source of enjoyment to
all the people. A budget kept distinct from the general park budget, a super-

intendent not only experienced but visible to the public, will help fix accountability. If there is attrition in the work force, or deferments of capital improvements, these will be known. At present the cuts too often occur by slow degrees, and the worsening condition of the park is not evident until it gets out of hand.

A sense of decline and shabbiness keeps people out of a park; so to an even greater extent does a feeling of personal insecurity. The amount of crime in major parks is probably exaggerated in the public mind, but the *fear* of crime is an ever-present fact not to be minimized. The landscaped park forms an environment particularly difficult to police, with its abundant shrubbery and the deep shadows of its trees. Olmsted, aware that safety after dark was not attainable in a heavily landscaped park, enforced the closing of Central Park at dusk. A later generation thought a better method of dealing with the problem was to cut down the shrubbery.

The visible presence of police in a park invariably pays off not only in added use by the people but in a better mixture of races and age groups.[23] In Forest Park, as in Piedmont Park, Atlanta, mounted police were responsible for maintaining the kind of confidence that allows varied elements of the city's population to mix comfortably. Officers in plain clothes, heavily relied on in New York, may have the effect of deterring would-be muggers and criminals; they do not, however, restore in the public the sense of confidence derived from a uniformed presence.

People in large numbers are in themselves an important provider of safety. Programs that draw the public, entertainments and events appealing to various audiences, banish the feeling of isolation in which fear is born; besides, the crowds become largely self-policing. An empty park always seems dangerous. Very probably it *is* dangerous.

Special Park Boards

The unique character of these central parks suggests that besides a budget and a superintendent of their own, they should, in certain cases at least, be within the keeping of a specially appointed park board.[24] Such a board would be particularly useful in a city like New York, where the park commissioner, directly responsible to the mayor, is without a board or commission related to his work.

In many cities a number of different departments have jurisdiction within parks—Highways, Recreation, Sanitation, Gas and Electricity, to name only a few. In Buffalo, eight different municipal departments share responsibility for Delaware Park. A stronger central authority is obviously required; but beyond that, in a park so deeply involved in history and in the values of the community, a board of guardians could play an essential role. It should include leading citizens, members of the landscape and architectural professions, and representatives of the surrounding communities.

Irreparable damage may be done to the character of a historic park by introducing into it forms of lighting, highway signage and fencing, play equipment and benches that may be entirely satisfactory in parks of a different nature. Standard maintenance procedures, such as the use of blacktop for pathways or asphalt tile for roofing, may be disastrous when applied to a carefully designed landscape environment. Similarly, a thoughtless change in plant or tree material can destroy a delicately conceived and long-nurtured visual effect.

In all such matters a board of guardians would exercise a constant surveillance and would have a final say. In the making of long-range plans, the raising of funds from public and private sources, and the maintenance of the park's image, it would play a part as important as the authority and dedication of its members makes possible.

In contrast to a park director, who may have hundreds of parks and playgrounds under his control (in New York City the number is close to a thousand), the board would have one park. Safe from political interference, undistracted by the clamor of special groups, it would have one task—to make sure that nothing is done in the present which betrays the past and that all is done which may assure for the park in the future a distinguished civic role.

8 Park Systems

THE ESTABLISHMENT OF MAJOR PARKS brought the city a long way beyond
the historic square. But it was not to be the end of the road. The planners
of open space were impelled beyond the isolated or rigidly circumscribed
pleasure ground; from the beginning they sensed the need for a continuity
of green space, for an interpenetration of urban and rural elements. They
were to reach outward to shape the systems of open space that will be described in this chapter. Their successors were to overleap the bounds of the
existing city and to organize greenbelts on the scale of megalopolis.

Respect for topography was one factor leading beyond the traditionally
conceived park. If the underlying bones of the urban form were to be kept
visible, if its natural assets were to be captured for recreation, green was the
color to be applied liberally to the map. The green would run along shores
and ridges, touch hilltops and the steeper slopes, spill over into wetlands. The
park domains of such cities as Seattle and Washington, D.C., have been
described in an earlier chapter to indicate the way physical geography affected the evolution of open space. That evolution tended toward open
spaces linked by corridors of green.

Such was the result when a *naturalistic* approach was applied to park planning. We shall now look at what happened when the approach was primarily
urbanistic. This chapter deals with parks systems that arose from a sense of
the city's inadequacies, from the felt need to make it a more congenial place
to live and work.

192

Breaking Through the Wall

The building of Central Park did not satisfy Olmsted's ambitions for New York. That bounded landscape, walled, ringed with trees, stood apart from the city almost as an act of defiance. Subtle approaches to this oasis, varied routes of dispersion toward other green spaces, would extend the park's influence and would ultimately transform the city. As his thinking matured, Olmsted moved toward this goal. He began to make accessible from the park the open spaces along Manhattan's rocky spine and those on the shore of the Hudson River.

In this he was not to be entirely successful. As has been noted, social and economic factors kept the areas north of Central Park from the kind of development for which Olmsted was reaching. In Brooklyn a better opportunity presented itself, and he approached the challenge of Prospect Park in full command of the new vision. The park would profit from what he conceived to be the shortcomings of his pioneering effort: not only would active sports and cultural institutions be banished to adjacent spaces, but the park would be linked by a linear green system to other parts of Brooklyn and to the sea. He even hoped that one day his two masterpieces—Central and Prospect—would be so joined. Unfortunately, the system Olmsted envisaged for Brooklyn was not completed, but one major segment of it, Ocean Parkway, we have already met up with in our discussion of Brooklyn's sequence of urban spaces.

Olmsted's supreme achievement of a unified and continuous system, however, was to be Boston's inner greenbelt. This was followed by his scheme for Buffalo and similar accomplishments by H. W. S. Cleveland in Minneapolis and George Kessler in Kansas City. What these men were doing in the America of the last century went far beyond park-building in the ordinary sense. They were planning cities; they were determining not only where structures would be excluded but the location of residential areas and neighborhoods. The spirit in which they acted was later to be expressed by Lewis Mumford: "Park planning is part of the broader process of ordering the human environment in such a way as to make the most of its varied possibilities," he wrote in his famous "Report on Honolulu." "Park planning, in other words, cannot possibly stop at the edges of the parks . . . The park system is thus the very spearhead of comprehensive urban planning."[1]

The early park planners thought in such large perspectives, but their arguments were cast in more traditional terms of beauty, "sanitation" (meaning health) and common enjoyments. Reading between the lines of Kessler and Cleveland, we detect their interest in a concept of urban planning still waiting to be formulated, while they appear to be urging only the advantages of healthy physical exercise or the pleasures of a shaded afternoon drive. Like all true prophets, they had their message for the multitude, while below the surface they kept a subtler appeal to the initiated, both of their own and of future generations.

The Concept of Parkways

The park-builders connected their parks and formed their greenbelts by developing boulevards and parkways. Modern traffic has so completely altered the nature of transportation routes that we must by an effort of the imagination put ourselves back a century in time if we are to understand how the park systems were intended to function.

Carriage roads were not generally thought to be incompatible with a park environment. Indeed, a major reason for building parks was to give people a pleasant place to drive. In New York's Central Park the roads were planned to exclude through traffic. But as late as 1917 the Minneapolis city plan could assert that in new parks "effective appreciation of the requirements of through-traffic should be shown." When an existing park impedes traffic, "the wise park enthusiast," we are told, "will be the first to seek the best method of conducting that traffic through the park, *whether it be vehicular or foot traffic.*"[2]

As for foot traffic, the report suggests that walking will be healthy, morning and evening, for working men and women going to and from their work. Meanwhile "hastening businessmen," presumably riding in their carriages, "will be cheered by the sight of the park"!

Olmsted recognized the importance of carriage drives, yet in the end concluded that "the walks of the park are more used than its wheelways." He urged that some of the best scenery of any park should be capable of being viewed only from its pedestrian paths. His reason, however, was not because horses would go fast and kick up the dust, but rather that it would be good for people to "take walking exercise."[3]

The attitude toward traffic in parks being thus ambiguous, and certainly on the whole lenient, it is not surprising that the park-builders should have grasped the opportunity to shape linear green spaces designed principally for carriages. They were not very clear in their writings about the difference between the *boulevard*—usually broad and straight, intended to be bordered by houses behind dense rows of trees—and the *parkway*, which was inclined to be sinuous and to follow natural contours. They used the two words more or less interchangeably. But in either case they had created for themselves an open space device of charm, and potentially of great significance to the form of our cities.

The parkways were conceived of at one level as an agreeable way of getting to parks, and a way of getting from one park to another. But more subtly they were seen as basic form-givers to the emerging cities. "What are called parkways, if judiciously designed," wrote Olmsted to the park commissioners of Minneapolis in 1886, "are likely to become the stems of systems of streets which will be the framework of the permanent residence quarters of our cities in the future." This in fact occurred. To this day Minneapolis neighborhoods have been stabilized and given identity by their relation to an arrangement of parkways and boulevards laid out a century ago.

The weakness of the romantically designed parkway, like the weakness of the classical Beaux Arts avenue, was that it lent itself so readily to being taken over by the automobile. The change in use and nature of the route was not immediately apparent and people went on believing the old ideas about the parkway when in fact an entirely new situation had come into being. The incompatibility of automobile roads and parks becoming finally apparent, the battle against the invader was inhibited by the parkmen's traditional tolerance of wheeled traffic. In the end a Robert Moses could become the great advocate of both automobiles *and* parks. The damage to parks would be immense as noise and pollution increased. In some cities older boulevards or parkways were taken over as routes for expressways or commercial avenues.

Origin of the Boston System

As New York's Central Park was the standard against which all other landscaped parks had to be judged, so the Boston greenbelt, also designed by Olmsted, became the standard for judging park systems.

Olmsted had moved to Boston when a long-simmering park enthusiasm culminated in an act of the state legislature opening the way to park acquisitions. At that time Boston possessed no major parks except the Common, going back to 1634, and the later Public Garden. Broad-based support

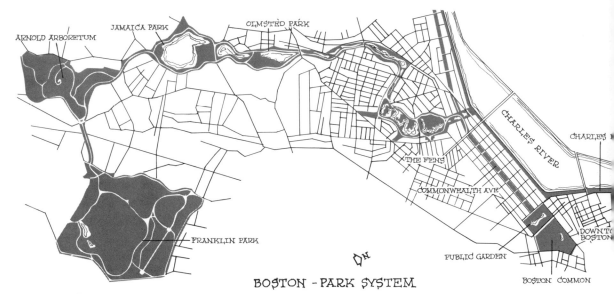

BOSTON - PARK SYSTEM

The Boston park system is strongly rooted in the central city, thrusting outward from the Common in a great arc climaxed by Franklin Park. The continuous greenbelt has been insensitively broken at several points.

existed for a system of green spaces linked by corridors and encircling the existing city. The Boston Parks Commission gave Olmsted the charge of carrying out the concept.

The system, graphically illustrated in the accompanying map, has its roots in the city's core and extends in a wide semicircle to the south. (Olmsted had hoped to complete the circle to the sea.) The actual greenbelt takes off from the juncture of the Charles and the Muddy River—the latter an insignificant stream that had been nothing but a nuisance until Olmsted made it the principal feature of his Fens park and the spine of his related parks and parkways. Along this spine are Jamaica Pond and the park now named after Olmsted. Continuing the greenbelt are the Arboretum and Franklin Park.

Olmsted's skill and sensitivity to nature are indicated by the way he treated the fen area. The city had planned a flood control and reservoir system for the unsightly and odorous mouth of the Muddy River, which, seeping in a wide delta into the Charles, had bothered the residents of the newly created Back Bay. Olmsted met the practical requirements posed by floods and sewage, and at the same time created a delightful park. Sewage was diverted; the mud flats were depressed by grading to a point just below low tide, while a high rim of encircling land provided a storage area for flood waters. A tide gate permitted a normal ebb and flow.

Within this ecological and engineering framework the art of the landscape artist was deployed. Codgrass cultivated on the submerged mud flats, trees planted around the rim, were supplemented by park drives, paths for horsemen and pedestrians, shelters and bridges.

The other parks of the greenbelt were designed and developed with similar imagination. Connecting them were drives or promenades designed each to have its own character—as each had its own name—and to invite a leisurely exploration of the whole system. Going beyond this, plans were made for the development of the Charles River basin as an area of mixed recreational and institutional use, running more than eight miles from the mouth of Boston Harbor upstream to Watertown.

The System in Trouble

These related open spaces provide the Boston of today with an unusually handsome park environment. Along the greenbelt, major institutions, including the Boston Museum of Fine Arts, have found a natural setting; and residential communities have maintained a special character. One unfortunate high-rise development has reminded the city of the absolute necessity to enforce the existing height limitations upon all buildings adjacent to parks.

Looked at more closely, the system shows deterioration and misuse at critical junctures and through most of its developed length. The decline began a generation after Olmsted finished his work. In 1910 a dam was built across the Back Bay fens. The original salt-water environment, washed by tides and sustaining the precious codgrass, became the site of a sterile fresh-water lake. Marshes were filled in to create conventional recreation space. The Muddy River was constrained within a hard-edged channel.

Highways have become the principal factor altering the relationship between man's open spaces and nature's. The Fenway, the Riverway, the Jamaica Way—segments of interconnected park roads which at the slow speeds of the nineteenth century could each be experienced individually—gradually coalesced into one continuous stream of fast-moving traffic. A route designed for pleasure became part of a modern transportation system facilitating the inner-city worker's escape to the suburbs. Minor physical changes and repeated widening further eroded the green space. In the 1960s park interests narrowly averted a plan to change the nature of the open space system by straightening the original drives and removing thousands of trees.

Not averted, however, was the construction of a maze of ramps and overpasses at the point where the open space system meets the spaces of the Charles. Here the Muddy River suffered the final humiliation of being placed underground in a culvert. Despite the millions of dollars that went into structures for moving automobiles, nothing was spent for bridges or underpasses for the far less demanding pedestrian. Today, as noted earlier. he cannot pass from the green spaces of the river to those of its tributary.

A 1973 study has gone into some of the conditions that currently mar the Olmsted system.[4] Jamaica Pond and sections within Brookline are most heavily used and are comparatively well maintained; the Arboretum is a model of good management. But in other areas rats are often the most prevalent form of wildlife. The path network is poorly maintained; the original picturesque light fixtures are inoperable or destroyed; statues and monuments show the result of long neglect. Within the 115 acres of the Back Bay fens, once the gem of the whole system, pollution and road noise destroy the park atmosphere.

What went wrong? Somewhere along the way the original vision failed. What followed occurs wherever city governments forget that parks are fragile creations and need constant preservation and upkeep. Broad social developments have played their part—new urban trends, new forms of transportation, changing neighborhoods and life styles. Yet if the original concept of the park system had remained vivid, a new generation could surely not have permitted such incongruities as the barrier of the cloverleaf at the mouth of the fens; or—a smaller but no less excusable defection—the Sears, Roebuck parking lot that breaks the greenbelt's continuity.

In the process of restoration upon which Bostonians now seem determined, a first move should be to make clear to the public by maps and graphics the essential nature of the greenbelt. Well-designed signs together with a consistent style of ornamental lights and benches could help, at the very least, to stimulate a remembrance of the vanishing Olmsted system. The citizens may then find the will and energy to make major repairs, and even to re-examine such basic matters as the development of new arterial traffic routes to spare the parks some of their present burden.

What has happened to the Boston park system does not warrant the conclusion that this form of open space is obsolete. The city possesses a major resource created by earlier generations. As with all of man's achievements, there is a choice: either it can be allowed to decline and gradually disappear, or it can be saved and renewed. If the latter course is successfully pursued it will be a lasting benefit to Bostonians and also an example to other cities with a similar heritage.

Kansas City—A System That Grew

Three examples of park systems related to Boston's but playing particular roles within their cities will now be examined. Each of these remains a significant part of the modern city, though with varying degrees of effectiveness.

The system of parks and boulevards in Kansas City, Missouri, was conceived by an ambitious park group and designed in 1893 by a newcomer from Texas. Two maps illustrates what is perhaps the most striking fact about this system, its capacity to extend itself so as to keep pace with the growing city, maintaining its basic outline and identity while serving a broader area than was conceived by its originators.

The 1893 map is drawn to the same scale as the existing system. Such features as North Terrace Park and Penn Valley are still intact, and indeed play an important part in the city's life. The main boulevard of the Paseo continues beyond the Parade for eight and a half miles to the outskirts of the present city limits. New features have been added, but the scale of the large grid has been preserved and wherever possible the principle maintained of tying in the green spaces with topographic features. It is a remarkable achievement and makes Kansas City one of the most interesting urban environments of the country.

George Kessler, who was asked to design this park system for Kansas City, had left his native Dallas to study forestry, botany and engineering abroad. There he had opportunity to see at first hand the old cities and under a private tutor studied civic design. Our readers have already met him briefly as a Central Park gardener. Kessler was well grounded in Olmsted's landscape principles and he rejoiced in the opportunities provided him by Kansas City's "topographical eccentricities."

Kessler and his first park board were convinced, nevertheless, that their contribution would depart from Olmsted's.[5] While appreciating the effect of his scenic parks in "correcting and opposing the evil results of life in crowded cities," they saw Kansas City as having other needs. The young midwestern metropolis wanted public squares and local parks; it wanted the embellishment of notable urban points and a primary system of parkways.

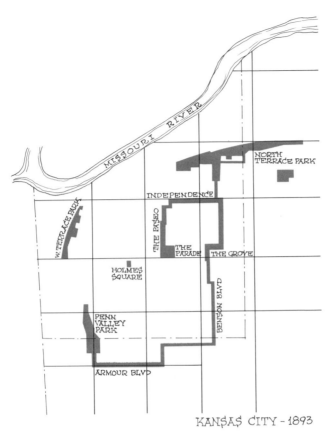

George Kessler's 1883 plan for a park system in Kansas City.

Kessler's success was in combining the city's natural endowments with an artificial structure to make the city more urbane—or as the good citizens of that time would have put it, more beautiful. To this day Kansas City has a strong sense of civic adornment. A far-reaching program for increasing its already numerous fountains is combined with the acquisition through public funds of contemporary sculpture to be placed in the broad malls of its boulevards.

The achievement of a coherent park system was not without its dramatic moments and its eccentric characters. The 1890 battle for the establishment of a park and boulevard authority was at bottom the age-old fight between two concepts of the city. On the one hand were land speculators

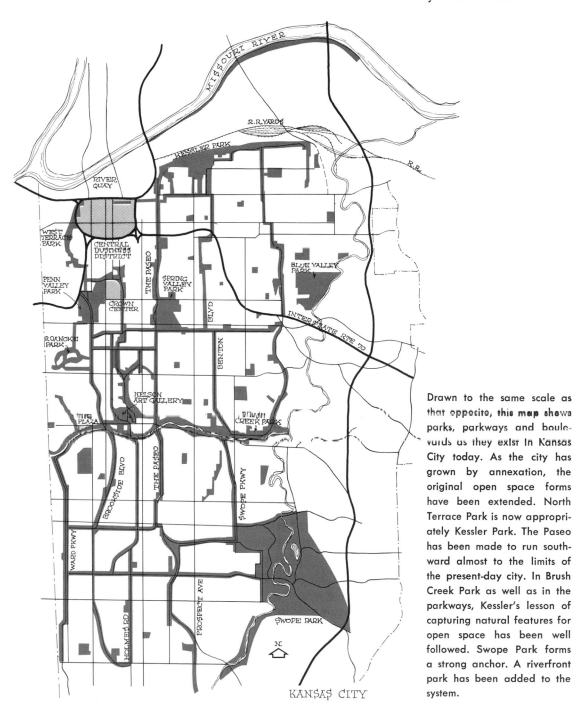

KANSAS CITY

Drawn to the same scale as that opposite, this map shows parks, parkways and boulevards as they exist in Kansas City today. As the city has grown by annexation, the original open space forms have been extended. North Terrace Park is now appropriately Kessler Park. The Paseo has been made to run southward almost to the limits of the present-day city. In Brush Creek Park as well as in the parkways, Kessler's lesson of capturing natural features for open space has been well followed. Swope Park forms a strong anchor. A riverfront park has been added to the system.

—those who put growth above all other goals and set as a foremost value their capacity and that of their brethren to enrich themselves. On the other side were those with an image of what a decent city for living might be.

In the course of rhetorical exchanges the speculators declared parks to be places "where scented dudes smoke cigarettes and play croquet with girls as silly as themselves." They spoke of boulevards as "streets decorated for the wives and daughters of millionaires to drive on." But they met their match in the park forces. A crucial amendment to the city charter was carried in 1895. "Kansas City is going to move on," cried the park leaders of the day. "The new age dates from the election of yesterday, when the mossbacks went down before the forces of progress."[6]

The large outlying park that Kansas City needed to anchor and to complete its system was acquired under picturesque circumstances. Colonel Thomas A. Swope, described as "a wealthy dyspeptic recluse," had been among the most vigorous opponents of what he called "this park foolishness." He was a large landowner and fought the increased real estate levy as long as he could. But in the end he capitulated with a grand gesture. He purchased a 1,134-acre expanse of pasture and woodlands and gave it to the city for a public park. It was nine miles from the business center and Kessler thought it was too distant to be of much use. A decade later, when the city had grown to the edge of the park, he recalled this judgment with amusement.

Swope himself was disappointed by the skepticism that greeted his gift. The man crept deeper into his shell, while his relatives would hear him mumbling under his breath, "Too far out, too far out." A quiet, wispy man, Swope died a violent death: he was murdered along with two other members of his household by a nephew by marriage, Dr. Bennett Clark Hyde. The sensational trial associated with his name has been largely erased from memory, but Swope Park survives. The city, shocked and saddened by the donor's death, tolled its bells and schoolchildren followed the route of the funeral march.

Kansas City has long felt that it got nothing but good from its parks. It attributes to the boulevard system the tendency for residents to disperse evenly, making Kansas City one of the least densely populated cities in the country. Desiring to live as close as possible to a park or boulevard, people have had a wide choice of location. In 1910 a group of conservative real estate men compared the valuation of ground frontage on Kansas City boulevards with that of ground fronting on adjacent streets. They found the difference in favor of the boulevards to be considerably greater than the entire cost to the taxpayers of all the parks and boulevards in the system.

More recently, when so many cities have been plagued by declining neighborhoods and incipient violence, Kansas City has felt that the boulevards stabilized key areas of the city.

Touring the system today,[7] one is disappointed to find the continuous system illustrated on the map narrowed at several points and its borders taken over for commercial uses. Yet strong park support remains, and a Kansas City park commissioner, backed by a united board, can feel safe in taking on other city departments and will be assured of public backing on central issues. Beyond the embellishment upon which civic leaders have set their hearts, there is need for the difficult, often expensive repairs to the system and full restoration of an unbroken green circuit. If Kansas City can keep the spirit it has shown in the past, it will remain an outstanding city. It will be able to claim that parks underlie its success to at least as great a degree as more spectacular downtown improvements.

Buffalo—A System Aborted

Delaware Park has been considered as a single central park. It is in fact part of a larger system. We now focus on that series of interconnected parks and roads threading its way through Buffalo, which Olmsted felt might well become the most complete and extensive within any American city.

The Buffalo park system is shown on the map on page 204. One is struck by the way Olmsted's plan supplemented and overlay the design of the earlier city. Buffalo had been laid out by Joseph Ellicott, the brother of L'Enfant's successor as planner of Washington, D.C.[8] Converging on Buffalo's Niagara Square were diagonals comparable to those of the capital city. Olmsted's approach to Delaware Park was in his familiar Romantic style; his boulevards, however, are wide and straight, leading into formal intersections.

Besides the key Delaware Park, the parks of the new plan included the Parade on the east and the Front on a low bluff two miles nearer town, above Lake Erie. Boulevards were conceived as ways of connecting these parks as well as of extending them through green corridors. Olmsted hoped other parks would be added later, and was particularly interested in a large park at the south end of town, on either side of the railroad tracks, for extensive beaches and watercourses as well as for rifle ranges and the ever-present militia.

Olmsted, in short, foresaw the need for waterfront development. This

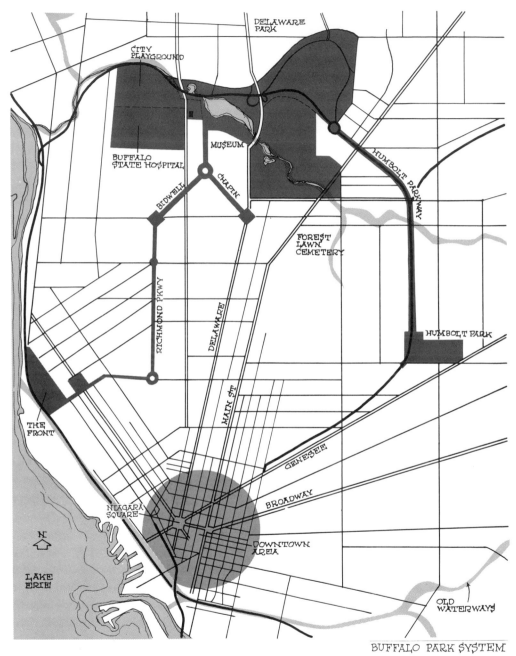

The Buffalo park system, designed by Olmsted, is shown in relation to the contemporary city. The structure of open space remains, though the boulevards with their neglected mansions and heavy traffic play an ambiguous role today. Expressways have eaten away at parks and parkways.

would wait a hundred years before becoming part of a sweeping proposal for a new development on the lake—a proposal that would once again be frustrated.[9] He also saw the need of a place for the kind of active sports that he hoped would be accommodated otherwise than by alterations in the character of Delaware Park.

Buffalo began with many of the ingredients necessary to the attainment of an effective park system.[10] A strong mayor, William F. Rogers, took a personal interest in the early stages of planning and land acquisition. A committee of substantial and influential businessmen formed an active park constituency. Olmsted himself, on the basis of his experience in other cities, urged going forward at full speed, warning that with the growth of population, parkland would become at once more essential and more difficult to acquire. The city council, however, found it politically popular to deplore the fiscal extravagances of the park board, and for three crucial years in the 1880s voted no funds for the maintenance of the growing system.

The council claimed its charges of extravagance to have been substantiated by the discovery in the kitchen of a park building of a list of tools which included silver spoons, ice picks and lemon squeezers—obviously the fixings for some wild tea parties. The commissioners were on firmer ground; they countered with arguments showing increased assessments in areas located near parks, from $37 million in 1870 to $104 million in 1884.

In the end, only half of the Buffalo plans came into being, and of this a substantial portion has since been lost, mainly to new traffic lanes. The expressway not only cuts across Delaware Park but runs down the route of one of the principal old boulevards, obliterating the Parade. The Front is also bisected. Other boulevards remain, still wide and tree-lined, but now bordered by mansions of a size and vintage that make them obsolete for family residences. Boulevard traffic, moreover, renders frontage less attractive for living than the side streets. A study has been made of the feasibility of restoring these mansions and adapting them to new uses, but the difficulties seem formidable.

At one of the intersections, Symphony Circle, stands the famous music hall designed by the elder Saarinen, an architectural monument in scale with the boldness of Olmsted's original planning.

Today Buffalo—its pride shaken by economic difficulties—has extensive schemes for reshaping its downtown area, enlisting its Main Street as a pedestrian mall and making it the center for a rapid transit system. Thus on top of the Baroque concept of Ellicott and the Romantic concept of

Olmsted will be laid (if all goes well) the entirely contemporary concept of a tightly organized city core scaled to the pedestrian.

Minneapolis—A Still-Vital System

A third park system, that of Minneapolis, has had a happier history and remains a vital force both in the city's recreation and in its physical organization. The map delineates it—a belt, broken only by one incompleted section at the east, which surrounds the city at its outer limits. The route ties in with the Mississippi riverbank and with the remarkable series of lakes on the city's outskirts.

This system is the work of H. W. S. Cleveland, one of the small group of outstanding nineteenth-century landscape architects. Cleveland came to Minneapolis from Chicago and the superintendency of the new South Park. Before that he had established a solid reputation in Boston practicing in partnership with Robert Morris Copeland. (Copeland was another unsuccessful competitor in the design of Central Park.) Cleveland had made his own recommendations for the Boston park system and subsequently supported and encouraged the Olmsted plan for that city. In Minneapolis, a city in 1880 of 50,000, he found the opportunity to put into practice his most cherished beliefs.

Cleveland had long been troubled by the way the towns of the West were being settled. Thoughtless repetition of the grid, he felt, betrayed the character of the land and sacrificed chances for giving cities their own form and character. He would break the grid in Minneapolis—break it permanently and decisively by his system of parks and parkways. The natural features of the city were favorable to his schemes—not only the river and the lakes, but the less evident interconnected drainage pattern of swamps, creeks and small ponds. Out of such natural elements he would fashion for the citizens a series of parks, and along the new roads create a continuously changing landscape and a variety of pleasing views. All this was to be rooted in an inner-city system of ornamental boulevards."[11]

The outer system created in the 1880s has been added to over the years and has lost virtually nothing.[12] The idea of inner-city boulevards did not work out and this was perhaps fortunate, for it left later generations to construct their own core, dense and compact—a strong focal point for the greenbelt to surround, a wholly man-made environment to contrast with the environment of nature.

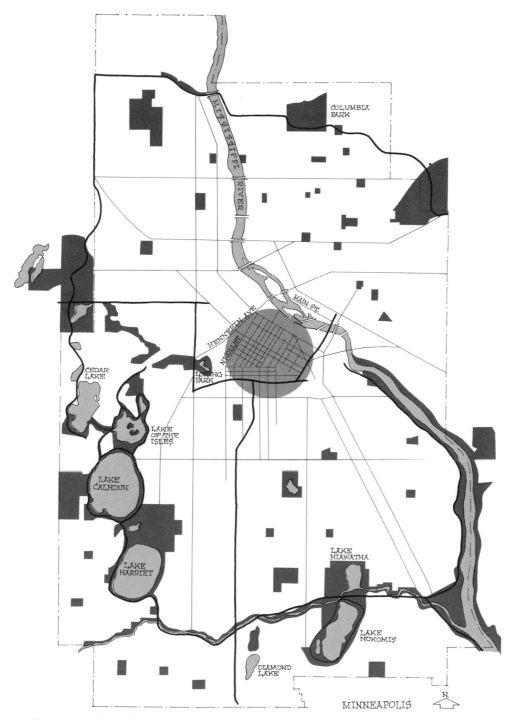

The Minneapolis park system as it exists within city borders, designed by H. W. S. Cleveland in 1883 and virtually unchanged today. The principal organizing feature of the scheme is water—lakes and the river.

In 1971 a study of the Minneapolis parkways[13] confirmed the basic validity of the system. It meets four goals: providing visual relief from the man-made city structures; defining the "edges" that give form to the city and identity to its neighborhoods; serving as a waterway drainage system; and not least, supplying an important recreational experience. Recommendations made in the study are in keeping with these objectives. Improvement and restoration of the parkways are advised not in order to enlarge their traffic capacity, but to strengthen the route's character as a corridor of natural scenery within the city.

In a section-by-section consideration of the route, recreation is stressed but only insofar as it can be adapted to the landscape without destruction of its intrinsic qualities. Swimming, hiking, bicycling and boating receive particular attention.[14] Warnings are sounded about adjacent land uses, and the proposal is made that the park board be a part of any review process for these areas. To screen the parkways from noise and air pollution is judged no less essential than to screen them from visual blight.

Today the parkways preserve their character as scenic routes. Parking is being concentrated and restricted rather than encouraged. An important referendum in the autumn of 1973 provided necessary funds for the work, and a strong park commissioner and board now doggedly back a plan that is adverse to the interests of motorists intent on speed alone.

Going through the parkways, one is impressed by their visual continuity and the general standards of design. At significant points along the way, maps indicate one's position within the system and, more importantly, stand as reminders of the concept as a whole. Here, at least, men once thought in large terms, and here they continue to keep the overall vision in mind.

A Culmination—The Kessler Plan

The ideal of an integrated park system, incorporating as in Boston a fenway or in Minneapolis a chain of lakes, was strong in the minds of nine-teenth-century planners. Where was all this leading? The answer is almost breathtaking: it was leading toward an image of the city that did not merely contain parks, that was not merely penetrated by circuits of green, but of the city *as a park in itself*.

For two centuries urbanists have flirted with this idea. Central Park in New York with its elaborate substructure of drainage and irrigation, with its separation of grades for various kinds of traffic, with its formal center and its romantic environs, could be read as a sketch of the ghost of a city never to be built. Conversely, in his plan for the Chicago suburban development of Riverside, Olmsted built a residential area upon a park base. Ideal plans integrating park and city were later to be elaborated by men as different as Ebenezer Howard and Frank Lloyd Wright. But the audacity of Olmsted, Kessler and Cleveland was to take existing cities and within them to create park systems so large and comprehensive as ultimately to make indistinguishable the point at which park ended and city began.

For the most complete embodiment of this idea, and to conclude and sum up this chapter on park systems, we turn to the plan made for Cincinnati by George Kessler.[15] The original Cincinnati plan has been redrawn in contemporary techniques so as to help the reader see clearly the nature of Kessler's accomplishment. This represents not a quaint image but a dynamic grasp of topography and civic structure. Here is molded into one whole the open spaces and the built-up areas—the solids and the voids—of a living metropolis.

How far we have come from the square, an isolated break in the city's fabric; how far from the central park, a sylvan island in a sea of buildings! How far, even, from Kessler's own Kansas City plan. The Cincinnati scheme, presented to a park commission headed by L. A. Ault in 1907, keeps a perfect balance between the squares and malls of the central business district and the parks of outer residential areas; between movement and stability; between neighborhood and metropolis. The open space system possesses an integrity and harmony that make it a true work of art, surpassing in scale and complexity anything previously proposed for an American city.

Kessler recognized that in the Cincinnati land forms he had rich material to work upon. The downtown area lies between hills of four hundred feet or more in height, pierced by the valleys of Mill Creek and the Little Miami. The railroads, unable to reach the upper levels with their tracks, had left unbroken the principal residential areas. True, the lands along the Ohio and up the major streams had already been taken for industrial uses; any effort to recover these for recreational purposes seemed vain. But a circle of separate hills from Price Hill on the west to Walnut Hill on the east harbored separate communities, ready to be tied into the central business district and linked to each other by flowing green spaces. Kessler saw his opportunity to combine parks and parkways, residential and city-wide parks, into a kind of web that leaves such achievements as Central and Golden Gate parks isolated and almost sterile by comparison.

Kessler saw rightly that everything begins with the downtown area. He

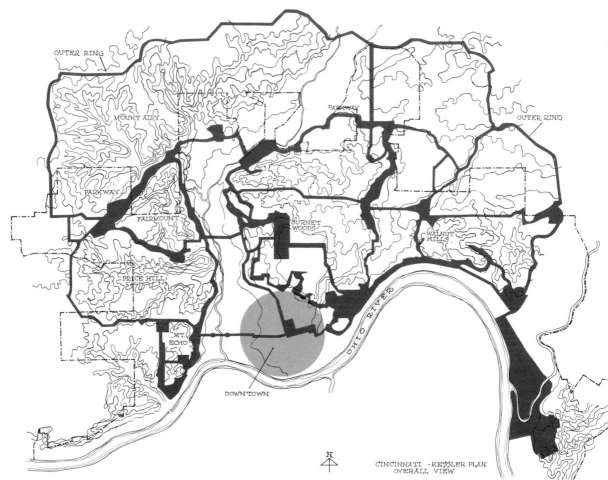

The Kessler plan for Cincinnati represents the culmination of traditional park planning. In effect, it turns the whole city into a park, with open spaces defining and giving form to the business and residential sections. Cincinnati today shows many elements of the Kessler plan, especially the hilltop parks and outlooks, but the parkway system did not develop and would have been self-defeating in the automobile age.

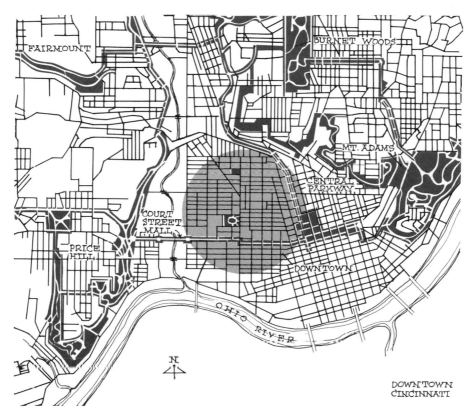

A striking feature of the Kessler plan for Cincinnati was the way it reorganized the down-town area in order to provide a base for the city-wide park system. The development of the mall and the creation of Central Avenue (in the bed of the old canal) created strong open space axes from which the parkways extending in various directions could be reached. Too rarely have the outer parks of a city thus modified and reshaped the town center.

seized upon the then largely unused Miami and Erie Canal, filling it in and setting a broad boulevard in its place. He hoped thus to create what he lacked in other cities, and what many were seeking to obtain at large costs of clearance and construction—"access along fine and easy lines into the very heart of the business district . . . an unsurpassed, main, central artery from the heart of the business portion of the city, connecting it with every residence district." Kessler's Central Parkway reached up into the hills, where it widened into a neighborhood park, or narrowed again as it moved through the next valley toward another hillside community with its own romantically landscaped green space.

The map on page 210 shows this central area of the city, penetrated by the parkway in the bed of the old canal, and crossed by the Court Street Mall; the whole focused on Burnet Park and including the nearest hillside communities from Price Hill on the east to Mount Adams on the west.

The map on page 211 shows the complete system, including the parkway proposed to ring the whole city. What can be only hinted at in such renderings is the elegance with which the parkways blend into parks, or yield to small areas devoted to city views.

By modern standards the plan is open to criticism. The central boulevard carrying traffic into the heart of midtown is at odds with the concept of a loop which arrests and disperses it. Today the 150-foot breadth of the boulevard creates a vacancy at the center of the town and divides the built-up areas. Moreover, through at least part of this way, the disappearance of the canal seems a definite loss. It would have been pleasing to see open water, even though it was no longer necessary for commercial purposes, and the canal could have provided a picturesque amenity at least equal to the proposed gardens of the boulevard.

The main shortcoming of the plan, however, is due to no fault of Kessler's, but to the new mode of automobile transportation which in 1907 was just at the point of bursting upon the cities and deeply transforming their lives.

This book deals with American cities as they are, not with visionary concepts or futuristic projects. Nevertheless, the Cincinnati plan earns its place in these pages, being so clear a culmination of ideas that were being put into effect in actual cities. It makes fully comprehensible what the nineteenth-century park-builders were trying to accomplish. It is, besides, an enchanting vision, reminding us of what our cities might have become had the invention of the internal combustion engine been delayed a few decades.

Cincinnati retains into the present the charm of a city of individual neighborhoods separated and identified by hills. Parts of the Kessler plan have been fulfilled and two important contemporary features have been added—the riverfront development and the 1,500 acres of Mount Airy Park, just outside the central city. But the grand design of a continuous park system has been lost, or lost so far as anything can be that so enduringly tantalizes the mind.

9 New Urban Opportunities

THE DAYS OF PARK-BUILDING are not over; beyond the tasks of preservation, maintenance and rehabilitation lie new possibilities for recreation within today's urban areas. A good deal of ingenuity is required if the opportunities are to be seized; often much determination if they are to be seized in time. Fortunately, many cities are today in the midst of imaginative open space planning and of acquisition, often setting themselves bold objectives and sometimes coming up with surprising results. In this chapter we shall consider some of the projects under way within city limits; next we shall look at the kind of planning that, going forward on a regional scale, aims to set up park systems adequate to contemporary patterns of settlement.

The Next Parks

Today's park planners cannot afford to be perfectionist in spirit nor always to insist upon a domain from which other uses are excluded. They will be dealing largely with bits and pieces of leftover land, with natural features that seem uninviting to the designer or inhospitable to the recreationist; they will be in fierce competition with other urban interests. Looking back upon the seemingly simple conditions in which older parks were created, the contemporary planner may feel envious. But he should remind himself that Golden Gate and Central parks were shaped from forbidding landscapes; that Swope and Forest parks were at first thought too far out to be useful; and that even at the height of the park movement powerful forces were in opposition, especially those favoring land speculation and unchecked growth.

214

Tracts of land available within the built-up areas of the cities are almost invariably serving some necessary urban purpose, such as drainage or flood control; or, like steep hillsides and other intractable natural features, they are not readily susceptible to development. These are not factors to discourage the open space advocate. Recreation of various kinds can be combined with public utilities, with transportation routes, even with conditions so apparently adverse as those produced by a waste-disposal plant.

As for the intractable natural object, it is worth remembering that park-builders were often happiest when contending with a gorge, a canyon, a mountainside or a fen. They were accustomed to take what other urban interests dismissed as unusable, enhancing the natural beauty of these unique natural sites. The difference today is that the residual landscape is often even more inaccessible or more challenging in the obstacles it presents to recreational use. It is true, also, that the forces promoting residential development are armed with a more formidable technology.

Proponents of active development have to be contended with, but the spokesmen for unspoiled nature may appear to stand equally in the way of recreational opportunities. The latter, if they had their way, would exclude people altogether from such remaining natural environments as mountain ranges or wetlands. They are at least half right. Today the recreational enthusiast should be kept from filling in a wetland to build a golf course, or padding a hillside to construct tennis courts. There are, nevertheless, important ways in which the natural scene may be opened to walkers, bird watchers, small groups of picnickers. In these cases the park user will not be accommodating himself to other forms of human activity, but to the requirements of the natural world.

In the main, the next parks will be put together from small patches of land, often elongated or irregular in form. In several cities military reservations or even an airfield wait to be released for other uses, but urban park-lovers stand at the end of the line in making claims to such a windfall. At best, they will have to share the land with other interests. In examples to follow we shall see some large areas falling at least in part to recreational purposes; but generally the park planner will do well to take advantage of smaller, less dramatic gains—the lands bordering a fen or small stream, the right of way of an abandoned trolley track, canal or railroad. He should not feel short-changed if he cannot claim at one stroke the several hundred acres of the ideal central park.[1]

The strip of land that so often becomes available as a result of changing transportation systems can, as a matter of fact, make a highly useful contribution to urban amenities. The nineteenth-century park-builders developed in their parkways a feeling for linear spaces; many stretches of the old parkway systems remind us of the benefits of the thin line of green. Opportunity for motion on foot or bicycle (or perhaps soon on revived trolley cars) is provided; the edge of trees or grass extends as a continuing natural presence through the urban context. Such linear spaces are often, besides, more easily protected and made safe than acreage solidly massed. The interior of large parks like Franklin in Boston or Crotona in the Bronx may become a no man's land while the bordering neighborhood extends its surveillance over the more modest, stretched-out green space.[2]

Mixed Use—Some Examples

Once urban parks are viewed in this way—shaped from odd pieces of land and subject to shared use—the opportunities for new recreational resources are various. Even highways, which we have judged so often in these pages to be the enemy of recreational facilities, can play a useful role. Acquisition of extra land during freeway construction, with the surplus then sold to the city for cost, can be an important source of new parkland; and where noise is not too much of an impediment, play and traffic can co-exist in the same right of way. Needless to say, high standards of landscape design, with careful grading and ample planting, are necessary for the achievement of such a result.

Examples follow of projects, some of them highly innovative, now under way or being actively considered in various communities.[3]

WATTS, greatly in need of recreational opportunities and notoriously deficient in parks, can take advantage of power-line rights of way to provide for skating rinks, football fields and other active-sports facilities as well as for gardening plots.

SANTA FE faces persistent pressure to open the Santa Fe Canyon for hiking and pedestrian access to the nearby mountains. This pressure should prevail against the overcautious policy which has kept the reservoir lands off bounds even to limited and carefully controlled use.

COHOES, New York, has been able to develop a linear park of great charm along the bed of the old Erie Canal. The little town on the Hudson plans for another park threading its way along a second canal bed through a picturesque industrial landscape.

SAN FRANCISCO has seen a park built in the East Bay area, in conjunction with BART, the new rapid transit system. Made possible by one of HUD's first Urban Beautification Demonstration Grants, the area selected was a 2.7-mile elevated portion of the right of way. A landscaped linear parkway containing bicycle and pedestrian paths, play spaces and sitting areas, proved so successful that it has been extended beyond the limits of the demonstration area.

NEW ORLEANS finds one of its famous trolley lines running out to the Garden District down the middle of a broad greenway accommodating benches and bicyclists. Grass obscures the tracks and the trolleys pass through unobtrusively.

LOS ANGELES in the north Hollywood area confronts the dry, littered bed of the Los Angeles River channel—120 feet wide with twenty-foot banks. Studies are being made for possible sewage treatment plants to be located nearby which would allow clean water to be discharged into the channel, creating a recreational water resource.

LOS ANGELES is also looking into possible recreational use of spreading grounds—earth basins as large as a hundred acres into which storm water is diverted from flood control channels. Use of deflatable dams could make these available in summer for swimming, small boats and flishing. Additional water may be supplied by locating a water reclamation plant in the vicinity of the spreading grounds.

Where there is multiple use, there is also capital funding from multiple sources. There may even be funds for maintenance drawn from other than park budgets. Putting together a project calling for support from more than one city agency, and often including state and federal sources, is a complex, time-consuming task. Yet there may be no escape. American cities are finding that the day of easy bond issues is over. Even citizen groups most loyal to the park cause hesitate when parks must be put above such other priorities as police and hospitals, or when a new tax must be levied. The limits of park development in the future may well be measured by the ingenuity with which recreation enthusiasts appeal to allied interests and to means of funding outside the orthodox park budgets.

The examples above illustrate another important aspect of the newer parks: they not only take advantage of existing city facilities but play a role in making these facilities visible and comprehensible. That citizens be aware of the power lines which feed their everyday needs, that they walk over lands set apart to keep the river under control and see the machinery constructed to tame it, should be an objective of rational city planning. Appreciation of these things should be in itself a kind of recreation.

The walker in the city may feel nudged and bothered by some of these industrial or engineering works, intruding on what in older parks was supposed to be a scene of unspoiled nature. But he will gain a better understanding of his total environment. Seattle is inspired by a sound goal when in one of its new parks an obsolete gasworks, instead of being demolished or masked by trees, is emphasized as a piece of vast sculpture on the landscape. Similarly, in New York a former asphalt plant and an abandoned electric powerhouse are conceived as embellishments rather than as visual distractions within their proposed parks. The celebration of such works of man, no less than the works of nature, should be an element of imaginative park planning.

National Urban Parks

Yet nature makes its claims and is still faithfully served by its devotees. Among novel developments in recent years has been entrance of the National Park Service into two major cities, with plans for park developments on a massive scale. In the past, for understandable reasons, the National Park Service was dominated by wilderness concepts. Its top management and its major constituency saw the city as the enemy, with national parks existing to assure that some lands remained unspoiled. In recent years the Department of the Interior, which is responsible for the Park Service, has begun to recognize urban needs, and through its Bureau of Outdoor Recreation and its Land and Water Conservation Fund has played a significant role in improving urban open spaces. The direct involvement of the National Park Service indicated a radical change in view. It was initiated by leaders convinced of the urgency of bringing recreation close to the inner cities.

In the 1960s, under secretaries of the interior Stewart Udall and Walter Hickel, and under mayors John V. Lindsay and Joseph Alioto of New York and San Francisco respectively, two immense national parks were conceived, both essentially urban in location and use. The first of these, known as Gateway National Recreation Area, acquired by transfer from New York City and from the state of New Jersey important but noncontiguous lands which it is amalgamating into one system. As the parts of this system become linked by water transportation, as major land areas are made accessible by public transport and suitable development proceeds, a national park of 26,000 acres will emerge on New York City's doorstep. Besides its obvious recreational possibilities, from bird watching in Jamaica wetlands to surfing on the Rockaway beaches, the national park preserves portions of the scenery through which millions of immigrants first came to these shores.

On the West Coast the Golden Gate National Recreation Area, taking in all of the San Francisco ocean shore and parts of Marin County, is a similar effort of the federal Park Service to preserve a particularly beautiful shoreline in close proximity to a large metropolitan center. San Francisco Bay was missed by Drake on his journey around the world and lay for another two hundred years unglimpsed by any European. Now the entrance-way will be preserved for future generations in something like its natural state.

In their scope, in the co-operative efforts required to establish them, and in their preservation of natural features, these two parks are illustrative of the newer park concepts being applied in American cities.

Mountains in the City

Similar concepts are visible in the efforts of several cities to make recreational use of mountains and mountain ranges within their borders. Such wild lands were thought until recently to be immune to residential development and were largely ignored by recreationists. Today it is recognized that such development will proceed unless steps are taken to forestall actions bound to deface the natural environment. It is seen, too, how advantageously these areas can be put to use for limited active recreational purposes.

The kind of mountain we speak of may be found in Portland, Oregon, within a ten-minute drive of downtown. This six-thousand-acre area has been set aside as a park—Forest Park—though once it was open to whole-sale development. In 1904 the Portland Fair was drawing visitors to the city in large numbers and creating a land boom. Would-be settlers were taken by boat down the Willamette River and sold lots on sight by unscrupulous agents. Purchasers later discovered how unsuitable these lots were for building. The lands reverted to public ownership except for the houses a few hardy souls had constructed on the wild slopes. Today the problem is not that of incipient development but of finding a sensible recreational use.

Close to downtown though it is, the mountain of Forest Park stands remote from the city's life. It is crossed by a single dirt road, the Leif Ericson Drive, which is subject to mud slides in wet weather and on occasion must be closed. Within the park wildlife of various forms thrives, including (it is reported) bears. Many Portlanders seem unaware of the park's existence, and when we found our way up to the summit of the mountain in 1974, we saw no sign of life other than some youths evidently playing hooky from school. One of them replied to our questions: "We know this place, but we don't know what sort of place it is."

Given the woods and mountains accessible to Portlanders in the nearby area, it is perhaps as well that this in-city mountain should remain with its recreational possibilities at least temporarily unexploited. But in other cases the two-pronged problem of residential and recreational development must be faced in the immediate present. Two examples may be looked at, one in California and one in Arizona.

The Santa Monica and the Santa Susana mountains rim the north of Los Angeles's vast urban expanse, a natural resource still virtually untapped. The pressures of urbanization lap at their base, and will soon cause housing to climb the steep slopes. Planning for the future of these mountains is absolutely essential, as has been stressed in the discussion of Los Angeles's topography.

An equally critical case of an in-city mountain is presented by the chain running northwest along the outskirts of Phoenix, Arizona. These mountains rise from the desert to a height of 2,700 feet, naked, rugged and craggy, fissured by canyons and valleys running north and south from the main spine. They were long considered outside the town and impervious to settlement. But Phoenix expanded enormously after World War II and repeated annexations of contiguous land took place. When the city came to grips with the problems and opportunities posed by the mountains, it was found that instead of being publicly owned, as was widely assumed, most of the twenty-three square miles of the mountain area was in private possession.

The preservation of these mountains, and their development for limited uses by the public, has provided a particular challenge to the population that chose to live in Phoneix and its surroundings. A few years ago the refugees from more crowded urban conditions were surrounded by citrus groves and well-kept farms, with the mountains providing an unspoiled natural background. Beyond the irrigated areas stretched the untrammeled desert. All this seemed (as indeed it was) God-given. Few of the Phoenicians were ready even to think about such measures as might be necessary to save this heritage from being man-destroyed. Yet today the farms and groves have retreated before the ever-pressing march of development; the air is no longer pure; the desert is often littered.

The Phoenix Mountains offer a highly visible and dramatic target for preservation. A 1966 open space plan prepared co-operatively by Phoenix's Parks Department and Planning Department established the concept of a general open space preserve, lightly developed for recreation and crossed by a scenic drive. It waited for later studies to go beyond mere graphic presentations, dealing with the difficult problems of setting precise boundaries,

of acquiring control over lands not owned by the city and of providing up-
dated ordinances to control development.

The current open space plan,[4] on the basis of which 70 percent of the
designated lands have been acquired for the public, begins with the assumption that the Phoenix Mountains should form one open space system.
It examines piece by piece the areas within this system, determining the
best use to be made of each.

The plan is interesting because it arrives at definition of boundaries by
criteria largely based upon the steepness of slopes within this mountainous
area. Thus all land with a 40 percent natural slope gradient is given to unobstructed open space, even though some of this has been platted for
development. Undeveloped land of more than 20 percent natural slope
gradient is made part of the open space system *except* for areas that because
of topography or location are held suited for limited development. Finally,
some lands of more level nature are judged as necessary and desirable for
open space, because of their importance to flood control or public recreation,
or because of their role in the preservation of natural, scenic and historic
qualities.

The open space system thus defined turns out to be approximately 9,700
acres in extent—of which 3,000 acres are still in private hands, waiting to
be acquired by fee purchase, easement dedication, gift or other means.
What is to be done with this vast in-city area? A scenic highway is seen
running along the length of the mountain range—but a highway specifically
designed for leisure driving, with commercial traffic excluded and with
width maintained at two lanes. Frequent overlooks would allow for stops
along the way. Recreational development would be barred from the steeper
slopes, but farther down the mountains provisions are made in the plan
for hiking and equestrian trails, picnic grounds (mostly quite small units
for individual families) along with provisions for archery, a nature
study center, and a few other facilities that will draw limited crowds and
provide minimum disturbance to the landscape.

This is open space on a grand scale—park-making of a modern kind.
The question is whether the values of open space here (as in similar
situations) can prevail against contrary pressures. The higher the lands
in these mountains, the more attractive they are to real estate developers.
The damage to ecological processes caused by change in land use is not
immediately discernible, and even the visual blight advances slowly. Not surprisingly, the course of perservation has not been a smooth one and has
received a serious setback.

16. The Phoenix Mountains seen from a downtown park and (17) within the urban complex.

18. The Santa Monica Mountains of Los Angeles, threatened by urban encroachments.

Opportunities for open space provided by strong natural features.

19. The bayou at Houston, a green approach to the central city.

20. The flood plain of the Trinity River in Dallas, surprisingly close to downtown.

Although two-thirds of the lands proposed for acquisition by the city had come under public ownership by 1975, these were not contiguous; they depended for their importance to the open space system upon completion of the program. A bond issue of that spring would have provided the necessary funds. Unfortunately, it was defeated, the influential *Arizona Republic* opposing it on the grounds that, while obviously desirable, "the costs at this time pose the inevitable question of whether they cannot be delayed." Yet delay is the one thing that in such a case cannot be justified. It is a signal to private interests to hasten development and to consolidate their hold on the land.

River System in Fort Worth

Comparable to in-city mountains in land area as in their dramatic possibilities for recreational development are the flood basins of river systems that are to be found in several major cities. Lacking in immediate appeal, they present a special challenge. In the raw state to which the Corps of Engineers reduces them, the flood basins are likely to be an indeterminate swath lying across the built-up urban fabric. Often reduced to concrete channels, they are barred by the inevitable chain-link fence from public access.

In somewhat different circumstances, the flood plain has been inadvisedly built upon. Low-grade commercial structures and marginal housing risk sporadic inundation; while massive levees and pumping stations are constructed in an attempt to protect investments that should not have been made in the first place. Federally subsidized flood insurance adds to the social costs of misusing the land.

Recently the short-sightedness of these practices has begun to be acknowledged. In planning for Woodlands, the new town north of Houston, use of concrete channels and storm sewers was found to be considerably more expensive than preservation of a natural system of drainage[5]—$18.2 million as compared with $4.2 million, with the added dividend of an attractive open space system. In one case in Texas it was found cheaper to relocate into Houston suburbs 1,150 households rather than call upon elaborate engineering to protect them in their existing location. With the basin thus freed of construction (which a wiser land-use policy would have prohibited initially), the area will be given over to a bird refuge and passive recreation.

Neither a fresh start nor relocation being possible in most cases, open space planners must begin with conditions as they exist—a mixture of favorable and unfavorable elements requiring long-range policies. Two excellent examples of such an approach are to be found within the cities of Fort Worth and Dallas, through each of which—though in a markedly different form—the Trinity River passes.

In Fort Worth the river wanders for eight miles through the city, channeled and leveed by the Army Corps of Engineers, with almost all its adjacent lands controlled and maintained by the Tarrant County Water District. The levees are as much as a hundred feet apart and the land between is designed to be inundated to within four feet of their top. Little in the way of change or permanent construction can be permitted within the confines of this existing flood control system. This might have seemed an unpromising situation and one that scarcely lent itself to the concern of the most dedicated open space enthusiasts.

Yet to a group of Fort Worth's leading citizens the Trinity River has seemed a major challenge. In 1970 Lawrence Halprin undertook a study of the river section by section.[6] He approached his task modestly, accepting the conditions imposed by the natural conditions and working in close association with the Corps of Engineers. The plan's basic concept is treatment of the eight-mile flood plain as a continuous corridor, with pedestrian, equestrian and bicycle trails running its full distance, linking points of interest and areas designed for particular activities. Access is provided along the way, despite the many industrial and other specialized uses which now tend to cut off the public.

In parts this river is, it must be admitted, quite characterless and uninviting, crossed by numerous railroad bridges, bordered by industries and freeways with their massive interchanges barring access to the neighboring communities. Even in such areas, principally east of the business district, Halprin doggedly continues his pedestrian trails and finds compensation for the poor surroundings in the fine view of Fort Worth's skyline. Where the river leaves the city to the east he proposes a gateway park, beckoning those who come in from the airport, with a restaurant spanning the turnpike and a stable for those who, wishing to abandon their cars, are ready to proceed on horseback down his greenway.

The Same—Dallas

When the Trinity River comes to Dallas, thirty miles to the east, an even greater opportunity presents itself.[7] The map of Dallas on page 66 indicates the scale and the location of the flood basin—a large circle ex-

tending around two sides of the central city. The basin has long been subject to study and discussion, and since 1908 planners have seized upon it as
the greatest open space resource offered by the city. In that year a devastating flood inundated a large portion of the downtown area; George
Kessler, the famous Kansas City park-builder, a native of Dallas, was
invited to prepare a master plan. Elements of Kessler's work guided the
city through a series of subsequent park plans, all of which pressed for
land acquisition in the flood plains and continued to see the Trinity River
as the spine of an open space system.

Development of the river with its tributaries and drainageways offers
Dallas today the chance for a greenbelt more spacious than in any comparable city and a park system unsurpassed in its many uses and its close
proximity to the central core. To achieve this, there must be a determined
program of acquisition and—no less important—for development of the
river in ways that are ecologically sound. The cause of recreation will derive
major benefits, but recreation in the end will be a partner along with the
other legitimate interests and needs.

The land itself varies dramatically along the river's route. North of the
city is a natural wooded valley. Here flood control programs have already
created a series of parks and multi-use reservoirs. As the river passes west
of the city a different situation prevails. The channel lies within concrete;
all large trees have been cleared. Downtown Dallas is separated from the
floodway by a half mile of railroad tracks, freeways, major thoroughfares
and industrial uses which make pedestrian access to the levee seemingly
impossible.

A widened navigation channel and a proposed freeway pose further
problems as the river passes downstream from the central business district.
Here, too, is the sewage treatment plant as well as the lock operations for
the heavy boat and barge operations.

Even such conditions do not discourage today's planners. A pedestrian
route from downtown to the levee is contemplated as an ultimate necessity.
The widened transportation rights of way leave strips of 900 and 1,200 feet,
which are viewed not as leftover space, but as opportunities for linear parks
devoted to a variety of recreational activities. The busy scenes connected
with the barge traffic, rather than being screened from the park user, are
to be displayed for his benefit from special viewing points. In addition, a
pool along the navigation channel is proposed for the Town Lake residential
development.

Through many less difficult areas parks provide a natural land use. A fifty-mile trail system is entirely feasible, bringing the city walker through a wide variety of scenes, past places of commerce, through locks and levees, around a man-made lake, and out into areas where the parks already own a large domain.

The key to such a development is a combination of land uses. The drainageways of the Trinity system can be single-purpose ditches, or they can be developed as multipurpose linear open spaces to which public and private projects relate. It is a striking goal, bold enough to muster the energies of a great city.

Saving the Bayous

Problems and opportunities similar to those of the Trinity River occur in connection with the Texas bayous. But the bayous are interesting in themselves, and they so vitally affect the open spaces of Houston that they will be considered separately.

The bayous are the wild rivers of Texas, flowing from west to east and cutting channels through the level land. One of these, known as Buffalo Bayou, makes a direct advance toward Houston's business district and cuts through the central core. (The map on page 65 indicates its general flow.) Coming from Memorial Park and into the heart of the city, the bayou is today a tree-lined strip of green with its own hiking trail and with several small parks along its course. Yet in the name of flood control this stretch of natural woodland and free-flowing water was threatened with destruction by bulldozers. The portion of the bayou that once ran through Herman Park has in fact been buried under concrete.

The paving of the bayous began following a severe flood in the 1930s when the Army Corps of Engineers was summoned to come up with a flood control plan. Their recommendation was to "rectify" the bayous and to build two holding dams above Buffalo Bayou. Rectification is a process that involves straightening the bayou as much as possible, cutting down all the trees and ground cover in an area approximately three hundred feet wide and paving a seventy-five- to one-hundred-foot center section. A tree-lined stream thus becomes a concrete ditch.

In the case of the Buffalo Bayou, the holding dams were built and the work of rectification was begun. It progressed unimpeded until a small group of citizens formed the Buffalo Bayou Preservation Association. Headed by Mrs. J. W. Hershey, the group went about educating themselves as well as city and county officials in the ecological implications of various methods of flood control.

To protect the bayous, the preservation group pleaded for the so-called gabion method as an alternative to rectification. Under this procedure the bayou area is lined with gabions, rectangular baskets of wire filled with stone and arranged so as to form retaining walls. The trees remain and the running stream is preserved.

"It is good to prevent floods; it is good to make parks for people. It is better if a single resource can be made to serve both purposes." This was the argument of the Buffalo Bayou Preservation Association. Flood plain management was to be used to preserve areas of unique ecological value and recreational opportunity.

The combination of persistence, passion and hard facts prevailed. According to A. Heaton Underhill of the Bureau of Outdoor Recreation,[8] Mrs. Hershey was directly responsible for changing the Corps of Engineers' plans for rectifying Buffalo Bayou and encouraging the city of Houston to develop a 26,000-acre park in the Addicks-Barker Reservoir area. The success of her efforts gave heart to other struggles and led in particular to the preservation of Armand's Bayou, one of the few remaining in its almost primitive state.

Armand's Bayou begins in the city of Pasadena, Texas, and meanders unfettered seventeen miles southward to Clear Lake, adjacent to Galveston Bay. The area is a mixture of natural habitats, making it a unique watershed within an urban community, and presenting an opportunity to preserve a complete working ecological system. Again there was a leader to serve as catalyst. What Terry Hershey was to Buffalo Bayou, Hana Ginzbarg was to Armand's Bayou. It was she who sounded the alarm, mobilized public opinion and persuaded public officials.

This bayou had seemed safe as it wound its way unchanneled; the surrounding area had not been touched. But there was reason to believe that the oil company that owned the land was about to begin developing it for housing and commercial purposes. The sides were drawn, with the preservation committee determined that the city and county acquire the land as the only alternative to untrammeled development. Their successful campaign is summed up by Mr. Underhill: "The Armand Bayou project alone is a monument to citizen endeavor. Mrs. Hershey and Mrs. Hana Ginzbarg of Houston have worked so effectively that they have managed to raise more than a half-million dollars. Their efforts have caused one of the nation's largest industries, Humble Oil and Refining Company, to change its plans for the Armand Bayou area drastically." Their efforts also induced the Bureau of Outdoor Recreation to make a crucial grant of funds.

These sketches of particular cases illustrate the diversity of conditions in which modern parks and recreation areas are being created. They suggest the importance of public participation, the need for confronting the bureaucracies involved with the possibility of more methods, and the importance of timely action. Neither the "fish and game" approach of the older conservationists, nor the tennis and ballfield fixation of the newer recreationists, is adequate for dealing with a mountain or a flood basin—or with related opportunities that present themselves within today's urban context.

10 Open Space
of Megalopolis

THE EXPANDING SCALE OF OPEN SPACE NEEDS was fully recognized by the end of the last century, and became a frequent theme of park planners. "The outer park system of yesterday is the boundary park system of today," the Minneapolis report of 1917 says, for example; "*it will be the interior park system of tomorrow.*" Open space resources for the growing cities were looked for far afield, and as early as the 1890s new governmental agencies were shaped to cope with a domain that exceeded the bounds of cities and of individual counties.

The Regional Scale

This study has been dealing with the city in its traditional aspect—a center of population, its encompassing terrain relatively uncrowded and still in a more or less natural state. For such cities the open spaces and parks beyond their borders are clearly important, providing as they do a kind of recreational resource not available within the city. But for the new and expanded metropolis such open spaces play a different role. Being no longer remote but part of the city itself, they become subject to novel pressures and invite different uses.

The development of American cities has repeatedly shown the enlargement of scale that changes outer space to inner space. Parks originally located on a city's outskirts and then absorbed within a highly built up area can be reduced in their social and even visual effect to something like a city square. Thus New York's Central Park, once in an undeveloped section of the city, plays a role today not altogether dissimilar from that played earlier by such a confined area as Madison Square. The wide green-belt of the Bronx parks, formerly thought of as existing in semirural regions, has been domesticated and brought within the intense life of the urban mass. Meanwhile in the upper expanses of the Hudson or the farther reaches of Long Island are sought the natural spaces that men need upon their horizons. These, too, will soon become surrounded by the endless accretions and extensions of humanity.

The meeting of open space needs in the future city obviously cannot be left to localities. Towns and cities must continue to provide spaces for play and relaxation for their citizens, but other activities of growing popularity —hiking, picnicking, camping and boating—call for a wider framework and a more extensive grant of power. Large-scale open space, with its protection of natural features and its provision of recreational opportunities for a vast population, must be regional in scope and must be planned before development has congealed. Planning for the Boston region affects no less than one hundred cities and towns and extends outward to the circumference defined by such cities as Lawrence and Lowell. The famous New York Regional Plan includes within its purview parts of three states; the plan for the Cincinnati region takes in part of Kentucky and Indiana as well as Ohio.

A pioneer in the formulation of a broad regional plan and of a governmental structure capable of implementing it was Charles Eliot, whom we have met as Olmsted's apprentice and then his partner. In cooperation with publicist Sylvester Baxter, Eliot in his twenties set out on a campaign to convince Bostonians of the need to preserve large areas of natural beauty within their region.[1] He first sought to use private funds to secure for the public major areas of natural beauty or historic importance. Later he worked for a state commission on the establishment of a regional park system.

In the Metropolitan Sewerage Commission, established after growing pollution of streams and water sources had proved that the problem was beyond being solved by individual localities, Eliot found the model for a park organization with broad regional authority. Scenery, like sewerage, depended on more than local action. A town on one side of a river could hardly be expected to keep the riverbank open to the public if a town on the other side gave over the land to low-grade uses. Both, moreover, would lack the kind of funding available to a metropolitan authority.

In 1893 state legislative action established a Metropolitan Park Commis-

sion for the Boston area. Within a year the commission acquired properties
totaling seven thousand acres, including mountains, thirty miles of riverbanks and ten miles of ocean shoreline. Embracing more than a hundred
governmental units of cities and towns, it was suggestive of a form of
metropolitan government organized on a wholly new scale.

The work of Eliot and Baxter continues in Massachusetts under the Metropolitan District Commission, which combines the sewerage and water boards
with the Metropolitan Park Commission. Today the joint agency serves a
total population of 2.5 million and embraces an area of nearly six hundred
square miles. Within the MDC the Division of Parks and Recreation operates
a park system according to policies laid down in the 1890s, policies that
are still, according to a 1975 report, "entirely appropriate for the metropolitan area." In addition to managing the parks, the MDC has cosponsored
extensive long-range regional plans, which will be discussed later in this
chapter.

Cleveland's Emerald Necklace

By the 1890s, Minneapolis and Kansas City had established systems of
parks at the outer limits of the existing cities. Early in the twentieth
century Cleveland cast a wider ring, taking in an entire county. Its Emerald
Necklace is in concept an important bridge between the older park system
and the new metropolitan planning.[2] The chain is unusually complete in
its circumnavigation of the city, is well maintained, and is still subject to
growth and expansion.

Cleveland was fortunate in being encircled by a series of natural valleys
and ravines lending themselves to park development. These were taken over
by top designers and improved within a well-conceived political and administrative structure. Today Cleveland's outer park system is looked upon
as a major source of pride by the citizens. In the autumn of 1974, when
bond issues for parks were seldom being approved, a successful campaign
for $35 million provided for additions to the system as well as funds for
upkeep.

Local myth has it that General William T. Sherman, fresh from the
destructive victories of the Civil War, announced upon a visit to Cleveland
that the scenery of the Rocky River valley was equal to that of any of the
great landscapes of the world. This aroused the interest of the citizens in
preserving the valley, along with the valleys of Euclid Creek, Chagrin

River and Tinker's Creek. In 1911 a statute of the Ohio General Assembly established a county board of four members empowered to accept as gifts any land donated within designated areas, and in 1915 county appropriations were permitted.

Immediately the process of design was begun. Frederick Law Olmsted, Jr., worked with W. A. Stinchcomb of Cleveland upon plans that were to be largely naturalistic, intended to bring within the new park system areas stretching from ridge to ridge of the numerous ravines and gorges, and also to place restrictions upon land use on abutting and contiguous areas.

The semicircle of green was launched almost entirely with donations of land. This was in the heyday of enlightened park interest. It was often easy to persuade landowners that they would not be the worse off having donated lands inaccessible to farming and frequently subject to floods.

Over the years the Emerald Necklace has grown to eighteen thousand acres and to a length of eighty-five miles. During much of this time—from the beginning to his resignation in 1957—William Stinchcomb was a guiding spirit, one of the park men, disciples of Olmsted, who along with Kessler, Cleveland and McClaren was responsible for enduring monuments of green. A Clevelander, born in 1878, Stinchcomb had campaigned for the Emerald Necklace as early as 1905. Under the reform mayor Tom L. Johnson, he was given his first public opportunity. His legacy was to be an almost continuous route of parks and parkways following the outer limits of the city.

The Emerald Necklace today retains much of its original quality of wilderness. Later roads have crossed it, but no expressway pre-empts or parallels it. The combination of automobile roads with recreation space presents here as elsewhere inevitable problems, with the increasing speed and pollution of the cars tending to vitiate the park atmosphere. Yet at least in the areas seen at first hand, the roads have been kept narrow and the temptation to turn them into speedways has been resisted.

Suggestions are regularly made to banish cars altogether. Certainly there are some areas that should be restricted to bicyclists, with carefully designed parking areas provided for those who come by car. Constant efforts at encroachment have thus far been successfully resisted by the Park District. The fact that the whole is maintained by proceeds from a special tax ensures a level of upkeep that the ordinary city park cannot reach.

Meanwhile in a far wider ring, encompassing counties out to the edge of two states, plans are being considered for a greenbelt of linked natural features, incorporating new national parks, which will do for the city of tomorrow what the Emerald Necklace has achieved for today's metropolis.

Forests of Megalopolis

The large-scale open spaces of the Ohio planners may be seen as oases upon the outer rim of the cities. Observers relate them to the historic city with its population center, describing them in terms of their distance from the core. Yet with a different perspective such open spaces become central —no longer on the periphery of the old city, but in the middle of a new one: a megalopolis comprising a vast configuration of settlements broken by greenbelts and bordering upon inland seas of nature.

In a classic study Jean Gottmann designated as Megalopolis the north-eastern seaboard of the United States. An area running from Portland, Maine, to Richmond, Virginia, revealed to him a continuous pattern of settlement comprising a population of more than 33 million people. Within this area were nodes of special activity—as intense as was to be found any-where in the world. There were also lands not built upon, and much open space running through the inhabited land.

In Gottmann's chapter on the woodlands many were surprised to learn that there were forests within this emerging supercity of the future. Even more surprising was the fact that this heavily built up and highly urbanized region of the United States possessed more forest land in 1960 than it had a generation before—and that indeed it suffered from a surfeit of deer and wildlife. The cause of this was the lag between an old and a new economy. Farming was declining and farmers allowed natural growth to take over while waiting for real estate values to increase. (They were at the same time benefiting from certain secondary sources of income, including govern-ment payments.)

The abundance of woodlands, Gottmann wrote, "results from the im-balance between expanding urbanization and shrinking agricultural lands. More formerly tilled farm land acreage is being abandoned and is reverting to wooded growth than is being consumed by urban and related social uses."[3] This had been going on for some time and by the late 1950s, excluding parks and gardens, woodlands made up 48 percent of the land area of Megalopolis.

This overall figure has not changed during the period of the 1970s, even though new expressways were then making it possible for settlement to ex-pand in a homogeneous pattern across the countryside. A study twenty years later of the same counties as had figured in Gottmann's original work showed in fact a slight increase in forest land, from 48 to 49 percent.[4]

The effect of this lag in land use is to suggest a sort of beneficent harmony between various forces at work within the metropolitan region. At the very least it induces an unjustified complacency. In fact, the open spaces of the outer city are being rapidly consumed—visibly where changes in use take place on pre-existing farmlands, and invisibly where land valuations and tax assessments become so high as to render the land usable only for development. A piece of land lying idle and producing a small new forest is actually part of the developed area, taken out of its wild state by economic forces if not yet by the bulldozer. Only a serious food shortage—conceivable now if it was not in the 1960s—could cause the more usable forest land to be put back into agricultural production.

Gottmann is a geographer, describing facts as they exist within a particular urbanized region. His book is not basically concerned with prescriptions for action or forecasts of future trends. As urbanists see it, however, the existence of megalopolis requires strong action programs if adequate open space is to be preserved. Modern cities, wherever they spread and coalesce, need to preserve natural areas, sensitive portions of the landscape, points of historic interest or of special ecological concern. Energy shortages or a declining birth rate may slow the expected expansion of cities, but the long-range trend is toward an ever greater consumption of land for housing, for commercial and industrial uses, for utilities and transportation.

Apart from the need for recreation, active and passive, there exist within every geographic area places *not to build.*[5] The sites of most early urban parks were chosen simply because land was not immediately attractive for construction—it was too steep, or too boggy, or too subject to flooding. By a fortunate coincidence many of these sites were also of prime natural beauty. Modern large-scale planners change the emphasis. They do not restrict themselves to taking over available lands, but make a basic decision as to what areas are to remain immune from development. They may be immune because they perform certain vital ecological functions or because they possess inherent and irreplaceable aesthetic values. A change from the existing natural land use may be totally barred, or the lands may be marked for restricted development and limited forms of recreation. In either case the message is to tread lightly in these areas. They are to be acquired for public use where possible, or restricted under easements, zoning or other forms of control.

In modern conditions, where technology permits construction even in the most seemingly adverse situation, such a basic "hands off" policy is a necessity. An awareness of places not to build is the beginning of any open space system scaled to megalopolitan needs.

Toward New Systems

For open space planning at the megalopolitan scale we may take as an example what is being done in the Southeast Michigan region.[6] Here can be seen the outline of an open space system comparable to that which nineteenth-century planners accomplished for the bounded and more sharply defined cities of their time. Focused on Detroit, the Southeast Michigan area takes in a wide grouping of towns and lesser cities embracing seven counties and working together under a council of governments. The objective of this plan is stated to be effective restrictions on development for urban purposes of natural areas and ecological preserves; also strict regulation of access and use in such fragile resource areas as flood plains, wetlands and woodlands. Resources for active recreation are sought. From the whole a wide park system is to be shaped, accessible to all the people of the region.

Agricultural lands are a characteristic resource of this area. Their erosion and uncontrolled fragmentation are a primary open space concern, for without planning the disappearance of farmlands from this area of Michigan is foreseen by 1990. Use of zoning, tax incentives and contractual agreements are among the ways recommended to preserve agricultural resources.

The scale of the plan is indicated by the following open space goals:

- 25,000 acres of public recreation facilities within an hour's driving time of all heavily populated points, including Detroit.
- Twenty miles of Great Lakes shoreline under public administration. (Eight miles are now publicly administered.)
- 10,000 protected acres of fragile natural areas, in addition to the 35,000 acres protected at present.

In addition, the planners envisage the perpetuation of 300,000 acres of farmland; 300,000 acres of flood plains and drainageways; and 300 miles of slow-speed parkway.

What is significant here is the planning process, not the achievement of a fully functioning and neatly defined open space system. It would be gratifying if we could point to a finished series of parks; but given the nature of the problem, this is not possible in Michigan, nor is it possible in any other part of the country. The open space system is an ongoing development, relying for its achievement on the activities of many governmental bodies and upon the capacity to seize opportunities of various kinds. Nevertheless, the Michigan plans are based upon an already existing network of publicly owned or regulated lands, as the acquisition program is based upon a wide range of available tools, legal and governmental.

The authority to act, in Michigan as elsewhere, exists more often than the actual funding, and the price of the designated land rises at a disconcerting rate. But at least the need of expanded recreational resources is plain, and the vision is as firmly written into the twentieth-century mind as were the visions of adequate municipal parks in the thinking of the late nineteenth century.

Open Space vs. Sprawl

Not recreation alone—nor even recreation primarily—is in the minds of a school of contemporary planners which sees new open space systems as a means of shaping the form of the modern city. The need for compactness, the danger of sprawl, take the place of such earlier open space objectives as preserving natural beauty or providing mass recreation.

In virtually every open space plan obeisance is made to this conception of controlling urban growth; in some it becomes clearly paramount. Thus the Ohio, Kentucky and Indiana Report speaks of a "skeletal framework" of vegetation, green space and water areas throughout the area—"a vehicle for guiding the physical development of the OKI region."[7] The plan for the greater Madison region (Dane County, Wisconsin) makes it a policy "to recognize open space, whether for active or non-recreational purposes, as a major device . . . for directing urban growth."[8]

In accepting this responsibility the open space planners are repeating on a more ample canvas what the early park-builders sought to accomplish. They, also, saw as part of their responsibility the shaping of the city. They knew they were establishing edges to communities, barring construction in unsuitable places, and forming the future pattern of density. At the middle scale, the in-city open space of the Phoenix Mountain chain has been recognized as channelizing the otherwise pervasive flow of settlement. However, the audacity of planners within a megalopolitan region exceeds by far these earlier efforts. It does nothing less than pit itself against almost overpowering developmental forces.

Urgent as it is to curtail sprawl, serious questions must be raised about the efficacy of open space planning in achieving this result. Whether the pattern of open space takes the form of a greenbelt, wedges or linear corridors, the plan is apt to look better on a map than it does in actual achievements. Configurations that appear beguiling in their logic run up against forces that open space cannot by itself resist. As has already been indicated, the forest lands that can be nudged into shape to serve the needs of the planners are often less an indication of open space permanently preserved or easily acquired for public purposes than they are evidences of the land's availability to developers. Farmlands, similarly, are often being kept in production as a means of reducing tax burdens for a limited period. Meanwhile the forces of development bide their time, holding back or advancing according to the economic conditions of the moment.

Open space tied to important recreational or conservation areas has a chance of surviving—far less, open space per se, whose value to the public is not self-evident. However much such space may serve the planners' objective of controlling regional growth, its preservation has little popular appeal. Too often, as a matter of fact, it is simply not very inviting as a recreational source and, to the passer-by, conforms ill to standards of natural beauty. If the designation of open space upon a regional map is actively reinforced by other policies—by the laying out of transportation routes and sewer lines, for example, or by the promotion of housing—the desired configuration may have a chance of emerging into reality. Without such reinforcement, the best-laid open space plans gather dust on the shelves.

Two ambitious schemes for restraining sprawl and giving form to the city have come up against precisely these difficulties. Both Washington and Boston have a long tradition of metropolitan planning; both of them have made ambitious plans for the year 2000—and both have seen precious green acres so encroached upon as to reduce their imposing designs to a hodgepodge.

The Washington Year 2000 plan was widely hailed in the early 1960s. Basically, this conceived a pattern of settlement along corridors radiating from the central city, each corridor to be served by rapid transit and a freeway. Between these corridors would be large wedges of open space—buffers against the advance of development. By the 1970s this strict configuration had been abandoned. (Officially, it had been "refined.")[9] The population figures for the area had vastly exceeded the original projections; the price of land had risen on an acreage by more than 25 percent per year and in some localities by considerably more. When the Washington rapid transit system was laid out it largely ignored the corridor concept, and by then the period of freeway building had come up against the twofold obstacle of popular opposition and funding difficulties.

The revised plan of 1971 asserted that the "wedge must no longer be thought of as an open space responsibility." Instead the areas adjacent to those of intensive development could support many development objectives and be the joint responsibility of many policy-making bodies.

The Greater Boston Plan of 1969 was equally explicit in determining patterns of settlement defined and reinforced by open space.[10] The planners looked at four possibilities: the web, the wedge, the greenbelt and the satellite structure. Each was seen to have its practical as well as conceptual difficulties. The web, presupposing settled nodes each outlined by green space, would lead to homogeneity. The wedge called for major green spaces of indeterminate use. These and the two other concepts—the greenbelts and the satellites—suffered mostly, however, from the increasingly evident fact that desired open spaces had already been pre-empted by developmental sprawl.

Sensibly enough, the Boston planners, instead of opting for any single solution, adopted in 1969 a combination of them all. A system of wedges and greenbelts would define major metropolitan forms, while web patterns would define space at the scale of the locality. The wedges would represent less actual open space than areas of relatively low development stretching outward along Boston's well-established system of radial routes.

Even this comparatively relaxed approach was to prove inadequate to controlling events. In the 1975 revision[11] the classic concepts and forms were given no more than lip service, while the emphasis shifted to the charting and acquisition of natural sites within the organization's 101 local authorities. It could be said that a portion of the acquisitions had been determined by the overall considerations of the earlier plan; it could also be hoped that the acquisition made for the sake of preserving natural scenery, historic sites and ecological features would in the end conform, at least in some measure, to the formal concepts of web, wedge and greenbelt. But the primary concern had altered. It was admitted by the planners that the best way of acquiring open land was to acquire it for recreation and natural conservation.

The 1975 Boston revision places heavy emphasis on the riverbanks and stream beds that intricately lace this old and densely settled part of the land. This is a reassuring return to earlier ideas about recreation planning. If it is less grandiose than the vision the open space planners had embraced a decade previously, it gives promise of measurable and rewarding achievements. Streams and rivers, as the Washington planners somewhat plaintively observed, do not always follow the scheme laid down by open space advocates. But their value as recreational resources can nevertheless be immense.

The same is true for such obvious natural and ecological features as steep slopes, wetlands, forest stands, canyons and coasts, as well as for such man-made treasures as historical and archeological sites. The green pattern that takes its own shape, aided by strategic connections and linkages, will serve the objectives long associated with park systems, and may as well have a not inconsiderable influence upon the ultimate form of the city.

A Summary

Thus we have passed on our journey through various forms and types of open space in the city—from the small square to the regional structure.

The scale expands and the forms vary, but it is the tendency of each form to enlarge itself through connections and extensions and to become part of a more complete whole. At its best the city square does not remain isolated, but is linked to other squares and other openings in the urban fabric. The central park, first conceived as a walled enclave, reaches outward through boulevards and related green spaces, until the idea of a park system inspires the original park-builders. Their successors lay hold upon massive elements of the landscape to shape parks of multiple use and large dimensions.

Finally, at a new scale of conceptualization, the open spaces of megalopolis take shape—separate preserves of nature growing toward a total system.

In these unfoldings and extensions of open space—this progression from the town square to the megalopolitan structure—there is ideally a continuing relationship and an inner harmony. The square at the city's heart leads the imagination outward to the largest green spaces at the city's limits. The big parks are joined physically or in the mind's eye with open spaces on a far larger scale and at a greater distance from the core. The city thus tends to become an organic whole, with open space as a major element in the shaping of its physical life.

PART THREE

The Central City

11 The New Downtown

WE NOW SHIFT THE PERSPECTIVE of our study, and returning from what might be called outer space, focus attention through the remaining chapters on American downtowns. Here we shall find the open space of malls and plazas, markets and courtyards contributing to a new kind of urban environment. Such open spaces at their best form the heart of contemporary downtown life and the key to economic development.

The role and importance of the newer open spaces cannot be measured except in relation to the decline of downtown in almost every city in the post–World War II era. The centers of older cities like Baltimore, Rochester, Philadelphia, Louisville were dying. Urban amenities of an earlier day had faded. Streets built for the transportation of another age had become clogged by the automobile, while municipal services lagged behind the needs of a rapidly rising population. The physical substructure appeared beyond modernization.

Cheerlessness and decay were the chief aspects of most downtown centers. The predominantly nineteenth-century buildings seemed obsolete—not for another decade would it begin to dawn upon urbanists that these old structures could be an important civic resource, lending themselves to fresh uses and preserving the habitable scale of the city. Where new construction was undertaken it was without the exuberance or conviction springing from a strong architectural tradition. A brief interlude of neoclassicism after 1910 had left its mark on temples of commerce and banking, well-proportioned buildings ornamented with taste. The early skyscrapers arose. But in most American cities after World War II a general atmosphere of blight prevailed.

The physical neglect and dinginess were the reflection of country-wide social and economic trends. The post-1920 decade had seen suburban development throw the whole city off balance. Middle-class and high-income families left the residential sections of the central cities to find green space and freedom from congestion. Disillusioned with urban life, they did not seek to create new patterns of living so much as to recapture an image of the past. In suburbs outside the city limits they found at least the superficial qualities of a country existence.

The city they left behind was one weakened in its tax base, unable to supply services for the poor who remained or the new immigrants who poured in. The situation worsened as business followed residents to the suburbs. Older residential buildings were subdivided to house a new class of tenants; similarly, manufacturing areas became the site of leftover, marginal enterprises. Storefronts and the less attractive forms of commercial enterprise speeded the degeneration of once-handsome neighborhoods.

New Functions for Downtown

If the central city was to survive, a massive reconstruction of downtown was plainly essential. Basic to such a reconstruction would be the shaping of new open spaces and open space systems. Nothing could get started, however, as long as earlier ideas about the nature and function of downtown continued to dominate the minds of planners and builders. The flight to the suburbs was not likely to be stopped—nor a retail area revived or a residential street restored—by simply deploring the general deterioration or repeating time-worn shibboleths about the value of the central business district.

What did "downtown" in fact mean to the older generation of urbanists and city dwellers? It meant the shopping area of the city. In the smaller cities today people still think of downtown as the place where they go to buy things. This is not where they live, it is not where they usually find their doctor, and such secondary activities as having a meal or going to a movie are less ends in themselves than extensions of the shopping experience. The central business district was, in short, primarily for business.

Everyday perceptions of the citizen were reinforced by urban economists. In a view characteristic of the 1950s, an authoritative article defined the central business district in such a way as to exclude governmental and cultural institutions on the ground that these are not "business" enterprises.[1] Such institutions might be physically located within the central business district, but they were not part of its essential functions. In their book on the central business district Murphy and Vance even express doubt about including the regional offices of an insurance or oil company. In their view, these do not fulfill "necessary functions"; worse, "they *add to the crowding, and hence to the problems,* of the central business district." As for the idea of including a residential area within the definition of downtown, it would have seemed as unlikely to the authors as actually to live downtown was inconceivable to most ordinary people.

Retail areas of the central cities were, as it happened, the first to be hurt by the suburban exodus. Shopping facilities were quick to trail the fleeing residents, and only later were they followed by other services, by entertainment, and finally by the offices and factories that supplied jobs. Stores were plainly needed in the suburbs; and the suburbs provided merchants with the precise advantages that central-city locations lacked—customer parking and the large floor space required by new marketing techniques. The traditional downtown thus received a blow in the very area where it considered itself supreme.

If the central business district was not to be a focus of retail trade, what was it to be?

The answer, made evident within the decade of the 1960s, was that downtown had a far more complex and diverse function than had earlier been acknowledged. It was a center for shopping, yes. But it was also a center for government, for the arts, for education, for voluntary institutions, for wide-ranging banking, insurance and financial services. It was a forum for the kind of human interchange required by modern business transactions. It was a magnet for tourists and conventions. It was a place where at some stage in the life cycle many people would choose to live.

These various functions, overlapping and in their physical embodiment often combined, constituted a new kind of downtown with a dense and compact spatial organization.

Toward the Regional Capital

The central business district has changed its character in becoming more diverse and including a greater number of interacting elements. It has also changed in becoming more modest in certain of its claims. Once an imperial place, unchallenged in its ascendancy over all aspects of the city, downtown today tends to be a center among several lesser centers, a dominant node among the nodes that constitute the modern urban complex. Its monopoly in the field of merchandising is challenged by outlying shopping centers; in trade and commerce by the office park; in entertainment by the suburban university and the local movie house. In two aspects, nevertheless, the major city's downtown is unique and retains its dominance over other centers.

First, it combines and juxtaposes the variety of functions that in the suburbs are sorted out and given a more or less exclusive setting. The wider city is characterized by separation and specialization; downtown by proximity and mixture. Retail center, recreation center, cultural center, financial and governmental center—often, too, a residential center—the city core gains from each and from the relationship of each to the others.

Second, it provides a wealth of special services not only to the city as a whole but to a region often far more extensive than its own boundaries. This is particularly evident in the field of government and finance; it is hardly less so in the arts, in medical research, in education.

Decentralization in the delivery of all kinds of services is a desirable goal, and for this reason alone the new form of the city is to be encouraged. Yet the originating impulse, the stimulus in art and in other fields, will usually come only from the center. Entertainment in the form of local movie houses or bowling alleys exists in every neighborhood; but the performing arts insofar as they rely on the comparative handful of actors, dancers and singers of genius, as well as on a distilled and critical audience, seek the most vibrant downtowns of the major cities. Museums can and should be decentralized; but the artists whose work will ultimately be contained in the museums find the conditions for creativity at the core.

The contemporary downtown becomes, then, not merely the chief center within a congeries of centers—in a city like Los Angeles the skyscrapers of downtown visibly outreach those of the city's other nodes—but also the capital of a wider region. The institutions of this regional capital require a degree of organization and a body of manpower outstripping the forms in which their more locally oriented predecessors were housed. As a result, the building programs of the 1950s and 1960s became sufficiently broad in scope to remake many of the downtowns of older cities, and to create a novel form of downtown in those newer cities whose role as regional capital was clear from the start.[2]

Men and women living in the suburbs may assume, being so comparatively comfortable and self-sufficient, that they have no need of the central city with its downtown core. This independence is an illusion. Apart from anything else, the psychological value to the individual of being connected with a recognizable place—of living "in no mean city"—should not be minimized. Beyond that are important administrative and economic links between city and suburb. The money that goes into suburban developments is generated in the central city; most of the jobs filled by suburbanites still exist within it; the image and the vitality of downtown attract the business from which the suburbs profit.

If the picture today is not of a commanding center surrounded by faceless bedroom communities, it is of something more significant: a flow of services, an interlocking of interests. Within this web of the city the downtown area continues to show strength. Within the larger context of the region it is pre-eminent.

Three Effective Downtowns

The new downtown begins to reveal itself to those who know what to look for. In one city after another its form is emerging—no longer a single retail and office center, but a group of related centers with varied functions, strung upon a framework of open space and bounded by a clear change of land use. Each function generates to some degree or other its own form of open space: the city hall, its square; the commercial buildings, their plazas; the shopping area, its malls. In the most successful downtowns the separate open spaces are united by a pattern of parks and multi-use streets.

The aim of Part Three is to give an account of the open spaces in the new American downtowns—their form, their interrelationships, their functions. It is important to see them as stimulators of development as well as a vitalizing influence on the downtown area. The next chapters will deal, among other things, with the open spaces of living, the open spaces of commerce, the open spaces of the arts. Before entering upon this examination, it seems well to take a few downtowns as they now exist, seeing how the pieces fit together. For our immediate purposes we select Minneapolis, Baltimore and Rochester. As well if not better than others, these enable us to illustrate and comment upon the new downtown as we have defined it.

These downtowns and many others are roughly similar in size. The ideal distance from rim to rim is approximately two miles, allowing a pedestrian to walk to the center from any point of the circumference in not much more than fifteen minutes. The three cities, as may be seen in maps drawn to the same scale, conform to that criterion.

As for the ideal "mix" for a downtown, it should include open space in the form of parks, plazas, malls. It should include a retail and office center;

CULTURAL CENTER

ELLIOT PARK

GATEWAY PLAZA

HOSPITAL COMPLEX

CIVIC CENTER

MISSISSIPPI R.

INDUSTRIAL MUSEUM

FEDERAL RESERVE

CONVENTION HALL

HENNEPIN AVE

NICOLLET MALL

PEAVEY PARK

ORCHESTRA BLDG

LIGHT INDUSTRY

SKYWALKS

TRANSIT STATION

PARKING

LORING GREENWAY

LORING PARK

N

WALKER ART CENTER

MINNEAPOLIS CENTRAL BUSINESS DISTRICT

GUTHRIE THEATRE

cultural, financial and government institutions; a downtown residential development and educational facilities. The existence of these various institutions not only breeds open spaces, but supplies the human factor that populates and enlivens them. The three cities chosen for illustration possess these attributes and combine them in various ways.

MINNEAPOLIS In its capacity to put everything together (some of the projects are still in the planning stage), Minneapolis is probably the best downtown in the country.

The adjoining map shows a downtown roughly triangular in shape, bounded by major traffic arteries and with the Mississippi River running through it. Main Street with its still unrestored historic façade is north of the river. A strong axis is formed by the Nicollet Mall with the enclosed court of the IDS Center midway down its length. Along the mall, or in close proximity to it, are strung out the major retail stores and high-rise office buildings, and Hennepin Avenue, the entertainment section of the city, runs parallel to it. The new music center has its own square, providing a happily conceived subsidiary space.

Loring Park is included within the circle of downtown and forms a fitting anchor to one end of the northeast axis; the river forms the other. Housing is projected along the river at right angles to the mall and also in the still-undefined area where Hennepin Avenue turns to meet Loring Park.

Various details shown on this map are discussed elsewhere. Here the objective is to see them as a whole, an image of the new downtown. To be noted are the skywalks, important elements in assuring a mix of the various elements, as well as the plan for powerfully shaped parking ramps to intercept traffic coming off the main arteries. It must be recalled, finally, that the core of Minneapolis is surrounded by a wide and well-functioning system of parks and parkways inherited from the last century.

BALTIMORE This border city shows a contemporary downtown effectively accommodated within an old framework. The core is walkable and its spatial organization is readily comprehensible. At its heart is the thirty-three-acre pedestrian space of Charles Center, with office towers, apartment houses, public plazas and a theater, one of the more civilized urban renewal projects to be found anywhere in the country. To the north, rehabilitation and restoration are going forward in the area around Mount Vernon Square, where leading cultural institutions are clustered in handsome Greek Revival buildings—the Historical Society, the Peabody Institute, the Walters Art Gallery.

The major north-south axis remains historic Charles Street. From Mount Vernon Square the pedestrian moves easily into Charles Center, coming

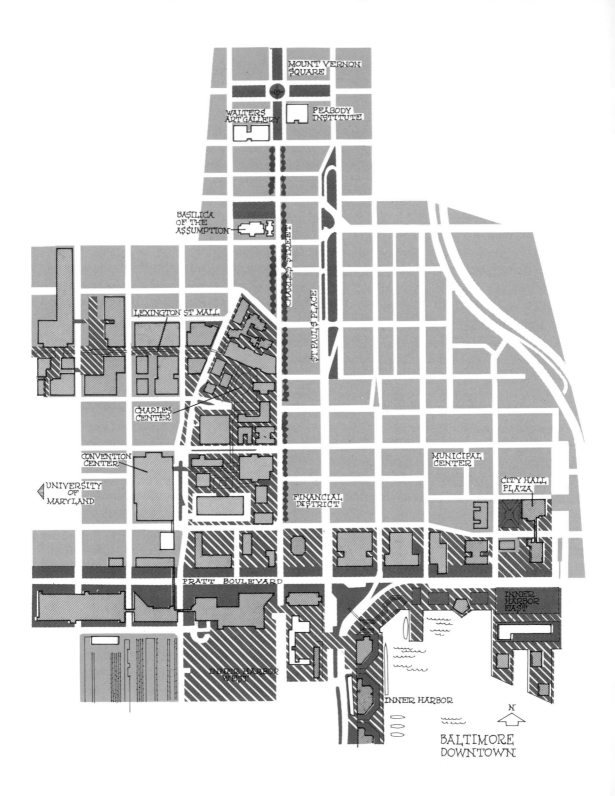

out once again at Charles Street and continuing to within a few blocks of the Inner Harbor. Here the city is constructing a major new downtown residential and commercial development to include a marina and new waterfront park.

Flanking Charles Center to the east are the financial and government centers with their related parks and plazas. Along St. Paul's Street a linear park, one of the city's original green spaces, extends for seven blocks. On the west are the retail shops and the well-used Lexington Mall. To the southwest lies the downtown campus of the University of Maryland.

Especially attractive is the way the human scale of the city is respected. The new office towers of Charles Center are less than skyscraper height. The best of the old buildings have been kept and the new have avoided over-assertiveness. The topography of the city is visible in the varied levels of Charles Center as well as in the hilly streets that descend, sometimes steeply, to the river.

Downtown Baltimore is ringed with parks and residential areas reached by diagonal boulevards, once grand, now reflecting changes in the neighborhoods through which they pass. Nevertheless, a movement to revive the old neighborhoods is under way and some, like Bolton Hills, are already attracting families to their restored town houses and brick-paved streets.

Baltimore today faces grave social and economic problems: the traditions of the old city are severely challenged. But it possesses a downtown congenial to a mix of people and interests, an open space environment that may demonstrably help the city in solving its problems.

ROCHESTER   A third map shows the unusually vivid organization of Rochester's downtown. Like the two others, it is contained, this time by a loop specifically designed to make it inviting to use for internal circulation. The resulting circle is crossed east-west by Main Street and north-south by the Genesee River. The riverbanks have recently been cleared of residual industrial uses and the area is a focus for office, hotel and residential developments. It is a new kind of downtown park.

West of the river along Main Street are the financial and civic centers, and to the east the retail center. The latter is strongly pinned down by the well-known Midtown Shopping Mall, a roofed-over "town square" designed by Victor Gruen. Within the area is the site of the important Southeast Loop residential project with a new park forming a link between it and the retail center.

The map does not indicate the disturbing amount of land within this comparatively small downtown area that has been cleared for development and is now being used for parking lots. Rochester's core requires heavy

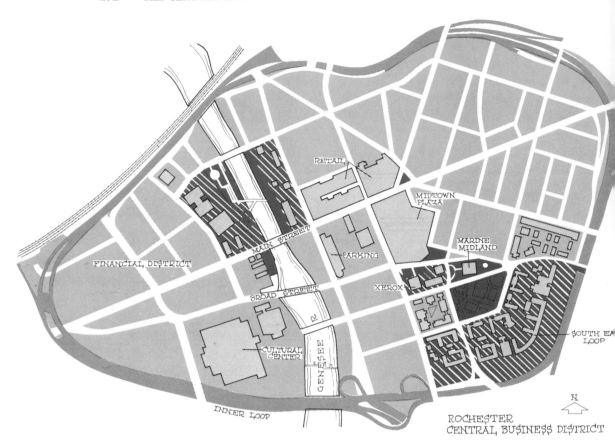

ROCHESTER
CENTRAL BUSINESS DISTRICT

investments before it can live up to its central river space and to the promise given in a few of its individual features and institutions. In the somewhat abstract delineation presented here, the core presents, nevertheless, an almost ideal portrayal of the way downtowns have been developing in new forms and fulfilling new functions.

A Further Sampling

More briefly now, we sketch the cores of ten representative cities. A traveler to these and other cities would do well to make it a practice to pick out the various components, sense their relationship to one another, and fix the open spaces in his mind. Each city is unique, even though the planners of the 1960s, in their reliance on wide-scale clearance procedures and the introduction of similarly designed centers for various functions, sometimes seemed intent on making them as much like one another as possible.

CINCINNATI   A boldly scaled waterfront development keeps links with the core and with the open space of Lytle Park. Downtown focuses on Fountain Square, its skywalks extending through the surrounding area. Governmental and cultural services are housed in pleasantly restored old buildings, but the city hall lacks any adjacent open space and the music hall seems detached from Washington Park. The German section, "Over the Rhine," is being sensitively preserved and the Findlay Market has been restored. Residential areas crown surrounding hills.

DENVER   Classically designed city and state buildings frame a well-used park, with a library and an extremely busy museum nearby. The high-rise Mile-High Center pioneered as a hotel, office and shopping complex with related open space, but turned its back on the adjacent park. The main thoroughfare is receiving new plazas and efforts are under way to establish a mall. Larimer Square recreates a historic setting; a multilevel environment with important open spaces is projected in the Skyline development. Nevertheless, at this time Denver's downtown seems formless and the links between its parts have not been clarified.

FORT WORTH   Although the Gruen plan for a compact pedestrian core ringed with parking garages inside a tight band of highways was never implemented, today's Fort Worth downtown lies within a strongly defined inner loop. Visual anchors stand at both ends of Main Street—a handsome courthouse on the north, a convention center on the south. Development, however, has tended to concentrate at the southern end, leaving much of Main Street sadly dilapidated. The city hall is an attractive contemporary building with an interior plaza. A dazzling new water garden provides a focus for development in the area behind the convention hall but just within the loop. Plans call for a mall on Houston Street, parallel to Main, and for a park and multipurpose complex where the Trinity River meets downtown. Museums are set in their own green space at some distance from the core.

KANSAS CITY   Contemporary office buildings and plazas are rising in the once-vigorous but lately run-down central business district. A loose collection of governmental buildings stands at the rim. Old waterfront lofts and warehouses are beginning to enjoy a life of mixed uses in the River Quai development. The "worst" square at the civic auditorium and new convention center is being redesigned to make for easier access and more amenable activity. A tradition of decentralized shopping has existed since the 1920s at the Plaza and continues today at Crown Center. In-town parks stabilize old residential areas.

LOUISVILLE   Almost 620 acres in area, this is one of the most loosely patterned, least comprehensible of U.S. downtowns. Some order has been imposed by the new Belvedere development along the river and by the Fourth Street Mall, but these wait to be connected by an exhibit center planned for the north end of the mall. The dignified old government center and the new hospital complex are disparate elements requiring linkages to other downtown activities. Just outside the core St. James Court and Belgravia form a charming residential enclave.

MILWAUKEE   A mature downtown, a pleasant mixture of old and new architecture in predominantly dark reds and browns, is penetrated by the Milwaukee River. Recently cleared banks reveal the charming old building of the County Historical Society fronted by a new park; across from it, with steps going down to the river, is the handsome complex for the performing arts. A strong axis, Kilbourne Avenue, extends from the Milwaukee Art Center east to the Saarinen War Memorial in Lake Park. A restored town hall and historic theater provide, along with Cathedral Square, a focus of activity in the heart of downtown. While high-rise housing has been provided, the old residential area on the bluff retains its popularity as an agreeable place to live in-town.

PHOENIX   A downtown for a city in motion, Phoenix is scaled to the automobile and to the big grid which its inhabitants prefer to the usual pattern of freeways. Down the high-rise corridor of Central Avenue stretch the commercial and retail areas, hotels, the museum and library. Pedestrian space is at a minimum, though nearby Encanto Park is pleasantly landscaped and residential streets run behind the façade of high-rise buildings. A governmental mall, primarily for vehicular traffic, is beginning to emerge from the planning stage and will provide a strong cross-axis from the performing arts center to the existing state capitol. An existing park and cemetery will be incorporated in the green spaces of this mall.

PORTLAND   Although the Willamette River divides the city, downtown lies intact on the west bank. A tradition of amenities—parks, squares and fountains—gives Portland a special character. A series of park blocks pierces the city, organizing cultural institutions and penetrating Portland State University, to become a campus shared by students and nearby residents. Lawrence Halprin's Forecourt Fountain fills a square block opposite the Civic Auditorium. Portland Center adds Pettigrove Park and the Lovejoy Fountain. Young professionals have discovered the waterfront district and the area with its historic Skidmore Fountain is being rehabilitated for shops, offices and restaurants.

SAN DIEGO   The core of the city is compact and agreeably low-key. City hall and the performing arts center share open space. The retail district is linked visually to the governmental center by special paving carried from the building line to the curb and across the wide streets. C Street, at the heart of the shopping area, has been embellished with planters and benches and converted to a semi-mall with one lane reserved for traffic. Proposed redevelopment of the area around historic Horton Square will open up the bay frontage, which is poorly used at present. The architecture downtown is pleasant but ignores San Diego's southwestern heritage. Balboa Park with its museums and zoo is within easy reach.

SEATTLE   Downtown Seattle stretches along the shores of Elliott Bay, running from the historic district at Pioneer Square to the grouping of cultural institutions at Seattle Center. It is an area of mixed and often incongruous uses. Flophouses and pawnshops survive among the restored buildings and new squares. Office towers shadow the jumble of sheds that house Pike's Place Market. Recent high-rise construction has not been kind to the picturesque urbanity long associated with Seattle, nor has it shown the traditional deference to residents on the nearby hills. The destruction of a particularly inviting block of small-scale stores is imminent, making way for an aggressively designed commercial plaza with an elevated podium. Yet Seattle's downtown keeps its own charm, in part because of its waterfront location, in part because of a past which has not yet been completely erased.

INDIANAPOLIS A classically conceived city on a flat midwestern plain. Monument Circle in the heart of downtown sits within a square from which radiate four major avenues. Contemporary plans retain the historic circle with its towering Soldiers and Sailors Monument and strengthen nodes of activity surrounding it. Just north of the circle, the four-block War Memorial Plaza adds a ribbon of green. The ambitious Lincoln Square development in one quadrant contains a new Hyatt House with its obligatory atrium, an office building and retail shops, all within easy walking distance of downtown, and linking it with the Convention Center and new Sports Arena. Flanking the high-rise City-County Building on the east, the City Market has been rehabilitated and is expected to spur development in an old commercial district. Playing a similar role is the landmark pink brick Romanesque Revival Union Station, which the city purchased just in time to save from the bulldozer. An old canal in this landlocked city is being studied as a possible site for a park, and housing is being considered for the area close to the city university. Long-range plans call for a broad transit mall on Washington Street.

12 Downtown Parks and Development

THE OLDER DOWNTOWNS were strikingly poor in parks. The reason was obvious. Downtown was strictly a place for business; recreation and delight were to be sought in other parts of the city. Historic squares, surviving from an earlier day, played a continuing role, but when large or small parks came to be created they were placed outside the retail zones. As a result, the commercial areas of such cities as Denver, Rochester, Dallas and Pittsburgh were—at least before recent efforts at renewal—devoid of significant green spaces.

In a few cities downtown parks did exist; but this was not because they had been fostered or supported by commercial interests. They were residues, created in a period when the area was residential. The open lands remained as business life developed around them, often adapting themselves awkwardly to the changed milieu.

In Syracuse, New York, Fayette Park presents an example of an old park in the process of this changeover. A single remnant of the fine old residences once surrounding the park still stands; and the green space with its wrought-iron fence and formal walks seems to be of use neither for family enjoyments nor as a magnet for business. In New York City, Madison Square was once encircled by residences; skyscrapers housing the offices of insurance companies have taken their place. The office workers use it sparingly; and the park rests between worlds, its large trees and its once well-kept lawns playing no defined role within the community.

Where such parks are found amid changed surroundings they can become valuable assets of a modern commercial district. In many cases a historic green place, preserved with its original sculpture and fencing, and so far as possible with its growth of old trees, provides a business neighborhood with something of the character it once gave to a residential area. When the oldest New York City park was recently rehabilitated, its historic form and details (down to the missing iron balls which had been converted to ammunition during the Revolutionary War) were restored. Thus Bowling Green stands today within the shadow of skyscrapers and at the heart of New York's financial district.

In other cases a contemporary treatment may well be justified, as more in keeping with the surrounding buildings and with modern uses of the green space.

The question remains, however, whether downtown parks cannot be deliberately created to give breathing spaces within the city's densely built up areas, to make the experience of shopping more agreeable, and to permit the kind of sociability that is at the heart of so many of today's business transactions. These parks would be different from the plazas that will be discussed later. They would be larger (though still small by the older standards of park-building); in general, green, where the plazas tend to be hard-surfaced, and belonging to the whole community rather than to a particular business development.

As a matter of fact, there are a number of instances of just such new parks being carved out of downtown environments, sometimes as gifts of the business community and sometimes by the public authorities. They form a distinct species of open space and exert a vital influence over the developmental and renewal processes in the business areas where they are located.

Changed Business Attitudes

Merchants and shopkeepers not only lacked interest in parks but were often actively opposed. They saw them as a waste of land that could be put to more profitable use, and as a refuge for vagrants and undesirables. The courthouse could have its square; for themselves, they preferred the traffic-laden street. Louisville, Kentucky, possessed a downtown open space, known as Lincoln Park, following the destruction of a custom house in the 1920s; a group of citizens wished to keep the space permanently for the public. But the business community was opposed, and its voice was heeded.

A certain Mr. A. J. Stewart spoke on behalf of businessmen of a generation ago. "The city," he said in 1944,[1] "has more parks and recreation centers than it can make use of. . . . Parks in 100 percent retails sections are an affliction rather than a blessing." Given a choice between a park and a parking space, the average merchant usually opted for the latter.[2]

In recent years the attitude of the business community has been changing. Merchants have seen shopping centers with their courts and walkways luring away customers; they have seen the point reached where more than half the retail business of the country is being carried on outside the central cities. A response of the more enlightened business leaders has been to support planning for pedestrian amenities of all kinds. An old, leftover park begins to seem a potential asset, worth having refurbished, policed and programmed with appropriate events.

A few far-sighted businessmen led the way in setting a new value upon open space. In the 1930s the builders of Rockefeller Center attached enormous importance to leaving a significant part of its prime real estate free of structures. Today, while sophisticated observers appreciate the architecture of its clustered towers, masses of ordinary people from all over the world glory in the simple fact that in the very heart of town there is a great space free of buildings. When the chairman of the Chase Manhattan Bank, David Rockefeller, determined a generation later to give the Wall Street area a new lease on life, he saw that a big open space could be the crucial factor in stabilization and renewal. The new headquarters building of the bank is one among the many skyscrapers in the Wall Street area; the open space it carved out, as large as the piazza of St. Mark's in Venice, remains unique.

Similarly, in Pittsburgh Richard Mellon saw a new park as an essential element in downtown renewal. The block of open space set on sloping land above a parking garage, pleasantly walled by buildings of harmonious scale, became the key to millions of dollars of new investment in a previously decaying business district. "And do not people now travel for miles," asks Lewis Mumford, usually so severe a critic of the empire builders, "of an evening, from the outskirts of Pittsburgh, just for the pleasure of a stroll in Mellon Square?"[3]

The new feeling among businessmen for the possibilities of open space was to have a dramatic effect—usually for the good—upon the high-rise buildings and multipurpose developmental schemes of the 1960s. A later chapter will take note of this. Hardly less significant is the changed attitude to parks themselves. Instead of following Mr. Stewart of Louisville in opposing parks within the central business district, businessmen have actually been creating them for the community. They see in their gifts a means of gratifying the public. They also see a way of enhancing real estate values and stimulating downtown development.

Parks Gratefully Received

One such gift of a new park is in Atlanta. The downtown area of the city has long been poor in open space. At Five Points, where old transportation routes came together, a jumble of rundown buildings occupied what should obviously have been a visible civic focal point. While the Trust Company of Georgia considered a major high-rise building for its offices at this site, an anonymous donor" offered to purchase an acre of adjoining land, clear it, and donate it to the public as a green space.

Everyone in Atlanta knows that an "anonymous donor" of so princely a gift is almost certain to be the Coca-Cola foundation. It is also known that in Atlanta the business community is bound by close ties and is geared in with the city's projected civic improvements. It was not considered strange, therefore, that in the end the Trust Company of Georgia found itself bordering on a previously nonexistent public space; nor that the plans for the new rapid transit system, when they were revealed, showed this to be the site of a major underground station.

Atlanta's central park exists in its present condition as the result of a simple but effective design by the Atlanta park department. The land had been acquired at a cost of more than $9 million; the development costs were only $250,000. A simple system of pathways links the interior with the irregular pattern of the surrounding streets, and grassy mounds or berms, combined with trees, give an agreeable sense of green. The park is well used. On a good day people pass through it on foot in all directions; others pause to lunch or enjoy the outdoors. A lack of benches was evidently conceived as a way of keeping vagrants from making the place their home. Fortunately, the berms provide ample sitting space.

A feature of this successful park is the programming of musical and other events which draw people at the lunch hour. To its credit, the Trust Company of Georgia has supported these programs, not being too fearful of either the noise or the sight of so many people.

So much loved already is this small patch of green at the heart of the city that one hears Atlantans speaking of it as if it were sanctioned by old custom and tradition. Any change in its landscaping or use is decried. Yet the present design of the park was intended to be temporary, and *Central Atlanta*—the city's striking downtown plan[4]—shows this space as occupied by a multilevel plaza providing pedestrian amenities along with entrances to the central station of the new subway system. The plaza is in the style of today's typical downtown improvement. Meanwhile the public is enjoying very much its small, old-style park.

Other downtown parks donated by private interests include the following:

THE FORT WORTH WATER GARDEN   Donated by the Amon G. Carter Foundation, the three-acre fantasy of water and landscaping designed by Philip Johnson is a major attraction in itself. But its location precludes, at least for the present, its playing a significant role in giving form and focus to downtown's renewal. Fort Worth's downtown has a pedestrian-scaled Main Street of nine blocks terminated at one end by the convention hall. Within this area upgrading and the provision of new amenities is urgently needed. Unfortunately, the water garden is at the *rear* of the convention hall and in close proximity to encircling expressways. A new hotel and other facilities are, however, being developed on the land rendered more valuable by the little park.

DALLAS'S THANKSGIVING PARK   Donated by businessmen and built on city land with a publicly financed parking space beneath, this is precisely where such a park should be—at the center of intensive activity, in a highly built up area desperately needing the amenity of a little open space. Also designed by Philip Johnson, it will undoubtedly be a successful park—an example of how open space can be carved out from an existing urban milieu—not inherited as an old square might have been, nor built in conjunction with large-scale development, as in examples to be seen later.

TWO "POCKET PARKS" IN NEW YORK CITY   Donated by individual philanthropists, Paley Park on East Fifty-third Street and Greenacre Park on East Fifty-first Street greatly enhance the public scene. Existing on land that continues to be privately held, both are in lively retail and commercial sections of the town where they exist as grace notes and charming increments rather than as a means of rejuvenating a neglected downtown area, as in the parks above.

For grateful shoppers and office workers they are a boon, providing a place to lunch or to rest in a convivial setting which is nevertheless serene. Both parks have been stylishly designed and use water as a backdrop to mute the sounds of traffic and soothe the weary visitor. Both are endowed, are kept in an awesome state of cleanliness and repair by their donors, and are regarded by the commercial tenants of their respective blocks as admirable neighbors.

These parks are not easily duplicated in either the public or the private sphere. Since they are of necessity situated on prime real estate, their cost alone is daunting. They do, however, suggest the desirability of small oases on the crowded streets of busy retail areas and the refreshment to the spirit of even a modest place to pause in a busy day.

Cities Take the Initiative

The public has not been dependent on private gifts, but has created its own downtown parks—instruments of renewal and also witnesses to the vitality of downtown. State and federal funds have joined with the contributions of the cities to make possible these new open spaces. In every case they have been well used, they have been maintained at a high level and have been considered safe. Despite problems faced by the older central parks in our cities, the new downtown parks seem to have been relatively free of controversy and trouble. In every case, they have served to give a new atmosphere, and new economic benefits, to the central business district.

In addition to the privately donated Mellon Square, Pittsburgh has its remarkable Point State Park, within easy walking distance of downtown and adjacent to the Golden Triangle complex. At the juncture of the Allegheny and Monogahela rivers, these thirty-six acres were at the end of World War II a confusion of railroad tracks and related facilities, lost to use by the city dweller. A combination of business and political leadership succeeded in getting the Pennsylvania Railroad to dispose of its properties and to make the land available for park use.

The boldness of the vision that liberated this historic land dramatized all the city's other efforts of renewal—the cleansing of the air, the construction of new office space, the restoration of an attractive environment at street level. The new park and the new downtown are one, witnesses to the same civic will and imagination.

Portland, Oregon, provides another interesting example. Already possessing the famous park blocks—one of the finest systems of inner green places in any American city—Portlanders turned naturally to the idea of a park for the renewal of downtown. And what a park it turned out to be! Lawrence Halprin was commissioned to design it, and his preparation for the work

21. and 22. The Fountain fills the square in front of
    Portland's performing arts center.

23. The fountain at the heart of San Francisco's new Embarcadero park.

Fountains form a natural gathering place within the urban scene.

24. A relatively small fountain, but one blessed by tradition,
gives Cincinnati's central square its name and theme.

25. In Fort Worth, a privately donated "water garden."

was not the examination of classic plazas but of waterfalls and cataracts in the northwestern forests. The result is something between a city fountain and a natural wonder. Water falls over crags and ledges, rests in pools, and renews its descent amid spruce and laurel. No restraining barriers, no obvious stairs, protect or guide the public, which has full access to the interior of this unusual park. People find their own places to pause, sitting on diminutive green meadows or outcroppings of seemingly natural rock.

This block-square park is not the result of a rich patron's fancy, but of a realistic decision by planners responsible for the city's future. Massive efforts at urban renewal, already undertaken in Portland Center, needed to be crowned and stabilized. Halprin had designed one fountain in the Portland Center project. This had proved so popular with the young that nearby town houses had to be converted to office space, less sensitive to nocturnal serenades. It seemed natural to turn to Halprin again—this time for design of a park at the edge of the neighborhood.

The new park works as had been planned and anticipated, and provides the bonus of being the major water attraction in a city already famous for its many fountains. Unfortunately, the surroundings of the square—its essential "wall"—do not measure up to their functions. On the east is the civic auditorium, to which the park provides a "forecourt"; but on the three other sides are an office building which turns an inhospitable podium toward the plaza, an apartment house whose base seems designed as a fortress against potential invaders, and a parking garage. None of these provides the kind of amenities at ground level—shops, a restaurant, an outdoor café— that add to the life of a park. Even the auditorium is cut off by the unmodified continuation of a through street. Some form of mall at this point would have formed an appropriate entrance to the walkways of Portland Center, lying just beyond. It would also have provided an attractive stage for outdoor noontime performances.

Yet the park works even though it is not fed and enhanced by the buildings immediately surrounding it. It is in itself so strong a feature that it draws people from the whole downtown and indeed from the wider region. It is a notable example of a new park carved with immense benefits out of the economically valuable downtown land, adding to the total assessments.

An Ideal New Square in Cincinnati

One of the liveliest spots in any city of the country is Fountain Square in Cincinnati, a small park created out of a traffic island at the very heart of downtown. It is a new place, yet blessed by tradition, for upon the island stood the well-loved Henry Probasco fountain with its picturesque symbolism of water in all aspects and uses. Here an annual flower fair had long been held. How this strip at the center of a flow of traffic was converted into an intensely used city park is a fascinating story.

Cincinnati came into the 1960s without a downtown plan. The 1948 master plan, following the characteristic thinking of that period, concentrated on the outer sections of the city, leaving the core to develop or not to develop pretty much in its own way, according to the decisions of merchants and retailers. A Victor Gruen proposal calling for a totally malled downtown ringed by large parking garages lacked support. Federal programs, meanwhile, were making available for the central business district a total of $32 million. How was this to be spent?

Suggestions were many and varied, but no one could come to a decision. An improbable method in the end worked out admirably. A so-called Review Committee was formed, composed of a majority of the City Council, the chairman of the City Planning Commission, the developer who had involved himself in the project, and the Downtown Development Committee, representing the business community. The Review Committee selected design consultants,[5] who also worked out the planning process. Meetings of the committee were held every two weeks and covered all aspects of policy from parking to sidewalk widths. Decisions were ratified between meetings by the City Council and City Planning Commission, so that by the time the plan was completed it had already been adopted.

Within this planning process Fountain Square was conceived. It resulted not from an initial decision to create a downtown open space, but rather as the end product of solutions to a number of key problems. Once the basic traffic decision was made to maintain the grid, the question of parking was raised. Should it be central or peripheral? Should it be above ground or below? In each case a compromise was accepted. Decentralized parking was to be supplemented with one major facility at the center; the entrance into a podium would be kept at street level, with drivers going below to park.

At this stage the planners were asked to design an underground parking facility with a public space above it, and Fountain Square was born. One of the traffic lanes was to be closed and the area added to the square. The adjacent block was to be cleared and new towers built to frame the park on two sides. Skywalks would link the park to the whole downtown area.

The plan required the historic fountain to be relocated slightly to the north and turned around so that it faced the traffic coming up Fifth Street, the principal traffic artery. Uprooting the fountain was a potential source of protest which could have disrupted the entire project. Trouble was averted by bringing community representatives into the planning process.

Today the fountain in its new location, placed upon a pavement with a pattern fanning out from it like waves, subtly lighted and with an abundant flow of water, is more than ever a beloved focal point of urban life. The raised pedestrian entrance to the underground parking makes a stage for music or oratory, as well as an entrance to the skywalk system. Contemporary sculpture is used effectively and a wrought-iron flower stall recalls the traditional fair.

San Antonio's Linear Park

Another group of new downtown parks have not so much been created as they have been discovered. This has been in connection with rivers flowing through the central business district.

The in-town rivers of half a dozen cities had, like waterfronts, been obscured by industrial uses and lost as a civic asset. Their recovery, the clearing of their banks and the provision of pedestrian amenities, form an important chapter in the renewal of their respective downtowns. The recaptured rivers have at their best become linear parks. They have become the focus of important urban renewal projects. In one city, San Antonio, the river walk is a tourist attraction for which the city is widely known.[6]

The San Antonio River extends in a loop through the business district. The river at this point flows below the street level, so that descending by steps, one enters upon a contained world entirely different from that above. The commercial signs, the traffic, the parking spaces are forgotten; the grid of the city block exists no more. A setting for small waterborne vehicles, the river winds between banks whose pedestrian paths open to the terraces of restaurants, small shops, an outdoor river theater. Carefully designed bridges carry overhead the seemingly remote hum of the workaday world.

Periodic floodings were climaxed in 1921 when fifty people lost their lives and property damage mounted into the millions. A plan was then launched to cover over the cut, putting a street above, with the riverbed serving as a sewer. Citizen protest mounted; the engineers were instructed to find a better way of preventing floods. In the end a flood-retention dam was built at the Olmos basin; the worst curves were removed from the river above, and the downtown stream was saved. In 1924, the citizens who had fought together formed the San Antonio Conservation Society, determined to preserve and to enhance what they had won.

The aesthetic possibilities of the river could now be explored. Taking advantage of WPA interest in a project for San Antonio, government officials and a citizen group commissioned the planner-architect Robert H. H. Hugman to prepare designs for the river downtown. The walks, the arched bridges, the steps and various entrances—all painstakingly detailed—were accomplished with WPA funds between 1939 and 1941.

The commercial potential of the river was realized more slowly. A chamber of commerce study of renovation of buildings along this river was rejected as being too carnival-like. Better received was a recommendation to set up a historical preservation commission comparable to that which has protected the Vieux Carré in New Orleans. Today the River Walk Commission has jurisdiction over all building permits within the river bend area. Color, lighting, signage and materials come within its power of review.

The result is not without its flaws. The very attractiveness of this area below street level calls attention to ominous blight and excessive parking spaces in the downtown core. The riverbanks suffer from being abutted by a few heavy or unimaginative buildings and in the newer sections a somewhat arid atmosphere results from declining use of HemisFair Plaza, once the site of an important fair. Yet the river walk as a whole stands as a model of what can be done when city officials, business leaders and other public-spirited citizens work together, using open space to give life and color to the heart of their town.

Further Examples

Among cities that have profited from San Antonio's example the following may be cited:

SANTA FE The city's downtown is in effect a single historic district, maintained in its existing state by statutes strictly limiting densities, building heights and structural materials. Through it runs a small but important river carrying waters from the Santa Fe Canyon. In recent years its banks have been cleared within the downtown core and continuous small parks established along its course. In this case the need has been for historic preservation, and the river has been thought of less as contributing to development than as stabilizing the quality of the urban environment.

ROCHESTER, NEW YORK The Genesee River (see map, page 252) passes

Rivers in the city—an attractive form of linear park.

26. An effort in Chicago to clear its river bank.

27. A portion of the Genesee River in Rochester, cleared to encourage major economic development.

28. The River Walk in San Antonio, a pioneering accomplishment in creating a greenway below the level of the city streets.

29. Milwaukee's dramatic opening of its river, with the new cultural center at left.

directly through the downtown area, a rapidly flowing body of water broken by falls. Yet through much of the city's existence, this scenic attraction was all but invisible. Main Street advanced across the river on a bridge that, like the old London Bridge, carried an unbroken line of buildings. "Certainly it has the negative virtue," said an observer of the Rochester bridge at the start of the century, "of preventing an intrusive interruption by the purely industrial and hideous."[7] Only recently has the bridge been opened up. What one now sees up and down the river is a park with walkways, pedestrian overpasses and the structures of a major urban renewal effort.

Developers along this linear park, working in co-operation with the local urban renewal office, have built hotels, office buildings and the first in-town apartment house. The most striking contribution to the area, however, is a small riverside park contributed by the Lawyers Cooperative Publishing Company. With unusual sensitivity to the environment, the company restored a group of nineteenth-century buildings, moving out printing machines and converting them to office space. The old brick, cleaned and repainted, speaks of the city's past and forms the background for the well-designed green space.

Thus, through liberating and developing its river, Rochester has not only gained a linear downtown park. It has attracted investments within the urban renewal area totaling $35 million.

BINGHAMTON   The bridges of the Chenango, passing through this upstate New York business district, are readily traversed by pedestrians. Four blocks of its length, between two principal bridges, form an area at the city's core of great potential value, aesthetic and commercial. The opportunities on both sides of the river were brought to the attention of the city fathers as long ago as 1911, when Charles Mulford Robinson, the early champion of urban amenities, made his report *Better Binghamton*.

Unfortunately, when serious planning was undertaken in the late 1950s, improvements involved only the east bank, which could be characterized as a slum and cleared under the existing standards of the federal urban renewal law. Today a major civic center has been constructed on the east bank (still waiting to be tied in with elevated walkways to the river); a new bank and hotel carry on their river side a public walkway of considerable charm; and a major department store has reoriented itself so as to take advantage of the pedestrian traffic. Studies of the west bank are now under way.

CHICAGO   Besides its magnificent lakefront, Chicago possesses an in-town river, long neglected though it played a crucial role in the city's development and early history. A breakthrough in recovering this heritage was not achieved until Marina City, a bold complex of downtown apartment buildings and offices, was constructed in 1964. For the first time in this century it became possible to go pleasantly by boat from the very heart of the city to the lake.

Since then, progress has been made toward achieving a continuous river walk. Freeing the banks of the Chicago River from outlived and secondary uses is a first priority and is emphasized in the Chicago 21 downtown plan.[8] It is also important to mark by appropriate open space the confluence of the river and the lake. If open space is to play its full role, it should celebrate a city's essential form, clarifying separate components for the citizen and the visitor. The juncture of two bodies of water is the kind of natural feature too often obscured by massive roads and bridges. Only as the meeting of the related waterways in Chicago finds a visible affirmation will the potentialities of its in-town river be fully realized.

Open-Space Planning for Downtown

Fountain Square, it will be recalled, evolved from a group of decisions only indirectly related to open space. Nobody on the Cincinnati Review Committee set up as a major objective the shaping of a new downtown park at the center of the business district. Similarly, in Santa Fe the river development occurred more by chance than as a major open space commitment. Comprehensive planning for downtown open space is, indeed, comparatively rare. A salient feature may be seized upon by the planners and then imaginatively exploited. A residual open space may be made into a focal point. But mostly the planners have trusted to the developers, prodded in various ways, to include adequate and appropriate open space within their projects.

In New York City a 1961 zoning ordinance granted bonuses to builders who left space at the foot of their buildings. This created problems of its own in the proliferation of isolated plazas and randomly broken building lines. In the late 1960s the New York City Planning Commission pioneered again in setting up special zoning districts in which open space standards were written block by block into plans available to prospective developers. Plazas, pedestrian overpasses, arcades and vistas were incorporated within the obligations any future builder was required to meet. Jonathan Barnett, who as a member of the planning department was active in developing this approach, has called it "designing cities without designing buildings."[9]

Small open spaces can be the making of a central business district.

30. San Diego's unpretentious Horton Plaza—where public transport lines meet and a relaxed clientele sees the days go by.

31. Union Square, standing a little awkwardly on top a parking garage, but possessing a somber elegance dear to San Franciscans.

32. Atlanta's Central Park, donated by local businessmen— the nerve center of downtown.

33. Cleveland's Public Square at the confluence of principal streets—a landmark, but not made for comfortable lingering.

34. Park Block in Portland, Oregon penetrates the state university to become a downtown college green.

The most comprehensively planned of the districts was the Greenwich Street Special Zoning District in lower Manhattan. How well the plan works depends upon whether building activity is resumed at a level comparable to that of the 1960s. It depends also upon the capacity of officials in the future to resist pressures for exceptions and to maintain the zoning restrictions on the various parcels of land.

A different type of downtown open space planning is characteristic of the work of Lawrence Halprin. In Cleveland, where an old and slowly changing urban environment is involved, planners have reviewed the city's commercial area with the active participation of citizens groups and leading businessmen. They seek the latent possibilities inherent within the existing downtown scene: a street that might be malled, a closed courtyard that might be opened to public use, a linkage that might be clarified or a park that might profitably be redesigned. In this process the perceptions of the ordinary citizen are given weight along with the sophisticated judgments of the professional.

The 1971 open space plan for downtown Dallas[10] is more conventional in approach, coming as it does from that city's own planning department with its excellent urban design group. Not uncharacteristic of its Texas background, the plan makes grandiose claims, implying that better parks will alleviate most urban shortcomings. "Majestic parks," begins the report, "are crowning embellishments of the cities of the world." Its own proposals are on the modest side, calling for the "longitudinal parks" created by planting trees along principal traffic arteries and for the landscaping of plots no one of which is more than four acres in extent. Most of these are within the ramps and under the elevated structures of the freeway system.

Within the city's core are projects for green oases—monuments and unexpected pedestrian malls. The crucial triangle forming Thanksgiving Park and the new park in front of City Hall are included. The fact that so much of the green space system is for the motorist rather than for the pedestrian is no reason for denigrating it. To seek within an existing framework means for giving the business district a recognizable form—to use green space to influence land use and to mark the city's entrances and exits—is the kind of creative planning that older park-builders would have approved.

Important concepts now in process of being implemented in Dallas include a greenbelt within the swath of the encircling freeway; "portal parks" where the ramps descend, and green areas to define access to nodes outside the central business district.

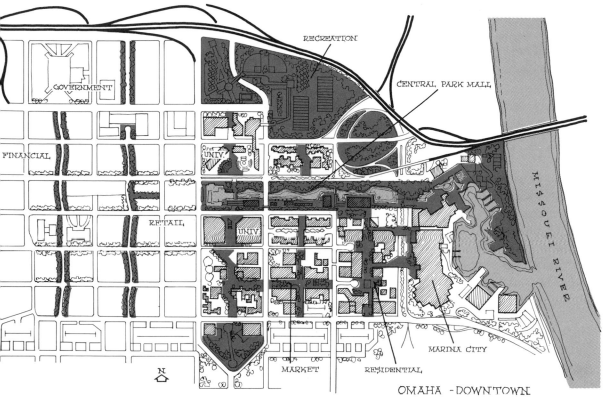

A traditional grid becomes the means of linking by landscaped walkways the various centers of urban activity, with the whole becoming one continuous open-space experience. The central mall connects the plan's separate elements.

Downtown as an Urban Park

One more plan for downtown open space may be noted, this prepared for Omaha, Nebraska.[11] Here Lawrence Halprin orchestrated the work of half a dozen architectural and engineering firms, showing his usual concern for reconciling the view of the citizen with that of the expert. The result is the use of open space to create not only a revivified downtown but one conceivably unique in the clarity with which its essential functions and nature are developed. It goes beyond the concept of a downtown park or system of parks to make the whole central core a place of changing visual experiences and a stage for passive recreation.

Omaha, with its street pattern an unbroken grid, its riverfront lost to citizen use, appears on the surface an unprepossessing, colorless American city. Buildings from the nineteenth century loom darkly amid typical office buildings from the boom of the 1960s. Within this downtown area, nevertheless, are older areas not only worth saving but capable of being converted to colorful contemporary uses. The two principal ones are the old market and the warehouse district—the former seen by the planners as a center of specialty shops, restaurants and galleries; the latter as a mixed-use in-town residential area. In addition are such existing "neighborhoods" as comprise most of today's central business districts—financial core, retail core, and auditorium-government center. Two projects, a large housing development on the riverfront and a downtown campus, will complete the internal nodes.

Courts, plazas and malls exist or will exist within each of these neighborhoods. The crux of the plan, however, is not in these separate spaces, but in the pedestrian network that ties them all together. At the center a large new park, called the Mall, provides the spine from which these pedestrianways branch out.

The underlying philosophy of the plan is striking. It transforms the central business district into one great space containing within it a number of individualized spaces. As the unfulfilled Kessler plan for Cincinnati turned the city of that day, with its outlying hills and residential areas, into a romantically landscaped park, so this turns the modern downtown into an *urban* park. The pedestrianways are not to be "read" as mere links between neighborhoods. Bordered as they are by shops and services of the town environment, they are in their way as much an element of the park as are Kessler's parkways or Olmsted's rural walks.

The old market, the university campus, the warehouse residential district, can of course be seen as discrete units in themselves; but in the perspective of open space they become the larger openings, the areas of special interest, within the overall pedestrian experience. Entering any one of these neighborhoods, the walker in this urban park finds different views and pleasures: in one the sight of students at their traditional pursuits and relaxations, in another the small specialty shops with their arcades, courtyards and inviting interiors, in another the mixed uses and domestic scenes of a neighborhood predominantly of loft and apartment dwellers. So it is, too, with the more traditional centers of trade, finance and government.

The open space plan depends for its effectiveness on the Mall, for which land is now being acquired and cleared. A Central Park in miniature, urban rather than pastoral, with a fountain at one end similar to that in the square at Portland (only this time extending in a waterway toward the river), the Mall is carefully composed to provide a diversity of city pleasures. One older building within the site was considered worth retaining and forms part of the structured southern edge of the park. This contrasts with the "softer" green edge to the north. The waterway is at a level that allows pedestrian bridges to cross over it, at a different scale serving the same function as Olmsted's sunken transverse roads in Central Park.

With the Omaha plan we come full circle—from the dense urban environment laboriously hollowed out so as to form a small park or public square to the environment made permeable by open space. This is the direction in which downtown open space planning must go. Streets must be seen as both corridors for movement and open space; the separate centers must be seen as part of one whole. As this is accomplished, the new downtown begins to fulfill its true function—a total environment within which the tasks and transactions of the modern city can be efficiently carried out.

13 Open Spaces
of Regional Institutions

THE CONTEMPORARY CITY is a regional city, and its downtown is a regional capital. Its most characteristic open spaces are those derived from institutions regional in scope. Old cities like New York and Boston will retain parks created when urban facilities existed chiefly to serve their immediate residents. But the new cities, of which Los Angeles and Phoenix may be taken as prototypes, are distinguished by the kinds of open space generated by administrative, cultural and business services made available to a population more dispersed and far more numerous than is contained within the central city itself.

Institutions of the Regional Capital

Today's urban planners recognize and constantly reaffirm the regional nature of the new downtown. "The central city must be viewed in the context of the entire region. . . . It is most appropriately suited to playing a highly specialized role as the location of business, commercial and government operations which require a trade area of metropolitan size and a convenient central location." The words are from the St. Louis Development Program of 1973; in one form or another they may be found wherever men have given serious consideration to what differentiates a true city center from lesser towns and from the suburban nodes. The St. Louis planners go on to say (as the planners of any regional capital would do) that major cultural institutions are by their nature located in the city; also medical centers, libraries and universities.

Significantly, all these central-city functions are, or should be, generators of open space. Government buildings have almost always had space around them. Museums have either been in a park or made their own park, as if they wanted to keep themselves a little away from the workaday world and at the same time show off the fine façades of their buildings. Business has not traditionally been known as a contributor to the public realm. Yet banks have often enough been styled like small palaces, with at least the remnant of a forecourt or garden. Modern business structures have developed ambitious plazas. In the same way, libraries, medical centers, universities, tend to exist within a space of their own.

What is often a matter of surprise on visiting one of America's smaller cities is the imposing scale of the institutions it contains. Binghamton, New York, for example, is a city of some 64,000 inhabitants. Yet its civic center —a combination of governmental buildings and convention hall—is conceived with a lavishness that would be at home in one of the major Old World cities. Are these delusions of grandeur? one asks. Then it becomes apparent that the facilities are serving a population not of 64,000, but of at least a quarter of a million in the surrounding area. And so one walks up the grand stairway, and through the elevated courts, past sculpture by Louise Nevelson and Arnaldo Pomodoro, feeling that one is in a strange sort of downtown, but not one that is necessarily irrational.

In far larger cities the power within the major institutions of government and finance is immense; and the capacities for creating a new physical environment are proportionately large. The way the new spaces interlock and relate make the inner city what it is. Residues of an earlier form of central city will survive, as in Los Angeles's Pershing Square and in its gracefully balconied, sky-lighted Bradbury Building. In addition, new services develop —an in-town shopping center, a cluster of residential units. But these amenities are not the essence of the regional capital. People who search for residential streets here, who expect large retail centers, are disappointed on not finding them and declare Los Angeles (or Phoenix or Jacksonville) to be without a central core. They say the suburbs have taken over. But the core is present and very much alive, only in a new guise and providing new, larger-scaled services.

Within this core it becomes essential to make full use of the opportunities for open space that the regional institutions suggest. The urban environment will be dead if it consists merely of massive structures, governmental, cultural or commercial; it will not be greatly helped if these are placed at distances from each other with decorative areas between them. The essence of the new downtown is that the spaces be in themselves a source of vitality. A plaza or forecourt is alive in proportion as it is the expression of people's activities, the reflection of their daily chores and errands.

In the examples we shall now be considering we shall see repeatedly a subtle but important distinction between the open space that is merely an architectural extension of the structure, and one that serves a basic need generated by the downtown institutions. A museum park that brings art and spectators together outdoors; a city hall square that provides the stage for assemblage, participation and protest; a commercial plaza that is the scene of informal transactions and exchanges—these are the true open spaces of the regional capital. Where they exist the urban scene has a new meaning. To create such spaces the architect and planner must add to their more routine skills a capacity to heed the citizens' behavioral patterns and to create a stage on which these can be fully realized.

THE SPACES OF GOVERNMENT

The presence of governmental authority can have a transforming effect upon the spatial organization of a city. A capital city, whether a Williamsburg or a Washington, is shaped throughout by the capacity of power to reflect in physical dimensions its nature and its ambitions. Williamsburg was never just a charming eighteenth-century town; and L'Enfant, when he was commissioned to design the young nation's capital, was not just designing a new city. In both are visibly embodied the ideals of political theory and the mysteries of freedom and control. More modestly, and with more extraneous elements, other major cities reflect what men think about politics.

The Governmental City

Let us glance first at the way Williamsburg spaces reflect the colonial concept of government.

Williamsburg's dominating spatial element is a main street of a length permitting it to be taken in at a glance or to be traversed in a brief walk. The street is given form and definition by being bounded at one end by the

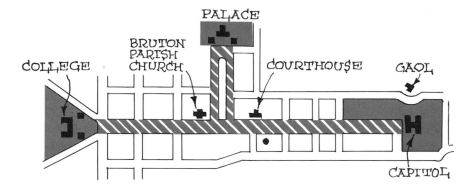

COLLEGE · BRUTON PARISH CHURCH · PALACE · COURTHOUSE · GAOL · CAPITOL

WILLIAMSBURG

five-acre green of the Virginia capitol. Bounding the other end—by its presence perhaps suggesting that the people still have much to learn—is the College of William and Mary. Midway along this street, between the parish church and the courthouse, a vista opens at right angles, revealing a third and ultimate source of power, the governor's mansion. As one continues down Duke of Gloucester Street the glimpse of that austere but beautiful building vanishes. Yet for the eighteenth-century citizen, the consciousness of another power would remain, an ultimate authority speaking for a distant king.

Washington is scarcely less explicit in making its spaces reveal the character of government. Its message, however, is more complex and has changed subtly with the years. To interpret its original meaning one does well to go back to L'Enfant's explanation of what he was trying to accomplish. After noting that his "Grand Edifices" and "Grand Squares" were placed where they could "command the most extensive prospects," L'Enfant goes on to say that avenues have been devised "to connect the separate and most distant objects with the principal, and *to preserve through the whole the reciprocity of sight.*"[1] Could there be a better description of the eighteenth-century concept of democracy? The "Grand Edifices" with their squares speak for the balance and division of powers; the "extensive prospects" for the kind of authority required to rule a new nation.

The "reciprocity of sight" animating the whole speaks for a mutuality of interest uniting the separate powers, and perhaps even more for the ultimate authority of the people. The "most distant objects" are connected with the "principal": the individual citizen is involved in every act of his government.

A hundred years after Washington had been established, a commission re-examined the L'Enfant plan in the light of a new century's needs. The McMillan Commission of 1900 was composed of such famous names as Daniel Burnham, Augustus Saint-Gaudens, and Frederick Law Olmsted, Jr. Its report[2] found the L'Enfant plan essentially sound and concentrated its aim (apart from certain important recommendations for parks outside the downtown area) upon organizing more tightly and more monumentally the central complex of open spaces and government buildings. American government now had a history, to be expressed in the reorganization of the Mall with the careful siting of the Washington and the new Lincoln memorials. It was now an imperial power, to be expressed in new federal buildings along Pennsylvania Avenue and around Lafayette Square.

In one striking reversal of the original intention, views of the river from the White House and the Capitol were cut off under the McMillan plan. The imperial capital was to look inward upon itself. The "reciprocity of sight" to which L'Enfant had attached so much importance would be minimized.

Contemporary Plans for Washington

More recent planning for Washington has emphasized spaces shaped to the pageantry of government, to the comings and goings of the great men of the world. Pennsylvania Avenue was the traditional scene of historic processions. Here Presidents had passed in state between the Capitol and the White House—on days of their inauguration, on occasions of policy-making and on the last passage home. Yet nothing in the form or the details of Pennsylvania Avenue marked its role. During the nineteenth century it had failed to attract notable buildings, remaining long unpaved and without trees. The new century saw the building of a row of monumental structures on its southern side (the Department of the Interior, the National Archives, the National Gallery), but to the north it was still bounded by a row of buildings neither in scale nor in function suited to so potentially grand a space. Its terminal points were, moreover, poorly defined.

In the 1960s the redesign of Pennsylvania Avenue was called for by

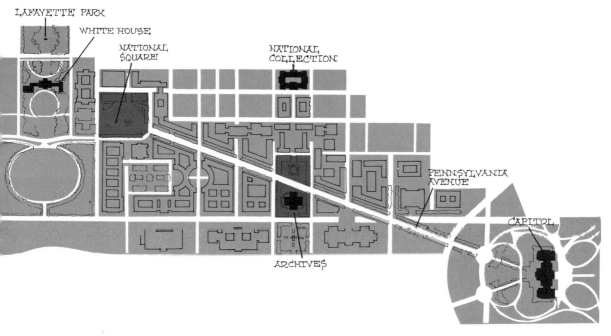

PENNSYLVANIA AVENUE PLAN

President Kennedy. The plan of the President's Council on Pennsylvania Avenue (1964) is interesting in the force and clarity of its concept; and also (in its original version) for failing to grasp certain of the values that had begun to control urban design. It conceived of an open space organized so as to provide both movement and repose—an avenue with a beginning and an end, punctuated midway by an opening surrounded by public buildings. In landscaping, in the detail of its pavement and street furniture, it was to declare itself as a significant place.[3]

The plan ran into difficulties in its attempt to deal with the awkward elbow occurring where Pennsylvania Avenue makes a turn to pass around the Treasury Building. Here was projected National Square, a great space within the city of spaces, a site for vast gatherings and a focal point for historic occasions. But by then popular judgment had grown wary of the grandiose and sought spaces more humanly scaled. Where the designers had envisioned the pageantry of mass events, the Washington public saw a space that would be alternately windy or sun-baked and vacant through much of its existence. Besides, it would have entailed the destruction of the old Willard Hotel and other familiar landmarks.

The same emphasis on the spontaneous and the small-scaled that preserved Lafayette Square as an intimate forecourt to the White House, that initiated the conversion of F Street to a pedestrian way and programmed the great Mall with music and craft shows, now caused the National Square to be redesigned more modestly. If monumentality was to be built into the country's capital, so were the more humane values which cities across the continent were attempting to achieve.

City Hall Parks

In the average city one does not, needless to say, find written so clearly in spatial forms the nature of government and the changing values of the people. Williamsburg and Washington have each been primarily a governmental city and each was shaped in a sort of morning light, when men's ideas were particularly strong and lucid. Washington, moreover, has seen successive generations apply their best talents to reorganizing its outward aspects as the spirit within changed. Yet a story may be read in the way cities handle the spaces around their city halls, and then in the way they combine the setting of local authority with the more wide-ranging powers of the county, state and federal governments.

A negative lesson is often obvious. Those city halls that exist in nondescript buildings, without a public place to set them apart, are usually the product of a long disregard for politicians and for public authorities. Here business interests have been predominant and city hall has been at best a junior partner. Seattle is a city that has never rated its political spokesman very high. Its city hall is indistinguishable from an office building of medium size. Overnight, a decade ago, Detroit destroyed a city hall of historic and architectural note, placed handsomely upon a public place. The present city hall is difficult to find amid a maze of other governmental offices, all lodged in a high-rise building which in the banality of its design and lack of surrounding space seems to be an indication of how much less important it is than the edifices of business power.

Pittsburgh, to take one more case, has its offices well housed in a massive stone landmark, but in front of it is an uncovered private parking lot.[4] The city that has shown itself superior to most others in its capacity to organize public space to serve and enhance the business community cannot find the funds to purchase the available land and convert the parking lot into a decent setting for city hall.

The desirability of a square or other appropriate open space in front of the seat of city government needs to be stressed. Tradition has decreed this arrangement, and today's political values confirm it. Nothing suggests so well as a pleasant forecourt the relationship of the citizen to his local authorities. Here is a visible proof that government adds to the life of the citizenry. This space is made for ceremonies, festivals, protests. Let the traditional Christmas tree be lit, or a visiting celebrity come to town, no place is so appropriate for the event as a small park in front of city hall. None is better for a musical program or a poetry reading in the lunch hour. Perhaps most important, groups can gather here to protest or to support the wide spectrum of causes with which city government is involved.

New York's City Hall Park has served in its time as a grazing field, a jail, a place for public hangings and a parade ground. It looks down toward the skyscrapers of Wall Street, yet manages not to be dominated by them. The famous Woolworth Building is at hand, as well as historic St. Paul's Church. Adjacent to the early-nineteenth-century city hall is the Tweed Courthouse, a somber building carrying to this day the smell of the notorious scandals that accompanied its construction. Behind that the Municipal Building rises ornately to skyscraper proportions; courthouses, jails, a new police department headquarters enclose a new square built over traffic lanes.[5] From the midst of these many related but diverse elements the Brooklyn Bridge rises appropriately, perhaps the only structure noble and eccentric enough to hold them all in one frame.

City Hall Park itself is of quite ordinary design, with wide asphalt walks, benches neither modern nor antique, and fences of welded pipe. In summer a patch of flowers decorates the southern tip of its roughly triangular form. It is used as it should be. In addition to being the scene of almost daily picket lines, it harbors habitués of the area and visitors on various errands. In short, it is a very typical city hall park, a model of old-fashioned democracy.

Elsewhere, in various ways, the basic requirements are met. It is pleasant in Houston, amid so much that is heartless and unshaded by tradition, to find city hall facing upon a small park whose donor stipulated that bums and vagrants should not be expelled from it. Officials have subtly manipulated the tilt of the benches, hoping to discourage, since they cannot ban, these users. But they return—and their presence is one of the best possible reminders of the limits of bureaucratic power.

In Philadelphia the old city hall stands foursquare at the center of town, occupying one of Penn's original open spaces. Around and through the building, crisscrossing its large interior court, people pass in crowds, making government seem indeed the nexus and center point of the common life. Baltimore's city hall faces a large square. But unfortunately city hall turns its back upon the other points of liveliness within the downtown core, and the park stands too much alone to be entirely successful as a meeting place. Yet the space is programmed and is seen as being closely related to the functions of city government.[6]

Creating a New City Hall

The right combination of authority and democratic ease, of tradition and progressive innovation, is more often found within an existing city hall and city hall square than in ones newly conceived. Dallas is building both on new ground from designs by I. M. Pei. The large open space, built over a parking garage, may work as intended; but at least for the present it is to be inadequately walled and contained, and its surface design appears uncongenial to the Texas climate.

The most striking new plaza for a city hall is in Boston. This is worth looking at as an example of how people, rather than buildings, are the true creators of open space. Controversy in regard to the plaza has run vigorously since the new city hall was completed in 1969.

A strong statement in concrete showing the influence of Le Corbusier and Perret, the structure has had the capacity of all good buildings to stir discussion and opposition. Yet in many ways the most notable thing about it is its plaza. The plaza's size was fixed by the government center's master plan, and within the predetermined space the dimensions of the future city hall were laid down—a building 275 feet square, between 100 and 130 feet in height. Thus the plaza was envisioned from the beginning; remarkably, its construction was carried through with only minor modifications.

This plaza is not open space "left over" after the city hall was constructed. It is not a forecourt to the building nor an opening to detach it from its surroundings. It was conceived as the element in which an object was to be placed—the milieu within which the building was to exist. Thus understood, the strong sculptural form of the building makes sense. People object to it in almost the precise terms they would use in objecting to a piece of contemporary art. Actually, the building does serve much the same function as a work of art in any plaza, giving it liveliness and focus, making the surrounding void more interesting. Thus by a fine paradox the plaza becomes more important than the building. It is the ultimate reality, which the structure completes. Its existence predates the city hall, as the people are anterior to their government.

The question, then, is whether this major plaza plays its role as a stage for the people—indeed, as the expression of their corporate being. The answer is not altogether clear. The architects chose to make it a "hard plaza." Gardens, they felt, abound in Boston; this was to be a civic place with no greenery to trample. It has been criticized for that reason. The lack of trees and comfortable benches, the wide expanse of open space to cross in Boston's summer heat or winter cold, have led to insistence that the plaza was never made for people.

The plaza is busy enough during the hours the city hall is busy. An average day brings two thousand city workers to cross it and at least five thousand visitors. But at night and on weekends it is empty. The sensible reply of the designers is that in a crowded city it is good that some places be empty some of the time; they refer to the charm of Wall Street's deserted canyons on a Sunday.

For special events and for great occasions the plaza is used as it should be. When the Boston Bruins won the Stanley Cup in 1972, the place was solid with human beings. Antiwar rallies and other protest meetings make this a natural point of convergence. At lunchtimes in summer the mayor's office of cultural affairs arranges exhibits, festivals, concerts in great number by professional and amateur groups. Yet according to a survey of the plaza three years after its completion, people still did not get a hold on this as a consciously designed and bounded space.[7] Emerging from the narrow streets into this sudden expanse of brick steps and terraces, they were apparently confused rather than liberated.

May it not be that failing to feel the space that is more basic than the building, they failed, too, to sense their own unformulated power? They saw the outward form of government, but ignored the root from which authority is derived.

The Government Complex

The Boston city hall is part of a governmental complex of county, state and federal offices. In such a conjunction of political and administrative facilities lies the opportunity for open space planning on a grand scale. The city hall with its accompanying park or plaza can make a significant point of impact in the city. The larger complex can shape the downtown of a regional capital.

The concept of government buildings placed together, on a formal axis with open courts, is at least as old as the City Beautiful movement.[8] In Cleveland Daniel Burnham created the prototype—a wide plaza to be surrounded by classical façades and walled at one end by a railway station. In Denver the most popular open space in the city remains the park created in 1920 as the central court for a group of harmoniously designed governmental buildings. San Francisco determined on French Renaissance architecture for its civic center and managed to get it built despite the interruption of the earthquake. It retains a forecourt a little too formal to make people feel at home, but elegant with flowers, fountains and flags. Buffalo has long possessed a taste for the Baroque. Its civic center is built around Niagara Square, with vistas in several directions opening down broad diagonal avenues.

All these centers have shown a healthy capacity to adapt themselves to the cities' changing needs. Buildings incorporating new federal services have been located in proximity to older state, city and county offices—too often, unfortunately, lowering rather than raising the architectural standards. (In San Francisco, for example, the federal building contributes a regrettably inappropriate wall to one side of the Renaissance garden.) Cultural facilities have also been added in some cases. The new Denver Museum is built opposite the library at the edge of the governmental mall. An exhibition hall and civic auditorium have been added to Cleveland's classic center, and San Francisco has its museum and opera house in the shadow of city hall's fantastic gold dome.

Significant and imposing as are these older assemblages, a greater interest attaches to recent projects. Here there has been a real chance to introduce into the urban maze a measure of rationality, and into its often ugly commercialism an oasis of beauty. The results are of varying success. It seems hard for an architect or group of architects to design an official building that is authoritative without being dull. Where a group of such buildings is called for, constructed for diverse clients and under bureaucratic limitations, the product can be disastrous. Undoubtedly the worst plaza and the worst buildings—reminiscent of what might have been done under a second-rate dictatorship—appear in Rochester. Atlanta worked hard to carve out a landscaped park of originality and beauty, uniting the state capitol with city and county office buildings. Unfortunately, the jinx was at work.[9]

Though its underground garage is used to capacity, the park failed to attract the public to its terraces and watercourses.

The Albany Mall

No large governmental center has been conceived more audaciously than the Albany Mall, or (as its originators prefer it to be called) the Empire State Plaza. As governor of New York, Nelson Rockefeller felt the need to impart a fresh image to what was admittedly a decaying upstate capital. With Brasilia as his inspiration, he determined to make Albany "the most spectacularly beautiful seat of government in the world." Ninety-three acres in the heart of the city were cleared. Within this area a group of office buildings for state workers was planned, together with a museum and a convention center. The heart of the project is a landscaped mall extending a quarter of a mile from the south front of the capitol. The major buildings rise from this substructure, which also contains shopping arcades and parking.

After many delays and a rise in costs which by itself made the project highly controversial,[10] the virtues and defects of the still-incomplete mall could be seen in late 1975. That it was "spectacular" could hardly be denied. The large reflecting pool, the planting and sculpture, certainly invite tourists and in good weather will provide an agreeable concourse for governmental workers. Five identical buildings punctuate the space on its western edge; to the east rises a tall office tower and the bizarre but challenging convention hall, held aloft like an egg upon its slender pedestal. A museum whose steep steps double as an amphitheater stops the mall at its farthest end, while the capitol, a fantastic building combining Romanesque and Renaissance architecture, provides a highly sculptural southern wall.

From the perspective of open space planning this mall is subject to serious criticism. It stands by itself, at places sixty feet above the surrounding city, defying the need for connections and linkages with the surrounding community. Divorced from the city which it dominates brutally, it is a prime example of space architecturally imposed rather than growing out of the needs and activities of the citizens.

The degree to which the mall is cut off from the texture of the surrounding city is emphasized by the nearby presence of the Bar Association headquarters, a project far smaller in scale, but nevertheless faced from the start with some of the same problems. A series of connected buildings and courtyards

Governmental complexes provide a variety of spaces around them.

35. A group of Renaissance-style buildings frame an enchanting court between San Francisco's City Hall and two of its cultural institutions.

36. The Albany Mall.

37. New York City gains a delightfully informal plaza,
the Municipal Building and its new Police Headquarters.
carved from previously unusable space between

38. The nightmare of dead
space—Rochester's Civic Plaza.

39. Denver's classically conceived governmental complex
provides a much-used downtown park.

introduces a new note into downtown Albany, yet keeps one foot planted solidly in the existing community. Indeed, the façades of old houses along Lafayette Park have been retained by the new headquarters. Entering through a traditional door, one finds oneself in space that expands into entirely contemporary vistas. The government mall rejected such accommodation with the community in favor of its isolated grandeur.

With the money ultimately spent on the mall, much could have been done to enhance the existing spatial features of the old town. State Street, running down the hill from the capitol of the old railroad station, still bordered with buildings of strongs architectural character, could well have been the nucleus of the necessary development. High-rise buildings, as in Lafayette Square in Washington, could have been placed behind the existing structures. The street itself would have then become a mall, its steep slope made a virtue through some such transportation system as cable cars. Such a possibility among others was rejected at the start, and the result shows what happens to open space when it is designed without being solidly meshed with the urban environment.

The government complex at Binghamton is equally ambitious (at least for a city of its size) and it has its chilling aspects. But in comparison to the Albany Mall it shows several advantages. It is linked effectively to the old courthouse square and one day will be linked to the river walk. It opens across a footbridge to the city's major high-rise bank building and to the convention center. If plans for an adjacent in-town shopping center reach fruition, the open spaces of the government complex will come fully alive, as the Albany Mall may never do.

Regional Capitals—The Pure Type

In two western cities, both "new" cities and the very type of regional capitals, we see governmental complexes capable of complementing existing downtown spaces. Phoenix's is still largely in the planning stage, a mall more than a mile in length on a cross-axis from Central Avenue and terminating in the state capitol. Like almost everything else in Phoenix, this mall is scaled to the automobile: it is to be driven down, not traversed on foot. In the context this seems acceptable planning. Attention is given to parks and pedestrian green spaces along the route. The relation of the mall to the rudimentary downtown retail section, to the new music hall and exhibition center, and to the uptown commercial buildings assures a city plan as uncrowded as Phoenicians seem instinctively to like and one scaled to the oversized grid of its street system.

Los Angeles's government center is more complex and is woven into the web of an increasingly mature central business district. An odd and eclectic skyscraper dominates the series of government buildings. This is the home of city hall. If it stood by itself it might be considered a typical product of Los Angeles's exuberance. But the building reaches out by malls, gardens and covered bridges so as to make itself in truth a center. At right angles in one direction, open spaces extend across a street to a block-long plaza of shops and restaurants; from here a further bridge is planned to cross the freeway and penetrate the historic Pueblo. In another direction the spaces mount over terraced garages, park by park, to the cultural complex on Bunker Hill.

The concept puts government at the heart of the city where it ought to be. The official buildings neither dominate nor exclude, but give form to a large area of downtown and provide as a bonus many unexpected, human-scaled amenities. All this, be it noted, in a city where the automobile is supposed to reign supreme, and where a downtown is not even supposed to exist!

OPEN SPACES OF THE ARTS

It has been noted that more than one of the governmental centers are related to facilities for the arts. In Cleveland, in San Francisco, in Los Angeles, the homes of the performing or visual arts are neighbors to the seats of power. This appears to be part of a general practice to group large elements which can be planned together and for which land can be readily cleared. It has the added advantage of drawing upon a combination of funding sources. In complexes where the demand for parking can be spread over day and night users, real economies are achieved. Finally, the possibilities of creative development of open space are enhanced when the maximum number of units are combined.

The Los Angeles approach realizes these various benefits in juxtaposing its governmental and cultural center. With one at each end of a common mall, vistas as well as green sitting places can be shared. It does not appear that many government workers climb the steep incline to the hilltop site of the performing arts facilities. But the possibility of such a journey exists. The center itself borders an open square where a fountain by Lipchitz proclaims the cause of world peace. The buildings are in the architectural style which in the 1960s was thought appropriate to culture—travertine with residual columns.

Most interesting is the Water and Power Building, which closes the vista on the west side of the square. This might have been a disaster, an officious bulk dominating the adjacent scene. Instead it is what the British critic Reyner Banham has called "the only gesture of public architecture that matches the style and scale of the city."[11] Projecting floor slabs, especially when viewed from close by, impart a feeling of shelter and depth; the whole is lifted very lightly upon its columns and stands in a pool of water large enough to give the structure repose. Banham is especially impressed by the building at night—"this brilliant cube of diamond-cool light riding above the lesser lights of downtown."

If it is something of a miracle that a Water and Power Building should thus give to a cultural center a final touch of grace, it is a miracle, too, that the cultural center should have been placed downtown. It would have been easy to build the complex out on Wilshire Boulevard, along with the Los Angeles County Museum, perhaps sharing Hancock Park, with its sculptures of dinosaurs. The question of whether Los Angeles was to have a downtown was settled once and for all when the Music Center, under the resolute leadership of Mrs. Dorothy Chandler, was built on its present site.

It is surely good for the performing arts to be located amid the tensions and the essentially dramatic contrasts of a downtown location. These arts have always flourished in the city, and the greatest cities have seen them at their best. Conversely, it is good for downtown. They bring a nighttime audience into the streets and restaurants; they impart an air of gaiety to the urban scene. The development of necessary new facilities can, if they are well conceived, add significantly to open space forms. From the scores of cultural complexes built in the 1960s, examples are taken from three American cities:

- In Houston, a flower-filled square climbs by terraces to a small arena where open-air recitals are staged. This square at the downtown core is the setting created for two principal institutions: the Jesse H. Jones Hall for the Performing Arts, where the Houston Opera and Symphony play, and the Alley Theater.
- In Milwaukee, a wide opening was secured along the banks of a hitherto obscured river as a site for the city's new performing arts center. The buildings are well integrated with the river's edge, with steps mounting from the water as if a part of the audience were to come by boat. (Massive bollards, adding a fine sculptural note, have been installed, presumably, to make the boat fast.) Land for a conventionally designed new park has been cleared

on the other side of the river. Altogether, the effect of this open portion of the river where it lies between two bridges surrounded by the busy town, with the handsome theater rising from its banks, is one of the most charming of any American city today.

• In Akron, the Edwin J. Thomas Performing Arts Center accommodates different functions and audiences of different sizes within one hall subject to changing configurations. Its exterior terraces are well integrated with the building's strong shape, and indoor and outdoor spaces tend visually to merge. But from our point of view the most interesting aspect of this center is the fact that physically it creates a hinge between the University of Akron and the downtown core. Its open space is a bridge between two forms of spatial systems.

Washington and New York

While so many cities were succeeding in creating fertile new spaces in connection with their performing arts centers, the nation's capital missed its opportunity. The site for what was then to be known as the National Cultural Center was chosen under the Eisenhower administration. The first scheme, which came for review to Eisenhower's successor, John F. Kennedy, was rejected on the grounds that it was too ambitious a concept—a vast undulating roof covering three separate halls with covered spaces between them. In the revised plans the spaces disappeared and a monolithic building enclosed all the performing arts activities. A single oversized "grand foyer" connected them. The building was placed on a podium which provided a narrow balcony on three sides, widened to form a terrace on the riverfront.

While the new center was in the planning stage, possibilities of intensifying the use of Pennsylvania Avenue were being examined. Would it not have been a good idea to change the location, as well as the projected form of the cultural center, and to make it a key element of the new Pennsylvania Avenue? It would, among other things, have brought life to the area after government workers went home. President Kennedy was tempted by this idea, but rejected it, feeling that to abandon the preliminary work and to give up the acquired site would delay the project, eliminating the chance to have it completed during his years in office. Actually, the new center, now named for the assassinated President, was officially opened in October 1972, after Kennedy's successor, Lyndon B. Johnson, had retired to private life.

Contained between the Potomac River and a maze of freeways, the center's site precludes its playing a role in the pedestrian movement of the city or in the vitalization of downtown. Its rigid form is at odds with the river's gentle sweep, and even its monumentality is dwarfed by the Watergate complex, directly to the west. A magnet for tourists and a highly successful stage for the performing arts in Washington (which prior to the construction of the center had lacked virtually all facilities), the building contributes to the city virtually nothing in the way of usable open space.

Lincoln Center[12] in New York avoids many of these shortcomings, but has certain defects of its own. The way it originated and the results it achieved form a major chapter in American open space planning.

The old Metropolitan Opera House on Broadway and Thirty-ninth Street had by the early 1950s long outlived its usefulness. Conventionally appealing in its interior, graced by memories of outstanding performances by singers on the stage and (hardly less important) by society leaders in the boxes, it was a relic for which a substitute location had long been sought. Virtually no storage facilities existed for scenery or costumes; offstage the singers prepared for their roles in primitive conditions; and the whole was virtually unreachable through the maze of midtown and garment-center traffic. When Rockefeller Center was being planned in the 1920s there were proposals for including a new opera house. Later, plans were discussed for robbing Central Park of a slice of land at Columbus Circle.

By the 1950s the New York Philharmonic symphony orchestra was ready to join in a move, having visions of something grander than Carnegie Hall despite its congenial form and excellent acoustics. The lack of central facilities for drama, dance and chamber music inspired various groups and individuals to participate. What seemed necessary to crown the venture was an intellectual core. This latter need was to be supplied by having as part of the complex a branch of the New York Public Library that would contain its fine collection of prints and literature on the performing arts—and finally by including Julliard, the famous graduate school of the performing arts.

The land for all these facilities was amassed in a fourteen-acre area on the West Side ripe for clearance under urban renewal procedures.[13] The city agreed to the closing of a through street and undertook to use its bonding power for the construction of a large underground garage. In addition, the city insisted upon obtaining within the area land for a two-acre park. The problem was then to weave all these elements into an ordered form of open space and structure.

A team of architects was convoked, each to work on an individual building under the general chairmanship of Wallace Harrison. A wise and patient man, Harrison had performed a similar role in constructing the United

Nations headquarters. The disposition of space and volume was laid out, uniform cornice lines and a single building material, travertine, were agreed on. Within this frame six separate architects (including the architect of the park and its band shell) went to work. The object of this study is to appraise not the buildings, but the spaces between them. Nevertheless, it must be noted that the siting of the major components of the design, the marmoreal covering of the walls and terraces, and the accepted proportions of the building blocks, led inevitably to architectural pseudo-classicism. This was not likely to provide the kind of spaces congenial to varied, everyday use by the neighborhood or by the mixed audience that comes from afar.

The principal approach to Lincoln Center is from the east at Broadway. A plaza six hundred feet in length is bounded by Philharmonic Hall (now called Avery Fisher Hall) on the right; the New York State Theater, originally designed for ballet, on the left; with the Metropolitan Opera House closing the vista. At the center is a fountain, playing a repertoire of varying configurations. It is not a hospitable space. Devoid of green, with the containing wall of the fountain too high for comfortable sitting, it misses its chance to be one of the great squares of the city. The Chagall murals within the opera house shine through the large glass areas of the façade and are an unexpected boon when viewed from the plaza.

Attempts to humanize the space with banners during summer festivals are only partially successful, and the placing of outdoor tables for a summer restaurant leaves diners feeling exposed and dwarfed. Street theater and certain other events have been brought for performances in this space, but the players are done in by the large scale and the classic axis. Happily, arcades provide the pedestrian with a shelter from the elements along the fronts of the two facing buildings.

At the west end, as one nears the opera house, glimpses open up of the spaces lying to the left and right of the main plaza.

Moving through the opening to the left, one is in Damrosch Park, built over the parking garage, a concession wrenched by Park Commissioner Robert Moses from the Lincoln Center planners. A large band shell, the gift of a private foundation, dominates the design of this area. Once again as a result of scale, formality and a strong central axis, we find opportunities precluded for the more intimate forms of presentation.

The space to the right (or north) of the opera house is of a more varied and dynamic composition, and indeed constitutes the jewel of the Lincoln Center complex. This plaza is bounded by the side wall of the opera house, the side wall of the hall housing the orchestra, and then by the two major

40. In New York, Lincoln Center's main square is neo-classically bland, but
(41) entering from the north, the pedestrian confronts a striking juxtaposition of
forms bordering a large reflecting pool.

architectural successes. Across a bridged street stands the façade of the Juilliard School, an intricate and subtle orchestration which manages to wring vitality from the elsewhere cold and passive travertine. To the west, finally, is the Vivian Beaumont Theater, wrapped around and integrated with the library and museum, a happy relief from the monolithic structures that form the rest of Lincoln Center. In the middle of this plaza, in a large shallow pool, the sculptor Henry Moore first experimented with having his mysterious forms made doubly mysterious through reflection in water.

These spaces within Lincoln Center benefit from the size of the complex and the number of units that compose it. If these cultural facilities had been decentralized and scattered about the town (as many critics have wished), several small forecourts might have been achieved, but not this impressive assemblage of open spaces. This is a major argument for the present arrangement, even though one may conclude that the architects and planners failed in the ultimate task of humanizing the interlocked squares and plazas.

What about Lincoln Center's physical connections with the community around it? Hopes were once held to cut through the structures east of the center and to connect it by a broad esplanade to Central Park. Not altogether unfortunately, this scheme failed: the space would have been windy and perhaps empty. So the great square of Lincoln Center opens to busy traffic and to a haphazard collection of buildings over the design of which the city has had no control.

At least it does open in this direction, and its influence on the development of offices, restaurants and high-rise apartments in its immediate vicinity is evident. A different story unfolds toward the west. The Center turns its back on what the local police refer to as the "casbah," an area of public housing which was part of the original urban renewal project. Graffiti on the pure travertine surfaces, the threat of muggings combated by hidden cameras and a costly private police force, testify to a continuing problem. But the problem might have presented itself differently if the complex had been so designed as to make its open spaces a more friendly meeting place for diverse racial and economic groups.

Central Park where it meets Harlem on its northern edge shows no difference in form or landscaping from its affluent southern end. In this the park is truly central; while the nation's chief home for the performing arts is not absolutely a center—neither in its design nor in its spirit of accommodation.

Museums and Parks

These examples have dealt mainly with the performing arts; it is for them, indeed, that the newer downtown cultural centers have mainly been built. To a greater degree than museums, theaters and music halls seem to belong downtown. Internal economics usually dictate the museum's being closed in the evening hours. It does not, as a result, play the same role as do the performing arts in bringing people downtown at night to reinforce the patronage of restaurants or to give the streets and squares a lively appearance. Besides, it has long been written into popular superstition[14] that great art is to be viewed apart from the press of daily business, in a building that is more or less like a temple and in a setting as much as possible like a park.

Various good reasons may be adduced as to why this superstition should be abandoned. A museum downtown is easily accessible to shoppers, tourists and office workers. Its physical proximity to theaters brings out the inherent relationship between different forms of art. It may well be the instigator, as are the Museum of Modern Art and the Metropolitan Museum in New York,[15] of small but much appreciated open spaces.

The fact remains, however, that most museums *are* in parks, where they occupy valuable land and often cause special problems. Earlier in the century, Forest Park in St. Louis found itself under severe pressure to introduce trolley cars to make the museum more accessible. The Metropolitan Master Plan for expansion was subject to prolonged agitation by park groups.[16] In Dallas the Museum of Fine Arts, along with other sports and cultural facilities, shares a park with an annual cattle show. Prize specimens have been known to be in danger of impaling themselves on the outdoor contemporary sculpture.

San Diego's massing of museums and exhibitions in Balboa Park, in buildings left over from the Panama-California Exposition of 1915, creates a picturesque and harmonious series of spaces. Regrettably, the central square, which should be a pedestrian mecca, is given over entirely to parking. Similarly in Seattle, former fairgrounds provide the setting for major cultural institutions. As in almost all parks originally planned for a fair, there remain a disproportionate amount of blacktop and too many buildings of an incongruous nature. But Seattlites are proud of their well-located fairgrounds and patronize enthusiastically its opera house, theater and art gallery.

In Cleveland a somewhat different solution prevails. Three and a half miles from the Public Square, moving eastward along Euclid Avenue through a section of run-down or abandoned housing, one comes to the extensive green opening of University Circle. Here are gathered some two-score major cultural, educational and medical institutions, including the Museum of Art, Severance Hall (home of Cleveland's famous symphony orchestra), the Garden Center, the Museum of Natural History and many others. Together they form their own park, and the walk from any one of these to any other should be pleasant and easy. Unfortunately, in recent years a pall of fear has lain over the neighborhood,[17] and its value as an open space has been negated.

Even more original in that it is not placed in a park but is itself a park is the Oakland Museum, a model of how such an institution can be sensitive to its physical surroundings. The citizens of Oakland were ambitious for a large community museum. Kevin Roche, chosen as the architect, envisioned a series of terraces richly planted and adorned by sculpture, reached by easy steps and providing views over the surrounding city.

A problem of the contemporary museum or theater is that we do not know what its appearance should be.[18] No forms handed down by tradition and validated by an inherent logic speak to us of the basic function. Lincoln Center, widely imitated, gave a quite arbitrary idea of how a symphony hall or opera house should appear. Even Philip Johnson, who has put his stamp on American museums, cannot quite arrive at an authentic image. Roche solved the problem in Oakland by making the museum invisible—or at any rate making it visible only in the way that a park is.

At the base of rising terraces and scarcely distinguishable from them is an area of natural ground ideally suited to the festivals and exhibitions that are regularly programmed. The roof at the lowest level of the underground museum insensibly abandons its role as shelter to become a slightly elevated extension of the park. From here one mounts according to one's mood and inclination, always amid landscaped vistas. The topmost point looks down to the crowd gathered on the greensward below, or out to where Lake Merritt, the largest body of fresh water to be entirely contained within any American city, is alive on a breezy day with what seem a thousand small sailboats.

OPEN SPACES OF COMMERCE

Regional institutions of business and finance, for reasons somewhat different from those of government and the arts, have created their own spaces.

42. Oakland Museum.

In the contemporary downtown these become a dominant feature, the result partly of a business ethic which recognizes communal obligations and partly of the imperial pride that marks the new merchant princes as it did the old. But there is an additional reason, derived from the special building form in which modern businesses tend naturally to house themselves. The high-rise tower is itself a symbol of pride; it is also a species of structure that, conforming naturally to the office economy, has a tendency to create space around it.

Land values at the center of downtown make it attractive to build to a maximum height; and height induces the need for setbacks of one kind or another, to admit light to the street and to the building's own lower floors. This implicit need has been defined and reinforced by public policy. The traditional zoning envelope was responsible for the wedding-cake pattern characteristic of much of New York's urban landscape. The pattern began to change in the 1960s when a new zoning law allowed sheer towers with a setback in the form of a plaza at their base.

The plazas, which became a major feature of New York, were copied by virtually every downtown and have helped create a new spatial form at the core of the cities. This development has brought undoubted benefits; but as New York was the first to realize, it also had negative results. The street line was broken by unrelated setbacks; builders taking advantage of the bonus in extra stories were too often content to leave open spaces devoid of the amenities that might have made them a genuine public asset. Most serious of all, the skyscraper's effect on wind currents often created downdrafts that made the plaza unusable.

Two New York Models

How could the sheer tower best come into contact with the ground? What could most appropriately happen at the point where the skyscraper and the plaza joined? Practical and aesthetic answers to these questions were largely to determine the nature of downtown's most important new open spaces.

Two buildings in New York within a few blocks of each other on Park Avenue—the Lever and the Seagram buildings—set patterns for plazas which were to be widely emulated. Both of these were the result of predominantly aesthetic concepts and were conceived before plazas were fashionable or were profitable in terms of zoning concessions. Two differing approaches may be observed here in their pure form: the complex plaza, shaded, somewhat withdrawn, shaped by the form of the building itself; and the simple plaza resulting when a shaft is set down upon a plane.

In the first of these, the Lever Brothers building, a square "doughnut" lifted above the street on pillars leads the pedestrian toward a landscaped court at the center. Here the space soars upward, broken by the building's tower, which is again lifted on pillars and rises over one portion of the free-standing lower element. Besides the open space at ground level, there is a garden a few stories above the street on the roof of the "doughnut."

The Seagram Building is, by contrast, one exquisitely detailed tower, rising sheer from the street level and standing on a plaza almost unbroken in its severe expanse. Two barely perceptible steps define the plaza at the Park Avenue edge; two sheets of water lie at pavement level. No benches encumber the space, no trees shade it. The only seating space is along the steps or on two low parapets separated from the water by six-inch ledges.

The Lever Building plaza has never quite worked as it should, while the plaza of the Seagram Building has proved one of the most popular outdoor spaces in town. The former lacks sun; the containing wall of the landscaped area is too high for sitting, and the arcades created by the lifted doughnut seem cold and unwelcoming. By contrast, the Seagram Building's plaza is pleasantly sunny. Across the avenue, the low Renaissance-style exterior of a private club forms a handsome wall to the space. The building's architectural fame and its quite patent elegance must also draw men and women to its foot. Whatever may be the determining factors (such things are always mysteries in part), Seagram's plaza is the scene at the noon hour of all those activities and encounters which give zest to outdoor urban life.

The complex spatial relationships and the modulated sheltered areas of the Lever Brothers building were to find later embodiments in the Embarcadero development of John Portman in San Francisco, for example, and in such a building as 100 William Street, New York, where a fine, unenclosed space is carved from the lower stories of the high-rise. But the apparent simplicity with which the Seagram plaza achieved its effects, combined with its manifest popular success, were factors in fixing a new image. In every American city, forgetting Seagram's fortunate positioning and usually insensitive to its art, developers imitated this plaza. They reproduced its bareness. They almost inevitably lost its magic. Small windy patches of pavement, usually without planting and with something enthusiastic but inadequate in the way of sculpture or a fountain, came to break the average street line.

Three plazas in the Chicago Loop.

43. Federal Complex.

44. First National Plaza.

45. Civic Center.

Chicago's Triad

Chicago presents the example of three notable plazas at the base of high-rise buildings, grouped closely together along Dearborn Street in the Loop. The street acts as a linkage to these separate openings in the tight urban web, within the length of a few blocks providing the pedestrian with the thrice-repeated experience of emerging from a constrained and busy passage into a major space. Two of these plazas are, to be sure, governmental in their principal use; they might have been treated in the earlier section of this chapter. But the dominant buildings take the skyscraper form. They say something important about the relationship between this type of structure and the street from which it arises.

Moving along Chicago's Dearborn Sreet, the Federal Plaza created by Mies van der Rohe comes to view first. The discipline of the surrounding structural forms and the somber detail of the tower make a place of somewhat formal elegance, dark in tone, subdued in use. This is not a green to dance upon; it is not even a square in which to congregate, but one to cross on foot with an awareness of the federal government's ultimate but reserved authority.

A block farther down appears the free-standing tower of the First National Bank. This was constructed in the 1960s with the intent of forming a new symbol on the skyline and a new people-place around it.[19] In the latter respect (which is our concern) it has fully succeeded. The plaza draws crowds who spread themselves on its terraces, lie upon its low parapets, observe the changing pattern of its fountains and stare bemusedly at the sculpture. The effect is one of movement and brightness.

Again the city walker moves a block down Dearborn: this time he enters the Civic Plaza, dominated by the thirty-one-story Civic Center building. It was the first high-rise to use Corten steel, and the rust-brown color of its exterior reinforces the strong sense of presence imparted by the eighty-foot span of its girders. The plaza is well surrounded on three sides by a variety of new and older buildings, and on the fourth is contained by a Renaissance-style façade running unbroken along it. This building houses city hall and the county offices and is connected by an underground passage to the Civic Center.

It is one of the most successful of urban places, and it gains in significance from its relation to the other squares. The walker will have come from the austerity of Mies van der Rohe's great construction through the people-centered plaza of the First National Bank. Now on these grounds of the Civic Center occurs a succession of public events and manifestations which build up an audience almost daily. Carefully programmed, this open space fulfills its own function and imaginatively supplements the adjacent plazas and street life.

In these examples the sheer tower meets the single plaza; but the movement toward a more complex form may be discerned. The high-rise Federal building is balanced and completed by smaller-scaled buildings of similar architectural details; the plaza of the First National Bank is multilevel—showing, incidentally, that areas below street level can attract public use if effectively designed. The First National also flares dramatically at its base, and though the lofty space is for customers of the bank, it suggests later experiments at creating public places within the body of the structure.

Thus within a small area, at the heart of the city that has contributed so much to skyscraper design, we find outstanding examples of how the tower and the plaza can create excitement where they meet. We also see suggestions of the more varied and complex solutions to which the skyscraper lends itself.

Toward Increasing Complexity

Though Lever was a single building, it suggested in its carefully separated structural elements—the "doughnut," the tower—that spatial possibilities would be fulfilled within an assemblage of buildings containing various functions. The achievement of the planners' dream of linked open spaces as part of a landscape of towers and platforms came to realization in large-scale business centers combining high- and low-rise buildings, and embodying—along with the office space—hotels, parking garages, shops, restaurants and theaters. As we move into this type of development we find ourselves dealing with the truly innovative spaces contributed by business to the new downtown.

The pioneer of this kind of large-scale project was Rockefeller Center in New York. To this day nothing surpasses it in the way open areas are molded and spaces contained or released with deliberate art. The placing of the low buildings in relation to the higher, the subtle changes of scale and level in the areas between the buildings, develop all the dimensions of outdoor space. The system of arcades below the street creates a new pedestrian world.

The skyscraper creates a diversity of spaces at its base.

46. The TransAmerica Building in San Francisco may affront the skyline, but where it meets the ground it offers a suggestive relationship between interior and exterior spaces.

47. The Gas and Electric Building in Los Angeles floats serenely over its watery base.

48. The IBM Building in Seattle adorns its own garden.

49. The Federal Reserve Building in Minneapolis is engineered to leave 90 percent of the ground free and forms an important adjunct to the mall. (But its "benches" do not make for comfortable sitting!)

The linkages to the surrounding community were given much thought. Not only was the center situated at the heart of a vibrant network of streets and avenues, but its planners hoped to break through the existing street structures to the north, cutting a midblock walkway to Central Park. In this they were unsuccessful,[20] but a generation later they tied to the original system of spaces and tunnels new plazas across the Avenue of the Americas. The second phase of the Rockefeller Center construction, running from Forty-seventh to Fifty-third Street along this avenue, is disappointing in its open spaces; it reverts to the single tower on the more or less isolated rectangle. Yet the lined-up plazas work better than might have been anticipated, providing a startling display of trees and waters and resulting in a few unexpected small parks and passages at the towers' rear.

A later attempt to combine office buildings within a coherent, pedestrian-scaled space was begun in the late 1950s in Constitution Plaza at Hartford. Not in this case a single dominant interest, but the business and financial leaders of a community long known for civic responsibility, took the initiative; they worked within the legal framework of urban renewal to transform a twelve-acre area running along the Connecticut River. A platform bridges the on-grade streets, with the related buildings opening upon this at their mezzanine level. A campanile and a fountain organize the space; shops and a restaurant open upon it. Two of the structures that pierce the plaza, Wallace Harrison's "double-ender" for the Phoenix Life Insurance Company and Skidmore, Owings and Merrill's vigorous adjunct to the Travelers' building, are sculptures in themselves.

Constitution Plaza, nevertheless, fails to attract the foot traffic essential to its life. Only in the finest weather and during public ceremonies does it draw people other than office workers from the buildings themselves. The plaza lies at the edge of downtown rather than at its center. To the east it abuts the expressway; along its western border the plaza suffers from lack of the pedestrian bridges that should have tied it in with the city's major retail area. Thus Constitution Plaza provides an unfortunate example of how an open space conceived with imagination and carried out with immense civic dedication can fall far short of its potentialities—and that for one reason. It does not observe the first rule of effective open space, namely that it must be tied in with the widest possible community and linked to other foci of pedestrian activity.

A somewhat comparable achievement of the 1960s, which avoids this pitfall and capitalizes brilliantly on its position at the center of various civic functions, is Charles Center in Baltimore. As has been noted in the description of Baltimore's downtown, this congeries of office buildings, old and new, supplemented by diverse services for entertainment and by two residential towers and a hotel, lies at the juncture of retail, governmental and educational nodes; it feeds into them and from them draws its own intense life. The open spaces, instead of being uniformly elevated upon a platform, follow the varying levels of the land; while an upper system of pedestrian bridges and walkways provides for easy communication and for changing visual experiences. The Charles Center is conceptually as far removed from the buildings grouped on Hartford's Constitution Plaza as it is from the independent skyscraper on its pocket of open land.

Space on a Podium

The platform from which arise the towers of Hartford's Constitution Plaza is not unique, nor is it by any means an aberration of the planners. It is a condition to be found in every city, being in most cases an expression of the need to provide accessible parking space. The base that houses the automobile, with a tower rising from it, is an inviting structural form, and has the advantage of allowing for a landscaped plaza on the roof of the podium. The trouble is that the podium is not part of the street and requires a psychological effort to mount to it. Even where the raised platform is intended primarily for use by the office workers of the building itself it will fall short of its purpose. For the office workers turn out to be unappreciative of even the most luxurious plantings, if the spaces lead nowhere and are not enlivened by cross-currents of humanity.

Efforts to draw people to such elevated plazas can be ingenious. The podium of the Alcoa Building in San Francisco is dramatically recessed at one point, to form a small courtyard with escalators tempting one to move upward. Overhead, as one mounts, the lifted tower of the main building is a sheltering presence. The plaza is then linked by pedestrian bridges to the Embarcadero Center and to the Gateway housing development. It is a pleasant sight upon a weekend to find young boys, escaped from the adjacent residential area, playing ball upon Alcoa's austerely landscaped and perfectly maintained plaza.

Even more elaborate are the devices used to lure people upward to the elevated plazas of John Portman's adjoining Embarcadero Center. Here, too, the combination of offices, hotel and shopping requires a podium, and poses the problem of how to make its surface fully useful. A series of so-called

50. The complex podium at Embarcadero Center.

people scoops—free-standing translucent passageways or tunnels—lead people from street level into a low-roofed open space. Escalators carry one to a second level, still confined in height but now considerably brightened by light falling through openings in the deck above. At one point a vertical stainless-steel sculpture pierces this deck, carrying the eye aloft and serving to unify the different levels.

Shops and small offices as well as main entrances to the high-rise buildings are found at this second stage of the upward climb. Finally at the top, in the free air but sheltered by wide overhangs and surrounded by the Embarcadero's towers, the pedestrian moves through alleys and courtyards, over bridges, and into variously shaped small courtyards.

From the lowest level the way has been brightened by flowers and fountains and variously lit by light falling from above. Despite so much evident care, the scheme is not entirely successful. The entrances at street level are into spaces that seem excessively low and that invite the San Francisco winds. The organization of the complex as a whole and the entrances into the main buildings do not readily explain themselves. As for pedestrian use of the upper level, it raises questions which will only be answered when the center has been completed and all its linkages are in place.

New Approaches

The pause in office construction after the overbuilding of the 1960s provides a much-needed opportunity for second thought in regard to the spaces of business institutions. New York, which had led the way in encouraging the plaza, revised its zoning law in 1975[21] to assure a higher standard of usefulness for these spaces. The provision of trees in a specified number, of comfortable seating areas (nothing above thirty-six inches or lower than twelve), the inclusion of small stores and kiosks, were included in the amenities for which construction bonuses would be given. The zoning revision also encouraged open spaces on the side streets rather than on the avenues, where the building line was in danger of being eroded by relatively useless setbacks.

In place of the sharp separation between outdoor and indoor space, architects began to consider ways of providing shelter at the point where the skyscraper touched earth. In his IDS Center in Minneapolis and his Pennzoil Place building in Houston, Philip Johnson let his towers descend into a cascade of sheltering glass; in his plans for the IBM Building in New York, Edward L. Barnes placed the tower hard on the street corner and tucked behind it, at the interior of the block, glass-covered, balconied arcades. The once-uniform office shaft became, as with New York's Olympic Tower or Galleria complex, a megastructure housing various functions, business and residential, with something like an enclosed street at the entrance level.

Perhaps the most radical outcome of such a re-evaluation would be to question the need of the skyscraper itself. The skyscraper in one form or another has been the generator of the business community's special contribution to open space. But except in the most crowded cities, the advantage of the skyscraper may be challenged. In Kansas City, Crown Center resisted the temptation to erect a central office tower; its active and well-peopled square lies within a series of white low-rise buildings descending the steep incline, turning to form a second wall for the open space.

When a city like Louisville builds again it could well imitate Kansas City rather than New York. A loosely organized downtown core is in need of edges, not points of reference. The edges create walls within which open space can have a familiar dimension and an inviting microclimate.

14 Designed for Living

THE IMPORTANCE OF RESIDENTS within the central business district is felt instinctively by all concerned with the vitality of U.S. cities and is a constant theme of city planners. No matter how effectively the core may serve the interests of the executive, the office worker, the visitor and tourist, it remains a half-formed place so long as it does not include permanent city dwellers. A transient population in hotels, even a tower or two of luxury apartments, are not sufficient to support retail and entertainment establishments. Streets and parks still remain empty after working hours; the lack of neighborhood services makes a barren streetscape prone to crime. To be downtown over the weekend in a city like Houston, which has virtually no residents within the core, is to feel oneself isolated in a strangely hostile and inhuman environment.

The addition to the tax base provided by a residential section is important, but in the long run it is perhaps less essential to the well-being of downtown than the overall vitality and color imparted by people living there.

Transients Are Not Enough

The features that appeal to a transient population—convention facilities, exhibition halls, dramatically conceived hotels and shopping centers—lose much of their attractiveness when they are not rooted in a living community. The city core conceived principally for visitors becomes inevitably blatant and somewhat tawdry in its appeal. New York's Greenwich Village or New Orleans's Vieux Carré are instructive examples of how a harmonious environment can degenerate—slightly at first but fatally if the shift is not arrested—when the residential component is weakened. Local arts, exploited for the benefit of outsiders, become debased; pornography takes over bookstores and strip joints invade the erstwhile haunts of musicians. Long-established residents move away, and in the end even the stranger begins to look elsewhere for the authentic attractions of big-city life.

Not only does the residential community relieve the city's scale, break its grid, feed life into its streets and squares. In more subtle and extended ways it enhances the environment. A resident population demands water-front development providing more complex and varied facilities than the massive structures that commercial developers encourage. It insists on such amenities as local entertainment facilities, on small stores and walkways, on historic areas preserved. In all these the visitor finds unexpected pleasures for himself and tastes the urban experience he is in search of.

The desire to live downtown is, happily, reasserting itself among various groups of the population. Singles and young couples looking for diversions, older citizens for whom life outside the center can mean loneliness and isolation, are glad of an opportunity to return to what is essentially an old form of city living. Others want to be close to their place of work or simply to feel part of the urban scene. Easy access to cultural facilities and to specialized shops compensates them for the lack of suburban green.

Meanwhile rising fuel costs and generally poor public transportation—factors not likely to be quickly reversed—make the central business district increasingly attractive as a place of residence.

A market for downtown housing exists. Some of this is for "found" quarters in lofts and in more or less decaying residential quarters capable of being imaginatively rehabilitated. Some is in historic areas. A further demand is for modern town houses or for apartments in high-rise towers. Not only upper- and middle-income developments, but public housing of modern design, should contribute significant new open spaces to the community.

Humanizing Downtown

As business or the arts create spaces suited to their needs, so the residential community weaves its own web of openness. Before examining housing itself, we glance at some of the increments to open space stimulated by a residential community. Schools within the core become a necessary adjunct to housing; they have playgrounds which are often shared with the community. Churches have their churchyards. In downtown Hartford we observed young children playing happily among the tombs of a centrally located church. Well-used local shopping streets become more than traffic lanes and at their best assume the quality of a plaza or square.

Special open space opportunities, too often neglected by urban planners, are provided by the community college.[1] The tendency for any college to become an enclave can reveal itself in a downtown campus designed exclusively for the benefit of students. Yet with some thought the campus can be integrated with the core and made to enlarge its pedestrian spaces. In Omaha, in Minneapolis, in Madison, to take a few examples, this interpenetration is stressed and the college is seen as a community asset not only because of its educational services but because of its environmental contribution.

Portland, Oregon, suggests most happily how the open spaces of the two worlds of living and learning can be made to supplement each other. Interconnected park blocks, extending like fingers of green through the central business district, have long been proof of the essential habitability of Portland's core. One of these linear, heavily treed parks extends past churches and cultural institutions to become the open space spine of the new Portland State College. Physically the blocks are unaltered as they reach into the heart of the college; but the manner of their use changes. They now become a kind of campus; students are crossing or sitting on the grass, are reading or playing ball or Frisbee.

Housing itself, however, most naturally and on the largest scale provides the open spaces of the downtown residential area. Where people have made their homes within the city there has invariably been a looser spatial texture. On the old main street stretching immediately beyond the business district houses were traditionally set back upon lots sufficiently large to allow trees and vestigial lawns. Other housing configurations provided open space in the form of private backyards or of some residue of green around apartment blocks. Today in the best of contemporary housing conscious efforts have been made to provide various kinds of spaces, from those strictly for the use of owner or tenant to those serving the community. In a few cases these spaces have been imaginatively integrated with the wider space system of downtown.

Hierarchy of Spaces

The open spaces of housing are different from those created by the activities of commerce, government or the arts in that they must be designed to satisfy a more extensive spectrum of human needs. They must be conceived with private as well as public activities in mind.[2] These residential open spaces, indeed, must be seen in relation to the spheres of life, which may be defined as private, communal and public. Each sphere should have its own mode of activity, its own form of social contact, its own level of discourse. A legitimacy attaches to each and the danger in a particular society is that one sphere will be neglected at the cost of the others or that confusion may exist among them.

Applied to housing, this approach suggests a justification for spaces that are genuinely private—for balconies that do not look into a neighbor's balcony; for patios or backyards that are adequately screened. This is the stage for intimate family life, which suffers from exposure or display. At a second level are the spaces of the communal sphere, basically designed for those who live nearby. Here men and women meet as neighbors, children play together and young people intensify already easygoing relationships. In the enclosed courtyard that typifies this kind of place, people can be relaxed, can feel safe, and talk naturally about the concerns of their shared existence.

Beyond these two lie the public spaces of the city, related to housing and yet not directly part of it. In the public sphere the individual must be on his guard; he is among strangers, he is inevitably insecure and to some extent or other must play a part. As a compensation he finds there the excitement, the variety and ultimately the responsibility that accompany a public role. The street is the conventional form of public space associated with housing. The resident emerges from comparative seclusion into the full glare of the busy public artery, and what this street is like will strongly affect the quality of life within the housing itself.

In the design of much contemporary housing, as in much of contemporary life, spaces have not fully reflected the threefold nature of the citizen's role. Private spaces have been lacking or have been poorly arranged for their functions. Frequently the existence of the community of residents has simply not been manifested in outdoor spaces (indoor spaces may occasionally tell a different story); and the wider society of the city itself has been seen as something to be kept at a distance and so far as possible to be ignored. In a few examples we shall presently see how, at best, a respect for the differentiation between the communal and the public spheres can be respected and can be expressed in terms of spatial organization.

Housing shapes open spaces for tenants and for public.

51. Gateway Housing in San Francisco provides sheltered streets built romantically on a podium.

52. And at its base a new public park.

53. In St. Louis' Benton Place, old houses, now being restored, border a private street.

54. La Clede housing in St. Louis has its own lane primarily for its community of tenants.

Problems of Common Space

First, however, we call attention to the major difficulties faced by planners endeavoring to create effective community space in housing developments. Uniform slabs rising from superblocks—a form characteristic of the
1950s[3]—destroyed the very concept of the street; its walkways belonged
neither to the public nor to the residents and its grass plots were fenced off
against use. Not surprisingly there was little if any "spread effect" from
such housing. The area around remained as barren as it had usually been
before, with crime developing within the housing units and increasing
through the immediate surroundings. Families would forbid their children to
descend into the open spaces that should have been the scene of their
play and their arena of contact with a world outside the home.

First attempts to remedy these intolerable conditions focused on making
the open spaces more inviting and useable.[4] Shelters and playgrounds were
constructed within the open space between buildings; benches and planting
were introduced. The impersonal nature of the structures themselves, however, minimized social contacts between the residents and introduced the
same impersonal quality into the open spaces. Because the tenants did not
know each other, they did not know who was a stranger or intruder; and
the open spaces could never be considered truly safe. Not being communal or
public, they possessed the merits of neither, and the result was visible in
vandalism and graffiti.

More recent efforts have recognized the importance of maintaining the
street line and at the same time have endeavored to create community
spaces that serve the real needs of tenants. At best, however, the task has
not been easy nor the results always encouraging. A basic dilemma exists.
If the community space is kept exclusively for use of residents, cut off from
contact with the wider city, it tends to become boring and sterile and often
is not fully enjoyed. If, on the other hand, the space is opened to public
passage or public use, it may well become a no man's land. There is no
complete answer to this problem, and much depends upon the locality, the
quality of the neighborhood and the type of housing. So long as crime and
the fear of crime run through the city, the opportunities for creating true
community space are limited.

It is to this problem of community space that Oscar Newman's well-known
study *Defensible Space* addresses itself.[5] Obviously private space *is* defensible, and public space, with equal obviousness, is not. The middle area,

however, invites some interesting and imaginative proposals designed to provide a feeling for security among its users. Newman advocates in particular subdividing communal space into zones toward which adjacent residents can easily adopt proprietary attitudes. He proposes positioning apartment windows to allow residents natural surveillance of semipublic areas. Yet in high-crime neighborhoods such methods prove sadly inadequate.

At one of the sites of the Twin Parks housing in the Bronx, the common space, originally entered under piloti from the street and crossed by a neighborhood path, is now barred by heavy fences and locked gates. The space reserved for the tenants is accessible only through the heavily guarded apartment lobbies; and there is talk of closing off this space entirely. In the later 1199 Plaza housing in East Harlem the community open spaces were designed so as to be invisible from the exterior and to be approached only through building exits at the second-floor level.

Such conditions are pathological, and it is distressing to see community spaces in upper- or middle-class residential neighborhoods, where security ought not to be the sole consideration, designed as impregnable bastions. Both to the housing complex and to the wider city a visual and physical connection between the communal and the public sphere is highly advantageous. In the Laclede housing in St. Louis, for example, the communal spaces are enlivened by being semipublic and by having the character of small village squares. Greens between the housing units may be penetrated by the casual visitor, even though they are set more deeply into the interior of the block and give the healthy impression of being under the watchful eye of householders. In San Francisco the charming walkways of the Golden Gate Housing are not off bounds to the public, though the spaces are secluded and are lifted a level above the regular street system.

Community spaces concealed from the city and walled against its intrusions can be particularly deadly if, as is often the case, the housing units themselves are coldly functional and impersonal. Negative feelings of defensiveness, fear and suspicion tend to transform themselves from the interior environment to the outdoor spaces. Where people in the building know each other and work together—where a high level of social interaction exists —the atmosphere in a closed commons can be good. But even here it will lack the stimulation that comes from relatedness to the city; and the city will not benefit from pleasing vistas or from opportunities for casual explorations of the domestic environment.

Public Spaces

The best of contemporary housing has recognized the importance of stimulating favorable conditions in the territory immediately surrounding it and has made efforts to weave itself into the context of the city. Low-rise buildings and row houses are particularly dependent on the street as a kind of forecourt; the need is plain to enhance this public place at the very minimum by tree plantings and improved pavement.[6] In a good many neighborhoods the street becomes a place for children to play as well as for householders to meet amid the errands of day-to-day living. Where there are no community spaces, but only the private spaces of backyards and patios, the commonplace, old-fashioned sidewalk plays an important role.

In more complex and large-scale residential developments, the need to improve and enlarge public space has too often been overlooked. The superblock is conceived in defiance of the conventional street pattern, while isolated towers destroy the wall of the street line. More recent planning restores to structures their old role as an edge, and the street in one form or another is made to penetrate the development. It serves for play, for free passage, as a spine for shops.

Thus in Manhattan's Ruppert Housing the existing street pattern is carried through at grade, with brick pavement and bold planting used to distinguish it from the surrounding neighborhood. Through traffic is blocked by bollards. Similarly, in Harlem's Metro North a continuation of the existing street thrusts visually into the interior of the complex, to be dramatically ended in this case by the sculptural forms of an elementary school. In both these cases the housing has invigorated pre-existing public space, to the benefit alike of the housing complex and of the surrounding neighborhood.

In other instances the housing has created incremental open space specifically for the public at large. In the Ruppert Housing the avenue has been gracefully widened to accommodate local shops and a restaurant; the result will be a landscaped public square with banners, kiosks and low walls for sitting. Less successful is the public space contributed by the housing at 1199 Plaza, where a fountain and a sunken arena are cut off from public enjoyment by a wide, truck-laden avenue and where noise must fatally inhibit musical or other performances.

In three examples we shall now see how residential developments have been planned on a large scale so as to give new importance to the spatial organization of a major city's downtown. Here the public spaces have not so much been contributed by the development as they have been planned by the respective cities to constitute the matrix upon which the new residential community takes shape. In one case the public spaces have the form of pedestrian lanes; in another of a greenway, and in the third of a major new public street.

PORTLAND CENTER Undoubtedly one of the most successful developments in any American downtown is in Portland, Oregon—a complex that includes major components of offices and shops with the housing. The story of Portland Center's planning is interesting, for it shows that less by original intent than by an interplay of chance forces was the housing locked into a major downtown site and made a vital part of its open space system.[7] That the site, a dilapidated group of buildings on dreary streets, should be cleared was generally accepted by the community and by the city planning department. But the first demand of the citizens was that it be rebuilt with federal funds as a combination recreation hall and convention center. A site for the latter was then picked across the Williamette River, notwithstanding the opposition of the federal authorities. In the ensuing controversy and delays, the deterioration of Portland's downtown became evident to all. As in many comparable American cities, business was leaving downtown, suburban branch stores and shopping centers were draining away retail trade. In the end the promise of jobs, housing and new downtown economic activity won out over the recreation center. The firm of Skidmore, Owings and Merrill was engaged in 1960 to prepare a master plan for the site.

The first decision was in regard to the street system. Both for practical reasons—to preserve the alignment of underground utilities—and for urbanistic reasons—to keep open vistas into the surrounding city—it was decided to continue the established street pattern, but with many of the vehicular corridors replaced by landscaped malls. Portland's blocks are unusually small (a mere two hundred by two hundred feet), and so several of these were consolidated as building sites. The result was a satisfactory combination of the superblock bounded by traffic and of small-scaled pedestrian malls.

Development of additional open space was then considered. Anchoring the site at one end would be the famous Forecourt Fountain; to balance this at the edge farthest from downtown was a hard-surfaced square known as Lovejoy Park, built around a fountain whose cascading waters pour down over slabs of rocks into a still pool. Within the complex the berms of Pettygrove Park provide a tranquil break amid the landscaped routes lying in the beds of the older streets.

These public places give to the whole area a parklike atmosphere. In

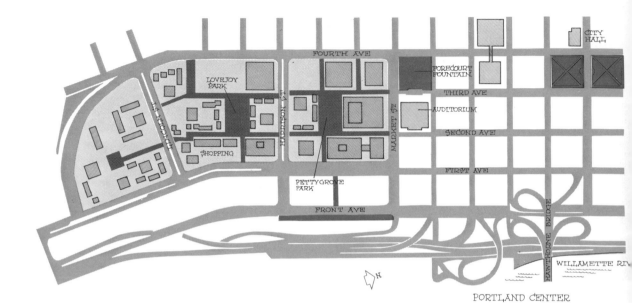

PORTLAND CENTER

55. In this mixed development pedestrian ways continue the street pattern of the surrounding city.

56. At Pettygrove Park it opens a new public space.

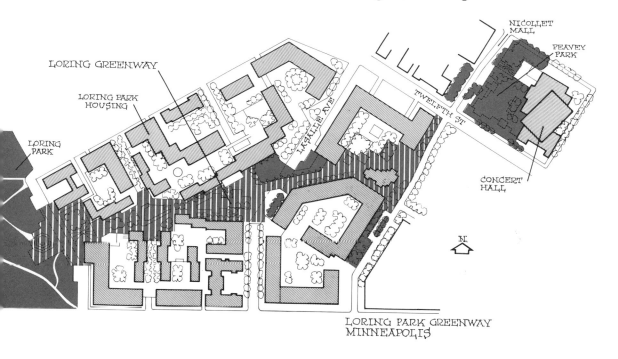

LORING GREENWAY

LORING PARK
HOUSING

LORING
PARK

LASALLE AVE

TWELFTH ST

NICOLLET
MALL

PEAVEY
PARK

CONCERT
HALL

N

LORING PARK GREENWAY
MINNEAPOLIS

smaller courts and patios, on terraces and balconies, exist the private and the community spaces of the development.

The continuity between the walkways of Portland Center and the streets of the surrounding downtown has been beneficial in economic as well as social and aesthetic terms. Here there has really been a spread effect, with the streets opening from the center being bordered today by new shops, headquarters for national industries and a major hotel. Prior to the development of Portland Center the annual tax return from the area was $143,000. By the 1972–1973 tax year this had mounted to approximately $3.6 million.

LORING PARK HOUSING   Unlike Portland Center, this downtown residential complex in Minneapolis is still in the early stages of development. But its principal open space, a public greenway completing the organization of Minneapolis's downtown, is being shaped.[8] The fact that the public space should come first is a striking indication of the values that determine the planning of this housing complex.

Loring Park itself is an old and particularly cherished green space, which had the rare good fortune of being included on the interior of the encircling expressway. It has stood somewhat apart, however, lacking a connection with the Nicollet Mall. The Loring Park housing complex was conceived as a way of providing for downtown a much-needed residential component and at the same time of assuring continuity for the walkway system that will ultimately connect the park and the river.

Housing on the two sides of the new greenway will be undertaken by private developers, but within restrictions that guarantee the most beneficial use of the new public space. The buildings must accommodate themselves to an arcade, which can be enclosed as the skyway system is completed. They must be of a design that provides windbreaks for the pedestrian as well as maximum sunlight. Community open spaces of the housing complexes must be maintained according to predetermined standards.

What the housing will thus support and contain is, in effect, a linear pedestrian park. It is composed of spaces carefully proportioned and arranged in sequence, as inviting to the residents of the new housing as it is important to the spatial structure of the central business district. Since it is built over a substructure through part of its length, its planting materials are necessarily restrained; the narrow width is appropriate to the rows of small shops on either side. Approaching Loring Park, the greenway widens. This section allows denser planting over earth fill and a drop in level is used to make possible a projected amphitheater.

Thus in one powerful and logical plan the old dream of bringing Loring Park fully within the scope of downtown is accomplished. Along with it is achieved the equally significant aim of making this part of downtown a place for residents. Here one sees clearly how various open space systems—a mall, a square, a famous old park and a new pedestrian concourse—can be woven into one whole so as to give the citizen a maximum diversity of urban experiences.

ROOSEVELT ISLAND HOUSING   When it was determined that the long-neglected island in New York's East River should accommodate four to five thousand units of housing, various conventional options were open to the designers. They chose to organize the structures so as strongly to define, and clearly to distinguish between, community and public places. The former take the form of courtyards within the U-shaped building forms. They work as community space because the general sense of security is high; the island families know one another and are less likely than in other circumstances to feel themselves subject to invasions by strangers.

57. Roosevelt Island—a strongly urban Main Street, shaped by housing.

The public spaces are striking and original, for from the beginning the buildings were shaped to create a curving central street. From this street, walkways were to open unimpeded views to the water and to connect with a bicycle path circumnavigating the entire island.

Unfortunately, the first stage of construction seems likely to stand alone through the foreseeable future, without the continuation of the central street into a proposed second "village" and an area of mixed commercial uses. Unfortunately, too, the views to the river have not been kept clear, nor the bicycle path built in its extended form. Yet Roosevelt Island, incomplete though it is, and with the mix of its population uncertain, shows the way the concept of housing has developed. From the vacant no man's land of the projects of the 1950s, from street levels devoid of stores and shops, we had come by the early 1970s to this shaping of the structures so as to form a genuinely public space, alive and busy, open but contained.

The master planners, Philip Johnson and John Burgee, worked with a highly sophisticated sense of external order, playing down architecture in favor of the spaces it enclosed. Any architectural expression (or at least, they said, "almost any") would be tolerable and capable of fitting within the defined framework. "The important elements of this plan," said the designers, "are its spatial and functional organization, its massing, the development of open and closed spaces."[9]

The shop-lined street of the Roosevelt Island housing presents in its three-dimensional form a pleasingly intimate urban environment—of sufficient length to express the curve and in some ways the more impressive because it is a street within a housing development rather than within the once-hoped-for new town. The height of the buildings, surpassing first projections, has been skillfully handled so as to avoid its becoming overwhelming. A landmark church, carefully preserved, has been converted to a community meeting house and, with its surrounding plaza, creates a satisfying break. Arcades and glass-sheltered entrances make the street an all-weather thoroughfare. The very fact that a certain number of cars (serving the hospitals still left on the island) pass through the street makes it seem like a "real" place and not a stage setting.

Open Space of Old Neighborhoods

The spaces we have been discussing exist in new neighborhoods; they have required for their construction extensive demolition and clearance.

Especially under early urban renewal procedures, structures that might have lent themselves to rehabilitation, and even structures of historical and architectural note, were destroyed wholesale by the bulldozer. People are still to be found who talk wistfully of a community that existed on the land where Constitution Plaza now extends in Hartford. Poor, squalid, subject to floods it admittedly was, yet it harbored a communal life which could not survive being transplanted. Similarly with the site of Portland Center. Some people think back to a community that might have been salvaged rather than replaced.

It is not always possible from a distance in time to judge whether particular communities might have been preserved; it is clear, however, that where preservation and rehabilitation are feasible, chances exist for open spaces at least as serviceable as those contrived by the urbanists. There may not be the kind of drama that designers like M. Paul Friedberg and Lawrence Halprin introduce into their new parks or walkways; but the older districts of downtown cores possess their own atmosphere and can add a refreshing note to the symphony of a city's large and small spaces. Usually such districts are responsible for a welcome change in scale, a limitation of building heights, a different street pattern. Squares or small parks which may have existed before the city itself remain in much their original condition.

As important as the formal open spaces, the streets of such a district, at their best, are pleasant to walk in and offer a variety of intimate views. For the city man a stroll through such a neighborhood can be at least as rewarding as one through a park. Indeed, a historic neighborhood *is* a sort of park, secure in its relationship to nature and the more stimulating to the senses because of its domestic uses. So it is in Boston's Beacon Hill or Brooklyn Heights. The quiet streets of Washington's Georgetown or Philadelphia's Society Hill are a tonic to jaded city nerves.

In many other cities historic areas wait to be discovered and defined.[10] Omaha's warehouse district would not at first glance appear a likely candidate for listing among historic places suitable for residential use. Yet the Omaha downtown plan seizes upon a four-block area, the oldest remaining section of the original city, consisting of brick warehouse buildings two to ten stories in height, as a resource for central-city housing. Cincinnati looks to the district known as "Across the Rhine" for buildings to be reclaimed and reused for dwellings.

Elsewhere the historic district shades off into neighborhoods that are simply old and run-down. Their houses built fifty or seventy-five years ago, these lend themselves to reasonably inexpensive rehabilitation, of a kind featuring modern interiors as often as period restoration. The Ohio City area directly across the river from downtown Cleveland, many streets in San Francisco or the Westport section in Kansas City, are examples of this kind of transition neighborhood.

The value of preservation and rehabilitation of such downtown districts is high in dollars and cents, and virtually incalculable in more elusive but generally acknowledged benefits—not least of these relating to open spaces. Yet the fact that such neighborhoods are often economically precarious (even the most solidly rooted historic areas were once thought to be so) has made banks reluctant to lend money for purchase or repairs. In other cases a contrary danger has existed. The appeal of the area to the wealthy and the fashionable has driven up rents and stimulated development of an incompatible nature.

From the open space point of view, the establishment of historic districts, with strong protective measures as in such key examples as New Orleans and Washington, are vitally important. In areas where the homogeneity of the district is not so complete, or its historic or architectural features so outstanding, greater flexibility should be allowed. A special zoning district can provide standards for in-fill housing, and under rational planning concepts can permit changes in form or a break in the building height. It is especially important in such zoning that attention be given to the open space. The street must be kept an agreeable place for walking, and nothing must be allowed to overshadow a square or destroy a containing wall of structures.

15 Meeting Place
and Forum

NEVERTHELESS, AND IN THE END, the city is not to be identified with any single interest—not even with the paramount and pervasive interest of those who make it their permanent home. If the core has need of the stability that residents give to it, it has need, also, of the motion and change provided by those who constantly come and go. To fulfill itself, the city must be a place of transactions, encounters, festivities. Its spaces must not only reflect these functions; they must provide a stage upon which they can be visibly enacted.

To Express the Civic Function

The heavy emphasis placed by downtown boosters upon facilities to attract visitors and tourists is to be understood as part of their reaching toward the city's ultimate role as magnet and catalyst. Yet these efforts are too often naïve, and if carried forward insensitively can fatally dehumanize an urban scene. The qualities of the city that make it attractive to visitors, its contrasts and its inner harmonies, have too often been destroyed before the welcome mat is laid down.

Physical clearance of older structures and neighborhoods is hardly less dangerous to the urban balance than the effect of undigestible crowds. New Orleans is convinced it strengthened downtown by the Superdome and its

331

attendant facilities. Still too early to tell, however, is the impact of the sports fans and conventioneers upon the delicate equilibrium hitherto maintained within the Vieux Carré. The question is whether Bourbon Street will sink further into tawdry commercialism, with residents of the area moving out. Similarly to be feared is the effect of placing Seattle's new sports stadium directly adjacent to Pioneer Square. The low rents and modest establishments of this historic section will have difficulty surviving the added strains and pressures.

The problem is made worse by the fact that the structures of tourism are often blatant or deadening in style. Culture and government may at best make a lively contribution to the environment; by contrast, the exhibition halls, convention centers and stadiums tend to be sterile boxes set unfeelingly within the urban frame.[1] Their open spaces are likely to be nothing better than asphalt seas of parking space; their vast interiors are cold and inaccessible except when taken over by exhibitors.

Athletic spectacles and big conventions remain, nevertheless, important elements of downtown life, and a sampling of such facilities across the country shows it is not impossible to integrate them into the downtown core. New Haven's exhibition hall and sports arena is a noble structure carrying parking facilities high upon its back; Hartford's is slipped sensitively into downtown. In the renewal area of Niagara Falls Philip Johnson's powerfully shaped exhibition hall has been responsible for the creation of a new park. The Busch Stadium of St. Louis, if ever surrounding development permits its parking to be concealed, will become an integral part of the central business district.

Where such accommodations have been achieved, the benefits are equally demonstrable for downtown and for the functions themselves. To hold conventions within an airport hotel, to stage great sporting events on the outskirts, is to rob the cities of an influence equally important from the point of view of economics and of urban drama. It is to reduce these events, moreover, to something less than their full potentiality. Part of the relevance and enjoyment is lost when such communal occasions take place outside the urban environment.

A crucial role of the city is precisely this: to set the comings and goings of men within a frame that enlivens them; to impart to events and occasions a dimension beyond themselves. Who wants to parade in the isolation of a countryside? Who, for that matter (and despite all common complaints), wants a city in which parades no longer occur?

The contemporary downtown is groping, often unconsciously, for ways to express this civic function. Planners conceive and developers construct new hotels and shopping centers; conservationists fight to save an old marketplace or landmark building; artists discover outdoor settings where they can perform or which they can enhance with banners, sculpture or murals. All, in one way or another, are saying that the city is more than a collection of isolated men and women engaged in entirely personal tasks. They begin to see it once again as a place where ordinary pleasures are heightened and common events given an added perspective. To walk in the streets should be to experience the arts; to shop should be to take part in something like an old-fashioned marketplace. Above all, the movement of men and women as they go about their daily pursuits should be visibly expressed in a kind of pageantry.

In all this the public spaces of the city are crucial. This concluding chapter looks at innovative spaces of movement and meeting, at novel points of procession and celebration. Some of these will be found embodied in unexpected forms. For example, the shopping center becomes a town square, the hotel lobby becomes a public gallery. In these spaces, many of them still imperfectly expressing their deeper role, lies an important aspect of the contemporary city.

The Hotel Lobby as a Plaza

The lobbies of large hotels have in the past served as grand pedestrian ways and meeting places; they are again beginning to do so. Conceived architecturally to be as much public as private space, the lofty ceiling of the old hotel would rise above a focal point comparable to the fountain in a town square. Not infrequently, smaller spaces lined with shops led out in the manner of streets. Peacock Alley in the old Waldorf Astoria hotel really was an alley; the new Waldorf, though not averse to people passing through, has more the aspect of a large indoor hall. "Meet me under the clock" has long been a New York password, referring to the central point of the Biltmore Hotel lobby.

In the Sheraton-Peabody hotel in Memphis there was until recently a grand public space, done in the Italian style with columns reaching two tall stories in height and carrying a balcony, which formed an arcade beneath. At the center was a fountain with a small surrounding pool. Here took place a twice-daily ceremony of public import, for which a dozen or so habitués and out-of-town visitors would regularly gather. Four ducks, long-standing guests of the establishment, would descend by elevator in the morning from their penthouse residence. At precisely three in the afternoon, ambulating across a specially laid red carpet, the ducks again entered the elevator and were borne aloft. In this tiny but significant way was the passing of each day marked and the ceremonial nature of civic life affirmed.

The day of these public-private indoor plazas seemed coming to an end, as indeed it did come to an end for the Memphis Sheraton. Who could afford to build them, or would desire to maintain them? The newer hotel lobbies seemed designed to keep people out, or, without any intervening common space, to shuttle guests from the public street to the privacy of their room or meeting hall. But a surprising reversal was in the making. The essential nature of downtown asserted itself, and its spirit was caught by an imaginative architect-developer, John Portman of Atlanta.

In his home city, and in his prototype achievement, Portman found he could roof over and air-condition at comparatively small extra cost the central court, bounded by four more or less conventional blocks of hotel rooms. In the resulting space he created a genuine concourse, colorful and festive. Light falls from a glass roof twenty-one stories above the lobby floor. Balconies upon which open the doors of the hotel rooms lend a strongly sculptural effect to the walls of the court; flowers and free-standing structures within the space add excitement. Most importantly, the elevators, freed from the necessity of being housed in shafts, rise and descend in full view, brightly outlined in lights.[2] Dramatizing the vertical motion, these elevators pierce the roof to ascend in glass-enclosed tubes to a restaurant seeming to float above the structure.

Portman's contribution in restoring to the hotel its primary wonder and excitement went deeper than the monumentality of his space or the drama of its decoration. Most significant in the Atlanta Hyatt Regency are the various entrances and connections of its lobby. The main entrance from Peachtree Street is conventional, past a powerful-looking individual dressed like the bouncer of a London club. The effect on the unprepared visitor, as the vast space confronts him is, nevertheless, striking. More original is the skillfully designed series of spaces through which one mounts after leaving one's car in the parking space below. In addition, a lateral extension reaches outward from the main lobby, crossing Benton Street in a translucent bridge, to penetrate the inner courtyard of a second building of the Peachtree complex. Here again is skylighting, and again the dramatization of upward motion, this time through a chain of flashing lights outlining the escalators. Exits reach out through various levels of terraces and squares, some open

Two notable indoor spaces.

58. The original Atlanta Regency Hyatt.

59. Minneapolis' IDS Building.

and some enclosed, to a small plaza forming a break in the projected Peachtree mall.

Taken in reverse, the journey is even more interesting, ending as it does with the burst of light and activity in the hotel lobby.

Versions of the Portman hotel are to be found in a number of cities, several of them an improvement on the original, yet in their urbanistic role not quite the equal of the first Atlanta achievement.

The Houston Hyatt Regency, designed by the firm of Caudill Rowlett Scott, its great court more sophisticated than the prototype in overall design, develops interesting linkages by pedestrian overpasses to a free-standing parking garage and to the second level of an adjacent office building, as well as underground to the tunnel system connecting many of Houston's skyscrapers. At the start of the working day a considerable part of the skyscraper population may be seen moving through the Hyatt Regency lobby to disperse itself in the clustered towers of downtown.

The San Francisco Embarcadero hotel falls short as a concourse, though its architecture has been highly praised. Part of a complex of office towers and shops designed by Portman, it has created a powerful terminus to Market Street and has brought into being the highly successful and much used Embarcadero Park. The public-private interior space of the hotel may find its role when the complex is completed and its linkages are all in place. However, while major office towers remained unbuilt, the entrances and connections of the hotel were confused. Within the magnificently contrived environment, where the designer's gifts of showmanship have been fulfilled and his architectural talents spectacularly displayed, the conventioneer is still removed from city life, safe and encapsulated, but not quite part of the action.

Today no downtown, not even New York's Times Square, considers itself complete without a new hotel in the Portman style. Local businessmen are prepared to make large commitments to secure such an advantage. It is important that the real function of these vast enclosed spaces be grasped, for they will otherwise become a cliché, a mere symbol of local pride like the skyscraper. The public will not continue to be dazzled by the scale or by the dramatic amenities of these developments. What counts in the end is their ability to intensify the urban experience. The features that really distinguish them are not the hanging balconies or the indoor trees, but their capacity to become part of downtown's spatial organization.

Cincinnati is on the right track when it plans for an interior public space of this kind as the vivifying factor in its extended skywalk system. Houston, by contrast, has shown a failure of nerve in refusing to make a connection between the lobby of the Hyatt Regency and the new Allen complex to the north. The way these open spaces connect with the public environment of the street is crucial; their life is in the linkages to downtown by bridges and passages or by secondary enclosed or open spaces. Too large to be vitalized by the hotel clientele alone, they require for their own benefit and for the city's a substantial movement of people passing through on pedestrian routes or coming to make use of their shops and other services.

Toward Mixed Uses

The recognized need to create in such new spaces something like a town square or general meeting place has led to interesting experiments in which the hotel is an element of spaces larger than its own and one of many related functions. Thus in Los Angeles the Hyatt Regency is an element within a downtown shopping center, its cafés and eating places flooding into the enclosed street and its lobby becoming scarcely distinguishable from it. In Minneapolis the Marquette Inn is part of the IDS Center, its "lobby" claimed by the designer to be nothing less than the vast, busy space through which the whole town seems to pass in the course of the day.

Similarly, in Kansas City the exceptionally beautiful lobby of Crown Center, rising sixty feet to enclose a natural rock formation with gardens and a cascading waterfall, is part of many interwoven stores and restaurants. It becomes hard to say which is the dominant function of the center, its hotel or its shopping mall; and the mix will be further enriched as the housing for an ultimate population of ten thousand is completed.

An easy transition, therefore, leads from the hotel as a crossroads of the city to the shopping center. And from here a concluding step is made toward a few focal points where the life is unexpectedly enriched by being drawn into a public square of motion and contrast.

Shopping—The New Forum

That shopping should be more than a chore, and should have about it something of recreation and even of celebration, has been recognized since markets and bazaars first took form. The marketplace became in the European cities an open space coequal with those of the city hall and the cathedral; and it was, like them, a scene of animation, a point of meetings, a stage for the dramas and entertainments of civic life.

The market street could be a complement to the square, but was often dark and narrow, and later became defiled by wheeled traffic. In U.S. cities today certain streets manage, in spite of all, to enhance the function of shopping and in the process fall within the concept of open space used in this book. Madison Avenue, New York, on a Saturday afternoon, Maiden Lane in San Francisco, Fifth Avenue in Scottsdale, Arizona, are examples of the predominance of the street-for-shopping over the street-for-traffic. Elsewhere, as has been noted, traffic has been banned to make the modern shopping mall.

Roofed-over streets in the form of galleries became, as in Milan and Brussels, famous features of European cities. An American example of an early enclosed street is to be found in Cleveland, where small stores on several levels line a skylighted central court. Completed in 1890, the Cleveland Arcade runs between two principal shopping streets and is as much in the heart of town as it was nearly a century ago. It is of striking architectural interest, with the five gallery floors connecting two ten-story towers, and the wide skylight handled with the ease and grace characteristic of a period adept at building large conservatories and greenhouses.

Clevelanders recognize the Arcade as a significant urban treasure, yet the owners have done little to develop its potential. The major entrances at Euclid and Superior avenues are bordered by stores with cheap commercial signs so that, if anything, one is discouraged from entering. The shops within are agreeably small-scale and oriented toward everyday needs, but are totally lacking in distinction. A single, rather forlorn American flag hangs from the high roof, where one longs to see bright colors and banners. Yet this surprising structure speaks of a past insight into what made shopping an excitement and made the city into a place of human encounters. It suggests, too, what the future may increasingly become.

Efforts to restore some sense of pleasure to the modern marketplace began in the suburbs. Here it seemed easy to construct spacious facilities, with amenities to attract the shopper still shy of a new environment.[3] Fields of parking, however, usually without any attempt at landscaping, cut these new centers off from the community. The interior courts and malls existed as an oasis in a desert of cars; and, more deeply, as an enclave secure against the dirt and the muggings that were supposed to prevail in the real world.

Brought downtown, the shopping center often showed this same contempt for the surrounding community. Designers and developers failed to see that if it was to perform its true role within the city, the shopping center must be in some way a continuation of the street. Indeed, in an older shopping center like the Plaza in Kansas City, originally built in 1925, the configuration of the street persists, though romanticized by a uniform Spanish architecture and punctuated by squares and fountains. In one of the first in-city shopping complexes, Lloyd Center at Portland, Oregon, the street is again the dominant theme.

Approaching Lloyd Center, one is hardly aware of when it begins, so well integrated is it with the surrounding city. It avoids a sharp break in the urban fabric by disposing of parking in a variety of ways, no one of them calling for a large open expanse or a monolithic structure. Some of the parking is belowground, some on the roof, some of it slipped unobtrusively into small lots. The mall here is unroofed except for overhangs as wide as the average sidewalk, and the whole is agreeably unpretentious, keyed to the serious, everyday shopper. Nevertheless, elements of festivity are present, including water, flowers, trees—and the ice-skating rink, which seems to be a favorite device,[4] introducing into these complexes a kind of activity rewarding alike to participant and observer.

Rochester's Midtown Plaza

A center designed more deliberately to make shopping an urban diversion, tied in closely with downtown renewal and providing for the city an indoor square, is found in Rochester, New York. Later developments are more elegant or more architecturally sophisticated, but Midtown Plaza, designed by Victor Gruen and completed in 1962, stands as a unique accomplishment in terms of its civic role. It makes downtown Rochester a place to shop; and it makes shopping something of an adventure.[5]

Midtown Plaza was conceived by merchants, the two brothers whose B. Forman Company, the leading women's fashion store, was finding its position weakened by a deteriorating downtown area. Convinced that revitalization of the central city was essential for their own survival, the Formans brought their idea to McCurdy and Company, a full-line department store. These two establishments agreed to cosponsor a project of wide civic importance.

The heart of the development is the Midtown Plaza Mall, an animated pedestrian core covered and air-conditioned, serving to tie together the various elements of the complex. Some sixty retail shops are grouped on two levels around the one-acre mall. The pre-existing McCurdy and Forman stores were remodeled and expanded during the construction and are accessible from the mall on both levels. In addition to the retail facilities, Midtown includes office buildings, one in combination with a new hotel, and an underground garage, the only part of the project to be built with city funds.

The ensuing years have seen exactly the revival that the Formans hoped to stimulate. Today Midtown reaches out to connect by second-level pedestrian bridges with the new Xerox Tower and indirectly with the Lincoln First Plaza. Unfortunately, an additional major department store, Sibley's, chose to remain outside the development. Standing across Main Street from Midtown Plaza, Sibley's is surrounded by parking lots and run-down buildings; and Main Street itself, failing to share in the general improvement, still presents a shabby face to the world.

Meanwhile Midtown Plaza is plainly the hub of downtown Rochester. Not a day goes by without some program on the mall—a store promotion, a concert, a public service exhibition. Tropical-tree clusters, pots of flowering plants and a reflecting pool contribute a pleasantly unexpected note in that cold upstate climate. At the center of the mall a large mechanical clock makes itself into a new landmark, performing on the hour and twice daily indulging in a climactic display.

Other Meeting Places

The Rochester experience proves that a shopping center can be a fulcrum of development. It indicates also that shopping itself can be touched by some of the broader social and cultural implications that make downtown a forum. Within the new context, the hotel lobby has become more than a lobby; the once specialized and exclusive mall of the shopping center has come to belong to the citizen for his wider pleasures. A further concept may now be discerned. Within the functioning core certain spaces are to be constructed, preserved or discovered that have in them the makings of the town's natural meeting place. These places may have specialized or secondary functions, but their popularity derives from their role as a nexus. They hold a community together, give it form, impart a kind of unity to the otherwise scattered activities of its common life.

The large concourse of a railway station can perform such a function.

The terminal is, or has been, a place to contain the arrivals and departures of men; but time and human associations and the influence of the place itself have worked to create a symbolic value beyond its apparent function. People respond to an atmosphere that gives importance to the most routine errands, until gradually they come to think of this as a center of city life. The concourse, in turn, begins to take on services and facilities answerable to a variety of needs. When such a place is destroyed, having outlived its primary and most obvious economic role, it leaves a gap in the urban fabric far more difficult to repair than is caused by loss of a physical monument.

A marketplace, or the dramatic pavilion of an office complex, can also exert such an influence on downtown. One serves, essentially, man's urge to buy and sell; the other his need for economic transactions. But both can rise above these primary functions in their service to the community and to man's quest for celebration and encounter.

The Seattle Market

Let us take a market first. In downtown Seattle a rickety and visually unimpressive group of nonbuildings, a congeries of sheds and halls, half-open, half-closed, run along the waterfront, occasionally catching startling views across Puget Sound. Here some sixty farmers bring daily their fruits and vegetables from the nearby rich river bottom of the Green River; here are stalls for meats, cheeses, fish. The fresh salmon, the lute fish, the Alaska king crab, oysters, octopus and gweduc are lovingly displayed next to collections of pomegranates, papayas, persimmons. In other small shops are coins, books, junk of various sorts, antiques.

The best account of the market and the fight to save it[6] lists among the particular objects to be seen at one time: lanterns, mirrors, keys with hollow ends, busts of Douglas MacArthur, a boa constrictor skin, copies of *Colonel Todhunter of Missouri* by Ripley D. Saunders—and so on almost endlessly. Eating places nestle in among the merchandise, and people of all kinds—the lawyers of the town, businessmen, housewives, farmers, lumberjacks, Indians, blacks, Chinese, students, fishermen—crowd the market's narrow ways and stalls. Victor Steinbrueck, professor of architecture at the University of Washington and chief guardian of Seattle's urban tradition, describes the market's role in the most comprehensive terms: "a broad social mixture going about its business in a natural and uninhibited way."

60. Seattle's market as seen by Victor Steinbrueck.

Devotees of this, the Pike Place Market, perhaps overdramatize its charm. To avoid disappointment, one must visit it with a mind open to hidden values and sensitive to the cross-currents that make a city live. A few years ago the city planners and virtually the city's whole establishment saw here —as the uninitiated tourist might—only a group of undistinguished buildings and an irrational maze of small shops and stands. They proposed an urban development of a style familiar in cities across the country. On land cleared by the city and sold back below cost to the developer, a group of apartment towers, office buildings and a major hotel would be erected.

When pressed, the developers maintained that the market would be housed in better quarters—"revitalized" by the presence of new convention facilities. The city council adopted the plan, the city's two major newspapers supported it, the business community was united behind it. What was there in the dozen or so dilapidated buildings of Pike Place Market that could stand in the way of so manifest an improvement? Nothing—except what Victor Steinbrueck called "the soul of Seattle."

Under Steinbrueck's leadership, the Friends of the Market were organized. The ensuing battle was fought on a scale and with an intensity worthy of a confrontation of historic forces. A rival committee "to save the market" proved a front for the developers, and ended by launching a $65,000 campaign to defeat the initiative that the Friends had succeeded in placing on the ballot. In the approaching election, preservation of the market became the chief issue. The initiative was carried by twenty thousand votes and great was the celebration that night at the headquarters of the Friends, the Brasserie Pittsbourg then in the historic Pioneer district.

The victory had wider implications than for the market itself. Forces in Seattle that valued the humane tradition of urbanism had mustered and felt out their strength; even those who were defeated seem to have found within themselves a new awareness of the intangible qualities that go into the make-up of a functioning downtown. Since then the planners have been careful not to repeat an effort at indiscriminate clearing. The press has been more sensitive to issues of conservation and the business community—though never in Seattle tending to move very fast—has for better or worse moved even more slowly.[7] In saving the market, the city in unexpected ways had quite truly saved its own soul.

The market's future is, nevertheless, still uncertain. In the end it will perhaps be determined as much by what happens to those sixty farmers out in the Green River valley, who find the value of their land constantly rising, as by the continuing concern of the market's friends. Local resistance has been effective, but perhaps the crucial element in deferring the urban renewal projects has been the federal government's cutback of funds. As a matter of fact, this part of the city—the so-called regrade area—calls for important improvements. The market itself should not be thought immune to rehabilitation, provided it is undertaken with sensitivity to its basic values.

Meanwhile the market continues to serve in its odd way as the kind of center we have found in the most creative of outdoor-indoor spaces, a place of many crossings and encounters, visible testimony to the web of relationships that make a city's life. Plans call for tying it in to other focal points in the downtown area. A people-mover will mount Pike Street to connect with the monorail to Seattle Center (the old world's fair grounds); at the juncture a small park is envisaged, bringing together the five major stores that exist somewhat precariously within a stone's throw of each other.

Further in the future the Seattle planners see a reconstruction of the water-front highway, thus tying the market more closely to the sea and to the other facilities and attractions that border it. If the essence of a true center is in its extensions and its connections with other elements in the urban scene, the Pike Place Market rates most favorably.

The Minneapolis Meeting Place

In Minneapolis in 1974 there appeared an enclosed space which promptly assumed a role as the heart of downtown. The IDS Center, designed by Philip Johnson, consists of an office tower, a hotel, and numerous shops and restaurants. It adjoins the Nicollet Mall and is situated amid some of downtown's principal office buildings and department stores. When those responsible for the project decided to join the two towers by a glass-covered plaza, they could have been reasonably certain the place would be busy. No one could have foreseen, however, the intensity of the activity focused in this area, or the civic pride and affection immediately lavished upon it.[8]

The roof of the plaza is formed of a three-dimensional grid enclosing large panes of glass. Giving the effect of a cave of stalagmites, the enclosure admits a light—broken and partially shaded, yet with intensity sufficient even for Minnesota's dark days. Below, the major entrances set up a diagonal pattern of foot traffic; and the placing of the escalators, rising to a broad balcony, extends the diagonal into the third dimension. A few box-shaped modules, independent of the structure, provide all that is needed in the way of casual seating and of planting.

This is not a place where one looks for hanging gardens or benches for dalliance; its inspiration is not a nineteenth-century conservatory but, more nearly, a nineteenth-century railroad terminal. It is a space for people in motion. The decorations lending the space warmth and color are the signs of quite ordinary commercial establishments. If people come to observe, which they do in large numbers—the rail of the mezzanine will be found at the lunch hour to be crowded with onlookers—it is mainly to see their fellow citizens doing such ordinary things as going in and out of banks and shoe stores, or heading purposefully for some destination at the farther end of a skywalk.

The IDS achievement required an unusual architect and an unusual client, working within the framework of a city thoroughly familiar with the values of urban life. The center would not have worked as it does if the Nicollet Mall had not been established. For its future vitality the center will require the extensions and improvements now envisaged for the mall, as well as the continued co-operation and economic health of the department stores to which it is physically linked.

The lesson to be drawn from the center, therefore, is not written in architectural or aesthetic terms (though there is much here it can teach); it is written in the degree of understanding shown by all concerned in regard to the nature of the city and the qualities of a validly functioning downtown area.

New York's Opportunity

Minneapolis built its downtown center; New York's still waits to be discovered and fully appreciated. Grand Central Station, at Forty-second Street, in its monolithic splendor is as different as could be imagined from the pleasantly confused jumble of buildings that comprise Pike Place Market; and in the slow accretions and changes of time it is almost equally different from the IDS Center's instant achievement. Yet it is capable in a superb degree of serving a role beyond that of a faltering railway depot or a setting for gaudy advertisements.

Completed in 1913 as a monument to Commodore Vanderbilt, in a style combining elements of the Roman and the classical French period, the station has stood so familiarly on its site that New Yorkers have ceased to see it in the full scope of its multifaceted activities.[9] Its value as a landmark is recognized; much less is its role as a great indoor space into which feed shops, office buildings and hotels—as well as an intricate transportation system. In many ways the most remarkable of all indoor spaces, it will depend for its preservation and its harmonious development upon an understanding among New Yorkers of the broad civic function it serves. Developers in other cities meditating plans for office, hotel or shopping centers can profit from what has been achieved here and what has been only partially discovered and understood.

Grand Central has long been acclaimed for its interior organization, which with seeming effortlessness, and with so little encroachment on the formality of the great hall, brought daily into the city's heart a vast mix of commuter, rapid transit and long-distance trains. The separate publics were sorted out and dispatched through ramps and passages with a lucidity that has evaded the planners of contemporary airports. Such a variety of transportation systems, with the consequent need to change trains, or to change from mass transportation to individual conveyance, was a condition that might have caused a whole city to arise; and indeed, around Grand Central there did grow up a network of services and dependencies generated by the traveler's needs. Shops, hotels, office buildings and restaurants made the real estate in the area of the terminal some of the most valuable in New York.

The great hall, 125 feet in height, with its central clock and information booth, has traditionally been a place of meetings and farewells. It has also been a place of pedestrian passage, for the terminal opens north and south and also connects on the east and west with Lexington and Vanderbilt avenues. More than 500,000 people pass through this space each day. Stores and eating places have long existed within it; an underground passage has brought travelers directly into the lobby of the Biltmore Hotel, while the Commodore has opened from the main level. In the past decades, with the decline in long-distance rail travel and with the increasingly intense development of this part of the city, significant changes have occurred in the nature, use and orientation of the terminal. Unfortunately, most of these have the effect of debasing and obscuring its true function.

To the casual visitor the most obvious changes affect the appearance of the central hall. Where there existed before World War II a space of great elegance and sobriety, free of distracting elements except for the crowds of people moving in silence upon their various errands, there is now a jumble of advertising signs and lights and of obtrusive booths serving miscellaneous purposes. It is understandable that with the decline of railroad-related business the owners of the terminal should seek all available sources of income. The lack of control over commercial intrusions is, however, distressing.

It can only be that the proprietors did not comprehend the nature of the great space within their control. In 1975 the chairman of the Metropolitan Transportation Authority "mused," according to the press,[10] that this could be one of the world's great shopping centers. Yet in general no one seems to have related it to the significant developments taking place in such distant cities as Minneapolis or San Francisco.

Grand Central, despite the superficial defilements, stands today as a superb mix of activities, with actual and potential connections to the surrounding city that are nowhere surpassed. In addition to the openings to the streets and hotels already mentioned, the terminal since the 1960s has been directly connected with the Pan Am Building, a good portion of whose twenty thousand office workers cascade daily down escalators into the midst of the great hall. Other existing connections need to be more sharply delineated.

The entrance from the direction of Madison Avenue needs, in particular, an imaginative touch. An earlier map (page 50) shows the sequence of spaces running from the Grand Army Plaza at Sixtieth Street and Fifth Avenue to a terminus in Grand Central. How comparatively easy it would be to mark by planting, by banners, by special lighting and narrowed sidewalks, the single block that runs eastward at Forty-fourth to the portals of the station concourse. There the existing sheltered arcade, now a taxi entrance, could be given over to such use as an outdoor café; the heavy doors obscuring the entrance could yield to a barrier scarcely causing a break between indoors and outdoors. Drawn forward to the balcony, one would be at the top of marble stairs overlooking the finest space to be found on this continent.

Unbelievably, this indoor space is gravely menaced. The owners of the terminal want to tear it down; even the frail protection afforded by its landmark status has been challenged.

The solution to the dilemma of Grand Central is plain. It is in keeping with economics and with landmark requirements. More significantly, from our point of view, it is in keeping with the essential character of this central place. However difficult the great hall, *taken by itself,* may be to maintain or to justify in economic terms, it presents a different face if it is viewed as part of an organic whole. The IDS concourse is possible only because of the complex of which it forms a part. Grand Central, too, is part of a complex, and many of the buildings that comprise it are under one ownership. Staged renewal of these buildings, with the air rights over Grand Central transferred to the neighboring properties, would permit construction to greater heights than would otherwise be feasible, while preserving the density allowed under the zoning laws.[11] The terminal itself would provide an "air park," assuring air and light to abutting buildings.

The magnificent inner space of Grand Central could then come fully into its own, not only saved but with its potentialities as a town center developed. In place of the present piecemeal and blatant commercialism, a controlled environment would combine services, shops and transportation. The great hall would be what it was once—a place of the city man's comings and goings, of his individual and communal celebrations.

The City as a Gathering Place

For the defense of familiar landmarks it is rarely impossible to arouse a constituency and provoke public support. More difficult is the preservation of a basic urban function. The object is seen; the function is felt only by those who have been made sensitive to urban values. A building bordering a historic square may be saved because it is recognized to be a structure of note: too few, by comparison, see its incalculable function as part of a wall giving the open space its special character. In much the same way a public space such as Grand Central will become a rallying point because of its aesthetic or antiquarian interest. But what will save it in the end—if, indeed, anything can save it—is a true perception of its place in the city's life.

Planners and developers mistook Pike Place Market in Seattle for a market merely and saw in its ramshackle buildings only an affront to civic order. Developers in New York make the same mistake when they see in Grand Central Station only a monument. Such gathering places in these and in many other cities are of far greater significance than their outward forms—whether the forms be of marble or of wood. What counts is their irreplaceable role as the stage upon which many of the city's most characteristic dramas are enacted. These central spaces penetrate the urban fabric ("people scoops," tunnels, bridges, walkways, are but the outward signs of this); in turn being penetrated, they become enlivened by more subtle forces than the most effective director of programming can account for. Let an enlightened citizenry rise up to defend such mysteries; it will be showing a true instinct for what makes the city live.

The city in the dream of open space planners came to be something like a park. In the dream of the contemporary urbanist, it becomes something like a fair. The quality of ritual and celebration, of wonder and wide-eyed surprise, that once made "going to the fair" a memorable experience should be capable of being in some measure recaptured by those who in the right spirit approach the modern downtown.[12] Here, too, are people engaging in various forms of transaction and amusement, intent and serious yet somehow aware that they are part of a total picture that has a sense of enjoyment, even of frivolity, at its core. As at every fair, spectators and participants become mixed. Those who carry on the business of the world are also those who delight in observing their fellow actors upon the urban scene.

In this image of the city, open space is the basic reality. The massive structures, the towers built in pride, are merely booths lining the common way. It may seem odd to conceive the great, troubled city in terms such as this. But in fact it is at its best (as it is most economically prosperous) when this element of enjoyment is present; and in fact no world's fair has ever been able to match an ideal city in excitement or beauty.

This study of open space concludes upon such a note. For open space, in all the variations that have been traced out, gives life to an otherwise inert human settlement; and it becomes the deepest source of its vitality, pleasures and meaning.

List of Maps

The Town Square

The City Park

Park Systems

The New Downtown

Open Spaces of Regional Institutions

Designed for Living

List of Illustrations

Notes

The Notes, besides indicating sources and enlarging on certain points in the text, form a bibliography of works whose ideas and critical approach have been particularly useful. The notes follow the practice of grouping citations that occur within a paragraph.

INTRODUCTION

1. The most commonly used standard for recreational space, established by the National Recreation and Park Association, is twelve to fifteen acres per thousand population, although in the larger cities of high density as many as twenty acres may be appropriate. (*National Park, Recreation and Open Space Standards*, ed. Robert D. Buechner, Washington, D.C.: National Recreation and Park Association, 1971.) It is above that of all cities and serves as a goal to encourage an increase in recreation space rather than as a practical standard. More useful as a planning tool are the standards for specific kinds of recreation space. Of these, the NRPA's criteria of five to twenty acres for a neighborhood park and 250+ acres for a regional park seem most useful. The best study of spaces for active recreation was undertaken for HUD by Dr. Diana R. Dunn (*Open Space and Recreation Opportunity in America's Inner Cities*, prepared for the U.S. Department of Housing and Urban Development by the National Recreation and Park Association). In her report, based on observation in inner-city areas of twenty-five cities with populations over 250,000, Dr. Dunn concludes that of far greater significance than the amount of open space per se are the location and physical condition of the space; the programs conducted and the quality of the supervisory personnel; and the relatedness of the open space to existing centers of community participation.

2. Cities visited include twenty-seven of the twenty-nine U.S. cities with population over 450,000. For our purposes the population figures for cities are more relevant than the figures for the Census Bureau's Standard Metropolitan Statistical Regions, since the major focus of the book is on open spaces in the midst

355

of urban densities. Nevertheless, even these figures can be misleading, for cities vary widely in area. St. Louis, for example, has sixty-two square miles with a population of 662,636, though the metropolitan region of which it is the center has a population of 2,410,163. Los Angeles, with its area of 463.7 square miles, has a city population conforming far more closely to the population of its metropolitan region. Cities with a population range of 100,000 to 300,000 often showed some of the most interesting and suggestive open space developments, and a number of these were visited with profit. Even smaller cities could in many cases be highly instructive. The following list of cities surveyed, all of which have influenced the study, is placed in categories according to size.

Over 750,000	450,000–750,000		Under 450,000
Baltimore	Atlanta	Milwaukee	Austin
Chicago	Boston	Minneapolis	Binghamton
Dallas	Buffalo	New Orleans	Fort Worth
Detroit	Cincinnati	Phoenix	Hartford
Houston	Denver	Pittsburgh	Louisville
Los Angeles	Indianapolis	St. Louis	New Haven
New York City	Jacksonville	San Antonio	Portland, Ore.
Philadelphia	Kansas City, Mo.	San Diego	Rochester
Washington, D.C.	Madison	San Francisco	Santa Fe
	Memphis	Seattle	Savannah
			Syracuse

3. George R. Collins and Christiane Grasemann Collins, *Camillo Sitte and the Birth of Modern City Planning* (New York: Random House, 1965).

4. The Park Questionnaire was drawn to provide information on the number of parks, their size, their facilities, etc., for some key cities. It did not seek to cover all cities whose open spaces were subsequently studied, and because of discrepancies, does not lend itself to statistical analysis. However, it is worth noting that in replying to the question on encroachments, a majority of the park directors were less troubled than might have been expected, feeling that they had effectively resisted intrusions on parkland while acknowledging the threat. Queried about park maintenance, most considered their parks in better condition today than ten years ago, a point of view that may perhaps be explained by their official responsibilities in this regard. Safety was another matter, and almost all concluded that the parks were less safe today, though one added parenthetically that the public streets were no better.

5. The two major legislative acts affecting urban space were the Open Space Land Program and the Urban Beautification Program authorized by the Housing Act of 1961, and consolidated, along with Historic Preservation, in the Legacy of Parks Program under Title IV of the Housing and Urban Development Act of 1970. By the end of 1973, before the categorical grants disappeared altogether with the Housing and Community Development Act of 1974, HUD had awarded $60,886,000 to some 4,585 projects in the total open space program. With these funds cities were enabled to acquire and develop parks, build swim-

ming pools and playgrounds and brighten the urban environment with a variety of amenities. An important feature of the grants was the requirement that open space projects be part of a Comprehensive Area Development Plan, causing many cities for the first time to engage in significant master planning. This book has made frequent use of these planning documents, some of which are of outstanding quality.

The best summary of the struggle to gain a commitment from the federal government to the improvement of the urban environment is in Mark I. Gelfand, *A Nation of Cities—The Federal Government and Urban America, 1933–1965* (New York: Oxford University Press, 1975).

1   CHANGING CONCEPTS OF OPEN SPACE

1. Jonathan L. Freedman suggests differences in preferred distances among various ethnic groups in *Crowding and Behavior* (New York: Viking Press, 1975), p. 72. See also E. T. Hall, *The Hidden Dimension* (Garden City, N.Y.: Doubleday, 1066).

2. For the nature of the classical and medieval city, see Howard Saalman, *Medieval Cities* (New York: George Braziller, 1968); Frederick R. Hiorns, *Town Building in History* (London: George G. Harrap, 1956); Lewis Mumford, *The City in History* (New York: Harcourt, Brace & World, 1961).

3. For the opening up of the medieval city, see especially Lewis Mumford, ibid.; Giulio C. Argan, *The Renaissance City* (New York: George Braziller, 1969); Pierre Lavedan, *Histoire de L'Urbanisme* (Paris: Henri Laurens, 1952), Chap. III; R. Wittkower, *Architectural Principles in the Age of Humanism* (London: University of London, 1949). (New York: 1965). Christopher Tunnard, *The City of Man* (New York and London: Charles Scribner's Sons, 1953), presents a humanistic approach to modern urban planning. The quotation is from a review by Anatole Broyard, *The New York Times*, October 10, 1973.

4. Haussmann's work is well described in Howard Saalman, *Haussmann: Paris Transformed* (New York: George Braziller, 1971). See also Françoise Choay, *The Modern City: Planning in the 19th Century* (New York: George Braziller, 1969); Siegfried Giedion, *Space, Time and Architecture* (Cambridge, Mass.: Harvard University Press, 1949).

5. For the approach of the modern planners see Giedion, op. cit., Part IX. The ideas of the Congrès Internationale Moderne (CIAM) are discussed in J. Tyrwhytt, J. L. Sert and E. N. Rogers, eds., *The Heart of the City: Towards the Humanization of Urban Life* (New York: Pellegrini and Cudahy, 1952). See also Ludwig Hilberseimer, *The Nature of Cities* (Chicago: Paul Theobald, 1955). "The space concept of our age is toward openness and breadth" (p. 221).

6. The description of "professional nomads" is based on Melvin M. Webber, "The Post City Age" in Martin Meyerson, ed., *The Conscience of the City* (New York: George Braziller, 1970). See also in the same volume, Kenneth E. Boulding, "The great problem of the central city today is that the people who make the decisions about it do not live there and do not feel themselves to be part of the community" (p. 27).

7. See Thomas S. Hines, *Burnham of Chicago, Architect and Planner* (New York: Oxford University Press, 1974); Charles Moore, *Daniel H. Burnham Architect, Planner of Cities*, 3 vols. (Boston and New York: Houghton Mifflin, 1921); Mel Scott, *American City Planning Since 1890* (Berkeley and London: University of California Press, 1971). The quotation on bigness is from Hines, p. 43.

8. The civic center plays its role in today's city (see pp. 152–154 for a discussion of its relation to Cleveland's public square). Unfortunately, Burnham's proposed relocation of the Union Railway Terminal to close his great plaza at the northern end failed of realization. Today, not inappropriately, a parking garage is planned for this site. An exhibition hall has been placed under a part of Burnham's plaza. The governmental buildings surrounding the square, which at one time promised to suffer from conformity, today suffer from a confusion of architectural styles.

9. Edward H. Bennett, *Plan of Minneapolis*, edited and written by Andrew Wright Crawford, prepared under the direction of the Civic Commission, Minneapolis, 1917. Quotations are from pp. 56 and 26.

10. City of Atlanta, Planning Department, *Urban Framework Plan*, 1973, p. 9.

11. Robert Venturi, Denise Scott Brown and Steven Isenour, *Learning from Las Vegas* (Cambridge and London, England: M.I.T. Press, 1972). See also Grady Clay, *Close-Up How to Read the American City* (New York and Washington: Praeger, 1973), for a stimulating discussion of social and economic forces behind the strip. "The strip," says Clay, "is trying to tell us something about ourselves . . . the value systems of the strip derive from the open road rather than the closed city" (p. 108).

12. Effects of pedestrianism on the urban environment are described in Simon Breines, and William J. Dean, *The Pedestrian Revolution: Streets Without Cars* (New York: Vintage Books, 1974). Emphasis on the pedestrian underlies much of Victor Gruen's planning; see especially his *The Heart of Our Cities* (New York: Simon and Schuster, 1964). A description of what the pedestrian's world might be, drawn largely from European examples, is in Bernard Rudofsky, *Streets for People* (Garden City, N.Y.: Doubleday/Anchor, 1969). An important study of the spatial needs of pedestrians and the impact of these needs on urban design is in Boris Pushkarev and Jeffrey M. Zupan, *Urban Space for Pedestrians*, A Report of the Regional Plan Association (Cambridge, Mass.: MIT Press, 1975).

13. On skyscrapers, see Winston Weisman, "A New View of Skyscraper History," in *The Rise of American Architecture*, Edgar Kaufmann, Jr., ed. (New York and London: Praeger, 1970). Weisman sees present-day skyscrapers as being in Phase 7—a multiblock complex with varieties of open space at its base. For Le Corbusier's views, see his *When the Cathedrals Were White* (New York: Reynal & Hitchcock, 1947) and *The City of Tomorrow and Its Planning* (Cambridge, Mass.: MIT Press, 1971).

14. Jane Jacobs, *The Death and Life of Great American Cities* (New York: Random House, 1961). Whyte's research on New York plazas has not yet been published, but see his article "The Best Street Life in the World: Why shmoozing, smooching, noshing, ogling are getting better all the time," *New York Magazine*, July 15, 1974, for a summary of his lively and penetrating views.

15. Translated by Charles T. Stewart, 1945. A French translation appeared in Paris in 1902 and was the source of considerable controversy. The CIAM group referred to Sitte's approach as "the Pack-Donkey's way. . . . He was a kind of troubador, ineffectually pitting his songs against the din of modern industry." For the contrast between the spatial concepts of Sitte and the CIAM group, see *Camillo Sitte and the Birth of Modern City Planning*, pp. 120ff.

16. *Architecture for the Arts: The State University of New York College at Purchase* (New York: Museum of Modern Art, 1971). The Drexler quotation is from p. 11.

2   SPATIAL ORGANIZATION OF U.S. CITIES

1. This analysis of the processional city owes much to Edmund D. Dacon. His *Design of Cities* (New York: Viking Press, 1967, rev. ed. 1975) is a pioneering work, based on analyses of European cities but focusing on Philadelphia, in whose spatial reorganization he played a crucial role as executive director of the Planning Commission, 1946–1970. To walk through downtown Philadelphia with Mr. Bacon is a spatial experience in itself. For an excellent presentation of the central city, see Richard Saul Wurman and John Andrew Gallery, *Man-Made Philadelphia, A Guide to Its Physical and Cultural Development*.

2. This parkway was designed by Jacques Auguste Greber. The energizing force of the City Beautiful concept is indicated by the fact that more than a thousand masonry structures had to be destroyed as the parkway was laid across the old grid.

3. *Central City Philadelphia*, Philadelphia City Planning Commission, 1963.

4. See *1965/1975 General Plan for the City of Boston and the Regional Core*, Boston Redevelopment Authority, Chap. XI. Also Roy Mann, *Rivers in the City* (New York: Praeger, 1973), pp. 214ff. For a valuable guide to Boston walking tours, see *This Is Boston*, ed. Dan Dimancescu, Erica Funkhouser and Robert Stephenson (Boston: Cities, Inc./Houghton Mifflin, 1974).

5. For the plan for Brooklyn, see *Plan for New York City, 1969, Volume 3: Brooklyn*, New York City Planning Commission. An excellent history of Brooklyn's spatial development is given in an unpublished dissertation by Donald E. Simon, "The Public Park Movement in Brooklyn, 1824–1873," New York University, 1972.

6. In 1974 it appeared that in order to gain federal funds for the much-needed repaving of the traffic lanes, these lanes would have to be widened to twelve feet each, involving the loss of many trees and a portion of the malls. "We will stick with the potholes if repaving means taking away one inch of our malls" —such was the battle cry raised by one forty-year resident and strongly supported by his neighbors. The federal bureau in charge of the repaving contract was forced to reconsider its hard-and-fast rules, and the parkway remains with its malls and tree intact.

7. Two early documents establish the theme of St. Louis planning. In *A Public Building Group—Plan for St. Louis*, City Plan Commission, 1919, Harland

Bartholomew sets forth a proposal for a mall to be lined with public buildings. Ten years later *A Plan for the Central Riverfront,* St. Louis, 1928, proposed extending the mall from the Old Court House to the river and included a riverfront plaza as an important feature. The contemporary waterfront is treated in *St. Louis Riverfront Development Plan,* City Plan Commission, 1967. See especially pp. 40–49.

For a sober assessment of the city in the 1970s and a comprehensive plan for the future, see *St. Louis Development Program,* City Plan Commission, 1973. Economic conditions affecting St. Louis's capacity to plan are analyzed in Barbara R. Williams, *St. Louis: A City and its Suburbs* (A Rand Report), Santa Monica, 1973.

8. Wolf Von Eckardt, *A Place to Live* (New York: Delacorte Press, 1967), p. 312, gives an account of how Chloethiel Smith attempted, without success, to deal with the Mall's western termination.

9. For an interesting application of techniques developed by Kevin Lynch in establishing the "imageability" of a city, see *Temporary Paradise? A Look at the Special Landscape of the San Diego Region,* a Report to the City of San Diego by Donald Appleyard and Kevin Lynch, 1974. This report, on the basis of its sampling, stresses the degree to which the sea remains the most positive factor in San Diegans' perception of their city.

10. Frederick Law Olmsted, *A Journey Through Texas* (New York: Burt Franklin, 1860), p. 148.

11. *The San Antonio River Corridor,* Skidmore, Owings and Merrill, 1973.

12. Houston, which prides itself on having no zoning laws, considers the haphazard placement of urban elements to be a sign of its vitality. See, nevertheless, *Preliminary Houston Downtown Master Plan Year 2000,* Houston Planning Department, 1973. An unusually good analysis of Houston as a city, with emphasis upon the visual aspects of its component parts, is *The Houston AIA Guide,* 1972.

3 THE ROLE OF TOPOGRAPHY

1. From "Diary of David McClure," in Richard C. Wade, *The Urban Frontier* (Chicago: University of Chicago Press, 1959), p. 13.

2. Charles Mulford Robinson, *Better Binghamton, A Report to the Mercantile Press Club,* Binghamton, N.Y., 1911.

3. The hillsides of Cincinnati have been studied in a series of reports issued by the Cincinnati Institute under Pope Coleman. See also *A Hillside Study,* City Planning Commission, Cincinnati, 1969.

4. *Detroit 1990: An Urban Design Concept for the Inner City,* Detroit City Plan Commission, undated.

5. Jonathan Development Corporation, *1974 General Development Plan,* p. 8, italics added. Masao Kimoshita, Sasaki, Dawson, DeMay and Associates were landscape architects for Jonathan. See also basic planning documents for an ambitious new town twenty-five miles north of Houston. Wallace, McHarg, Roberts and Todd, *Woodland New Community—Land Planning and Design Principles,* 1973, also *An Ecological Plan,* 1974.

6. For the topography of Seattle, see *Seattle Urban Design Report I; Determinants of City Form*, Department of Community Development, 1971. Victor Steinbrueck's *Seattle Landscape*, No. 2 (Seattle: University of Washington Press, 1973) is an invaluable discussion of the visual aspects of the city in relation to its natural forms.

7. The 1903 Olmsted Brothers report is printed in *Parks, Playgrounds and Boulevards of Seattle, Washington*, issued by the Board of Park Commissioners, 1902. We are indebted to Professor Steinbrueck for lending us scarce documents, as well as a rare 1911 map showing existing parks and boulevards together with those proposed in the Olmsted plan.

8. The relation of L'Enfant's plan to the natural site is well discussed in Mann, *Rivers in the City*, p. 181; also in Ian L. McHarg, *Design with Nature* (Garden City, N.Y.: Doubleday/Natural History Press, 1969), pp. 177ff.

9. For contemporary planning for Washington open space, see *Proposed Comprehensive Plan for National Capitol*, National Capitol Planning Commission, 1967. The work of Charles W. Eliot II and of early metropolitan planning is discussed in Scott, *American City Planning*, pp. 204–227.

10. *The Comprehensive Plan: Recreation and Open Space*, Department of City Planning, San Francisco, 1973.

11. The best account is in Katherine Wilson, *Golden Gate, Park of a Thousand Vistas* (Caldwell, Idaho: Caxton Printers, 1947).

12. Banham, Reyner, *Los Angeles, The Architecture of Four Ecologies* (New York: Harper & Row, 1971), p. 36.

13. Important documents issued by the Los Angeles Department of City Planning include: *The Visual Environment of Los Angeles*, 1971; *Open Space Staff Report*, 1973; *Open Space Proposed Plan*, 1973.

4 WATERFRONT SITES

1. For a charming account of the role played by the Battery in the social life of early-nineteenth-century New York see *A Season in New York, 1801, Letters of Harriet and Maria Trumbull*, ed. Helen M. Morgan (Pittsburgh: University of Pittsburgh Press, 1969).

2. These parks, acquired on the basis of a proposal by Olmsted in 1890 for a park system in Louisville, exist today with their original Indian names—Iroquois, Cherokee, Seneca, Shawnee and Chickasaw.

3. Herman Melville, *Moby Dick*, Chap. I (Modern Library ed.).

4. *Mississippi/Minneapolis—A Plan and Program for Riverfront Development*, Minneapolis, 1972, pp. 5ff.

5. The complete text of Cleveland's "Suggestions for a System of Parks and Parkways for the City of Minneapolis," which he read at a meeting of the park commissioners on June 2, 1883, is reprinted in *Minneapolis Park System 1883–1944*, Minneapolis, 1945, by Theodore Wirth. Drawing on his own experience and interspersing his narrative with reminiscences and personal observations, Wirth, who served as superintendent of parks from 1906 to 1935, has written a history of Minneapolis parks that is relevant to park movements elsewhere.

6. An important reason for the prevalence of expressways along waterfronts is the need to complete the inner loop system which is discussed in Chapter 5. The loop is suited to an inland city; but when the concept is arbitrarily superimposed upon a city bordering a sea, river or lake, the result is to make one portion of the encircling expressway system run along the shore.

7. *The Comprehensive Plan: City and County of San Francisco, Transportation,* San Francisco City Planning Commission, 1972, p. 22.

8. A good account of the development of the Chicago lakefront appears in the *Lakefront Plan of Chicago,* City of Chicago, December 1972.

9. *The Cincinnati Metropolitan Master Plan and the Official City Plan,* Cincinnati, 1948, p. 144.

10. The account of the origins of Renaissance Center is based on local interviews. The quotations are drawn from "The Challenge and the Reality," *Sunday News Magazine,* Detroit, June 24, 1973.

11. The story of the Seaport is well told in *South Street Seaport, a Plan for a Vital New Historic Center in Lower Manhattan,* published by the South Street Seaport Museum. The museum issues a quarterly newsletter, *South Street Reporter.*

12. *Progressive Architecture,* June 1975, is largely devoted to urban waterfronts and contains an excellent discussion of planning and architectural problems. See especially comments by Suzanne Stephens, pp. 42, 48–49. The special-district zoning approach has been developed in New York City and is applied to waterfront developments at Manhattan Landing and Battery Park City with emphasis on visual corridors from the center of the island to the Hudson and East rivers. The best description of this planning process is in Jonathan Barnett, *Urban Design as Public Policy* (New York: Architectural Record Books, 1974), pp. 58–67.

13. Op. cit. As of the end of 1975, the Minneapolis City Council had directed implementation of the downtown and St. Anthony Falls section of this riverfront plan. Community development funds and state open space funds had provided a start for the financing.

5   TRANSPORTATION SHAPES OPEN SPACE

1. Cited in Plan for New York City, 1969, No. 3, Brooklyn, pp. 74ff.

2. Charles Mulford Robinson, *Better Binghamton.*

3. For a discussion of the contemporary use of Grand Central Station in New York, see pp. 345–346.

4. "The Townless Highway," *Harper's Magazine,* 1931, cited in Lewis Mumford, *The Urban Prospect* (New York: Harcourt, Brace and World, 1956), p. 216.

5. *Cincinnati Metropolitan Master Plan,* p. 89.

6. For a discussion of expressway encroachments on parks, see Chapter 7.

7. Thomas H. MacDonald, cited in *Cincinnati Master Plan,* p. 87.

8. Cited in Helen Leavitt, *Superhighway—Superhoax* (Garden City, N.Y.: Doubleday, 1970), p. 6.

9. The expressway would have been novel in design, and one has some regret it was not built. Crossing downtown at a height of one hundred feet, it would have provided a kind of aerial gateway. Descent was to be not by the normal and space-consuming cloverleaf, but by a tightly coiled ramp known as a helicoil, which met all requirements of speed and safety yet occupied no more land than the roadway itself.

10. For a fuller account of this significant modification, see Nathaniel Alexander Owings, *The Spaces in Between—An Architect's Journal* (Boston: Houghton Mifflin, 1973).

11. It must be added that Robert Moses, notwithstanding his brutal doctrine and many of his equally brutal accomplishments, was responsible for such a masterpiece of sensitive engineering as that which created the esplanade on top of the Brooklyn expressway behind the old mansions of Brooklyn Heights.

12. For an illuminating report of the Advisers to the Federal Highway Administration, Michael Rapuano, Chairman, see *The Freeway in the City, Principles of Planning and Design*, a Report to the Secretary, Department of Transportation, Government Printing Office, 1968. Unfortunately, such "principles" were not often followed.

13. Engineering criteria, functions and size of the inner loop, are explored in Edgar M. Horwood and Ronald R. Boyce, *Studies of Central Business District and Urban Freeway Development* (Seattle: University of Washington Press, 1959).

14. *Movement in Midtown,* van Ginkel Associates, June 1970. Ulrich Franzen has also made a study of certain New York streets, separating out their particular character and function: *Progressive Architecture,* October 1975.

15. The former, the Lincoln Mall in Miami Beach, is considered a disappointment as far as retailers are concerned. The elderly on fixed incomes are without the buying power that business wants to attract. But for the elderly themselves, who come to pass the time of day, the mall may be said to work well. The other mall is in Burbank, California.

16. Cited in *Planner's Notebook,* vol. 1, no. 6 (September 1971).

17. Bicycling is still another mode of transportation with the potentiality of affecting open space. Its greatly increased popularity in recent years has stimulated citizen requests for specialized routes, usually parallel to other forms of transportation, as along parkways or park roads, but also reinforcing the linear spaces along riverbanks. In Seattle a bicycle path is planned for an abandoned railroad right of way; in New York City the aqueduct lands have been studied for a bike route leading from a major city park into upstate areas. The most comprehensive planning for bicycle routes within a city has been undertaken by Denver: *The Bikeway Plan,* Denver Planning Office, 1972. See also *Guidelines for a Comprehensive Bicycle Route System,* Department of Development and Planning, City of Chicago, 1971.

18. Washington, D.C., does not use its new rapid transit stations to mold or augment aboveground open space. Designers of the system claim the city is already sufficiently provided with circles, squares and triangles, and the subway entrances are unobtrusive sheltered openings in these, with escalators leading

below. The station points of New York's proposed new Second Avenue subway have been made special zoning districts, where anticipated private development is encouraged to add public space. Construction of the subway, however, has been postponed indefinitely.

19. Quoted in "Full Speed Ahead in Atlanta," *Christian Science Monitor,* March 12, 1974.

20. See *The Regional Center, A Comprehensive Plan for Buffalo,* prepared by Wallace, McHarg, Roberts & Todd, Philadelphia, 1971.

6   THE TOWN SQUARE

1. Giedion's description of London squares applies as well to their early American counterparts. "In the best of London squares a whole district is composed architecturally *around the existing countryside." Space, Time and Architecture,* p. 508.

2. For a good discussion of historic American squares see Chap. VI, by Carl Feiss, in Paul Zucker, *Town and Square—From the Agora to the Village Green* (Cambridge, Mass.: MIT Press, 1959).

3. New York City pioneered in the establishment of special zoning districts as a means of design control. The technique has been used in regard to specialized areas of the city and to streets and avenues, but it has never been applied to parks.

The various ways in which special district zoning has been used in New York is told by one of the architects who helped to develop the concept, Jonathan Barnett, in *Urban Design as Public Policy,* pp. 22–27, 43–67.

4. See Grady Clay, "Magnets, Generators, Feeders—The Necessities of Open Urban Space," *Journal of the American Institute of Architects,* March 1961, on the importance of the "mix" in generating lively open spaces. Clay had written earlier, in "What Makes a Good Square?" a chapter in *The Exploding Metropolis,* The Editors of *Fortune* (Garden City, N.Y.: Doubleday, 1958), p. 170: ". . . the most interesting open spaces were those in which several currents of life came together—working-class people, well-dressed junior executives, mink-stoled ladies at their shopping, and above all, children, who add a quality of noise, excitement, and vibrancy to the urban scene that is altogether indispensable."

See also the brilliant analysis by Jane Jacobs (op. cit.), showing how the squares laid out by William Penn in Philadelphia have taken on with time the nature of their immediate surroundings, each as different as the sections of the modern city in which they are situated. There is no better proof of the Jacobs thesis than a look at those same squares today. In at least one case, neighborhood renewal and the increasingly residential character of former commercial areas have caused changes in the clientele and use of the square so that the description so apt in 1961 no longer applies today.

5. For a description of Tompkins Square and its varied users in the turbulent summer of 1967, see August Heckscher, *Alive in the City* (New York: Charles Scribner, 1974), pp. 75–85.

6. The Fifth Avenue Association in New York objected strenuously when

the Parks Department with the cooperation of the Parks Council set up bookstalls on Fifth Avenue adjacent to the Grand Army Plaza. The Association, and in particular the nearby hotels, claimed that browsers were "undesirables," a characterization stoutly refuted by the then park commissioner. The well-designed bookstalls were a success with the public and remain to this day.

7. This account is based on local interviews and an article in a New Orleans newspaper: David Snyder, "True Grit: Fighting City Hall," *States-Item*, March 7, 1975.

8. For a picturesque description of the early square see William Payne, *Cleveland Illustrated: A Pictorial Handbook of the Forest City* (Cleveland: Fairbanks, Benedict, 1876).

9. An account of the square's history appears in the New Haven Redevelopment Agency's planning document *Wooster Square Design, A Report on the Background, Experience and Design Procedures in Redevelopment and Rehabilitation in an Urban Renewal Project*, New Haven, Connecticut, 1965, pp. 12–17.

10. Charles William Eliot, *Charles Eliot, Landscape Architect* (Boston: Houghton Mifflin, 1902), p. 307.

7 THE CITY PARK

1. *San Francisco Chronicle*, 1855, in Roger W. Lotchin, *San Francisco 1846–1856* (New York: Oxford University Press, 1974), p. 285.

2. Quoted in First Annual Report of the Board of Park Commissioners of the Cleveland Metropolitan District, 1918.

3. Quoted in *Plan of Minneapolis*, 1917. Napoleon III, builder of Paris's chief nineteenth-century parks, also believed he could improve the morals of the citizens. Haussmann, in his memoirs, declared he could not share the *"illusions genereuses"* of the emperor, but justified the expenditure for parks on grounds of rising land values and revenues from vendors and concessionaires.

4. See note 15 below.

5. Ben Whitaker and Kenneth Browne, *Parks for People* (New York: Winchester Press, 1971), p. 22.

6. For a breakdown of open space in these cities, see *Charles Eliot, Landscape Architect*, pp. 304–308.

7. Laura Wood Roper, *FLO, A Biography of Frederick Law Olmsted* (Baltimore: Johns Hopkins University Press, 1973), p. 420.

8. Olmsted's early career and later accomplishments are well told in Roper, ibid. For a consideration of his influence in the fields of landscape architecture and city planning, see Julius G. Fabos, Gordon T. Milde and V. Michael Weinmayr, *Frederick Law Olmsted, Sr., Founder of Landscape Architecture in America* (Amherst: University of Massachusetts Press, 1968). This book was intended to preserve in graphic form a traveling exhibition of Olmsted's life and work which the authors had assembled in celebration of the centennial year of the first use of the term "landscape architect."

9. For an interesting analysis of Olmsted's social philosophy, see *Landscape into Cityscape, Frederick Law Olmsted's Plans for a Greater New York City*, ed.

and with introd. by Albert Fein (Ithaca: Cornell University Press, 1968). See also Fein's *Frederick Law Olmsted and the American Environmental Tradition* (New York: George Braziller, 1971).

10. An excellent study of the park in its naturalistic aspects is Henry Hope Reed and Sophia Duckworth, *Central Park, A History and a Guide* (New York: C. N. Potter, 1967). In *Tree Trails*, Mrs. M. M. Graff has catalogued some 118 varieties of trees and shrubs to be found in Central Park today, most of them known to Olmsted. See also Elizabeth Barlow and Alex Williams, *Frederick Law Olmsted's New York* (New York: Praeger, in association with the Whitney Museum of American Art, 1972) on the occasion of the 150th anniversary of Olmsted's birth. For a discussion of the complexities of managing the park, see Heckscher, "The Central Park," in *Alive in the City*, pp. 245–268.

11. Frederick Law Olmsted, "Letter of Professor Olmsted. Relative to the General Duties of Park Commissioners and Incidental Matters," Fourth Annual Report of the Board of Park Commissioners of the City of Minneapolis for the Year Ending March 14, 1887, Tribune Job Printing Co., Minneapolis, 1887, pp. 15–25.

12. Roper, op. cit., p. 409.

13. Eliot, op. cit., p. 305.

14. Roper. op. cit., p. 420.

15. We are indebted to John Lindenbusch, director of the Missouri Historical Society, for background material on Forest Park.

16. Ibid.

17. A sympathetic account of the park and its problems is given in "Belle Isle: An Endangered Treasure," *MSA Monthly Bulletin*, June 1973, published by the Michigan Society of Architects.

18. *Delaware Park Comprehensive Development Plan Summary Report*, July 1973. The consultants were Building Science Inc., Planning Consultants; Castle Hamilton Houston Lownie, Architects; Decker & Borowsky, Architects-Planners, and Schnadelbach Braun Partnership, Landscape Architect.

19. In Norman T. Newton, *Design on the Land: The Development of Landscape Architecture* (Cambridge, Mass.: Belknap Press of Harvard University Press, 1971).

20. Where resistance to encroachment is not possible, in the face of undeniable city-wide need, compensation must be insisted on. Even a fair purchase price for the land is usually not sufficient. The demand should be for an equal amount of land in an area short of park facilities; and this land should be both acquired and cleared before the trade is consummated.

21. Among these are Forest Park in St. Louis; City Park, New Orleans; Cherokee Park, Louisville; Balboa Park in San Diego and Griffith Park, Los Angeles.

22. 401 U.S. 402, 1971, *Overton Park* v. *Volpe*. The decision shifted the burden of proof from those who want to keep highways out of the parks to those who want to put them in. Only if the cost or disruption resulting from alternative routes reaches "extraordinary magnitudes" or the alternative routes present "unique problems" will highway engineers be permitted to put their roads through parks.

23. A separate police force, under the control of the park commissioner,

has existed in some cities, but has been sacrificed to municipal economies. Such is the recent experience of Philadelphia and Baltimore. In New York, until 1968, the commissioner had control, largely theoretical, over police stationed within the park. A special police force trained to deal with a park's special problems reduces crime and also makes possible the enforcement of park rules. Police of a city-wide force show little interest in protecting trees and flowers, enforcing rules concerning dogs or otherwise maintaining a degree of civil behavior.

24. An interesting situation exists in Philadelphia, where the Fairmount Park Commission, a small, prestigious citizens' board created in 1867, not only runs Fairmount Park but is charged with maintaining four thousand acres of roads and boulevards, additional small parks and the city's historic squares. In recent years Philadelphia's energetic commissioner of recreation, Robert Crawford, became president of the Fairmount Park Commission as well, for the first time bringing under one authority responsibility for parks and recreation. Working with the Fairmount Park Commission is the Fairmount Park Art Association, formed in 1872 to guide the embellishment of the park. Over the years the Art Association has purchased or commissioned a large collection of outdoor sculpture, which can be seen throughout the park.

8 PARK SYSTEMS

1. The "Report on Honolulu" is included in Mumford, *The Urban Prospect*. The quotations may be found on pp. 99 and 130.

2. Bennett, *Plan of Minneapolis*, p. 134, italics added.

3. The quotations are from Olmsted's letter to the park commissioners of Minneapolis, op. cit.

4. *Olmsted Park System Study—Interim Summary of Findings*, prepared for the Boston Redevelopment Authority by the Metropolitan Area Planning Council, May 1973.

5. Report of the Board of Park and Boulevard Commissioners of Kansas City, Missouri, October 12, 1893.

6. The story of Kansas City's "climactic battle" to establish a park and boulevard authority is well told in Henry C. Haskell, Jr., and Richard B. Fowler, *City of the Future, A Narrative History of Kansas City, 1850–1950* (Kansas City: Frank Glenn Publishing Co., 1950).

7. The system endures, nevertheless. Returning in April 1974 from a two-hour drive around the city with Frank Vaydik, Kansas City's impressive commissioner of parks, we were informed that we had not once been off park land.

8. Earlier than most cities, Buffalo was aware of the need for parks. At least one effort, however, ended in tragedy. Joseph Ellicott planned a circle on Main Street, where he intended to place his own house and then bequeath it to the city for park purposes. In 1809 the city commissioners frustrated his plan by running Main Street directly through his lot. The stones of Ellicott's unbuilt house were removed and used to build a jail. Ellicott himself was so enraged that he left Buffalo and ended his days in an asylum, where he committed suicide in 1826.

9. The New York State Urban Development Corporation, author of this

proposal, was conceived as a bold scheme of state government for building large-scale housing developments. Financial problems racked the agency, aborting many of its projects.

10. For an account of the civic and political forces behind Buffalo's park movement, see *History of Erie County, 1870–1970,* ed. Walter S. Dunn, Jr., published by the Buffalo and Erie County Historical Society in commemoration of the Erie County Sesquicentennial 1971: Chap. VI. "Flexible Authorities Build the Parks."

11. Cleveland set forth his principles in *Landscape Architecture as Applied to the Wants of the West,* ed. Roy Lubove (Pittsburgh: University of Pittsburgh Press, 1965; orig. ed. Chicago: Jansen, McClurg & Co., 1873).

12. Robert Ruhe, Minneapolis's commissioner of parks and a staunch defender of his domain, confided to the author in 1974 that he was "having trouble" with his parkways, because of cars constantly increasing in speed and numbers. "What are you doing about it?" he was asked. "I am narrowing the parkways," was his pleasantly unexpected reply.

13. Eckbo, Dean, Austin & Williams, *Minneapolis Parkway System—Concepts for the Future,* June 1971, for the Minneapolis Park and Recreation Board.

14. Sections of the parkway system are closed to automobile traffic through the summer months and the bicyclist is provided with a guide pointing out scenic and historic features along the way.

15. *A Park System for the City of Cincinnati,* Report of the Park Commission of Cincinnati to the Honorable Board of Public Service of the City of Cincinnati, 1907.

9 NEW URBAN OPPORTUNITIES

1. William H. Whyte, in a brilliant and often polemical study of open space issues, discusses the value of acquiring small pieces of land in built-up urban areas and linking them with community parks, school sites and other existing open spaces to form an effective open space system. *The Last Landscape* (Garden City, N.Y.: Doubleday, 1968), pp. 185–205.

2. The author had opportunity as park commissioner to learn that while the tennis courts and playgrounds along the edges of Crotona Park were well used and could be kept in reasonably good condition, even the police were reluctant to patrol the interior, and Broadway Maintenance refused to go in to replace defective lights.

3. Opportunities for mixed land use, taking advantage of major features of the natural and man-made landscape, are imaginatively considered in *The Visual Environment of Los Angeles,* Department of City Planning, Los Angeles, California, April 1971.

4. *An Open Space Plan for the Phoenix Mountains,* City of Phoenix, Arizona, 1972.

5. The design of Woodlands is based on an ecological planning study undertaken for the developers by Wallace, McHarg, Roberts and Todd: *Ecological Planning Study for the New Community,* Houston, Texas, July 1971.

6. Halprin, Lawrence & Associates, *Fort Worth Trinity River Report,* pre-

pared for the City of Fort Worth with the cooperation of the Streams and Valleys Committee, 1970.

7. Springer, Marvin & Associates, *Open Space Development Trinity River System*, prepared for the Dallas Park Board, 1969.

8. We are indebted to A. Heaton Underhill, assistant director for State Programs and Studies of the Bureau of Outdoor Recreation, for making available to us his file on the Texas bayous.

10   Open Space of Megalopolis

1. An account of the work of Baxter and Eliot in promoting a metropolitan park system appears in Scott, *American City Planning Since 1890*, pp. 17–26.

2. For the origins of the Cleveland outer park system, see the First Annual Report of the Board of Park Commissioners of the Cleveland Metropolitan Park District, 1918.

3. Jean Gottmann, *Megalopolis—The Urbanized Northeastern Seaboard of the United States* (New York: The Twentieth Century Fund, 1961), pp. 342ff.

4. Neal P. Kingsley, research forester with the Northeastern Forest Experiment Station, has reviewed for us the recent survey. While it is true that the overall figure in the counties of Megalopolis is now 49 percent, he notes that there have been important shifts within individual counties and that New Jersey and southern New England counties indicate a reversal of the trend and a predictable decrease in forest land.

5. S. B. Zisman, Delbert B. Ward and Catherine H. Powell first developed this concept in *Where Not To Build, A Guide for Open Space Planning*, in a study of land use for Utah. (Technical Bulletin No. 1, U.S. Deparement of the Interior, Bureau of Land Management, Washington, D.C.)

6. Southeast Michigan Council of Governments, *1990 Regional Recreation and Open Space Plan*, Detroit, last amended March 1, 1974.

7. Regional Planning Staff, Ohio-Kentucky-Indiana Regional Planning Authority, *Open Space Plan*, 1973. Dane County Regional Planning Commission, *Plan for Parks and Open Spaces*.

8. The means of obtaining and preserving open space have been well researched. They include—in addition to outright acquisition by purchase or gift—easements, purchase and leaseback, zoning actions, the purchase of development rights and subdivision regulations. For a good discussion of these tools, see ibid., pp. 17, 18; also Department of City Planning, Los Angeles, California, *Open Space Staff Report, City Plan*, 1973, pp. 41–43.

9. The original Washington open space plan is contained in National Capital Planning Commission, National Capital Regional Planning Council, *A Policies Plan for the Year 2000*, Washington, D.C., 1961. For its revisions, see Metropolitan Washington Council of Governments, *Preliminary Open Space Plan and Program for Metropolitan Washington*, 1971.

10. The Commonwealth of Massachusetts: Metropolitan Area Planning Council, Metropolitan District Commission, Department of Natural Resources, *Open Space and Recreation Plan and Program for Metropolitan Boston*, Vol. I, 1969.

11. Metropolitan Area Planning Council, *Final Draft Open Space and Recreation Plan and Program for Metropolitan Boston,* 1975.

11   The New Downtown

1. Raymond E. Murphy and J. E. Vance, Jr., "Delimiting the CBD," *Economic Geography* XXX (July 1954), pp. 189–222.

2. For the city after World War II and the tools used to rehabilitate the core, the following are useful: Victor Gruen, *The Heart of Our Cities,* Charles Abrams, *The City Is the Frontier* (New York: Harper & Row, 1965); Jeanne R. Lowe, *Cities in a Race with Time* (New York: Random House, 1967); Wolf Von Eckhardt, *A Place to Live,* pp. 289–344. A suggestive chapter on downtown appears in Peter Wolf, *The Future of the City* (New York: Whitney Library of Design, 1974), pp. 12–16. Most cities have included the central business district as a component within their master plans and we have drawn extensively on these documents.

12   Downtown Parks and Development

1. *Louisville Courier-Journal,* May 19, 1959.

2. This was the case, for example, in Steinway Street, a busy but threatened shopping section of Queens, New York, in 1970.

3. *The Urban Prospect,* p. 104.

4. *Central Atlanta Opportunities and Responses,* City of Atlanta Department of Planning, 1971.

5. Taliaferro, Kostritsky, Lamb (TKL) of Baltimore were selected. Details of the planning of Fountain Square were provided by Peter Kory, formerly Director of Urban Development for the city of Cincinnati, who served as secretary to the working Review Committee. A good account of the development of downtown Cincinnati appears in Jonathan Barnett, "A New Planning Process with Built-in Political Support," *Architectural Record,* May 1966.

6. We are indebted to the Greater San Antonio Chamber of Commerce for a memorandum on the "History of the San Antonio River and Its Development."

7. Charles Mulford Robinson, *The Improvement of Towns and Cities,* (New York: G. P. Putnam, 1901), p. 6.

8. *Chicago 21, A Plan for the Central Area Communities,* Chicago Plan Commission, 1973.

9. *Urban Design as Public Policy,* Chap. 2. Ada Louise Huxtable discusses the Bankers Trust Building, the first major structure to build in these amenities within the Special Greenwich Street Development District, in "This is the Bank That Zoning Built," *The New York Times,* January 11, 1976.

10. *Dallas Central Business District, Boulevards and Green Spaces,* "a guide plan for the development of central area boulevards and green spaces including a system of major parks linked by landscaped boulevards," Department of Planning and Urban Development, City of Dallas, Texas, 1971.

11. *Omaha C.B.D.,* report prepared by the Omaha City Planning Department, 1973.

13 OPEN SPACES OF REGIONAL INSTITUTIONS

1. John W. Reps, *The Making of Urban America* (Princeton: Princeton University Press, 1965), p. 249.

2. For an account of the Senate Park Commission Plan for Central Washington, D.C., 1901, see Ibid., pp. 502–514.

3. A discussion of the plan and its genesis is found in Nathaniel Owings, *American Aesthetics* (New York: Harper & Row, 1969), pp. 133–139. A revised version of the Pennsylvania Avenue plan has been officially adopted. The first building to be constructed in conformance with it is the new FBI headquarters, named for former director J. Edgar Hoover, not precisely the kind of facility that symbolizes the republic or brings people by night as well as by day into the area.

4. Cincinnati, it is sad to report, also has a garage and parking lot directly in front of its landmark city hall. This must be the exception that proves the rule, for Cincinnati has long been a city distinguished by the important role played by its city council and by the respect shown to the men and women who serve in it.

5. This square, carved out with superior skill by Gruzen and Partners, provides an unexpected and highly successful people-place. It will be found lying behind the ornate tower of the Municipal Building, whose rear elevation had previously been lost to view. The plaza itself consists of a wide overpass constructed above the approaches to the Brooklyn Bridge, and is bounded at the east by the new police department headquarters building. Paved in brick, with water, sculpture and trees to enliven it, this space attracts daily a large crowd at lunchtime, along with carts selling various ethnic foods. A subtly formed passage leads from the plaza into the busy traffic of Foley Square, center of the city's court life.

6. Two city halls, in Hartford and Fort Worth, make good use of interior space, creating something like a streetlite under high glass enclosures. The former, designed by Davis and Brooks, dates from the early years of the century, and is graced by elegant ironwork and gilded details. The latter, the work of Edward Durell Stone, is in a contemporary form which, while adding little to the exterior environment, creates within certain aspects of a public place. For a discussion of other interior spaces that play the role of open space see Chapter 15.

7. Ellen Perry Berkeley, "The Boston City Hall," *Architecture Plus*, February 1973, pp. 72–76.

8. "Many cities seem to have felt they were not properly planned unless they had made provision, at least on paper, for an arrangement characterized by monumental buildings in rectilinear relationship, facing a broad open plaza." From the 1948 *Cincinnati Master Plan*, commenting on the abortive proposal for a government center set forth for the city in 1925.

9. When the park was visited in 1974, a sign at the base of a large stone sculpture warned the public to keep away. "This artwork is cracked," it said. Somehow that seemed to characterize both the hopes and the shortcomings of this well-intentioned open space.

10. For the financing and cost of the mall, see Eleanor Carruth, "What Price Glory on the Albany Mall?" *Fortune*, June 1971, pp. 92ff.

11. *Los Angeles, The Architecture of Four Ecologies,* p. 134.

12. The center is not named for the martyred President, and the Art Commission once turned down a statue of the barefoot log-splitter which Robert Moses had wanted to install. The name derives from a farmer who once owned the land.

13. For early planning and financing, see Richard A. Miller, "Lincoln Center —'a new kind of institution,'" *Architectural Forum,* August 1958.

14. See, for example, John Cotton Dana, *The Gloom of the Museum* (Woodstock, Vt.: The Elm Tree Press, 1917). Dana attacks the "spurious suggestion" that a museum gains in dignity by being aloof from urban life. He makes a special plea for not taking advantage of the museum's appeal "to encumber with it the fine, open spaces of a public park" (p. 19).

15. The garden of the Museum of Modern Art is accessible (except during a special summer program) only to those who have paid their entrance fee to the museum. As an open space designed in the contemporary style it is well worth the price of admission. The Metropolitan Museum, with its new steps, fountains and trees, has created a kind of elongated forecourt. "It's become the place where people congregate," says the museum's director, Thomas P. F. Hoving. "It's a real street fair with vendors and jugglers and musicians. It's begun to change the nature of our audience, bringing many more kids into the museum." Quoted by Grace Glueck, *The New York Times,* February 8, 1975.

16. The basic issue was a lease of 1878, approved by the state legislature, entitling the museum to occupy the land within which the expansion was to take place. The Master Plan of 1970 was, moreover, smaller in extent than a plan approved by Olmsted and Vaux, designers of the park. For an account of the controversy, see Heckscher, *Alive in the City,* pp. 263–268.

17. University Circle, a planning and administrative corporation serving this area, has established its own security forces. It also coordinates the institutions in working for the betterment of the neighborhood.

18. When the first, temporary stage for the Lincoln Center Repertory Theater was built near Washington Square, it was very sensibly sunk 90 percent underground. Since nobody knew what a theater should resemble in any case, it seemed entirely satisfactory that it should resemble an eight-foot fence.

19. In the planning stage of this plaza, a small group, which included the author, was assembled by the First National Bank and its architects, the firm of Perkins and Will, to give ideas upon how this plaza might gain maximum popular usage. The idea was discussed of creating a tropical microclimate (sure to attract citizens of that cold and windy city); also a festive public ceremony, heralded by trumpet blasts, which would mark the arrival and departure of the bank's funds. It was suggested that it would not only be more colorful, but also safer, to handle the money in this way rather than in concealed underground passages. The designers relied on more conventional means for winning the public.

20. The location of the Museum of Modern Art, nestled among skyscrapers in this busy commercial area, is a result of the failure of the plan for a midblock extension of Rockefeller Center's open spaces. The site of the present museum was in the possession of the Rockefeller interests when the Rockefeller-inspired

museum needed a new home. The museum would still have terminated a vista opening from the center had not the famous 21 Club refused to be budged from its midblock brownstone. (From a conversation with Wallace K. Harrison, August 1974.)

21. See *New Life for Plazas*, published in April 1975 by the New York City Planning Commission, John E. Zuccotti, Chairman, for a summary of the new rules and a revealing presentation of their underlying philosophy. New York zoning laws also give a substantial bonus of building space for each square foot of *covered pedestrian space*. Standards are set for the height and width of such space; also for the types of facilities that must border it in order to qualify for the bonus (no airline ticket offices or banks, and at least 50 percent of the frontage in shops no wider than twenty-five feet each).

14   Designed for Living

1. Not only community colleges must come to terms with the problems of establishing connections with the surrounding community. Universities, too, seek ways to avoid the charge of exclusivity and the danger of an enclave approach to planning. Writing in the Yale Alumni Magazine of December 1973, Henry Chauncey, Jr., secretary of the university, states the case in New Haven: "One of the vexing things that New Haven people mention most often is the existence of a large wall around Yale—an invisible wall which causes them to feel that they're not welcome. . . . Almost all our buildings are built in quadrangles which have lovely courtyards on the inside but large and offensive gates on the outside." Plans for two new colleges attempted to incorporate not only stores, but an open promenade through the college rather than a closed quadrangle. Unfortunately, the colleges were never built.

2. Hannah Arendt, in *The Human Condition* (Garden City, N.Y.: Doubleday Anchor Books, 1959), develops the classic concept of the household as primarily a place where the necessities of life are fulfilled. She contrasts it with the public sphere of action: "To leave the household," said Arendt, "[was] originally to embark on some grand adventure and glorious enterprise and later simply to devote one's life to the affairs of the city." Arendt sees the social or communal realm emerging when men and women have found ways of living together but before they have organized themselves for the heroic work of politics. This is the sphere where group life tends to predominate and where conformity tends to be a controlling virtue. For a book making somewhat similar distinctions between the private and the public spheres, see Edward A. Shils, *The Torment of Secrecy*, (Glencoe, Ill.: The Free Press, 1956). In August Heckscher, *The Public Happiness* (New York: Atheneum, 1962), the author has applied these concepts to many aspects of modern life.

3. Wolf Von Eckardt, in *A Place to Live*, provides a good introduction to housing developments in the 1950s.

4. For an attempt to convert the dead spaces of the typical housing project of the 1950s into a true common, opening to the city and shared by public and tenants, see Charles Goodman and Wolf Von Eckardt, *Life for Dead Spaces, The*

Development of the Lavanburg Commons (New York: Harcourt, Brace & World, 1963). The Lavanburg Foundation set out to create a prototypical commons in a new housing development in the South Bronx, New York, but with the change in atmosphere between the 1960s and 1970s the open space ended up as a locked and defensive enclave. M. Paul Friedberg's prize-winning park in the Riis Houses on New York's Lower East Side remains a model of community open space created within a pre-existing housing complex.

New York State's UDC proposed placing parking at a distance from entrances to the buildings to ensure that the buildings' open space would be policed by tenants walking to and from their cars, as they formerly walked to and from the local shops. A far-fetched device, but one that at least recognized the problem of dead spaces!

5. See, for elaboration of this concept, Newman, *Defensible Space—Crime Prevention through Urban Design* (New York: Macmillan, 1972).

6. Brooklyn's Bedford-Stuyvesant neighborhood goes further by developing certain streets as a play and communal area with vehicular circulation changed and through traffic eliminated.

7. We are grateful to Lloyd Keefe, former director of city planning for Portland, for serving as a guide to the city and for providing background information on the development of Portland Center.

8. Loring Park Development Task IV Urban Design Plan, Task VI Public Open Space Schematics Loring Greenway, M. Paul Friedberg & Associates, Landscape Architecture and Design, Barton-Aschman Associates, Inc., Transportation and Engineering, City of Minneapolis.

9. *Report of The Welfare Island Planning and Development Committee*, Benno C. Schmidt, Chairman. Submitted to John V. Lindsay, Mayor, City of New York, Feb. 1969. For the Johnson-Burgee plan, see *The Island Nobody Knows* (New York: Metropolitan Museum of Art, October 1969). The quotation is from the latter document, p. 15.

10. Other cities have followed New Orleans in designating historic districts, which are regulated by statute in regard to land use, demolition and new construction, and to such matters as building height, signage and design of renovation. Santa Fe's Historic Style Ordinance, San Antonio's River Walk Commission, Seattle's Pioneer Square Historic Preservation Board and New York City's Landmarks Preservation Commission all seek to preserve the historic and architectural character of unique areas within the city. In New York City, special district zoning has been utilized to stabilize transitional neighborhoods. An account of this process as applied to Little Italy and the Clinton area on Manhattan's West Side appears in *The Special District Zoning Concept in New York City*, ed. Robert E. Davis and Jon Weston, Center for New York City Affairs, New School for Social Research, 1975.

15 MEETING PLACE AND FORUM

1. A good discussion of the problems of designing and locating convention centers is in Carter B. Horsley, "Convention Centers: Another Kind of Show Business," *The New York Times*, January 25, 1976.

2. Interestingly, elements combined by Portman had been prefigured more than a century before in Atlanta's Kimball House. There, too, the lobby rose to an astonishing height, a full six stories; and an eye-stopping innovation in the form of the earliest elevators was introduced: whole "rooms" were described as moving up and down in full view. Norman Shavin, *Underground Atlanta* (Atlanta: Capricorn Corporation, 1973).

3. For a brisk history of the modern shopping center, its varieties and social implications, see "Spaced-Out at the Shopping Center," *The New Republic*, December 13, 1975.

4. Thus, for example, the ice-skating rink at the lower level of Houston's Galleria, a successful shopping center outside the core. The ice with its dark moving figures supplements the whiteness that pervades the large interior space. A further effect of kinetic sculpture is provided (free of cost) by joggers who circle a track on the roof, visible through glass to spectators below.

5. We are grateful to Angelo Chiarella and Mary Ellen Wood of Midtown Plaza for background information and a thorough tour of Midtown's facilities.

6. Patrick Douglas, "Up Against the System in Seattle," *Harper's Magazine*, April 1972, pp. 91–94.

7. When in 1973 *Seattle Landscape II* was published—Victor Steinbrueck's analysis in word and sketch of the mysteries lying at the heart of a city's vitality—it was a local best seller month after month, with a readership among groups not often reached by hard-cover books.

8. A pictorial account of the IDS building and its ties to the Nicollet Mall and the downtown circulation system is provided by "Grist and Gusto—The IDS Center in Minneapolis Leavens an Already Lively Downtown," *Architectural Forum*, November 1973, pp. 36–42.

9. The history of Grand Central, its influence on the development of the area and its contemporary problems are well told in James Marston Fitch and Diana S. Waite, *Grand Central Terminal and Rockefeller Center—A Historic-critical Estimate of Their Significance*, Division for Historic Preservation of the New York State Department of Parks and Recreation, 1974.

10. Carter B. Horsley, "Grand Central Getting a $1 Million Facelift," *The New York Times*, August 31, 1975.

11. Such an approach was worked out by the Landmark Commission of the city in the early 1970s, but it was undermined by the ensuing economic recession. For a discussion of the transfer of air rights and the creation of an air park, see John J. Costonis, *Space Adrift—Landmark Preservation and the Marketplace* (Urbana: University of Illinois Press, 1974).

12. See report of G. Holmes Perkins, Chairman, City Planning Commission, City of Philadelphia, to Mayor James H. J. Tate, April 7, 1964, for proposal to have the city itself, refurbished and with its permanent amenities completed, be the focus of the 1976 Bicentennial.

Index

Page references in italic refer to illustrations